Introduction to Biometrics

Anil K. Jain • Arun A. Ross • Karthik Nandakumar

Introduction to Biometrics

Foreword by James Wayman

 Springer

Prof. Anil K. Jain
Department of Computer Science
and Engineering
Michigan State University
East Lansing, Michigan
USA
jain@cse.msu.edu

Dr. Arun A. Ross
Lane Department of Computer Science
and Electrical Engineering
West Virginia University
Morgantown, West Virginia
USA
arun.ross@mail.wvu.edu

Dr. Karthik Nandakumar
Institute for Infocomm Research
A*STAR
Fusionopolis
Singapore
knandakumar@i2r.a-star.edu.sg

ISBN 978-0-387-77325-4   e-ISBN 978-0-387-77326-1
DOI 10.1007/978-0-387-77326-1
Springer New York Dordrecht Heidelberg London

Library of Congress Control Number: 2011942231

Printed on acid-free paper

Springer is part of Springer Science+Business Media (www.springer.com)

Foreword

In the 1901 debut issue of the journal *Biometrika*, founders of which included Sir Francis Galton and Karl Pierson, there appears an introductory editorial entitled, "Spirit of Biometrika".

It is almost impossible to study any type of life without being impressed by the small importance of the individual. In most cases the number of individuals is enormous, they are spread over wide areas, and have existed through long periods. Evolution must depend upon substantial changes in considerable numbers and its theory therefore belongs to that class of phenomena which statisticians have grown accustomed to refer to as mass-phenomena. A single individual may have a variation which fits it to survive, but unless that variation appears in many individuals, or unless that individual increases and multiplies without loss of the useful variation up to comparatively great numbers-shortly, until the fit type of life becomes a mass-phenomenon, it cannot be an effective factor in evolution.

In the first part of the 20th century, "biometrics" was about bringing statistical methods into the relatively new and rapidly developing field of evolutionary biology so as to increase knowledge about variance between and within large populations. "Biometrics" was about the statistical understanding of mass-phenomenon.

Sometime around 1980, the term "biometrics", by then well-established in the meaning of "active pursuit of biological knowledge by quantitative methods", was appropriated as a designator for what had previously been called "automated personal identification" (API). By 1980, the field of API encompassed such technologies as fingerprint, retina, voice, signature, face and finger-length recognition used for the purpose of differentiating individual humans. This use of the term "biometrics" in the narrower meaning of API turned the "Spirit of Biometrika" on its head: the individual is not of "small importance" as a single data point in a "mass-phenomenon", but is of all importance – a recognizable and unique entity distinguishable from the mass and addressable as a person. Biometrics in this sense is not about understanding mass-phenomenon within the context of evolutionary biology, but about understanding the distinguishing characteristics of individual persons for the purpose of recognition.

Introduction to Biometrics by Anil Jain, Arun Ross and Karthik Nandakumar uses the term "biometrics", in this more recent sense of individualization: the automated recognition of human individuals based on their biological and behavioral traits. This application, of course, is immediately personal. It is about recognizing (*re* again; *cognoscere* know/learn) me and you and each of those around us. This recognition occurs automatically, meaning by computers, so this "me"-directed outcome is being delivered almost immediately by impersonal machines, capable of both proper operation and improper errors. Therefore, biometrics in this new meaning involves more than population statistics and biology, but now encompasses computer science, computer vision, pattern recognition, law, sociology, human factors, philosophy and even religion.

In the 21st century, we now have these machines capable of quickly and efficiently recognizing individuals, even when "the number of individuals is enormous", and linking each of them to personal data. It is no wonder that the interest in biometric technologies has grown rapidly over the last 10 years, particularly in facilitation of international travel. But interest in itself is insufficient; advancing these technologies requires understanding based on analysis of real data. Additional research continues to be needed to explore the privacy, legal, and security implications of these technologies and increase their usability, reliability and accuracy. More importantly, we need to open discussion on which socially-positive, security and privacy enhancing applications should be created and to ensure that biometric technologies are used to empower individuals and not enslave them. Of course, careful consideration of these cross-disciplinary issues requires a comprehensive explication of the technologies, their capabilities and their risks, which leads directly to the need for this textbook.

Introduction to Biometrics takes a comprehensive look at the current major forms of automated personal identification, with particular emphasis on fingerprint, face, and iris recognition, in the context of how the technologies are being and should be used: to ensure individual security and privacy. This book fills a pedagogical gap in the literature, supplying a unified treatment of technologies, developed separately from different historical requirements, by emphasizing their algorithmic, system and application similarities. The approach of this textbook is very clearly technical, with emphasis on the pattern matching algorithms employed by the computer to make recognition decisions. This book engages technically-capable students who may have limited or no knowledge about biometrics and thus facilitates the generation of a more knowledgeable workforce. The text will also be a valuable reference for those already active in the field. As with previous books by these authors, it is destined to become a classic.

July 2011   *James Wayman*

Preface

A number of crucial societal applications like international border crossing, electronic commerce, and welfare disbursement require reliable person recognition systems. Traditional person authentication methods based on passwords and identity documents often fail to meet the stringent security and performance demands of these applications, which in turn has spurred active research in the field of biometric recognition. Biometric recognition, or simply biometrics, is the science of establishing the identity of a person based on physical or behavioral attributes such as fingerprint, face, iris, and voice. Biometric systems are based on the premise that many of the physical or behavioral attributes of humans can be uniquely associated with an individual. By capturing these attributes using appropriately designed sensors, representing them in a digital format, and comparing this recorded data against the data acquired from the same person at an earlier time instance, it is possible to automate the process of person recognition. Thus, biometric recognition can be viewed as a pattern recognition problem, where the machine learns the salient features (patterns) in the biometric attributes of an individual and robustly matches such patterns efficiently and effectively.

While biometric characteristics such as fingerprints have a long and successful history in forensics, the development of automated biometric systems started only in the later half of the 20th century. However, the deployment of biometric systems has been gaining momentum over the last two decades in both public and private sectors. These developments have been fueled in part by recent government mandates stipulating the use of biometrics for ensuring reliable delivery of various services. For example, the Enhanced Border Security and Visa Entry Reform Act of 2002 enacted by the United States Congress mandated the use of biometrics in the issue of U.S. visas. This led to the US-VISIT program (United States Visitor and Immigration Status Indicator Technology) that validates the travel documents of foreign visitors to the United States based on fingerprints. The International Civil Aviation Organization (ICAO) has unanimously recommended that its member States use Machine Readable Travel Documents (MRTDs) that incorporate at least the face biometric (some combination of face, fingerprint and iris can also be used) for purposes of verifying the identity of a passport holder. The Government of India has established the Unique Identification Authority of India (UIDAI) to implement a nationwide biometric infrastructure to combat identity fraud and provide access to social benefits for the underprivileged. It plans to issue each resident of India a unique 12-digit identification number called Aadhaar that will be based on 10 fingerprints and two irides. Thus, it is clear that biometric technology has the potential to profoundly influence the ways in which we are recognized for conducting various transactions on a daily basis.

Objectives

Despite its rapid proliferation, the study of biometric technology has mostly been restricted to a fairly small community of biometric researchers and practitioners due to two reasons. Firstly, biometric recognition is often considered as a rather specialized field and is typically taught only as part of a course on pattern recognition, computer vision, or image processing. However, it is important to realize that biometric recognition is a broad and important subject in its own right; challenges and issues involved in the design of biometric systems go beyond pattern recognition and encompasses a variety of other topics including applied statistics, sensor design, software engineering, information theory, and human factors. Secondly, knowledge about biometric technologies is primarily contained in research articles and books written for the research community, which are accessible only to those with a prior introduction to this field. In short, there is no biometric book that caters to undergraduate and graduate students who may not have an extensive background in biometrics. Since this is the first textbook on biometrics, our primary objectives are to:

- provide an introduction to the basic concepts and methodologies for biometric recognition; and
- build a foundation that can be used as the basis for more in-depth study and research on this topic.

To fulfil these objectives, we focus only on key illustrative techniques that are widely used in the biometrics community, rather than providing a detailed analysis of the state-of-the-art advancements. Our focus is primarily on three most commonly used traits, namely, fingerprint, face, and iris, although we discuss a few other biometric traits briefly.

Organization

- Chapter 1 introduces the generic concepts in biometric recognition, including an overview of how a biometric system works, the terminology used to describe biometric traits and systems, the ways in which a biometric system can be used, the factors affecting the design of a biometric system, and the measures to evaluate the performance of a biometric system. Chapters 2, 3, and 4 discuss how a biometric system can be implemented based on fingerprint, face, and iris characteristics of a person, respectively. These three chapters share a common structure. The sensing, feature extraction, and matching techniques for these three biometric identifiers are introduced in order, followed by a discussion on advanced topics that are specific to each identifier.

- Chapter 2 on fingerprints focuses more on the minutiae-based representation and matching algorithms. This chapter also includes details on topics like indexing large fingerprint databases, generation of artificial (synthetic) fingerprint images, and palmprint-based biometric recognition.
- Chapter 3 emphasizes the problem of face detection and the different approaches for matching 2-dimensional face photographs. Other issues in face recognition such as handling pose, illumination, and expression variations, matching of heterogeneous face images, and face modeling are also covered in this chapter.
- Chapter 4 deals with the problem of iris segmentation in detail, followed by a description of iris encoding and matching based on Gabor wavelets. Quality of the iris image is a critical issue in iris recognition, and techniques for estimating the iris image quality are also discussed in Chapter 4.
- Chapter 5 briefly describes the techniques for person recognition based on additional biometric attributes like hand geometry, ear, and gait. Soft biometric characteristics like scars, marks, tattoos, and periocular biometrics are also useful in identifying a person in some scenarios. The chapter concludes with a discussion on how these soft biometric identifiers can be used in person recognition.
- High-security applications and large-scale civilian identification systems place stringent accuracy requirements that cannot be met by biometric systems based on a single biometric identifier. Multibiometric systems overcome this limitation by intelligently combining the evidence from multiple biometric sources. A discussion on the taxonomy of such multibiometric systems and the different ways in which the information from multiple sources can be fused to obtain a reliable identity decision is the primary focus of Chapter 6.
- Finally, the common security vulnerabilities of a biometric system and the various countermeasures that need to be followed to address these threats are presented in Chapter 7. In particular, this chapter emphasizes two of the most well-studied vulnerabilities of a biometric system, namely, spoof detection and biometric template security.

The website for the book will be initially maintained at `http://www.csee.wvu.edu/~ross/BiometricsTextBook`. Homework assignments, reading resources, sample codes, links to biometric databases, and errata will be documented in this website. This website will be updated regularly for the benefit of the reader.

Intended Audience

This textbook has been designed for senior undergraduate students and first-year graduate students who have introductory preparation in linear algebra, probability theory, statistics, and computer programming. The book would also be useful to a wider audience, including developers of biometric applications, system integrators, and designers of security systems. Ideally, this text would be used in a one-semester course in introduction to biometric recognition. Some background in the fundamental concepts in statistical pattern recognition and digital image processing will be useful to easily understand some of the technical details, but this is not a prerequisite. If the instructor wishes to further elaborate on some of the techniques based on the references contained in the Bibliography section, it may be possible to cover only Chapters 1-4 and parts of Chapters 6 and 7 in one semester.

Biometric recognition is a rapidly evolving field with an active research and development community that continues to generate new technological innovations and create progressively better biometric systems. Since this book emphasizes the fundamental concepts, we hope that it serves as a good starting point for readers with little prior knowledge about biometrics and as a useful reference for biometric experts and security system designers.

Acknowledgements

We would like to thank a number of individuals who were instrumental in making this book a reality. Abhishek Nagar of Michigan State University provided exceptional assistance in the formatting and organization of the book and offered useful suggestions to improve its readability. Thanks to Kim Thompson for carefully proofreading the book. Our appreciation also goes to the following individuals for their help with the individual chapters.

- Jianjiang Feng, Tsinghua University and Soweon Yoon, Michigan State University, for the fingerprint chapter;
- Raghavender Jillela, West Virginia University, for the iris chapter;
- Unsang Park, Michigan State University, for the face chapter;
- Abhishek Nagar and Unsang Park, Michigan State University and Brian DeCann, West Virginia University, for the chapter on additional biometric traits.

We are also indebted to the following individuals for providing illustrations and short narratives for various chapters: Salil Prabhakar of Digital Persona Inc., Qijun Zhao and Brendan Klare of Michigan State University, Thirimachos Bourlai and Aglika Gyaourova of West Virginia University, Ayman Abaza of West Virginia High Technology Consortium Foundation, and Francesco Turroni of University of Bologna. We are grateful to Kar-Ann Toh and Andrew Teoh Beng Jin of Yonsei University and Rangachar Kasturi of University of South Florida for their valuable comments on individual chapters. Finally, we would like to acknowledge Jim Wayman of San Jose State University for not only agreeing to write the Foreword for this book, but also for kindly answering the many queries we had about biometrics.

June 2011   *Anil K. Jain*
                                                                                  Arun A. Ross
                                                                       Karthik Nandakumar

Anil Jain would like to acknowledge the support of WCU (World Class University) program funded by the Ministry of Education, Science and Technology through the National Research Foundation of Korea (R31-10008) and his affiliation with the department of Brain & Cognitive Engineering at Korea University, Seoul. Arun Ross is grateful for support from the US National Science Foundation (NSF) CAREER Program. Karthik Nandakumar would like to acknowledge the support of Institute for Infocomm Research, A*STAR, Singapore. The authors are very grateful to their families for their exceptional support during the writing of this book.

Contents

Chapter 1
INTRODUCTION

Sur un procédé d'identification permettant de retrouver le nom d'un récidiviste au moyen de son seul signalment, et pouvant servir de cadre pour une classification de photographies à la préfecture de police, à la sûreté générale, au ministé de la justice, etc.

Alphonse Bertillon, 1881[1].

About an identification process that enables finding the name of a repeat offender based on his description only, and that can be used in the context of a classification of photographies in the police headquarters, in the national security office, at the ministry of justice, etc.

English translation

The ability to identify individuals uniquely and to associate personal attributes (e.g., name, nationality, etc.) with an individual has been crucial to the fabric of human society. Humans typically use body characteristics such as face, voice, and gait along with other contextual information (e.g., location and clothing) to recognize one another. The set of attributes associated with a person constitutes their personal *identity*. In the early days of civilization, people lived in small communities where individuals could easily recognize each other. However, an explosion in population growth accompanied by increased mobility in modern society has necessitated the development of sophisticated identity management systems that can efficiently record, maintain, and obliterate personal identities of individuals.

Identity management plays a critical role in a number of applications. Examples of such applications include regulating international border crossings, restricting physical access to important facilities like nuclear plants or airports, controlling logical access to shared resources and information, performing remote financial transactions, or distributing social welfare benefits. The proliferation of web-based services (e.g., online banking) and the deployment of decentralized customer service

---

[1] A. Bertillon, "Une application pratique de l'anthropométrie, Annals de démographie internationale, 1881"

centers (e.g., credit cards) have led to the risk of identity theft[2]. Rising magnitude
of identity theft and heightened concerns about national security have reinforced the
need for reliable identity management systems.

1.1 Person Recognition

The fundamental task in identity management is to establish the association between an individual and his personal identity. One must be able to determine a
person's identity or verify the identity claim of an individual whenever required.
This process is known as person recognition. A person can be recognized based on
the following three basic methods (see Figure 1.1): (a) what he knows, (b) what he
possesses extrinsically, and (c) who he is intrinsically. While the first method relies
on the fact that the individual has exclusive knowledge of some secret information
(e.g., password, personal identification number, or cryptographic key), the second
method assumes that the person has exclusive possession of an extrinsic token (e.g.,
identification card, driver's license, passport, physical key, or personal device such
as a mobile phone). The third method establishes the person's identity based on
his inherent physical or behavioral traits and is known as biometric recognition.
Formally, biometric recognition can be defined as the science of establishing the
identity of an individual based on the physical and/or behavioral characteristics of
the person either in a fully automated or a semi-automated manner.

Knowledge-based and token-based person recognition rely on surrogate representations of identity such as passwords or ID cards, which can be easily for-
gotten/lost, guessed/stolen, or shared. Moreover, they cannot provide vital identity management functions like non-repudiation and detecting multiple enrollments
by the same person under different identities. For example, individuals can easily
deny (repudiate) using a service by claiming that their password had been stolen or
guessed. Individuals can also conceal their true identity by presenting forged or duplicate identification documents. In addition, traditional mechanisms like passwords
and tokens do not provide strong evidence for post-event person recognition, such
as suspect identification at a crime scene. Therefore, it is becoming increasingly apparent that knowledge-based and token-based mechanisms alone are not sufficient
for reliable identity management.

Biometric recognition, or simply biometrics[3], offers a natural and more reliable
solution to the problem of person recognition. Since the biometric identifiers are inherent to an individual, it is more difficult to manipulate, share, or forget these traits.
Hence, biometric traits constitute a strong and reasonably permanent link between
a person and his identity.

---

[2] Identity theft or identity fraud occurs when a person usurps the identity of another individual or
claims a false identity in order to access resources or services to which he is not entitled.

[3] The term *biometric recognition* is perhaps more appropriate than *biometrics*, because the latter
has been historically used in the field of statistics to refer to the analysis of biological (particularly
medical) data. For the sake of brevity, we use these two terms interchangeably in this book.

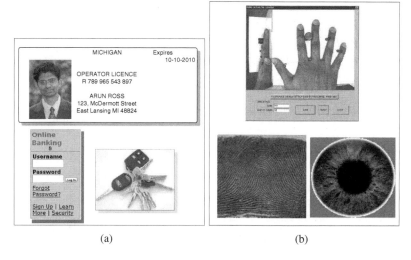

Fig. 1.1 Three basic approaches to person recognition. (a) Traditional schemes use passwords ("what you remember") and ID cards or keys ("what you possess extrinsically") to validate individuals and ensure that system resources are accessed only by a legitimately enrolled individual, (b) with the advent of biometrics, it is now possible to establish an identity based on "who you are intrinsically".

Any person who presents his biometric identifier to a biometric system for the purpose of being recognized can be called a *user* of the system. Since biometric systems require the user to be present at the time of authentication, they can also deter users from making false repudiation claims. Moreover, only biometrics can establish whether a certain individual is already known to the identity management system, although the individual might deny it. This is especially critical in applications such as welfare disbursement, where an impostor may attempt to claim multiple benefits (i.e., double dipping). Due to the above reasons, biometric recognition is being increasingly adopted in a number of government and civilian identity management applications either to replace or to complement existing knowledge-based and token-based mechanisms.

1.2 Biometric Systems

A biometric system measures one or more physical or behavioral characteristics (see Figure 1.2), including fingerprint, palmprint, face, iris, retina, ear, voice, signature, gait, hand vein, odor, or the DNA[4] information of an individual to determine or ver-

---

[4] DNA refers to deoxyribonucleic acid, which contains the genetic information necessary for the development and functioning of living organisms.

ify his identity. These characteristics are referred to by different terms such as *traits*, *indicators*, *identifiers*, or *modalities*. In this chapter, the various building blocks of a generic biometric system and the issues involved in the design, implementation, and evaluation of such a system will be discussed. The details on implementing a biometric system based on specific biometric traits will be dealt with in the subsequent chapters.

1.2.1 Enrollment and recognition phases

How does a biometric system identify a user based on his physical and/or behavioral traits? This process consists of two main phases, namely, enrollment and recognition (see Figure 1.3). During the *enrollment* phase, the biometric data is acquired from the individual and stored in a database along with the person's identity. Typically, the acquired biometric data is processed to extract salient and distinctive features. In many cases, only the extracted feature set gets stored, while the raw biometric data is discarded. During the *recognition* phase, the biometric data is re-acquired from the individual and compared against the stored data to determine the user identity. Thus, a biometric system is essentially a pattern recognition (or a pattern matching) system consisting of four basic building blocks, namely, (a) sensor, (b) feature extractor, (c) database, and (d) matcher as shown in Figure 1.3. These four modules will now be discussed in turn.

1.2.2 Sensor module

A suitable user interface incorporating the biometric sensor or reader is needed to measure or record the raw biometric data of the user. For example, an optical fingerprint sensor may be used to image the friction ridge pattern at the tip of the finger. The design of a good user (or human-machine) interface is critical for the successful implementation of a biometric system. An intuitive, ergonomic, and easy to use interface may facilitate rapid user habituation and enable the acquisition of good quality biometric samples from the user.

The quality of the raw biometric samples also depends on the characteristics of the sensor used. For most biometric modalities, the raw biometric data is in the form of two-dimensional images (e.g., fingerprint, face, iris, etc.). Exceptions include voice (1-dimensional amplitude signals), online signature (pen pressure, position, and velocity), odor and DNA (chemical-based). For image-based data, factors like resolution, frame rate, and sensitivity of the camera play an important role in determining the image quality. Figure 1.4 shows fingerprint images at two different resolutions obtained using different fingerprint sensors. One may also need to consider the demographic characteristics of the target population like age and gender, and other cultural issues (e.g., some users may be averse to touching a sensor sur-

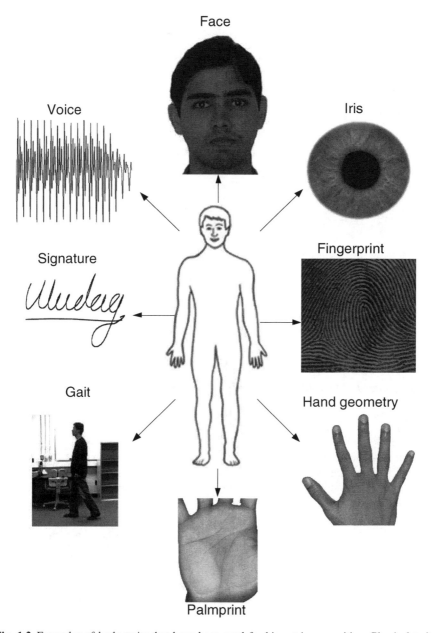

Fig. 1.2 Examples of body traits that have been used for biometric recognition. Physical traits include face, fingerprint, iris, palmprint, hand geometry, voice, and ear shape, while gait, signature, and keystroke dynamics are some of the behavioral characteristics. The distinction between a physical trait and a behavioral characteristic is actually not very important. This is because the biometric data captured from an individual is typically a manifestation of both the physical and behavioral aspects of the person. For example, while fingerprint is a physical trait, the fingerprint image acquired from a person also depends on how he interacts with the sensor, i.e., the user's behavior. Similarly, while gait may be a behavioral trait, it is to some extent defined by the physical characteristics of the human body.

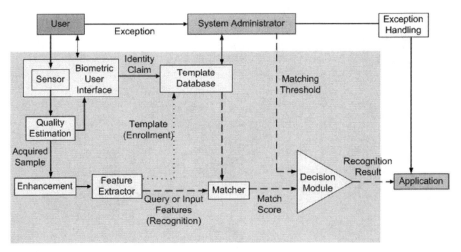

Fig. 1.3 Basic building blocks of a generic biometric system.

face) while designing the sensor module. Furthermore, factors like cost, size, and durability also impact the sensor design.

1.2.3 Feature extraction module

Usually, the raw biometric data from the sensor is subjected to pre-processing operations before features are extracted from it. The three commonly used pre-processing steps are (a) quality assessment, (b) segmentation, and (c) enhancement. First, the quality of the acquired biometric samples needs to be accessed to determine its suitability for further processing. If the raw data is not of sufficient quality, there are two options. One can either attempt to re-acquire the data from the user or trigger an exception (failure alarm) alerting the system administrator to activate suitable alternate procedures (typically involving some form of manual intervention by the system operator). The next pre-processing step is known as *segmentation*, where the goal is to separate the required biometric data from the background noise. Detecting a face in a cluttered image is a good example of segmentation. Finally, the segmented biometric data is subjected to a signal quality *enhancement* algorithm in order to improve its quality and further reduce the noise. In the case of image data, enhancement algorithms like smoothing or histogram equalization may be applied to minimize the noise introduced by the camera or illumination variations. Figure 1.5 shows a face image obtained after segmentation and quality enhancement based on histogram equalization. In some cases, the above pre-processing steps may be inseparable from the actual feature extraction step. For example, quality assessment in itself may entail the extraction of some features from the acquired biometric data.

(a) (b)

Fig. 1.4 Fingerprints scanned at (a) 1000 points per inch (ppi) and (b) 500 points per inch using different fingerprint sensors. The intricate details of the finger such as location of sweat pores can be more easily observed in the higher resolution fingerprint image shown in (a) as compared to the lower resolution image in (b).

Feature extraction refers to the process of generating a compact but expressive digital representation of the underlying biometric trait, called a *template*. The template is expected to contain only the salient discriminatory information that is essential for recognizing the person. For example, the position and orientation of minutia points (locations where the friction ridges in a fingerprint pattern exhibit some anomalies) are believed to be unique for each finger. Therefore, detecting the minutia points in a fingerprint image is a key feature extraction step in most fingerprint-

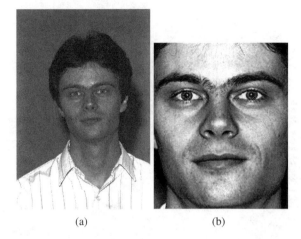

(a)   (b)

Fig. 1.5 Face segmentation and enhancement. (a) A face image of a person as captured by the camera and (b) the processed face image obtained after segmentation (removal of the background and other non-face regions such as hair and regions below the chin) and contrast enhancement based on histogram equalization.

based biometric systems. Figure 1.6 shows the commonly extracted features used to represent fingerprint, iris, and face images.

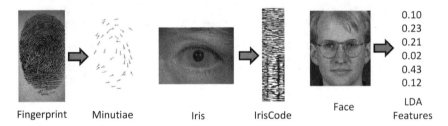

Fingerprint   Minutiae   Iris   IrisCode   Face   Features

Fig. 1.6 Common features extracted from fingerprints, iris, and face. Fingerprint is commonly represented as a set of points depicting the minutiae; iris is represented as a binary vector depicting the binarized response of an input image to Gabor filters; face is commonly represented as a vector of real numbers depicting, say, the coefficients of Linear Discriminant Analysis (LDA).

During enrollment, the template gets stored either in the central database of the biometric system or is recorded on a token (e.g., smart card) issued to the individual based on the nature of the application.

At the time of recognition, the template is retrieved from the database, and matched against the feature set extracted from the new biometric sample acquired from the user. This new feature set obtained in the recognition phase is usually re-ferred to as the *query* or *input*. In many image-based biometric systems (e.g., face or fingerprint), the raw biometric images may also be stored in the database along with the templates during enrollment. Such images are often known as *gallery images, reference images, stored images,* or *enrollment images.* The images acquired during recognition are known as *probe images, query images,* or *input images.*

The template of a user can be extracted from a single biometric sample, or generated by processing multiple samples acquired during enrollment. Thus, the minutiae template of a finger may be extracted after mosaicing (combining) multiple impressions of the same finger. Some systems store multiple templates in order to account for the large variations that may be observed in the biometric data of a user. Face recognition systems, for instance, may store multiple templates of an individual, with each template corresponding to a different facial pose with respect to the camera.

1.2.4 Database module

The biometric system database acts as the repository of biometric information. During the enrollment process, the feature set extracted from the raw biometric sample (i.e., the template) is stored in the database along with some personal identity information (such as name, Personal Identification Number (PIN), address, etc.) characterizing the user. One of the key decisions in the design of a biometric system is whether to use a centralized database or a decentralized one. Storing all the templates in a central database may be beneficial from a system security perspective, because the data can be secured through physical isolation and by having strict access control mechanisms. On the other hand, compromise of a central database would have far greater implications than the compromise of one of the sites in decentralized database. This is because malicious individuals (corrupt administrators or hackers) can abuse the biometric information stored in the database to compromise the privacy of innocent users.

1.2.5 Matching module

The purpose of a biometric matcher is to compare the query features against the stored templates to generate match scores. The match score is a measure of the similarity between the template and the query. Hence, a larger match score indicates greater similarity between the template and the query. If a matcher measures the dissimilarity (instead of the similarity) between the two feature sets, the score is referred to as a distance score. A smaller distance score indicates greater similarity. In a fingerprint-based biometric system, the number of matching minutiae between the input and the template feature sets can be considered as the degree of similarity (match score). The match score may also be moderated based on the quality of the presented biometric data. The matcher module also encapsulates a decision making module, in which the match scores are used to either validate a claimed identity or provide a ranking of the enrolled identities in order to identify an individual.

1.3 Biometric Functionalities

A biometric system can provide two types of identity management functionalities, namely, *verification* and *identification*. Throughout this book, the generic term recognition will be used when we do not wish to make a distinction between the verification and identification functionalities. Moreover, the term authentication will be used as a synonym for verification. Figure 1.7 shows the enrollment and recognition phases of a biometric system operating in the verification and identification modes.

1.3.1 Verification

In verification, the user claims an identity and the system verifies whether the claim is genuine, i.e., the system answers the question "Are you who you say you are?". In this scenario, the query is compared only to the template corresponding to the claimed identity (a one-to-one match). The identity claim is usually made through the use of a Personal Identification Number (PIN), a user name, or a token (e.g., smart card). If the user's input and the template of the claimed identity have a high degree of similarity, then the claim is accepted as "genuine". Otherwise, the claim is rejected and the user is considered an "impostor". In the biometrics literature, the terms "client" or "authentic" are sometimes used in place of the term "genuine". Verification is typically used in applications where the goal is to prevent unauthorized persons from using the services.

Formally, verification can be posed as the following two-category classification problem: given a claimed identity I and a query feature set $\mathbf{x}^A$, we need to decide if $(I, \mathbf{x}^A)$ belongs to "genuine" or "impostor" class. Let $\mathbf{x}_I^E$ be the stored template corresponding to identity I. Typically, $\mathbf{x}^A$ is compared with $\mathbf{x}_I^E$ and a match score s, which measures the similarity between $\mathbf{x}^A$ and $\mathbf{x}_I^E$, is computed. The decision rule is given by

$$(I, \mathbf{x}^A) \in \begin{cases} \text{genuine, if } s \geq \eta, \\ \text{impostor, if } s < \eta, \end{cases} \quad (1.1)$$

where η is a pre-defined threshold. If a distance score is used in place of the similarity or match score, the inequalities in the decision rule shown in equation (1.1) should be reversed. When the identity claim is deemed to be "genuine", the user is allowed to access the services provided by the system.

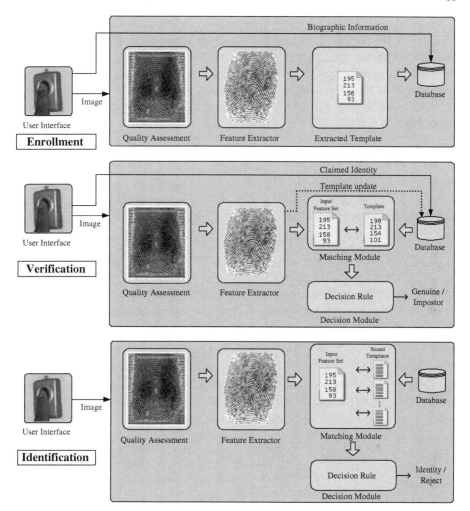

Fig. 1.7 Enrollment and recognition stages of a biometric system operating in the verification and identification modes. The dotted line in the verification module is an optional operation to update a specific user's template.

1.3.2 Identification

Identification functionality can be further classified into positive and negative identification. In positive identification, the user attempts to positively identify himself to the system without explicitly claiming an identity. A positive identification system answers the question "Are you someone who is known to the system?" by determining the identity of the user from a known set of identities. In contrast, the user in a negative identification application is considered to be concealing his true identity (either explicitly or implicitly) from the system. Negative identification is also known as screening and the objective of such systems is to find out "Are you who you say you are not?".

The purpose of negative identification is to prevent a single person from using multiple identities. Hence, screening can be used to prevent the issue of multiple credential records (e.g., driver's licence, passport) assigned to the same person or to prevent a person from claiming multiple benefits under different names (a problem commonly encountered in welfare disbursement applications). Screening is also often used at airports to verify whether a passenger's identity matches with any person on a "watch-list".

In both positive and negative identification, the user's biometric input is compared with the templates of all the persons enrolled in the database and the system outputs either the identity of the person whose template has the highest degree of similarity with the user's input or a decision indicating that the user presenting the input is not an enrolled user. Formally, the problem of identification can be stated as follows: given a query feature set $\mathbf{x}^A$, we need to decide the identity I of the user, where $I \in \{I_1, I_2, \cdots, I_N, I_{N+1}\}$. Here, $I_1, I_2, \cdots, I_N$ correspond to the identities of the N users enrolled in the system and I_{N+1} indicates the case where no suitable identity can be determined for the given query. If $\mathbf{x}^E_{I_n}$ is the stored template corresponding to identity I_n and s_n is the match score between $\mathbf{x}^A$ and $\mathbf{x}^E_{I_n}$, for $n = 1, 2, \cdots, N$, the decision rule for identification is,

$$\mathbf{x}^A \in \begin{cases} I_{n_0}, & \text{if } n_0 = \arg\max_n s_n \text{ and } s_{n_0} \geq \eta, \\ I_{N+1}, & \text{otherwise,} \end{cases} \quad (1.2)$$

where η is a pre-defined threshold. The above decision rule is commonly known as *open set identification*, because it is possible to return a result indicating that the user presenting his biometric trait is not among the N enrolled users. Almost all practical biometric identification systems (including screening systems) use open set identification. It is also possible to force the system to return one among the N enrolled identities, irrespective of the value of s_{n_0}. Such a scenario is called *closed set identification*.

In some practical biometric identification systems (e.g., latent fingerprint matching), identification is semi-automated. A semi-automated biometric system outputs the identities of the top t matches ($1 < t \ll N$) and a human expert manually determines the identity (among the t selected identities) that best matches the given query. The value of t could be determined based on the availability and throughput of the human expert(s). Against a large database such as the FBI's Integrated Automated Fingerprint Identification System (IAFIS), which has approximately 60 million users enrolled, the typical value of t could range from 20 to 50. Another approach is to return all identities whose corresponding match scores exceed the threshold (η) in equation (1.2). Since the number of enrolled users in the database can be quite large (e.g., FBI-IAFIS), the identification task is significantly more challenging than verification.

1.4 Biometric System Errors

The science of biometric recognition is based on two fundamental premises, namely, *uniqueness* and *permanence* of the underlying biometric trait. A biometric identifier is said to be unique only if any two persons in the world can be differentiated based on the given identifier. A biometric trait is permanent if it does not change over the lifetime of an individual. However, these two premises are seldom true in practical biometric systems. This can be primarily attributed to two reasons.

Firstly, the physical trait itself may not be unique. For instance, when fingerprint recognition systems gained popularity at the beginning of the 20th century, press reports claimed that fingerprints were truly unique.

"Only once during the existence of our solar system will two human beings be born with similar finger markings" - *Harper*'s headline, 1910.

"Two like fingerprints would be found only once every 10^{48} years" - *Scientific American*, 1911.

Such claims were accepted over time, not because of rigorous scientific evidence in their favor, but rather due to a lack of contradiction and relentless repetition. In the last two decades, the claims about the uniqueness of fingerprints have been challenged by both the scientific and legal communities. Similarly, the uniqueness or individuality of other biometric modalities has not been clearly established.

The genetic similarity between related individuals (e.g., twins, father and son) may also contribute to the lack of uniqueness of some biometric traits. For example, the facial appearance of identical twins is almost the same. Modalities such as DNA, where the genetic constitution of the individual largely determines their biometric characteristics are referred to as genotypic factors/features. In contrast, the modalities whose characteristics are determined by other sources of randomness in nature (e.g., fingerprints) are referred to as phenotypic factors/features. Figure 1.8 shows the fingerprint, face, and iris images obtained from identical twins.

Furthermore, the notion that the biometric traits are permanent is also not an established scientific fact. The effects of body growth (especially during childhood and adolescence) on common biometric identifiers like face, fingerprint, or iris, have not been studied in detail. Even casting aside possible natural changes in the physical traits, practical biometric systems face a much more challenging problem. Biometric systems rely only on the digital measurements of the body characteristics, and not the real physical traits. This process of measurement (sensing) introduces variations in the samples of the same biometric trait of a user obtained over a period of time. Consequently, the feature sets obtained from different samples of the same biometric trait of a user are seldom identical.

The variability observed in the biometric feature set of an individual is known as *intra-user variations* or *intra-class variations*. This variability may be due to reasons like imperfect sensing conditions (e.g., noisy fingerprint due to sensor malfunction), alterations in the user's biometric characteristic (e.g., respiratory ailments impacting

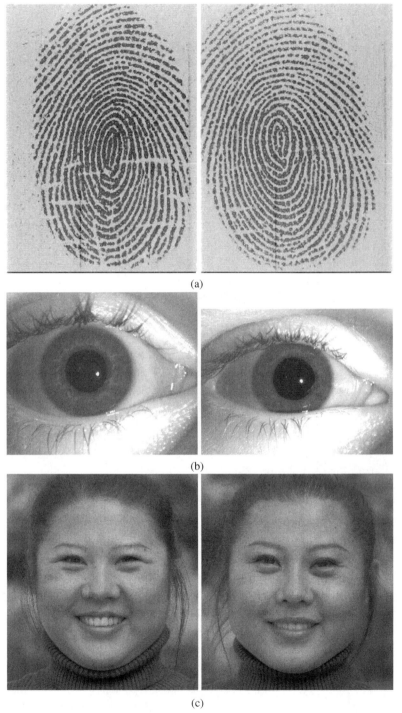

(a)

(b)

(c)

Fig. 1.8 Biometrics of twins. (a) The right index fingerprints of a pair of twins; (b) right eyes of a pair of twins; (c) face images of a pair of twins.

speaker recognition), changes in ambient conditions (e.g., inconsistent illumination levels in face recognition applications), and variations in the user's interaction with the sensor (e.g., occluded iris or partial fingerprints). As an illustration, consider two impressions of the same finger obtained on different days shown in Figure 1.9. These impressions differ in terms of the geometric distortions and amount of overlap caused by factors such as placement of finger on the sensor, applied finger pressure, skin condition, and feature extraction errors. Similarly, Figure 1.10 shows the intra-user variations in the face images of a person due to changes in pose and other attributes such as facial hair.

Fig. 1.9 Illustration of intra-user variability in fingerprints. Two different impressions of the same finger obtained on different days are shown with minutia points marked on them. Due to differences in finger placement and distortion introduced by finger pressure variations, the number and location of minutiae in the two images are different (33 and 26 in the left and right images, respectively). The number of corresponding/matching minutiae in the two images is only 16. Some of these correspondences have been indicated in the figure. The concept of minutia points will be described in the next chapter.

Intra-user variations are even more prominent in behavioral traits since the varying psychological makeup of an individual might result in vastly different behavioral characteristics at different time instances. For example, depending on the stress level of an individual, the voice sample presented by the person at the time of authentication may be significantly different from the enrolled template. Similarly, an inebriated person's gait and signature may be substantially altered.

Given the variability in the acquired biometric traits, it is factitious to expect a perfect match between any two biometric feature sets, even if they come from the same individual. In fact, if two feature sets are indeed identical, it may be a strong indication that the biometric data actually comes from an adversary who is replaying the data recorded at an earlier time. Therefore, there is a fundamental difference between password-based authentication systems and biometric systems.

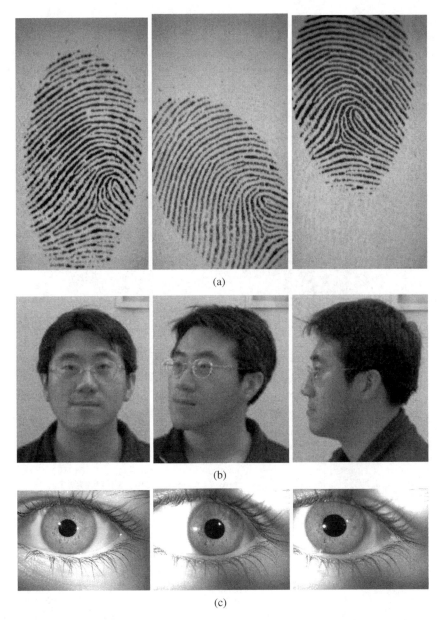

(a)

(b)

(c)

Fig. 1.10 Intra-user variations. (a) Variations in the fingerprints of the same person due to differ-ence in position and orientation of the finger printed, (b) variations in the face images of the same person due to changes in pose, and (c) variations in the iris images due to difference in dilation and gaze direction.

In a password-based system, a *perfect* match between two alphanumeric strings is necessary to validate a user's identity. On the other hand, biometric systems mostly decide on a person's identity based on a *close* match between the template and the query, where the strength of the match (or the degree of similarity) is represented by the match score.

An ideal biometric feature set must exhibit small inter-user similarity and small intra-user variations. In practice, both these conditions may not be fully met either due to inherent *information limitation* (lack of uniqueness) in the underlying biometric trait or due to *representation limitation* (problems in feature extraction). Practical feature extraction systems, typically based on simplistic models of biometric data, fail to capture the richness of information in a realistic biometric input resulting in the inclusion of redundant or spurious features, and the exclusion of salient features.

Due to large inter-user similarity and large intra-user variations, a biometric system can make two types of errors, namely, *false non-match* and *false match*. When the intra-user variation is large, two samples of the same biometric trait of an individual (mate samples) may not be recognized as a match, and this leads to a false non-match error. A false match occurs when two samples from different individuals (non-mate samples) are incorrectly recognized as a match due to large inter-user similarity.

1.4.1 Performance measures

The basic measures of the accuracy of a biometric system are *False Non-Match Rate* (FNMR) and *False Match Rate* (FMR). FNMR refers to the expected probability that two mate samples (samples of the same biometric trait obtained from the same user) will be falsely declared as a non-match. FMR is the expected probability that two non-mate samples will be incorrectly recognized as a match.

A False Non-Match Rate of 5% indicates that on average, 5 in 100 authentication attempts by genuine users will not succeed. A majority of the false non-match errors are usually due to incorrect interaction of the user with the biometric sensor and can be easily rectified by allowing the user to present his biometric trait again. This scenario is similar to the case where the user in a password-based authentication system makes a mistake while entering a password and is allowed to re-enter the password.

A False Match Rate of 0.02% indicates that on average, 1 in 5,000 authentication attempts by random impostors are likely to succeed. It is quite natural to consider how the FMR of a biometric system compares with the security provided by a password-based system. Consider a simple knowledge-based authentication system that uses a four-digit numeric PIN. Since a 4-digit PIN can take up 10,000 different values, 5,000 impostor attempts will be required, on average, to correctly guess the PIN. Does this mean that the security of a biometric system operating at 0.02% FMR is equivalent to the security provided by a 4-digit PIN? The answer is *no* because of two reasons. Firstly, it should be noted that the effective security provided by a

4-digit PIN is typically much less than 1 success in $5,000$ impostor attempts, because most users tend to use numbers that are easy to remember (e.g., 1234, year of birth, etc.) and such PINs can be easily guessed by the adversary in a few attempts. Secondly, while a single adversary can theoretically attempt any number of guesses for a PIN, he has only a limited number of biometric samples (say ten fingers or two irides) that can be tried physically. To overcome this limitation, the adversary can make use of an off-line database of biometric samples or templates. However, in order to input these samples/templates, he must circumvent a physical component in the biometric system (sensor, feature extractor, or communication channels). This circumvention can be made very difficult by securing the physical infrastructure of the biometric system.

1.4.1.1 Verification system error rates

In the context of biometric verification, FNMR and FMR are generally referred to as False Reject Rate (FRR) and False Accept Rate (FAR), respectively. Strictly speaking, FMR and FNMR are not always synonymous with FAR and FRR, respectively. This is because while FNMR and FMR are measured as a proportion of the number of biometric matching attempts, FAR and FRR are application level metrics that measure the proportion of successful or failed transactions (a transaction may involve one or more matching attempts). However, in this book we treat them as being equivalent.

A match score is termed as a *genuine* or *authentic* score if it indicates the similarity between two mate samples. An *impostor* score measures the similarity between two non-mate samples. As discussed in section 1.3, a verification system makes a decision by comparing the match score s to a threshold η. Therefore, given a set of genuine and impostor match scores, FRR can be defined as the proportion of genuine scores that are less than the threshold η and FAR can be defined as the fraction of impostor scores that are greater than or equal to η.

Consider a scenario where the biometric data (e.g., right index fingerprint) corresponding to N users is acquired. Further, assume that each user is asked to provide t samples of their biometric data. To generate a genuine match score, a pair of samples from the same user have to be compared using the matcher; to generate an impostor match score, a pair of samples from two different users have to be compared. Thus, using this biometric data, a total of $Nt(t-1)/2$ genuine scores and $(N(N-1)t^2)/2$ impostor scores can be generated by the matcher. Here, it is assumed that the matcher is symmetric in the sense that comparison of sample A against B gives the same score as the comparison of B against A.

In the subsequent mathematical notations, we will use the labels ω_0 and ω_1 to denote the impostor and genuine classes, respectively. Let $p(s|\omega_1)$ and $p(s|\omega_0)$ be the probability density functions of the genuine and impostor scores, respectively. Figure 1.11 illustrates the genuine and impostor match score distributions corresponding to a face biometric system. The FAR and FRR of the biometric system are given by

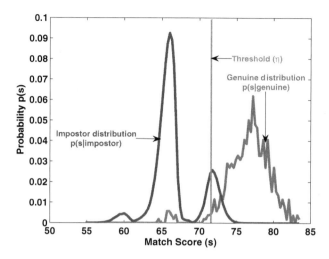

Fig. 1.11 The genuine and impostor match score distributions. In this illustration, the genuine and impostor match scores originate from a matcher identified as Face-G in the Biometric Score Set Release-1 provided by the National Institute of Standards and Technology (NIST). The threshold, η, determines the FAR and FRR of the system. Note that given these two match score distributions, the FAR and the FRR cannot be reduced *simultaneously* by adjusting the threshold.

$$FAR(\eta) = p(s \geq \eta|\omega_0) = \int_{\eta}^{\infty} p(s|\omega_0)ds, \qquad (1.3)$$

$$FRR(\eta) = p(s < \eta|\omega_1) = \int_{-\infty}^{\eta} p(s|\omega_1)ds. \qquad (1.4)$$

Both FRR and FAR are functions of the system threshold η. If the threshold is increased, FAR will decrease but the FRR will increase and vice versa. Hence, for a given biometric system, it is not possible to decrease both these errors simultaneously by varying the threshold.

The Genuine Accept Rate (GAR) or True Accept Rate (TAR) can be used as an alternative to FRR while reporting the performance of a biometric verification system. GAR is defined as the fraction of genuine scores that exceed the threshold η. Therefore,

$$GAR(\eta) = p(s \geq \eta|\omega_1) = 1 - FRR(\eta). \qquad (1.5)$$

Since the same biometric system can be operated at different thresholds (η) depending on the changing security level or different requirements of different applications, the FAR and FRR at different values of threshold η are measured and summarized in the form of a Detection Error Tradeoff (DET) curve. The DET curve plots the FRR against the FAR at various thresholds on a *normal deviate* scale[5] and interpolates between these points (Figure 1.12(a)). When a linear or logarithmic scale is used to plot these error rates, then the resulting graph is known as a Receiver Operating Characteristic (ROC) curve. In many instances, the ROC curve plots the GAR (rather than the FRR) against the FAR (see Figures 1.12(b) and (c)).

Given a set of match scores $\{s_i\}_{i=1}^{L}$, where the first L_1 match scores correspond to the genuine class, the subsequent L_0 match scores correspond to the impostor class, and the total number of scores is $L = (L_1 + L_0)$, the ROC curve can be computed using the following technique:

1. Generate a set of thresholds $\{\eta_j\}_{j=1}^{T}$ such that $s_{min} \leq \eta_j \leq s_{max}$, $\forall j = 1, 2, \cdots, T$, where s_{min} and s_{max} are the minimum and maximum scores, respectively, in the given set of match scores. A typical approach is to select thresholds that are spaced equally, i.e., $\eta_j = s_{min} + (j-1)p$, where $p = (s_{max} - s_{min})/(T-1)$.
2. At each threshold, η_j, $j = 1, 2, \cdots, T$, compute the FAR and FRR as follows.

$$FAR(\eta_j) = \frac{1}{L_0} \sum_{i=L_1+1}^{L} I(s_i \geq \eta_j), \qquad (1.6)$$

$$FRR(\eta_j) = \frac{1}{L_1} \sum_{i=1}^{L_1} I(s_i < \eta_j), \text{ where} \qquad (1.7)$$

$$I(x) = \begin{cases} 1, & \text{if } x \text{ is true,} \\ 0, & \text{otherwise.} \end{cases} \qquad (1.8)$$

3. The set of points $\{(FAR(\eta_j), FRR(\eta_j))\}_{j=1}^{T}$, connected using a smooth curve gives the ROC curve.

The best way to compare the performance of two biometric systems is to examine their ROC curves. If the FRR of one biometric system (say A) is consistently lower than the FRR of the other system (say B) for corresponding values of FAR, one can conclude that the matching performance of biometric system A is better than that of B. However, if the two ROC curves intersect, it indicates that system A is better than system B at some operating points (FAR values), while system B is better at other operating points. In this scenario, it is also possible to compare the performance of the two systems by estimating the area under the ROC curve (AUC). For a given set of match scores, the AUC is computed as

$$AUC = \frac{\sum_{i=1}^{L_1} \sum_{j=L_1+1}^{L} I(s_i > s_j)}{L_0 L_1}. \qquad (1.9)$$

The value of AUC ranges from 0.5 to 1, with 1 indicating that there are no errors.

It is important to note that the occurrence of false accepts and false rejects is not evenly distributed across the users of a biometric system. There are inherent

---

[5] In the normal deviate scale, the thresholds correspond to linear multiples of standard deviation of a normal (Gaussian) distribution. Consequently, if the genuine and impostor score distributions are Gaussian, the corresponding DET curve would be linear.

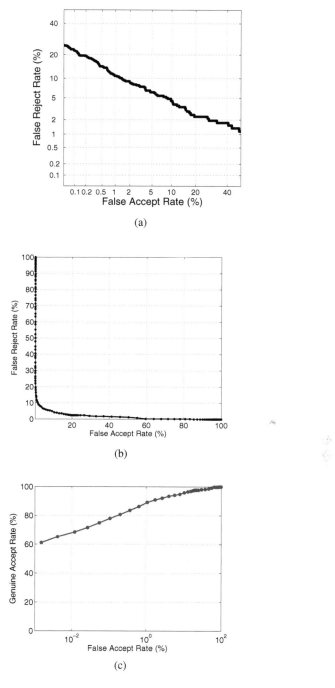

Fig. 1.12 The performance of a biometric verification system can be summarized using DET and ROC curves. In this example, the performance curves are computed using the match scores of the Face-G matcher from the Biometric Score Set Release-1 provided by NIST. The graph in (a) shows a DET curve that plots FRR against FAR in the normal deviate scale. In (b) an ROC curve plots FRR against FAR in the linear scale, while in (c) an ROC curve plots GAR against FAR, where FAR is in logarithmic scale.

differences in the "recognizability" of different users. Four categories of users are usually defined in the biometrics literature based on these inherent differences. Although this categorization (more popularly known as Doddington's zoo) was originally made in the context of speaker recognition, it is applicable to other biometric modalities as well. The four categories are:

1. *Sheep* represent users whose biometric feature sets are very distinctive and exhibit low intra-class variations. Therefore, these users are expected to have low false accept and false reject errors.
2. *Goats* refer to users who are prone to false rejects. The biometric feature sets of such users typically exhibit large intra-class variations.
3. *Lambs* are users whose biometric feature set overlaps extensively with those of other individuals. The biometric feature sets of these users have high inter-user similarity. Thus, a randomly chosen user (from the target population) has a higher probability of being accepted as a lamb than as a sheep. The false accept rate associated with these users is typically high.
4. *Wolves* indicate individuals who are successful in deliberately manipulating their biometric trait (especially behavioral traits) in order to impersonate legitimately enrolled users of a system. Since the wolves make a concerted effort to adopt the identity of another user, such an effort is often referred to as an *adversary attack* and it can increase the FAR of a system. Examples include forging the signature of another user or mimicking someone else's voice. This is in contrast to a *zero-effort* attack, where the biometric traits of an opportunistic intruder may be sufficiently similar to a legitimately enrolled user.

Apart from false non-match and false match errors, two other types of failures are also possible in a practical biometric system. If an individual cannot interact correctly with the biometric user interface or if the biometric samples of the individual are inherently of very poor quality (see Figure 1.13), the sensor or feature extractor may not be able to process these individuals. A fingerprint biometric system, for example, may fail to extract minutiae features in images obtained from a subset of people who may have cuts or bruises on their fingers, or whose fingerprints are worn-out due to age or hard manual labor. Hence, such users cannot be enrolled in the biometric system. The *Failure to Enroll (FTE)* rate denotes the proportion of users that cannot be successfully enrolled in a biometric system. User training or habituation may be necessary to ensure that an individual interacts with a biometric system appropriately in order to facilitate the acquisition of good quality biometric data. This necessitates the design of robust and efficient user interfaces that can assist an individual both during enrollment and recognition.

In some cases, a particular sample provided by the user during authentication cannot be acquired or processed reliably. This type of error typically occurs when the device is not able to locate a biometric signal of sufficiently good quality (e.g., an extremely faint fingerprint or an occluded face image). This error is called failure to capture and the fraction of authentication attempts in which the biometric sensor cannot capture the sample presented to it is known as *Failure to Capture* (FTC) or *Failure to Acquire* (FTA) rate. The FTA rate is also impacted by sensor wear and

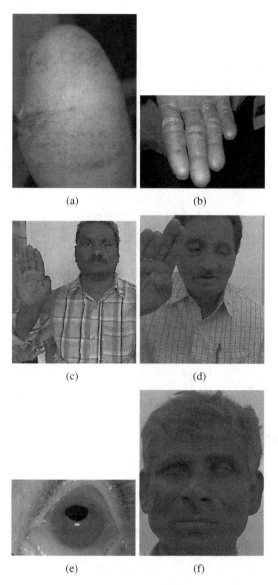

Fig. 1.13 Examples of biometric samples that lead to failure to enroll error. (a) and (b) show examples of degraded finger and hand, respectively, (c) and (d) show examples of persons with missing fingers, and (e) and (f) shows a degraded eye and a person with eye disease, respectively. (Source: Unique Identification Authority of India)

tear. Thus, periodic sensor maintenance is instrumental for the efficient functioning of a biometric system.

There is a tradeoff between the FTE rate and the perceived system accuracy as measured by FAR/FRR. FTE errors typically occur when the system rejects poor quality inputs during enrollment; consequently, if the threshold on quality is high, the system database contains only good quality templates and the perceived system accuracy improves. Because of the interdependence among the failure rates and error rates, all these rates (i.e., FTE, FTC, FAR, and FRR) constitute important performance specifications of a biometric system, and should be reported during system evaluation along with the demographics of the target population (e.g., age, ethnicity, occupation) using the system.

The performance of a biometric system may also be summarized using other single-valued measures such as the Equal Error Rate (EER) and the d-prime value. The EER refers to that point in a DET (or ROC) curve where the FAR equals the FRR; a lower EER value, therefore, indicates better performance. The d-prime value (d') measures the separation between the means of the genuine and impostor probability distributions in standard deviation units and is defined as,

$$d' = \frac{\sqrt{2}\,|\mu_1 - \mu_0|}{\sqrt{\sigma_1^2 + \sigma_0^2}}, \qquad (1.10)$$

where μ_1 (μ_0) and σ_1 (σ_0) are the mean and standard deviation, respectively, of the genuine (impostor) score distributions. A higher d-prime value indicates better performance. If the genuine and impostor distributions indeed follow a normal (Gaussian) distribution with equal variance (a very unlikely situation in practical biometric systems), then d' reduces to the normal deviate value. Another single-valued performance measure is known as the F-Ratio, which is defined as,

$$\text{F-ratio} = \frac{\mu_1 - \mu_0}{\sigma_1 + \sigma_0}. \qquad (1.11)$$

If the genuine and impostor distributions are Gaussian, then the EER and F-ratio are related according to the following expression:

$$\text{EER} = \frac{1}{2} - \frac{1}{2}\text{erf}\left(\frac{\text{F-ratio}}{\sqrt{2}}\right), \qquad (1.12)$$

where

$$\text{erf}(x) = \frac{2}{\sqrt{\pi}} \int_0^x e^{-t^2}\,dt. \qquad (1.13)$$

1.4.1.2 Identification system error rates

Suppose that a biometric identification system, with N identities enrolled, outputs a set of identities corresponding to the top t matches ($1 \leq t \ll N$). The identification rank is defined as the rank of a user's correct identity in the top t matches returned by the identification system. For instance, if a user's correct identity corresponds to the topmost match (highest score among all N match scores), we say that the user has been identified at rank one. Similar to the verification scenario, there are two types of identification system errors. A false positive identification occurs when an identity is returned for a user not enrolled in the system. This is analogous to the false match case in biometric verification. The expected proportion of identification transactions by users not enrolled in the system, where an identity is returned, is known as the *false positive identification rate* (FPIR). The FPIR depends both on the size of the enrollment database (N) and the threshold (η) used in equation (1.2).

False negative identification refers to a scenario where the transacting user is enrolled in the database, but his correct identity is not among those returned by the system. The expected proportion of identification transactions by users enrolled in the system in which the user's correct identity is not returned is called the *false negative identification rate* (FNIR). FNIR depends on the size of the enrollment database (N), the threshold (η) used for the match scores, and the number of identities t returned by the identification system. A quantity related to the FNIR is the *true positive identification rate* (TPIR), which is the expected proportion of identification transactions by users enrolled in the system, where the user's correct identity is among the t identities returned by the system. Therefore, FNIR $= 1 -$ TPIR. If the biometric system outputs the identities of the top t matches, the corresponding TPIR is also known as the rank-t identification rate, which we refer to as R_t. In particular, the value of TPIR for $t = 1$ is called the *rank-one accuracy* and this value is one of the most commonly used metrics to compare different biometric identification systems.

The rank-t identification rate for different values of t can be summarized using the Cumulative Match Characteristic (CMC) curve (see Figure 1.14), which plots R_t against t for $t = 1, 2, \cdots, N$, where N is the number of enrolled users. In general, it is difficult to infer the identification error rates (FPIR and FNIR) from the FMR and FNMR of the underlying biometric matcher. This is because identification involves finding the top match among the N identities in addition to comparing the top match score against a threshold. However, under some simplifying assumptions it is possible to estimate the performance in the identification mode from the FMR and the FNMR of the biometric matcher. Suppose that the identification system returns all the identities whose match score is above a threshold and these identities are found by sequentially comparing the query to each of the N templates in the enrollment database. Let us also assume that the same matching threshold (η) is used for both verification and identification scenarios. Under these assumptions,

- FNIR $=$ FNMR; in fact, the probability that the input is falsely declared as a non-match against the user's template is the same as in verification mode. In most identification systems, the number of returned identities is restricted to t due to practical constraints. When t is less than number of identities whose score is above the threshold, FNIR $\geq$ FNMR.
- FPIR $= 1 - (1 - \text{FMR})^N$; in fact, a false positive identification occurs when the input falsely matches one or more templates in the database. FPIR is then

computed as one minus the probability that no false match is made with any of the database templates. In the above expression, $(1 - \text{FMR})$ is the probability that the query does not falsely match a single non-mate template, and $(1 - \text{FMR})^N$ is the probability that it does not falsely match with any of the N database templates. Here, we assume that all the N matches are statistically independent. If we further assume that FMR is very small $(<< (1/N))$, FPIR can be approximated as FPIR $\approx N \times \text{FMR}$. From this expression, it is clear that FPIR increases when the value of N increases and often the increase is linear in the database size (N).

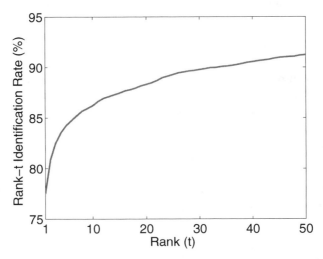

Fig. 1.14 Cumulative match characteristic (CMC) curve for the Face-G matcher in the Biometric Score Set Release-1 provided by NIST. In this example, the rank-1 identification rate is $\approx 78\%$, which means that for $\approx 78\%$ of the identification attempts, the correct identity of the user is selected as the best matching identity.

The above results highlight the tremendous challenge involved in the design of large-scale biometric identification systems as compared to verification systems. While an FMR of 10^{-6} (1 false match in 1 million attempts) is typically acceptable for a biometric matcher operating in the verification mode, the FPIR of an identification system with 10,000 enrolled users using the same underlying matcher under the same threshold setting would be about 1%. Suppose that such an identification system is used at an airport to screen passengers against a watch-list of 10,000 persons, 1 in 100 innocent passengers would be falsely matched against someone from the watch-list, causing inconvenience and potential embarrassment.

1.5 The Design Cycle of Biometric Systems

The design of a biometric system typically entails the following major activities, some of which are carried out iteratively. The foremost step in designing a biometric system is understanding the nature of the application and the performance requirements. This is followed by choosing the right biometric trait(s) for the application in hand. Given a specific biometric trait, one needs to collect biometric data from a subset of target population and design or train the core biometric modules, including the feature extractor and the matcher. Finally, the developed biometric system must undergo a thorough evaluation procedure to ensure that it meets the requirements of the application. Figure 1.15 presents an overview of this design cycle.

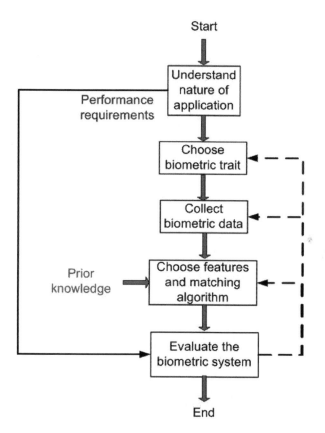

Fig. 1.15 The design cycle of a biometric system involves the key steps shown here. A part of the biometric data collected during the design stage is used for choosing the appropriate feature set and matching algorithm. The remaining part of the data is used to evaluate whether the designed biometric system satisfies the performance requirements of the application in hand. Depending on the results of the evaluation, some steps in the above process may need to be repeated until satisfactory results are obtained.

1.5.1 Nature of the application

The design of a biometric system completely hinges on the nature of the application in which the biometric system will be used eventually. In fact, the characteristics of the application determine whether a biometric system is required or even feasible in the first place. Prior to opting for a biometric system, one must also consider the existing security solutions (e.g., passwords, smart cards, etc.) in the application domain where the biometric system will be embedded. Biometrics does not have to replace tokens and passwords in all applications. In some applications, biometrics may be used to supplement ID cards and passwords, thereby imparting an additional level of security. Such an arrangement is often called a multi-factor authentication scheme.

Depending on the application, we may need to choose between the verification and identification functionalities. This choice need not be always mutually exclusive. In some applications such as large-scale national ID systems having a broad usage scope, one may need to perform negative identification during enrollment to prevent the possibility of the same user acquiring multiple identities. In the recognition phase, the system can run in the verification mode to deliver benefits or services only to the enrolled users. Apart from the type of functionality, biometric applications can also be classified based on the following issues.

1. **Cooperative** versus **non-cooperative users**: Cooperation refers to the behavior of the user when interacting with the system. For example, in a verification system, it is in the best interest of a genuine user to cooperate with the system and be accepted as a valid user. An electronic banking application is an example where enrolled users are likely to cooperate with the system in order to be recognized accurately. On the other hand, in a negative recognition system, a user may not cooperate with the system (e.g., may purposely apply excessive pressure when placing his finger on the sensor) to avoid being recognized. A terrorist attempting to conceal his identity from an airport screening application will be non-cooperative.

2. **Overt** versus **covert deployment**: If the user is aware that he is being subjected to biometric recognition, the application is categorized as overt. If the user is unaware, the application is called covert. Facial recognition can be easily used in a covert application (e.g., surveillance), while fingerprint recognition cannot be used in this mode (except for criminal identification based on latent fingerprints). Most commercial uses of biometrics are overt in nature.

3. **Habituated users** versus **non-habituated**: If the enrolled users interact with the biometric system quite frequently, they tend to get habituated in providing their biometric data. For example, a computer network login application typically has habituated users (after an initial "habituation" period) due to their use of the system on a regular basis. However, a driver's license application typically has non-habituated users since a driver's license is renewed only once in a period of several years. This is an important consideration when designing a biometric

system because the familiarity of users with the system can affect recognition accuracy since a habituated user is likely to provide good quality biometric data.

4. **Attended** versus **unattended operation**: Attended versus unattended classification refers to whether the process of biometric data acquisition in an application is observed, guided, or supervised by a human (e.g., a security officer). Furthermore, an application may have an attended enrollment operation but unattended recognition operation. For example, a banking application may have a supervised enrollment when an ATM card is issued to a user, but the subsequent uses of the biometric system for the ATM transaction are not attended.

5. **Controlled** versus **uncontrolled operation**: In a controlled environment, ambient environmental conditions such as temperature, pressure, moisture, lighting conditions, etc. can be moderated during the operation of a biometric system. Typically, indoor applications such as computer network login operate in a controlled environment, whereas outdoor applications such as keyless car entry or parking lot surveillance operate in an uncontrolled environment. This classification is also important for the system designer as a more rugged biometric sensor is needed for an uncontrolled environment.

6. **Open** versus **closed system**: If a person's biometric template can be used across multiple applications, the biometric system can be considered as open. For example, a user may use a fingerprint-based recognition system for entering secure facilities, computer network login, electronic banking, and bank ATMs. When all these applications use separate templates (databases) for each application, the system is considered closed. A closed system may be based on a proprietary template whereas an open system will need standard data formats and data compression methods to exchange and compare information between different systems (most likely developed by different commercial vendors).

All the above factors profoundly influence the design of a biometric system. Most of the commercial applications of biometrics, such as access to secure facilities, have the following attributes: verification, cooperative, overt, habituated, attended enrollment and non-attended authentication, and closed.

1.5.2 Choice of biometric trait

A number of biometric traits are being used in various applications. Each biometric trait has its pros and cons and, therefore, the choice of a biometric trait for a particular application depends on a variety of issues besides its recognition performance. In general, seven factors must be considered to determine the suitability of a physical or a behavioral trait to be used in a biometric application.

1. **Universality**: Every individual accessing the application should possess the trait. This factor determines the failure to enroll (FTE) rate of the biometric system.

2. **Uniqueness**: The given trait should be sufficiently different across individuals comprising the user population. Otherwise, the false match rate (FAR or FPIR) of the biometric system would be unacceptably high.
3. **Permanence**: The biometric trait of an individual should be sufficiently invariant over a period of time with respect to the matching algorithm. A trait that changes significantly over time is not a useful biometric because it will lead to a high false non-match rate (FRR or FNIR).
4. **Measurability**: It should be possible to acquire and digitize the biometric trait using suitable devices that do not cause undue inconvenience to the individual. Furthermore, the acquired raw data should be amenable to processing in order to extract discriminative feature sets. This factor significantly impacts the frequency of FTE and FTA failures and the recognition accuracy.
5. **Performance**: Apart from the recognition accuracy (FMR, FNMR, FTE, and FTA), the computational resources required to achieve that accuracy and the throughput (number of transactions that can be processed per unit time) of the biometric system should also meet the constraints imposed by the application.
6. **Acceptability**: Individuals in the target population that will utilize the application should be willing to present their biometric trait to the system.
7. **Circumvention**: This refers to the ease with which the trait of an individual can be imitated using artifacts (e.g., fake fingers), in the case of physical traits, and mimicry, in the case of behavioral traits. It also refers to the process of obfuscation, where a user deliberately alters his biometric trait to evade recognition.

No single biometric is expected to effectively meet all the requirements (e.g., accuracy, practicality, cost) imposed by all applications (e.g., forensics, access control, government benefits programs, etc.). In other words, no biometric is *ideal* but a number of them are *admissible*. The relevance of a specific biometric to an application is established depending upon the nature and requirements of the application, and the properties of the biometric characteristic. A brief introduction to some of the commonly used biometric characteristics (also shown in Figure 1.16) is given below:

1. **Fingerprint**: Humans have used fingerprints for personal identification for many decades. A fingerprint is the pattern of ridges and valleys on the surface of a fingertip whose formation is determined during the first seven months of fetal development. While fingerprints have been in use in forensic applications for over 100 years, the advent of low-cost and compact fingerprint scanners has spawned a large number of commercial applications in the past ten years. In applications requiring large-scale identification involving millions of identities, multiple fingerprints of a person (e.g., ten-prints used in Automated Fingerprint Identification Systems (AFIS)) can be used to improve the matching performance, though at the cost of more computational resources. Finally, fingerprints of a small fraction of the population may be unsuitable for automatic identification because of genetic factors, aging, environmental, or occupational reasons (e.g., manual laborers may have a large number of cuts and bruises on their fingerprints). Chapter 2 of this

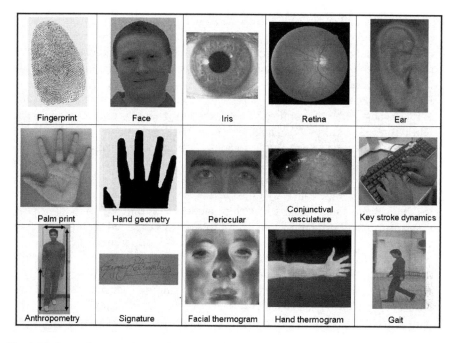

| Fingerprint | Face | Iris | Retina | Ear |

| Palm print | Hand geometry | Periocular | Conjunctival vasculature | Key stroke dynamics |

| Anthropometry | Signature | Facial thermogram | Hand thermogram | Gait |

Fig. 1.16 A set of commonly used biometric traits.

book addresses the various issues concerning the design and implementation of automated fingerprint recognition systems.

2. **Palmprint**: The palms of the human hands contain pattern of ridges and valleys much like the fingerprints. The area of the palm is much larger than the area of a finger and, as a result, palmprints are expected to be even more distinctive than the fingerprints. Since palmprint scanners need to capture a large area, they are bulkier and more expensive than fingerprint sensors. Human palms also contain additional distinctive features such as principal lines and wrinkles that can be captured even with a lower resolution scanner, which would be less expensive. Finally, when using a high-resolution palmprint scanner, all the features of the hand such as geometry, ridge and valley features (e.g., minutiae and singular points such as deltas), principal lines, and wrinkles may be combined to build a highly accurate biometric system. There is a growing interest in palmprint matching, particularly latent palmprint matching, among the law enforcement agencies. More details about palmprints are presented in Chapter 2 along with the fingerprints.

3. **Iris**: The iris is the annular region of the eye bounded by the pupil and the sclera (white of the eye) on either side. The visual texture of the iris is formed during fetal development and stabilizes during the first two years of life (the pigmentation, however, continues to change over an extended period of time). The complex iris texture carries very distinctive information useful for personal recognition.

The accuracy and speed of currently deployed iris-based recognition systems is promising and can support large-scale identification. Although early generation iris-based recognition systems required considerable user participation and were expensive, the newer systems have become more user-friendly and cost-effective. Iris recognition is the primary focus of Chapter 4 of this book.

4. **Face**: Face recognition is a non-intrusive method, and facial attributes are probably the most common biometric features used by humans to recognize one another. The applications of facial recognition range from a static, controlled "mugshot" authentication to a dynamic, uncontrolled face identification in a cluttered background. While the authentication performance of the face recognition systems that are commercially available is acceptable for use in some applications, they impose a number of restrictions on how the facial images are obtained, often requiring a fixed and simple background with controlled illumination. These systems also have difficulty in matching face images captured from two different views, under different illumination conditions, and at different times. The design of face recognition systems and the associated challenges will be discussed in more detail in Chapter 3.

5. **Hand geometry (shape)**: Hand geometry recognition systems are based on a number of measurements taken from the human hand, including its shape, size of palm, and the lengths and widths of the fingers. Environmental factors such as dry weather or individual anomalies such as dry skin do not appear to adversely affect the authentication accuracy of hand geometry-based systems. However, the geometry of the hand is not known to be very distinctive and hand geometry-based recognition systems cannot be scaled up for systems requiring identification of an individual from a large population. Furthermore, hand geometry information may not be invariant during the growth period of children. In addition, individuals wearing jewelry (e.g., rings) or with limitations in dexterity (e.g., from arthritis), may pose challenges in extracting the correct hand geometry information. The physical size of a hand geometry-based system is large, and it cannot be embedded in certain devices like laptops. There are a few commercially available systems that are based on measurements of only a few fingers (typically, index and middle) instead of the entire hand. These devices are smaller than those used for hand geometry, but still much larger than those used for acquiring other traits like fingerprint, face, and voice. Hand shape biometric is discussed in Chapter 5.

6. **Gait**: Gait refers to the manner in which a person walks, and is one of the few biometric traits that can be used to recognize people at a distance. Therefore, this trait is very appropriate in surveillance scenarios where the identity of an individual can be covertly established. Most gait recognition algorithms attempt to extract the human silhouette in order to derive the spatio-temporal attributes of an individual who is walking. Hence, the selection of a good model to represent the human body is pivotal to the efficient performance of a gait recognition system. Some algorithms use the optic flow associated with a set of dynamically extracted moving points on the human body to describe the gait of an individual. Gait-based systems also offer the possibility of tracking an individual over an extended period of time. However, the gait of an individual is affected by sev-

eral factors, including the choice of footwear, nature of clothing, affliction of the legs, and walking surface. The segmentation problem is particularly severe for gait-based recognition. More details are provided in Chapter 5.

7. **Ear**: It has been suggested that the shape of the ear and the structure of the cartilegenous tissue of the pinna are distinctive. The ear recognition approaches are either based on matching the distance of salient points on the pinna from a landmark location on the ear or based on the appearance of the ear. Ear recognition could be useful for identifying a person based on a profile photograph. See Chapter 5 for more details on ear biometric systems.

8. **Voice**: Voice is a combination of physical and behavioral biometric characteristics. The physical features of an individual's voice are based on the shape and size of the appendages (e.g., vocal tract, mouth, nasal cavities, and lips) that are used in the synthesis of the sound. These physical characteristics of human speech are invariant for an individual, but the behavioral aspects of speech change over time due to age, medical condition (such as common cold), emotional state, etc. Voice is also not very distinctive and may not be appropriate for large-scale identification. A text-dependent voice recognition system is based on the utterance of a predetermined phrase. A text-independent voice recognition system recognizes the speaker independent of what she speaks. A text-prompted system prompts the user to repeat a phrase generated dynamically, which offers more protection against fraud. A disadvantage of voice-based recognition is that speech features are very sensitive to factors like background noise and microphone characteristics. Speaker recognition is most appropriate in telephone-based applications but the voice signal is typically degraded in quality by the communication channel.

9. **Keystroke**: It is hypothesized that each person types on a keyboard in a characteristic way. This biometric is not expected to be unique to each individual but it may be expected to offer sufficient discriminatory information to permit identity verification. Keystroke dynamics is a behavioral biometric; one may expect to observe large intra-class variations in a person's typing patterns due to changes in emotional state, position of the user with respect to the keyboard, type of keyboard used, etc. The keystrokes of a person could be monitored unobtrusively as that person is keying in information. This makes it possible to "continuously verify" an individual's identity over a session, after the person logs in using a stronger biometric such as fingerprint or iris.

10. **Signature**: The way a person signs her name is known to be a characteristic of that individual. Although signatures require contact with the writing instrument and an effort on the part of the user, they have been accepted in government, legal, and commercial transactions as a method of authentication. With the proliferation of PDAs, Tablet PCs, and smartphones, on-line signature may emerge as the biometric of choice in these devices. Signature is a behavioral biometric that changes over a period of time and is influenced by the physical and emotional conditions of the signatories. Signatures of some people vary substantially: even successive impressions of their signature are significantly different. Further, professional forgers may be able to reproduce signatures that can fool the signature verification system.

11. **DNA**: DNA refers to deoxyribonucleic acid that contains the genetic information necessary for the development and functioning of living organisms. DNA is the one-dimensional unique code for one's individuality - except for the fact that identical twins have the same DNA pattern. It is, however, currently used mostly in the context of forensic applications for suspect and victim identification. Three issues limit the utility of DNA for several other applications: (a) contamination and sensitivity: it is easy to steal a piece of DNA from an unsuspecting subject that can be subsequently abused for an ulterior purpose; (b) automatic real-time recognition issues: the state-of-the-art technology for DNA matching requires cumbersome chemical methods (wet processes) involving an expert's skills and is not yet geared for on-line non-invasive recognition; (c) privacy issues: information about susceptibilities of a person to certain diseases could be gained from the DNA pattern and there is a concern that the unintended abuse of genetic code information may result in social discrimination, e.g., in hiring practices.

12. **Facial, hand, and hand vein infrared thermograms**: The pattern of heat radiated by the human body is a characteristic of an individual and can be captured by an infrared camera in an unobtrusive way much like a regular (visible spectrum) photograph. The technology could also be used for covert recognition. A thermogram-based system does not require contact and is non-invasive, but image acquisition is challenging in uncontrolled environments, where heat emanating surfaces (e.g., room heaters and vehicle exhaust pipes) are present in the vicinity of the human body. A related technology using near infrared (NIR) imaging is used to scan the back of a clenched fist to determine hand vein structure. Infrared sensors are currently expensive, which is a factor inhibiting widespread use of the thermograms.

13. **Odor**: It is known that each object exudes an odor that is characteristic of its chemical composition and this could be potentially used for distinguishing various objects. A whiff of air surrounding an object is blown over an array of chemical sensors, each sensitive to a certain group of (aromatic) compounds. A component of the odor emitted by a human (or any animal) body is distinctive to a particular individual. It is not clear if the invariance in the body odor could be detected despite deodorant smells, and varying chemical composition of the surrounding environment.

14. **Retinal scan**: The retinal vasculature is rich in structure and is supposed to be distinctive for each individual and each eye. It is claimed to be the most secure biometric since it is not easy to change or replicate the retinal vasculature. The image acquisition requires a person to peer into an eye-piece and focus on a specific spot in the visual field so that a predetermined part of the retinal vasculature could be imaged. The image acquisition involves cooperation of the subject, entails contact with the eyepiece, and requires a conscious effort on the part of the user. All these factors adversely affect the public acceptability of the retinal biometric. Retinal vasculature can reveal some medical conditions, e.g., hypertension, which is another factor deterring the public acceptance of retinal scan-based biometrics.

Table 1.1 summarizes the error rates of fingerprint, face, iris, and voice biometric systems obtained through various technology evaluation tests (see Section 1.5.5). In fact, these four biometric modalities are the only ones that have undergone extensive testing and evaluation so far. Although the error rates presented in Table 1.1 are dependent on a number of test conditions such as the sensor used, the acquisition protocol, the number and demographic profile of the subjects involved, and the time lapse between successive biometric acquisitions, they provide a good estimate of the accuracy of state-of-the-art biometric systems because these results are obtained by independent third-party testing of competing algorithms on common databases. The results of these evaluations clearly indicate that biometric systems have non-zero error rates and there is scope for improving the accuracy of biometric systems.

Table 1.1 False reject and false accept rates associated with state-of-the-art fingerprint, face, voice, and iris verification systems. Note that the accuracy estimate of a biometric system depends on a number of test conditions.

Biometric Trait	Test	Test Conditions	False Reject Rate	False Accept Rate
Fingerprint	FVC 2006	Heterogeneous population including manual workers and elderly people	4.2%	0.1%
	FpVTE 2003	U.S. government operational data	0.6%	0.1%
Face	FRVT 2006	Controlled illumination, high resolution	0.8-1.6%	0.1%
Voice	NIST 2008	Text independent, multi-lingual	12%	0.1%
Iris	ICE 2006	Controlled illumination, large quality range	1.1-1.4%	0.1%

One way to improve the accuracy of biometric systems is to use more than one biometric trait in a recognition application. For example, the face and iris traits, or the fingerprints from all the ten fingers of an individual may be used together to resolve the identity of an individual. Such systems are known as *multibiometric systems*. These systems are expected to be more accurate and reliable due to the availability of multiple pieces of evidence. The design of multibiometric systems will be addressed elaborately in Chapter 6.

1.5.3 Data collection

The next step in the design cycle of a biometric system is the collection of biometric data from a subset of the targeted population. This data is required both for designing the feature extraction and matcher modules as well as for the evaluation of the designed biometric system. However, before venturing into data collection, we first need to design appropriate sensors to acquire the chosen biometric trait(s). Factors like size, cost, ruggedness, and ability to capture good quality biometric samples are some of the key issues in biometric sensor design. In the case of more mature biometric modalities like fingerprint, the sensors must also be capable of satisfying certain industry standards such as minimum image resolution.

It is important to remember that the characteristics of the database such as data collection environment, sample population, and user habituation will greatly affect the performance of the biometric systems. Hence, care must also be taken to ensure that the database is neither too challenging (collected under the most adverse conditions) nor too easy (collected under the most favorable conditions). If the database is too easy (i.e., it includes only good quality biometric samples with small intra-user variations), the resulting recognition error rates will be close to zero and it will be very difficult to distinguish between the competing feature extraction and matching algorithms. On the other hand, if the database is too challenging (i.e., it includes only poor quality biometric samples with large intra-user variations), the recognition challenge may be beyond the capabilities of existing technologies.

Ideally, a database should include samples that are representative of the population and must preferably exhibit realistic intra-class variations (achieved by collecting data over multiple sessions spread over a period of time and in different environmental conditions). Further, due to the involvement of human subjects, legal and privacy issues must also be considered and approval of organizations like the Institutional Review Board (IRB) is mandatory in many countries. This makes biometric data collection a time-consuming, relatively expensive, and cumbersome process. On the other hand, careful planning and implementation of data collection process is likely to lead to successful and operational biometric systems.

1.5.4 Choice of features and matching algorithm

The choice of features and the matching algorithm to be employed is one of the most critical steps in biometric system design. Most of the research and development in the field of biometrics has been focused on this issue. Design of a feature extractor and matcher not only requires a database of biometric samples, but also some prior knowledge about the biometric trait under consideration. For instance, prior knowledge about the "uniqueness" of minutia points facilitated the development of minutiae-based fingerprint recognition systems. Similarly, the fact that a minutiae pattern is typically represented as an unordered set of points, drives the development of a suitable matching algorithm to match the minutia sets.

In some biometric modalities, incorporating prior knowledge may be difficult. Consider the example of a face recognition system. What are the features that makes a human face distinct from other human faces, especially if the faces belong to individuals with the same gender and ethnicity? Humans seem to have the capability to learn these distinctions easily, but it is challenging to elicit this information from the humans and then mimic this process in a machine. Since the features and matching algorithms are mostly modality-specific, these choices will be discussed in detail as we consider the individual modalities in the subsequent chapters.

Another important factor affecting the choice of features and matching algorithm is the *interoperability* between biometric systems. Most biometric systems operate under the assumption that the biometric data to be compared are obtained using the same sensor and, hence, are restricted in their ability to match or compare biometric data originating from different sensors. For example, a speaker recognition system may find it challenging to compare voice samples originating from two different handset (microphone) technologies such as electret and carbon-button. The performance of face recognition algorithms is severely affected when the images used for comparison are captured using different camera types. Similarly, fingerprints obtained using multiple sensor technologies cannot be reliably compared due to variations in sensor technology, image resolution, sensing area, distortion effects, etc.

Although progress has been made in the development of common data exchange formats to facilitate the exchange of feature sets between vendors, very little effort has been invested in the actual development of algorithms and techniques to match these feature sets. The US-VISIT program for example, obtains fingerprint (and face) information of millions of travelers arriving at U.S. airports and seaports. An optical fingerprint sensor is currently being used during the enrollment phase to procure fingerprint images. However, it is not guaranteed that a similar type of sensor will be used at a later time when verifying the same individual. It is possible that due to advancements in sensor technology, it may be more desirable and cost effective to use the current generation of sensors. The cost and time involved in re-enrolling individuals every time the sensor is changed will be tremendous, and could potentially lead to huge bottlenecks in the system, resulting in user inconvenience. In cases such as these, the need for feature extraction and matching algorithms that operate seamlessly across different sensors is paramount and will significantly impact the usability of the system over a period of time.

1.5.5 Evaluation

Evaluation of a complete biometric system is a complex and challenging task that requires experts from a variety of fields, including statistics, computer science, engineering, business, and psychology, as well as system designers and the end user community. In order to gain a thorough understanding of the performance of a biometric system, one must address the following questions.

1. What are the error rates of the biometric system in a given application? (matching or technical performance)
2. What is the reliability, availability, and maintainability of the system? (engineering performance)
3. What are the vulnerabilities of the biometric system? What level of security does the biometric system provide to the application in which it is embedded? (security of the biometric system)
4. What is the user acceptability of the system? How does the system address human factor issues like habituation and privacy concerns? (user concerns)
5. What is the cost and throughput of the biometric system and what tangible benefits can be derived from its deployment? (return on investment)

No existing biometric evaluation framework has addressed all the above questions in a systematic manner. In this section, we focus only on the matching performance of a biometric system. Ideally, the evaluation requires an independent third party to design, administer, and analyze the test. We can divide the matching performance evaluation of a biometric system into three stages:

1. **Technology evaluation**: Technology evaluation compares competing algorithms from a single technology on a standardized database. Since the database is fixed, the technology evaluation results are repeatable. The Fingerprint Verification Competitions (FVC), the Fingerprint Vendor Technology Evaluation (FpVTE), the Face Recognition Vendor Tests (FRVT), the Face Recognition Technology (FERET) program, and the NIST Speaker Recognition Evaluations (SRE) are examples of biometric technology evaluations.
2. **Scenario evaluation**: In scenario evaluation, the testing of the prototype biometric systems is carried out in an environment that closely resembles the real-world application. Since each system will acquire its own biometric data, care must be taken to ensure uniformity in the environmental conditions and sample population across the different prototype systems.
3. **Operational evaluation**: Operational evaluation is used to ascertain the performance of a complete biometric system in a specific real-world application environment on a specific target population.

Researchers have identified some best practices to be followed when evaluating the technical performance of a biometric system. There are recommendations available in the biometrics literature on a number of testing issues, including size of the test, volunteer selection, factors that may affect the performance of a biometric system, data collection methodology, estimation of the performance metrics, estimating the uncertainty of performance metrics, and reporting the performance results. A sound evaluation of the technical performance of a biometric system must follow these best practices as closely as possible and clearly explain any deviations from these recommendations that may be necessary.

1.6 Applications of Biometric Systems

Establishing the identity of a person with high confidence is becoming critical in a number of applications in our vastly interconnected society. Questions like "Is she really who she claims to be?", "Is this person authorized to use this facility?" or "Is he on the watchlist posted by the government?" are routinely being posed in a variety of scenarios ranging from issuing a driver's licence to gaining entry into a country. The need for reliable user authentication techniques has increased in the wake of heightened concerns about security, and rapid advancements in networking, communication, and mobility. Thus, biometric recognition is being increasingly incorporated in several different applications. These applications can be categorized into three main groups (see Table 1.2):

1. Commercial applications such as computer network login, electronic data security, e-commerce, Internet access, ATM or credit card use, physical access control, mobile phone, PDA, health record management, distance learning, etc.
2. Government applications such as national ID card, managing inmates in a correctional facility, driver's license, social security, welfare-disbursement, border control, passport control, etc.
3. Forensic applications such as corpse identification, criminal investigation, missing children, parenthood determination, etc.

Table 1.2 Recognition solutions employing biometrics can be used in a variety of applications which depend on reliable person recognition mechanisms.

FORENSICS	GOVERNMENT	COMMERCIAL
Corpse identification	National ID card	ATM
Criminal investigation	Driver's license; voter registration	Access control; computer login
Parenthood determination	Welfare disbursement	Mobile phone
Missing children	Border crossing	E-commerce; Internet; banking; smart card

Examples of a few applications where biometrics is being used for authenticating individuals are presented below (also see Figure 1.17).

1. **Airport security**: Biometrics is being used for authenticating passengers as well as employees at various airports. For example, the *Schiphol Privium* scheme at Amsterdam's Schipol airport employs iris scan smart cards to speed up the immigration procedure. Passengers who are voluntarily enrolled in this scheme insert their smart card at the gate and peek into a camera; the camera acquires the eye image of the traveler and processes it to locate the iris, and computes a feature set; the computed feature set is compared with the data residing in the smart card

to complete user verification. A similar scheme is also being used to verify the identity of Schiphol airport employees working in high-security areas.

The Ben Gurion International Airport at Tel Aviv has deployed a similar biometric security system called the Unipass Airport Management System. Under this system, the outbound passengers are required to provide fingerprints and facial images, which are stored in a smart card that is issued to each passenger. These smart cards are then used to track the passengers as they pass through different locations at the airport, such as security checkpoint, baggage screening, airline check-in, and finally, boarding the aircraft.

2. **Government applications**: A good example of a large-scale biometric system is the United States Visitor and Immigration Status Indicator Technology (US-VISIT). The US-VISIT program represents one of the security measures adopted by the Department of Homeland Security to identify visitors entering the United States. When a traveler from a visa waiver country enters the U.S. for the first time, a digital facial photograph of the visitor and fingerprints from all ten fingers are collected at the immigration booth prior to admission into the United States. The ten fingerprints are matched against a dynamic watch list containing up to a few million records in less than 10 seconds. This is an example of negative recognition, where the purpose is to find if the visitor has multiple aliases. If not on a watch-list, the visitor is admitted into the U.S. and the person's fingerprints are enrolled into the US-VISIT enrollment database for future matching. For travelers requiring a visa, the above process is completed prior to issuing a visa at the U.S. consulates. During subsequent visits into the United States, the person's fingerprints are matched against his previous records in the enrollment database (authentication) to verify the visitor's identity. Over 75 million visitors have been processed through this system since its inception in January 2004 and about 1,000 have been denied entry.

Another example of large scale use of biometric system is the Unique Identification (UID) project in India. The objective of this project is to significantly increase the efficiency and effectiveness of various welfare disbursement schemes initiated by the Government of India by improving the transparency of various transactions. The project involves collection of multiple biometric traits, namely, ten fingers, two irides, and face, as well as demographic information (name, gender, birthday, and address) from the residents of India and will provide each resident with a 12-digit unique identification number. The project is expected to enroll 600 million residents of India over a span of five years. This is an example of de-duplication (negative recognition) where a fusion of 10 fingers and 2 irides is expected to determine if the same person is trying to acquire two different identification numbers.

3. **Commercial applications**: Some of the major financial institutions in Japan have installed palm-vein authentication systems in their ATMs to help validate the identity of a customer intending to conduct a transaction. A contactless sensor is used to image the vein pattern pertaining to the customer's palm using a near infrared lighting source.

Another example of a high-throughput biometric verification system is the one used by the Walt Disney World Resort in Orlando, Florida to prevent ticket fraud. Every visitor to the resort must provide his index finger at the turnstile along with the ticket. The fingerprint provided by the ticket holder then gets linked to that particular ticket; if the ticket holder visits the resort again (either later the same day or on a different day if he has a multiple entry ticket) he must present the same finger that was used to validate the ticket. This prevents more than one person using the same ticket. The Disney system can handle a large number (around 100,000 per day) of visitors efficiently, and more importantly, this system works in all weather conditions because it uses a rugged fingerprint sensor that is able to capture good quality fingerprint images even in adverse imaging conditions. The personal details of the visitor are not associated with the fingerprint data in the database, which is regularly purged, thereby imparting security without compromising privacy.

1.7 Security and Privacy Issues

The United States Code on 'Coordination of Federal Information Policy' defines *information security* as "protecting information and information systems from unauthorized access, use, disclosure, disruption, modification, or destruction". Typically, there are four major aspects to be considered in information security.

- **Integrity** - guard against improper modification or destruction of the data and ensure non-repudiation and authenticity of information.
- **Data confidentiality** - prevent illegitimate access or disclosure of sensitive information.
- **Availability** - guarantee timely and reliable access to and use of information.
- **Authentication** - only legitimate and authorized users should be able to access the data and carry out specific tasks.

It is generally agreed that biometric recognition can effectively address the authentication problem. Since biometric traits cannot be easily lost, stolen, misplaced, or shared, biometric recognition offers a natural and more reliable authentication solution compared to other techniques such as passwords or physical tokens (e.g., ID cards). This is the reason why biometric systems are being increasingly deployed to control access to other information systems. For example, US legislation mandates that the entities (e.g., health care providers, health insurance companies) dealing with electronic health information must implement strong authentication procedures such as biometric recognition to prevent unauthorized exposure of sensitive health information. Furthermore, by implementing a non-repudiable biometric authentication scheme, it will be possible to track all the accesses to privileged information, thereby increasing the accountability of the transactions within the information systems.

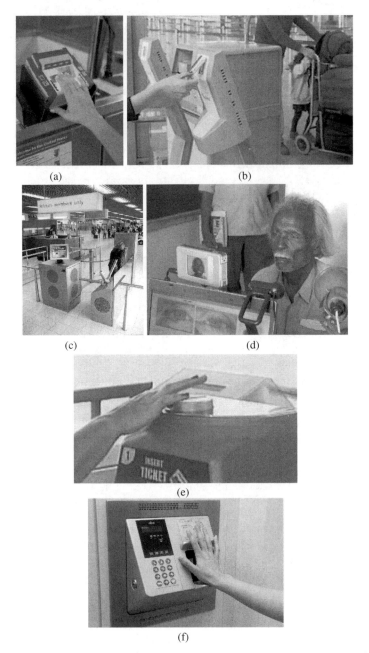

Fig. 1.17 Biometric systems are being deployed in various government and commercial applications. (a) The US-VISIT program currently utilizes all ten fingerprints to validate the travel documents of visitors to the United States, (b) the Ben Gurion airport in Tel Aviv uses the biometric-based Unipass System for security, (c) the Schiphol Privium program at the Amsterdam airport uses iris scans to validate the identity of a traveler, (d) Unique Identity (UID) Card project in India plans to enroll 600 million residents to facilitate efficient delivery of various welfare schemes, and (e) fingerprint information is used in Disney World, Orlando to ensure that a single ticket is not fraudulently used by multiple visitors, and (f) a new product by Fujitsu captures the vein pattern of the palm for verification.

However, it is important to realize that a biometric system is just one component of the overall information security solution because it address only the authentication aspect. Other technologies such as encryption, digital signature, etc. are needed to meet the confidentiality, integrity, and availability requirements of the total information system. Moreover, the biometric system can itself be considered as an independent sub-system within the complete information system. If the biometric system is compromised or circumvented, the security of the entire information system gets affected. Due to this reason, the security aspects involved in the design and implementation of a biometric system need to be analyzed carefully and independently, which is the focus of Chapter 7 in this book.

Unauthorized disclosure of sensitive personal information can cause both objective (e.g., financial fraud, denial-of-service) and subjective (where the mere knowledge of one's private information by a second or third party is perceived as an injury) harms. When the breach of security in an information system leads to personal and subjective harm to the person involved, it can be termed as loss of privacy. Privacy refers to the right of the a person to be left alone, i.e., the ability to lead ones's own life free from intrusions, to remain anonymous, and to control access to one's own personal information. Although the need for privacy is typically an individual preference, there are cases where disclosure of information may be required for the sake of larger societal interest (e.g., national security). In the words of privacy expert Esther Dyson,

"Privacy is not a one-size-fits-all condition: Different people at different times have different preferences about what happens to their personal information and who gets to see it. ⋯ Rather than attempting to define privacy for all, society should give individuals the tools to control the use and spread of their data. The balance between secrecy and disclosure is an individual preference, but the need for tools and even laws to implement that preference is general." - - *Scientific American*, September 2008.

Though biometric recognition can serve as a tool to preserve the privacy of individuals by restricting access to their personal information (e.g., medical records), the use of biometrics may itself create a privacy conundrum. This is because biometric identifiers provide an irrefutable link to the identity of a person. Consequently, the users of biometric systems have a number of legitimate concerns.

- Will the undeniable proof of biometrics-based access infringe upon an individual's right to remain anonymous? For instance, persons legally maintaining multiple aliases (say, for safety reasons) can be identified using biometric recognition. Furthermore, it is often possible to covertly recognize a user by capturing his biometric traits without his active involvement (e.g., face can be captured using hidden surveillance cameras). As a result, persons who desire to remain anonymous in any particular situation may be denied their privacy due to biometric recognition.
- Will the biometric data be abused for an unintended purpose (function creep), e.g., allowing linkage of identity records across systems without the knowledge

of the user? For example, a fingerprint template obtained from a bank's database may be used to search for that person's health records in a medical database. How to ensure that an information system is indeed exclusively using biometric recognition for the intended purpose (e.g., can it be provably demonstrated that the trusted system administrators cannot abuse the system)?

• Will the requirement of biometrics be proportional to the need for security, e.g., should a fingerprint be required to purchase a hamburger at a fast food restaurant or access a commercial website?

• Who owns the biometric data, the individual or the service providers?

The above privacy issues are thorny and do not have concrete answers. While one could stipulate some measures to protect user privacy, there are no satisfactory practical solutions on the horizon for either addressing the entire spectrum of privacy issues or how exactly these privacy issues need to be traded against the security issues. Fair information practice principles such as transparency, informed consent, use limitation, accountability, and auditing could be followed to limit the privacy concerns arising from biometric recognition. Since these issues are beyond the scope of technology, appropriate legislations must be put in place to enforce these principles. Self-regulation by the biometrics industry and autonomous enforcement of rules by independent regulatory organizations (say, a Central Biometric Authority) could also address the privacy fears of the general public.

1.8 Summary

Reliable person recognition is integral to the proper functioning of our society. It is now widely accepted that conventional recognition techniques based on credentials such as driver license, passport, password, or PIN are not sufficiently reliable to recognize an individual because they are easily vulnerable to theft and forgery. Biometric recognition, or simply biometrics, refers to the automatic recognition of a person based on his distinctive physical and behavioral (e.g., face, fingerprint, iris, voice) traits. Biometrics offers a number of advantages compared to token-or knowledge-based authentication: (a) discourages fraud and enhances security, (b) detects multiple enrollments, (c) cannot be easily transferred, forgotten, lost, or copied, (d) eliminates repudiation claims, and (e) increases user convenience. As a result, biometric recognition is now recognized as a powerful and necessary tool for identity management.

Considering the recent adoption of biometric-enabled national ID cards and e-passports by several governments, it is certain that biometric recognition will profoundly influence the way we are recognized in our daily lives. While biometric recognition has been successfully deployed in some niche applications, it is far from a solved problem. As observed from Table 1.1, there is clearly plenty of scope for improvement in the matching performance of biometric technologies. Researchers are not only addressing issues related to reducing error rates, but they are also looking at ways to enhance the usability of biometric systems. For example, the deployment of biometrics in many civilian and government applications has also raised questions related to the privacy accorded to an enrolled individual and the security of the biometric system itself. There is also a definite need for standardization of biometric systems in order (a) to facilitate interoperability between vendors, and (b) to ensure that biometric sub-systems can be easily integrated into a variety of applications.

Bibliographical and Historical Remarks

The use of biological traits to confirm the identity of an individual is certainly not a new concept. In the late 19th century, Alphonse Bertillon, a French law enforcement officer, advocated a personal identification system that associated a set of anthropometric measurements with an individual [1]. The Bertillonage system entailed the precise measurement of certain bony parts of the body (including the ear); a morphological description of the appearance and shape of the body; and a listing of peculiar marks such as moles, scars, and tattoos on the surface of the body (see Figure 1.18). These measurements were then recorded on a card and filed in a central repository that was partitioned into several categories based on the acquired measurements. This indexing ability permitted the quick retrieval of an individual's card when a repeat offender was booked by the police. But the system was cumbersome to administer uniformly (making it prone to error) and did not guarantee uniqueness across individuals. It was, therefore, abandoned in the wake of rapid developments in forensic fingerprint examination thanks to the pioneering works of Henry Faulds [6], William Herschel [10], and Sir Francis Galton [7]. Although the Bertillonage system cannot be considered as a biometric system because of its lack of automation, it has nevertheless laid the foundation for modern day biometric recognition systems.

The development of fully automatic systems for person recognition dates back to the early 1960s [36]. Mitchell Trauring published an article in *Nature* in 1963 on automated fingerprint recognition [35]. Furthermore, the advent of digital signal processing saw the design of automated systems in the 1960s that were capable of processing fingerprint images [9, 32]. The U.S. National Bureau of Standards (NBS), which later became the National Institute of Standards and Technology (NIST), started the formal testing of automated fingerprint recognition systems in 1970 [37]. However, what really boosted the popularity of automated fingerprint recognition systems was the rapid evolution of fingerprint sensing technology over the last four decades (see Figure 1.19).

The first work on automated face recognition reported in 1966 [2] used distances and distance ratios between manually marked landmarks on the face (eye centers, mouth, etc.). Other early face recognition systems followed a similar geometrical approach of finding anatomical facial landmarks and determining distance ratios [8, 16]. An appearance-based face recognition approach that decomposes the face images using principal component analysis, was first proposed in 1987 [33].

Fig. 1.18 The Bertillonage system, so named after its inventor Alphonse Bertillon, relied on the precise measurement of various attributes of the body for identifying recidivists. These measurements included the height of the individual, the length of the arm, geometry of the head, and the length of the foot. The process was tedious to administer and did not guarantee uniqueness across individuals.

(a)   (b)

Fig. 1.19 Evolution of fingerprint sensors. (a) an optical fingerprint sensor called the Identix Touchview that was in production in the 1990s; its dimensions were $125 \times 180 \times 60$ mm, (b) an optical fingerprint sensor, Digital Persona UareU, having similar capabilities that is widely used now; its dimensions are $65 \times 36 \times 16$ mm.

Other biometric modalities like voice [17, 30, 18], hand geometry [5, 21, 12], and signature [20] were also developed in the latter half of the 1960s or in the early part of the 1970s. By 1977, the field of biometric recognition technology had evolved significantly and the NBS formally published the "Guidelines on the Evaluation of Techniques for Automatic Personal Identification" as a Federal Information Processing Standard [22]. In the subsequent two decades, the availability of faster computers coupled with significant advances in statistical pattern recognition and computer vision resulted in the development of sophisticated schemes to process and match the biometric data of several modalities including iris [4], retina, and gait. Furthermore, advances in 3D modeling and graphics in recent years have paved the way for processing 3D biometric data such as range images of the hand, face, and ear.

While there are a number of overviews and reference books on biometrics, we recommend the following key readings to interested readers. References [24], [15], [13], [25], and [3] serve as a good introduction to biometrics and how biometric recognition compares to traditional authentication mechanisms like passwords and ID cards. The human factors (e.g. ergonomics) involved in the design of biometric systems and the privacy implications of using biometric technology are elaborately dealt with in [34] and [23], respectively. The general framework for technological evaluation of biometric systems is presented in [26] and the best practices to be followed in biometric evaluation, including the performance metrics to be considered, are summarized in [11] and [19]. More details about the well-known third-party technology evaluations listed in Table 1.1 can be found in references [38, 29, 27, 31].

References

1. A. Bertillon. *Signaletic Instructions including the Theory and Practice of Anthropometrical Identification, R.W. McClaughry Translation.* The Werner Company, 1896.
2. W. W. Bledsoe. Man-machine Facial Recognition: Report on a Large-scale Experiment. Techical Report PRI:22, Panoramic Research Inc., 1966.
3. R. Bolle, J. Connell, S. Pankanti, N. Ratha, and A. Senior. *Guide to Biometrics.* Springer, 2003.
4. J. Daugman. How Iris Recognition Works? *IEEE Transactions on Circuits and Systems for Video Technology*, 14(1):21–30, 2004.
5. R. H. Ernst. Hand ID System. United States patent number US 3576537, 1971.
6. H. Faulds. On the Skin Furrows of the Hand. *Nature*, 22:605, October 1880.
7. F. Galton. Personal Identification and Description. *Nature*, 38:173–177, June 1888.
8. A. J. Goldstein, L. D. Harmon, and A. B. Lesk. Identification of Human Faces. *Proceedings of the IEEE*, 59(5):748–760, May 1971.
9. A. Grasselli. On the Automatic Classification of Fingerprints - Some Considerations on the Linguistic Interpretation of Pictures. In S. Watanabe, editor, *Methodologies of Pattern Recognition*, pages 253–273. Academic Press, 1969.
10. W. Herschel. Skin Furrows of the Hand. *Nature*, 23:76, November 1880.
11. ISO/IEC 19795-1:2006. Biometric Performance Testing and Reporting – Part 1: Principles and Framework. Available at http://www.iso.org/iso/iso_catalogue/catalogue_tc/catalogue_detail.htm?csnumber=41447, 2006.

12. I. H. Jacoby, A. J. Giordano, and W. H. Fioretti. Personnel Identification Apparatus. United States patent number US 3648240, 1972.

13. A. K. Jain. Biometric Recognition. *Nature*, 449:38–40, September 2007.

14. A. K. Jain, P. Flynn, and A. Ross. *Handbook of Biometrics*. Springer, 2007.

15. A. K. Jain, A. Ross, and S. Prabhakar. An Introduction to Biometric Recognition. *IEEE Transactions on Circuits and Systems for Video Technology, Special Issue on Image- and Video-Based Biometrics*, 14(1):4–20, January 2004.

16. T. Kanade. *Picture Processing System by Computer Complex and Recognition of Human Faces*. PhD thesis, Department of Information Science, Kyoto University, November 1973.

17. L. G. Kersta. Voiceprint Identification. *Nature*, 196:1253–1257, 1962.

18. J. Luck. Automatic Speaker Verification Using Cepstral Measurements. *Journal of the Acoustic Society of America*, 46:1026–1031, 1969.

19. A. J. Mansfield and J. L. Wayman. Best Practices in Testing and Reporting Performance of Biometric Devices, Version 2.01. Technical Report NPL Report CMSC 14/02, National Physical Laboratory, August 2002.

20. A. J. Mauceri. Technical Documentary Report for Feasibility Study of Personnel Identification by Signature Verification. Techical Report SID65-24, North American Aviation Inc., Space and Information Systems Division, January 1965.

21. R. P. Miller. Finger Dimension Comparison Identification System. United States patent number US 3576538, 1971.

22. National Bureau of Standards. Guidelines on the Evaluation of Techniques for Automated Personal Identification. Publication 48, Federal Information Processing Standard, April 1977.

23. NSTC Subcommittee on Biometrics. Privacy and Biometrics: Building a Conceptual Foundation. Available at `http://www.biometrics.gov/Documents/privacy.pdf`, September 2006.

24. L. O'Gorman. Comparing Passwords, Tokens, and Biometrics for User Authentication. *Proceedings of the IEEE*, 91(12):2019–2040, December 2003.

25. J. N. Pato and L. I. Millett. *Biometric Recognition Challenges and Opportunities*. The National Academies Press, Washington, D.C., 2010.

26. P. J. Phillips, A. Martin, C. L. Wilson, and M. Przybocki. An Introduction to Evaluating Biometric Systems. *IEEE Computer*, 33(2):56–63, February 2000.

27. P. J. Phillips, W. T. Scruggs, A. J. OToole, P. J. Flynn, K. W. Bowyer, C. L. Schott, and M. Sharpe. FRVT 2006 and ICE 2006 Large-Scale Results. Technical Report NISTIR 7408, NIST, March 2007.

28. S. Prabhakar, S. Pankanti, and A. K. Jain. Biometric Recognition: Security and Privacy Concerns. *IEEE Security and Privacy Magazine*, 1(2):33–42, March-April 2003.

29. Biometric System Laboratory - University of Bologna. FVC2006: The Fourth International Fingerprint Verification Competition. Available at `http://bias.csr.unibo.it/fvc2006/default.asp`.

30. S. Pruzansky. Pattern-Matching Procedure for Automatic Talker Recognition. *Journal of the Acoustic Society of America*, 35:354–358, 1963.

31. M. Przybocki and A. Martin. NIST Speaker Recognition Evaluation Chronicles. In *Odyssey: The Speaker and Language Recognition Workshop*, pages 12–22, Toledo, Spain, May 2004.

32. C. B. Shelman. Machine Classification of Fingerprints. In *Proceedings of the First National Symposium on Law Enforcement Science and Technology*, pages 467–477, Chicago, USA, 1967.

33. L. Sirovich and M. Kirby. Low-dimensional Procedure for the Characterization of Human Faces. *Journal of Optical Society of America*, 4(3):519–524, March 1987.

34. M. Theofanos, B. Stanton, and C. A. Wolfson. Usability & Biometrics: Ensuring Successful Biometric Systems. Available at `http://zing.ncsl.nist.gov/biousa/docs/Usability_and_Biometrics_final2.pdf`, June 2008.

35. M. Trauring. On the Automatic Comparison of Finger Ridge Patterns. *Nature*, 197:938–940, 1963.

36. J. L. Wayman. Biometrics Now and Then: The Development of Biometrics Over the Last 40 Years. In *Proceedings of Second BSI Symposium on Biometrics*, 2004.

37. J. Wegstein. Automated Fingerprint Identification. Technology Note 538, National Bureau of Standards, August 1970.
38. C. Wilson, A. R. Hicklin, M. Bone, H. Korves, P. Grother, B. Ulery, R. Micheals, M. Zoepfl, S. Otto, and C. Watson. Fingerprint Vendor Technology Evaluation 2003: Summary of Results and Analysis Report. NIST Technical Report NISTIR 7123, National Institute of Standards and Technology, June 2004.

Chapter 2
FINGERPRINT RECOGNITION

"Perhaps the most beautiful and characteristic of all superficial marks are the small furrows with the intervening ridges and their pores that are disposed in a singularly complex yet even order on the under surfaces of the hands and the feet."

Francis Galton, *Nature*, June 28, 1888.

The pattern of interleaved ridges and valleys on the tip of a finger is referred to as a fingerprint. The systematic use of these patterns for personal identification was promoted in the late 19th to early 20th century, although the discovery of human fingerprints on a large number of archaeological artifacts suggests that ancient people were aware of the potential individuality of fingerprints. While fingerprints were originally acquired by rolling an inked fingertip on the surface of a paper, advances in sensor technology have resulted in the design of compact and low-cost optical and solid-state sensors that can rapidly image the fingertip and generate digital renditions of fingerprints for automated analysis. This chapter discusses the technologies used for fingerprint imaging, type of features extracted from digital images of the fingerprint, techniques for classifying fingerprint images, and methods for automated feature extraction and matching of fingerprint images.

2.1 Introduction

Unlike the skin on most parts of our body, which is smooth and contains hair and oil glands, the skin on the palms and soles exhibits a flow-like pattern of ridges and valleys (sometimes referred to as furrows), and contains no hair or oil glands. These papillary ridges on the finger, called friction ridges, help the hand to grasp objects by increasing friction and improving the tactile sensing of surface textures. The friction ridge skin is composed of two major layers: dermis (inner layer) and epidermis (outer layer). The ridges emerge on the epidermis to increase the friction between the volar (palm of the hand or sole of the feet) and the contact surface (see Figure 2.1). A typical young male has, on an average, 20.7 ridges per centimeter while a female has 23.4 ridges per centimeter.

Another important value of friction ridges is its use in biometric recognition. The pattern of friction ridges on each finger (Figure 2.1(b)) is claimed to be unique and immutable, enabling its use as a mark of identity. In fact, even identical twins can be differentiated based on their fingerprints. Superficial injuries such as cuts and bruises on the finger surface alter the pattern in the damaged region only temporarily. Indeed, the ridge structure has been observed to reappear after the injury heals. However, if the injury were to extend to the basal layer of the epidermis, it can obliterate the ability of the basal layer to regenerate cells in the damaged area. While the surrounding basal cells will attempt to repair such an injury, this process will result in a permanent scar on the surface of the friction ridge skin.

Although the possibility of using fingerprints as unique identifiers was recognized thousands of years ago, their systematic use in applications requiring person recognition did not occur until the early 20th century. Law enforcement agencies now routinely record fingerprints of criminals on tenprint cards (Figure 2.2), which capture rolled and plain impressions of all ten fingerprints. Two main purposes of the recorded fingerprints are (a) to identify repeat offenders who often use an alias to hide their true identity and (b) to perform background checks for employment or licensing. Another important application of fingerprints in law enforcement is to establish the identity of a suspect based on partial fingerprints left at a crime scene. These are called latent prints, or simply latents (see Figure 2.3(c)). Compared to rolled and plain fingerprints in Figures 2.3(a) and 2.3(b), latents typically have poor image quality. As the size of fingerprint databases began to expand to the millions, Automated Fingerprint Identification Systems (AFIS) were developed in the 1970s to improve the efficiency and accuracy of fingerprint matching. Currently, almost every law enforcement agency worldwide relies on AFIS to match fingerprints. Figure 2.4 shows the AFIS installed at the Michigan State Police facility. Growing concerns about homeland security and consumer fraud have prompted the use of fingerprint-based biometric systems in many non-forensic applications.

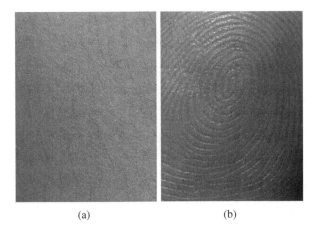

(a)   (b)

Fig. 2.1 There are two types of skin on the human body: (a) smooth skin and (b) friction ridge skin. The friction ridge skin is observed to have a pattern of ridges interspersed with valleys.

In fact, fingerprint-based biometric systems are so popular and successful that they have become synonymous with the notion of biometric recognition in the minds of the general public.

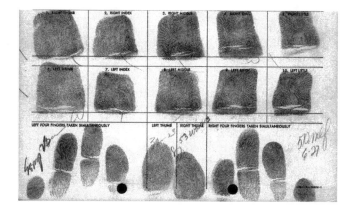

Fig. 2.2 A tenprint card. The top two rows show fingerprints acquired by rolling each finger from one side to the other (so called *rolled* fingerprints). The bottom row shows *plain* or *slap* fingerprints: slap impressions of four fingers (little to index finger) of the left hand acquired simultaneously are shown on the left part of the bottom row, two thumb prints are shown in the middle, and the slap impressions of four fingers (index to little finger) of the right hand acquired simultaneously are shown on the right.

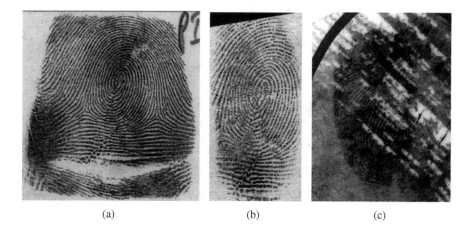

(a)	(b)	(c)

Fig. 2.3 Three different fingerprint impressions of the same finger. (a) Rolled fingerprint, (b) plain fingerprint, and (c) latent fingerprint.

2.2 Friction Ridge Pattern

Fingerprint recognition, whether done manually by a human expert or automatically by a machine, is predominantly feature-based (as opposed to image-based) and the features used have a physical interpretation. The terms *feature-based* and *image-based* are widely used in the computer vision literature to indicate the methods used for representing and matching images such as fingerprints. A feature-based method, as the name suggests, extracts explicit features from the image under consideration and encodes these features into a feature set, which is subsequently used for matching. An image-based method, on the other hand, directly uses the image for matching without explicitly extracting any features from it.

We first introduce the different types of features that can be extracted from a fingerprint, followed by a description of the histology of friction ridge skin and its formation. Knowledge of these two topics is essential in understanding the uniqueness and permanence of friction ridge patterns, which are the two fundamental premises in fingerprint recognition.

2.2.1 Features

The details in a fingerprint can be characterized at three different levels ranging from coarse to fine. Under ideal conditions, coarse level features can be derived from the finer levels of fingerprint representation.

Fig. 2.4 AFIS installation at Michigan State Police facility. This system was first installed in 1989; the database has 3.2 million tenprint cards and performs 700,000 searches each year.

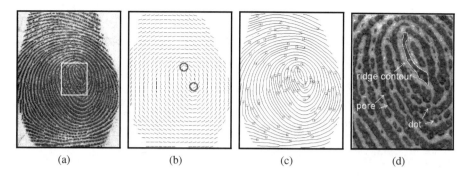

(a)   (b)   (c)   (d)

Fig. 2.5 Features at three different levels in a fingerprint. (a) Grayscale image (NIST SD30, A067_11), (b) Level 1 feature (orientation field or ridge flow and singular points), (c) Level 2 feature (ridge skeleton), and (d) Level 3 features (ridge contour, pore, and dot).

2.2.1.1 Level 1 features

At the first (coarsest) level, a fingerprint is represented as a ridge orientation map (see Figure 2.5(b)), which records the local ridge orientation at each location of the fingerprint, and a ridge frequency map, which records the local ridge frequency at each location in the fingerprint. A fingerprint is often referred to as an oriented texture pattern since its global shape and structure can be defined by the orientation and frequency of its ridges. In Level 1 detail, only the ridge flow and ridge frequency are observed; the exact location and dimensional details of ridges are ignored. Thus, low-resolution image sensors capable of scanning 250 pixels per inch (ppi) can be used to observe the Level 1 details of a fingerprint.

The local ridge orientation at a pixel (x,y) represents the tangential direction of ridge lines passing through (x,y). Ridge orientation is defined in the range $[0,\pi)$. Thus, the ridge orientation map can be viewed as a unit-length vector field whose direction is defined between 0 and π. The ridge orientation at a pixel p is illustrated in Figure 2.6. Local ridge frequency at (x,y) is the average number of ridges per unit length along a line segment centered at (x,y) and normal to the local ridge orientation. Ridge frequency is the reciprocal of the ridge period, which is illustrated in Figure 2.6. Generally, the ridge orientation information is viewed as being more important than the ridge frequency information for fingerprint matching and classification purposes.

A ridge orientation map typically contains some salient locations where the ridge orientations change abruptly - such locations are termed as singular points. There are two basic types of singular points - loop and delta - and they are visually distinctive. A loop-type singularity, also called the *core*, refers to a local area where a set of ridges enters from one direction and exits in the same direction (Figure 2.7(a)). A loop in a fingerprint can be used as a landmark point to align the fingerprint. *core* Generally, the core point corresponds to the north most loop-type singular point in a fingerprint; if a fingerprint does not contain any singular points (e.g., arch-type

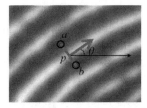

Fig. 2.6 Level 1 details pertain to coarse features of the fingerprint. These details capture the ridge orientation and frequency information in a fingerprint. This figure shows a portion of a fingerprint with ridges indicated as dark lines with the ridge orientation θ and ridge period $\overline{ab}$ (reciprocal of ridge frequency) marked at a pixel p.

fingerprints), the core usually refers to the point of maximum ridge curvature. However, the term *core* itself is often used to indicate a loop-type singularity in practice. A delta-type singularity indicates a local area where three ridge systems appear to meet (Figure 2.7(b)). The set of singular points in a fingerprint can be viewed as an abstract representation of the orientation map so that the orientation map can be roughly predicted based on the number and location of singular points. An even more abstract representation of the orientation map is the pattern type (often referred to as a fingerprint *class*), which can be deduced based on the number of loops and deltas, and the spatial relationship between them. Examples of six major fingerprint pattern types are shown in Figure 2.8, and almost all of the fingerprints fall into one of those classes. Singularities in most fingerprints are observed to satisfy the following constraints: (a) the numbers of loops and deltas in a full print are the same; in other words, loops and delta appear in pairs; and (b) the total number of singular points are either 0, 2, or 4. The procedure to determine the fingerprint pattern type based on the singular points will be discussed later in the chapter.

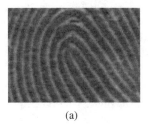

(a)

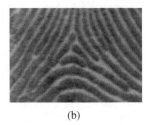

(b)

Fig. 2.7 Singular points. (a) Loop and (b) delta.

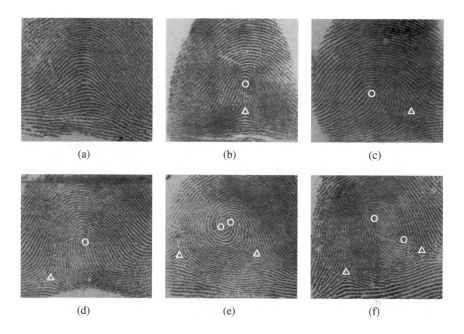

Fig. 2.8 Major fingerprint pattern types. (a) Plain arch, (b) tented arch, (c) left loop, (d) right loop, (e) whorl, and (f) twin loop. A loop is denoted by a circle and a delta is denoted by a triangle. Loop- and whorl-type of fingerprints are found most commonly; about 65% of fingerprints belong to loop-type, and 24% are whorl-type [52]. Twin loop, arch and tented arch account for approximately 4%, 4% and 3% of the fingerprints, respectively.

2.2.1.2 Level 2 features

In the second (middle) level, a fingerprint is represented as a ridge skeleton image in which each ridge is only one-pixel wide (see Figure 2.5(c)). At this level, the exact locations of the ridges are recorded, but the geometric and dimensional details of the ridges are ignored. The locations where a ridge emerges, ends, splits, or merges with another ridge are termed as ridge characteristics or minutiae. In addition to its location, a minutia generally has two other properties: direction and type. The direction of a minutia is along the local ridge orientation. There are two basic types of minutiae: ending (also called 'termination') and bifurcation (see Figure 2.9). Thus, each minutia can be characterized by its (a) location in the image, (b) direction, and (c) type. Level 2 details of a fingerprint can be easily observed in images acquired at a resolution of 500 ppi. The number of minutiae found in a fingerprint varies a lot according to the acquisition method and other factors. For example, the rolled impression of a finger shown in Figure 2.3(a) has 136 minutiae while its plain impression in Figure 2.3(b) has 56 minutiae extracted by a commercial fingerprint matcher. On the other hand, only 18 minutiae were found in the latent fingerprint in Figure 2.3(c) by a latent examiner.

A minutiae set, consisting of all the minutiae in a fingerprint, is an abstract representation of the ridge skeleton in the sense that the minutiae set captures most of the discriminative information at Level 2, and ridge skeletons can be approximately derived from the minutiae information alone. Minutiae-based representations are extensively used in automated fingerprint recognition systems, primarily due to the following reasons: (a) minutiae capture much of the discriminative or individuality information in fingerprints, (b) minutiae-based representations are storage efficient, and (c) minutiae extraction is reasonably robust to various sources of degradation. The spatial distribution of minutiae in a fingerprint is an interesting topic of study that has gained increased attention due to the need for assessing the individuality of fingerprints using minutiae information alone.

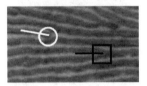

Fig. 2.9   There are two types of minutiae used to represent the Level 2 details in a fingerprint: ridge ending (denoted as white circle) and ridge bifurcation (denoted as black box). While the forensic literature alludes to other types of minutiae as well, ending and bifurcation are the most extensively used ridge anomalies in automated fingerprint recognition systems. The spatial distribution of these minutiae points in a fingerprint image is believed to be unique to each finger.

2.2.1.3 Level 3 features

In the third (finest) level, a fingerprint is represented using both the inner holes (sweat pores) and outer contours (edges) of the ridges. So the ridges are no longer viewed as being simple, one-pixel wide skeletal images. Rather, information embedded within the ridges are observed in detail. Incipient ridges and dots are also included at this level (see Figure 2.5(d)). Incipient ridges are immature ridges, which are thinner than mature ridges and contain no sweat pores. A dot is a very short ridge containing only a single ridge unit. With advances in fingerprint sensing technology, many sensors are now equipped with 1000 ppi scanning capability that is needed to capture the Level 3 details in a fingerprint. Figure 1.4 in Chapter 1 shows images captured at 500 ppi and 1000 ppi by a CrossMatch L SCAN 1000P optical scanner from the same portion of a fingerprint. Level 3 features are receiving increased attention due to their importance in matching latent fingerprints that generally contain much fewer minutiae than rolled or plain fingerprints. Figure 2.10(a) shows the Level 3 features extracted from a latent fingerprint that are also observed in the mated rolled fingerprint (Figure 2.10(b)).

(a)

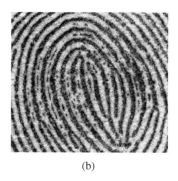
(b)

Fig. 2.10 Level 3 features observed in a latent and its mated rolled fingerprint. (a) Latent fingerprint with pores and incipient ridges and (b) the mated rolled print with the same configuration of the Level 3 features observed in (a).

2.2.1.4 Additional features

Fingerprints often have other features such as creases, cuts, and scars. While these features are not inherent to fingerprint formation, they may become permanent depending on the severity of cuts and scars. However, since these features are not as universal as the three levels of features discussed earlier, their utility in fingerprint matching is limited. In fact, such abnormalities are often the source of matching errors, as discussed later.

2.2.2 Formation

The exact process of friction ridge pattern formation is not fully known. Embryology research has shown that the epidermal ridges are preceded by the formation of volar pads that first appear at about the sixth week of fetal development. The friction ridges appear in about the fourth month of gestation as a result of the stresses during the growth of the fetus; the ridges are not elevated on the skin until about the eighteenth week. Minutiae are formed as ridges separate and create space for forming new ridges due to the growth of the finger surface.

The ridge flow on the boundary of a finger runs parallel to the fingernail furrow and the finger crease. The ridge flow pattern in the central area, also termed as pattern area, of the finger is governed by the shape, size, and placement of volar pads; higher and symmetric volar pads tend to generate whorls, flatter and symmetric volar pads tend to generate arches, and asymmetric volar pads tend to generate loops. It is generally understood and agreed that friction ridge patterns are not just influenced by genetic factors but also by random physical stresses and tensions during fetal development. These random effects during the morphogenesis of fingerprints are believed to impart uniqueness to the fingerprint.

2.3 Fingerprint Acquisition

The first step in fingerprint recognition is image acquisition - the process of capturing and digitizing the fingerprint of an individual for further processing. Traditionally, the ink-on-paper technique has been used to capture the fingerprint information from a person. It is a simple - yet powerful - acquisition and recording technique that has been in use since the late 19*th* century. However, the primary reason for the popularity of fingerprint recognition, particularly in non-forensic applications, is the availability of mature, convenient, and low-cost sensors that can rapidly acquire the fingerprint of an individual with minimum or no intervention from a human operator. These compact fingerprint sensors have also been embedded in many consumer devices such as laptops and mobile phones. Below, we discuss some of the sensing techniques that have been developed for acquiring fingerprints from a subject.

2.3.1 Sensing techniques

Broadly speaking, digital images of the fingerprints can be acquired using off-line or on-line methods (see Figure 2.11). Off-line techniques generally do not produce the digital image directly from the fingertip. Rather, the fingerprint is first transferred to a substrate (e.g., paper) that is subsequently digitized. For example, an inked fingerprint image, the most common form of off-line capture, is acquired by first applying ink to the subject's fingertip and then rolling or pressing the finger on paper, thereby creating an impression of the fingerprint ridges on paper. The impression is then scanned and digitized using a flatbed document scanner. The tenprint card (see Figure 2.2) used by several law enforcement agencies records the inked fingerprints of an individual. While the acquisition of inked fingerprints is still in practice, it is both infeasible and socially unacceptable in the context of non-forensic applications. Latent fingerprint development is another example of an off-line method. Latent fingerprints are lifted from the surface of objects that are touched or handled by a person (Figure 2.11(c)). This is achieved through a variety of means ranging from simple photography to more complex dusting or chemical processing.

In contrast, on-line techniques produce the digital image directly from a subject's fingertip via digital imaging technology (described below) that circumvents the need for obtaining an impression on a substrate. The resulting fingerprint image is referred to as a live-scan fingerprint.

Most of the popular sensors to obtain a live-scan fingerprint image are based on either optical or capacitive technologies. A brief description of some of the live-scan sensing technologies is presented below.

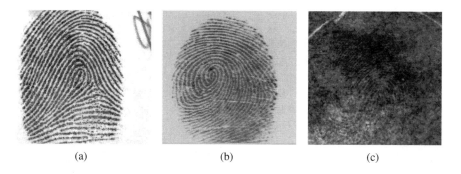

(a)   (b)   (c)

Fig. 2.11 There are different ways to acquire and digitize the fingerprint of an individual. (a) A fingerprint can be first transferred to a paper substrate by manually placing an inked fingertip on paper, and then digitizing the resulting impression using a flatbed scanner, (b) a live-scan fingerprint can be directly imaged from a finger based on a number of advanced sensing technologies, (c) a latent fingerprint can be lifted from objects in a crime scene using chemical or electrical processes.

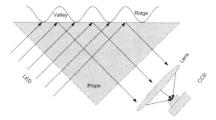

Fig. 2.12 FTIR-based fingerprint sensing.

(a) Optical Frustrated Total Internal Reflection (FTIR): This technique utilizes a glass platen, a LED (or a laser) light-source, and a CCD (or a CMOS) camera for constructing fingerprint images. When a finger is placed on one side of a glass platen (prism), only the ridges of the finger are in contact with the platen, not the valleys (see Figure 2.12). The imaging system essentially consists of an assembly of an LED light source and a CCD camera placed on the other side of the glass platen. The light source illuminates the glass at a certain angle and the camera is placed such that it can capture the light reflected from the glass. The light incident on the ridges is randomly scattered (and results in a dark image), while the light incident on the valleys suffers total internal reflection (and results in a bright image). It is difficult to have this arrangement in a compact form, since the focal length of small lenses can be very large. Further, image distortions are possible when the reflected light is not focused properly.

(b) Capacitance: Capacitance-based solid state live-scan fingerprint sensors are more commonly used than optical FTIR sensors since they are very small in size and can be easily embedded into laptop computers, mobile phones, computer peripherals, and the like. A capacitance-based fingerprint sensor essentially consists of an array of electrodes. In a typical arrangement, there are tens of thousands of small capacitance plates (electrodes) embedded in a chip. The fingerprint skin acts as the other electrode, thereby forming a miniature capacitor. Small electrical charges are created between the surface of the finger and each of these plates when the finger is placed on the chip. The magnitude of these electrical charges depends on the distance between the fingerprint surface and the capacitance plates. Thus, fingerprint ridges and valleys result in different capacitance patterns across the plates. The capacitance due to the ridges is higher than those formed by valleys. This differential capacitance is the basis of operation of a capacitance-based solid state sensor. This technique is susceptible to electrostatic discharges from the tip of the finger that can drastically affect the sensor; proper grounding is necessary to avoid this problem.

(c) Ultrasound Reflection: The ultrasonic method is based on sending acoustic signals toward the fingertip and capturing the echo signal. The echo signal is used to compute the range image of the fingerprint and, subsequently, the ridge structure itself. The sensor has two main components: the sender, that generates short acoustic pulses, and the receiver, that detects the responses obtained when these pulses bounce off the fingerprint surface. This method images the sub-surface of the fingerprint and is, therefore, resilient to dirt and oil accumulations that may visually mar the fingerprint. The device is, however, expensive, and as such not suited for large-scale production.

(d) Piezoelectric Effect: Pressure-sensitive sensors have been designed that produce an electrical signal when a mechanical stress is applied to them. The sensor surface is made of a non-conducting dielectric material which, on encountering pressure from the finger, generates a small amount of current. (This effect is called the piezoelectric effect). The strength of the current generated depends on the pressure applied by the finger on the sensor surface. Since ridges and valleys are present at different distances (heights) from the sensor surface, they result in different amounts of current. This technique does not capture the fingerprint relief accurately because of its low sensitivity.

(e) Temperature Differential: Sensors operating using this mechanism are made of pyro-electric material that generates a current based on temperature differentials. The temperature differential is created when two surfaces are brought into contact. The fingerprint ridges, being in contact with the sensor surface, produce a different temperature differential than the valleys that are away from the sensor surface. The sensors are typically maintained at a high temperature by electrically heating them up.

2.3.2 Image quality

The quality of the acquired fingerprint image has a significant impact on the performance of feature extraction and matching. Important factors that determine fingerprint quality include image resolution, finger area, and clarity of ridge pattern.

In most forensic and biometric applications, an image resolution of 500 points per inch (ppi) is necessary for successful processing and matching. At this resolution, the distance between adjacent ridges is approximately 9 pixels. Law enforcement agencies have now started scanning fingerprints at 1000 ppi in order to capture Level 3 features (see Figure 1.4 in Chapter 1 for comparison between fingerprint images captured at 500 ppi and 1000 ppi). In civilian applications, fingerprint sensors with resolution lower than 500 ppi are often used to reduce the cost of the sensor.

The captured finger area of a fingerprint image is also an important factor impacting image quality. Because of the finger's shape, plain fingerprints, obtained by simply placing the finger on the sensor surface, cannot capture the whole fingerprint. In law enforcement applications, where recording the whole fingerprints is important, the finger has to be rolled on the sensor surface to obtain the full fingerprint (this often requires a fingerprint examiner to hold the subject's finger during rolling). In consumer electronic products (e.g., laptops and mobile phones) where the cost and size of the sensor are important issues, swipe sensors that can be as narrow as 3mm have been introduced. To use this type of sensor, the user needs to swipe his finger across the sensor window, during which all captured slices are combined into a full fingerprint. Figure 2.13 shows an example fingerprint for each of the three operation methods. In law enforcement applications where all ten fingerprints need to be enrolled, fingerprint scanners that can capture the four fingers of a hand (thumb is captured separately) or even the whole hand simultaneously are preferred.

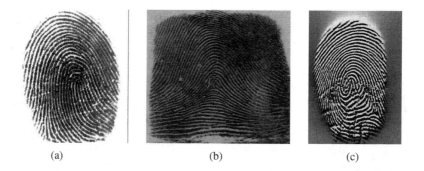

(a) (b) (c)

Fig. 2.13 Fingerprint scanner operation methods: (a) A plain fingerprint is obtained by simply placing the finger on the surface of fingerprint sensor; (b) a rolled fingerprint is obtained by rolling the finger from "nail to nail" on the surface of fingerprint sensor (this typically requires someone to hold the finger to assist in proper rolling); (c) a sweep fingerprint is obtained by combining narrow fingerprint slices (typically 3mm wide) while the user swipes his finger across the sensor.

The clarity of ridge pattern is another important determinant of quality. Both the finger skin and the sensor have a large impact on the ridge clarity. In a good quality fingerprint, ridges continuously flow and adjacent ridges are well separated. When the finger is moist, adjacent ridges may be joined; when it is dry, the ridges may have many breaks; and the inherent quality of some fingers is poor (see Figure 2.14). Fingerprint images obtained using live-scan or inked techniques are typically of better quality than latent fingerprints (see Figure 2.11).

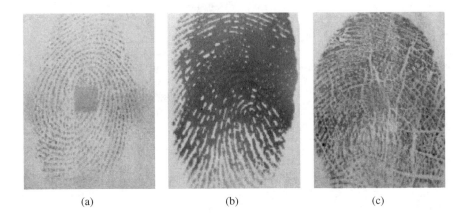

(a)   (b)   (c)

Fig. 2.14 Examples of low quality fingerprint images: (a) dry finger, (b) wet finger, and (c) finger with many creases.

2.4 Feature Extraction

Commercial fingerprint recognition systems are mainly based on Level 1 (ridge orientation and frequency) and Level 2 features (ridges and minutiae). Generally, Level 1 features are first extracted and then Level 2 features are extracted with the guidance of Level 1 features. Figure 2.15 shows the flowchart of a typical feature extraction algorithm which includes four main steps, namely (a) ridge orientation and frequency estimation, (b) ridge extraction, (c) singularity extraction, and (d) minutiae extraction. In the following subsections, these four main steps are described.

2.4.1 Ridge orientation and frequency estimation

Ridge pattern in a local area of a finger can be approximated by a cosine wave

$$w(x,y) = A\cos(2\pi f_0(x\cos\theta + y\sin\theta)), \qquad (2.1)$$

where A, f_0, and θ denote the amplitude, frequency, and orientation of the cosine wave. Then, the 2D Fourier transform of the cosine wave is given by

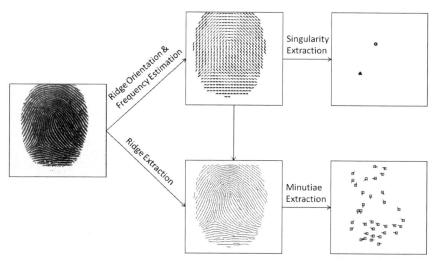

Fig. 2.15 Schematic diagram for the extraction of level 1 and level 2 features from a fingerprint image.

$$W(u,v) = \frac{A}{2}\left[\delta(u - f_0\cos\theta, v - f_0\sin\theta) + \delta(u + f_0\cos\theta, v + f_0\sin\theta)\right]. \quad (2.2)$$

It consists of a pair of impulses located at $(f_0\cos\theta, f_0\sin\theta)$ and $(-f_0\cos\theta, -f_0\sin\theta)$. The parameters of the cosine wave can be easily obtained by detecting the maximum value of the magnitude spectrum. Let $(\hat{u}, \hat{v})$ denote the location of the maximum magnitude. The parameters of the cosine wave are given by:

$$\hat{A} = |W(\hat{u}, \hat{v})|, \quad (2.3)$$

$$\hat{\theta} = \arctan\left(\frac{\hat{v}}{\hat{u}}\right), \text{ and} \quad (2.4)$$

$$\hat{f}_0 = \sqrt{\hat{u}^2 + \hat{v}^2}. \quad (2.5)$$

Since local ridge pattern is not exactly a cosine wave, its 2D Fourier transform, computed using the Fast Fourier Transform (FFT), contains a pair of blurred impulses (see Figure 2.16). To better estimate the parameters, the magnitude spectrum is first smoothed using a low pass filter and then the maximum value is detected.

In the presence of noise, such as creases on the finger surface, initial estimation of ridge orientation map and ridge frequency map may contain erroneous local regions. To recover the parameters of the correct ridge pattern, a smoothing operation with a proper window size is performed. It should be noted that although a frequency map can be smoothened using a low pass filter, such as Gaussian filter, smoothening an orientation field requires special consideration. Recall that ridge orientation of fingerprints in a local area is defined in the range $[0, \pi)$. Thus, a vector in 2D plane with an angle θ and another vector with angle $(\theta + \pi)$ correspond to the same orientation. As a result, a simple arithmetic averaging of the orientations does not give the desirable outcome. For example, the average value between $1°$ and $179°$ should be $0°$ rather than $90°$. To perform a meaningful orientation field smoothening, the following three-step procedure is used.

1. Construct a vector field $V = (V_x, V_y) = (\cos 2\theta, \sin 2\theta)$;
2. Perform low pass filtering on the two components of the vector field separately to obtain the smoothened vector field $V' = (V'_x, V'_y)$;
3. The smoothened orientation field is given by $\frac{1}{2} \arctan \left(\frac{V'_y}{V'_x} \right)$.

Figure 2.17 shows the effect of orientation field smoothening.

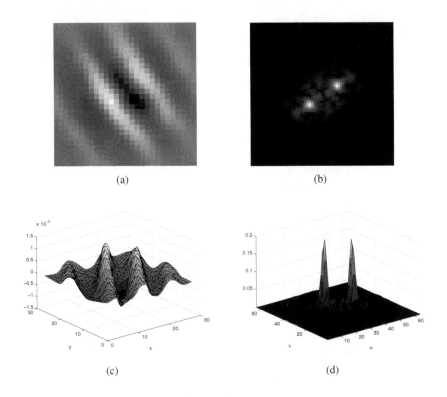

(a)   (b)

(c)   (d)

Fig. 2.16 Discrete Fourier Transform (DFT) of a local region in a fingerprint image. (a) Local ridge pattern of a fingerprint, (b) magnitude spectrum of (a), (c) local ridge pattern in (a) shown as a surface, and (d) magnitude spectrum of (a) shown as a surface.

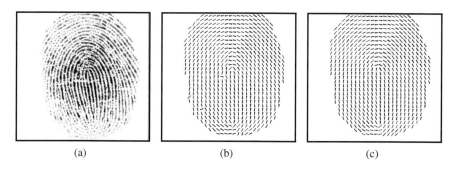

Fig. 2.17 Orientation field estimation and smoothing. (a) Fingerprint image, (b) initial (noisy) orientation field, and (c) smoothed orientation field.

2.4.2 Singularity extraction

Fingerprint singularity can be extracted from the orientation field using the well known Poincaré index method. Poincaré index refers to the cumulative change of orientations along a closed path in an orientation field. To accurately detect the location and type of singularity, Poincaré index is generally evaluated using the eight neighbors of a pixel. Let $O[i] \in [0, \pi)$, $i = 0, \ldots, 7$, denote the orientations at eight neighbors, counterclockwise sorted starting from any neighbor, of a pixel. The Poincaré index, PI, of the pixel is computed as

$$PI = \frac{1}{\pi} \sum_{i=0}^{7} \delta \left(O[(i+1) \bmod 8] - O[i] \right), \tag{2.6}$$

where $\delta(\theta)$ is defined as

$$\delta(\theta) = \begin{cases} \theta - \pi, & \text{if } \theta > \pi/2 \\ \theta, & \text{if } -\pi/2 \leq \theta \leq \pi/2 \\ \theta + \pi, & \text{if } \theta < -\pi/2. \end{cases} \tag{2.7}$$

Poincaré index of a pixel corresponding to a singular point can take one of four possible values: 0 (non-singular), 1 (loop), -1 (delta), and 2 (whorl). Figure 2.18 shows an example for non-singular orientation field and three orientation fields containing singularities. Note that whorl was not defined as a separate type of singular points in Section 2.2.1 since it can be viewed as a combination of two adjacent loops facing each other. Clearly, the Poincaré index of whorl is equal to the sum of the Poincaré indices of two loops.

Typically, more than one singularity is detected around a true singularity. A simple grouping algorithm is used to cluster the singular points that are close in location and are of the same type. The mean location of a cluster is used as the representative location of singularity.

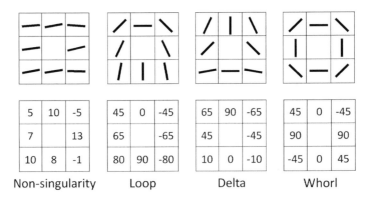

5	10	-5
7		13
10	8	-1
Non-singularity

45	0	-45
65		-65
80	90	-80
Loop

65	90	-65
45		-45
10	0	-10
Delta

45	0	-45
90		90
-45	0	45
Whorl

Fig. 2.18 Poincaré indices around non-singular flow, a loop, a delta, and a whorl are 0, 1, -1, and 2, respectively. The top row shows local orientation fields of the four cases and the bottom row gives the corresponding orientation values in degrees.

2.4.2.1 Direction of singularity

A singular point can also be assigned a direction. One approach is to define the reference orientation field for a loop and a delta, respectively. The orientation field around a true singular point can be approximated by a rotated version of the reference orientation field. The rotation angle is defined as the direction of the singular point. The reference orientation fields of loop and delta, respectively, are given by

$$RO_l(x,y) = \frac{1}{2} \arctan\left(\frac{x}{y}\right) = \frac{\theta}{2}, \text{ and} \tag{2.8}$$

$$RO_d(x,y) = -\frac{1}{2} \arctan\left(\frac{x}{y}\right) = -\frac{\theta}{2}, \tag{2.9}$$

where θ denotes the angle in the polar coordinate system. Figure 2.19 shows the reference orientation fields of loop and delta.

The loop reference orientation field rotated by α is given by

$$RO_l(x,y;\alpha) = \frac{\theta - \alpha}{2} + \alpha = \frac{\theta}{2} + \frac{\alpha}{2}. \tag{2.10}$$

The delta reference orientation field rotated by α is given by

$$RO_d(x,y;\alpha) = -\frac{\theta - \alpha}{2} + \alpha = -\frac{\theta}{2} + \frac{3\alpha}{2}. \tag{2.11}$$

Note that rotating a delta reference orientation field by $\alpha + n\frac{2\pi}{3}$, $n \in \mathbb{Z}$ (the set of all integers) gives the same orientation field.

The difference between the local orientation field around a singularity and the reference orientation field is given by

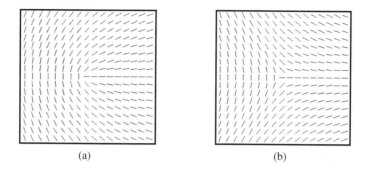

(a)   (b)

Fig. 2.19 Reference orientation fields of (a) loop and (b) delta.

$$D_{\{l,d\}}(x,y) = O(x\lambda + x_0, y\lambda + y_0) - RO_{\{l,d\}}(x,y). \qquad (2.12)$$

According to equation (2.10), the direction of a loop at (x_0, y_0) is computed by

$$\alpha = \arctan\left(\frac{\sum_{x=-r}^{r}\sum_{y=-r}^{r}\sin(2D_l(x,y))}{\sum_{x=-r}^{r}\sum_{y=-r}^{r}\cos(2D_l(x,y))}\right). \qquad (2.13)$$

According to equation (2.11), the direction of a delta at (x_0, y_0) is computed by

$$\alpha = \frac{1}{3}\arctan\left(\frac{\sum_{x=-r}^{r}\sum_{y=-r}^{r}\sin(2D_d(x,y))}{\sum_{x=-r}^{r}\sum_{y=-r}^{r}\cos(2D_d(x,y))}\right). \qquad (2.14)$$

The estimated singular points in three fingerprints are shown in Figure 2.20.

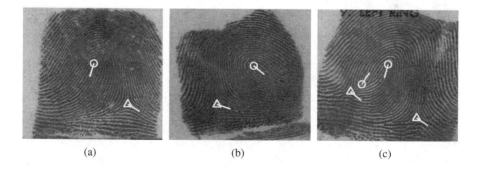

(a)   (b)   (c)

Fig. 2.20 Singular points and their directions. (a) Left loop, (b) right loop, and (c) twin loop.

Given a set of singular points in a rolled fingerprint, the following criteria can be used to classify the fingerprint into one of six major pattern types (as shown in

Figure 2.8). Note that arch and tented arch types are often put into the same category, called arch, because of the difficulty in distinguishing between these two types.

1. A fingerprint is classified into plain arch, if it does not contain any singular points.
2. A fingerprint is classified into left loop, if it contains one delta and one loop whose direction points to the left side of the delta.
3. A fingerprint is classified into right loop, if it contains one delta and one loop whose direction points to the right side of the delta.
4. A fingerprint is classified into tented arch, if it contains one delta and one loop whose direction points toward the delta.
5. A fingerprint is classified into whorl, if it contains at least two loops and two deltas where ridge orientation field around the two loops form a circular orbit.
6. A fingerprint is classified as twin loop, if it contains at least two loops and two deltas where the ridge orientation field around the two loops does not form a circular orbit.

It should be noted that the accuracy of the above classification algorithm depends on successful singularity extraction, which can be challenging in poor quality fingerprints. Further, it requires the fingerprint to be complete (i.e., a rolled fingerprint). Therefore, the pattern type of latent fingerprints obtained from crime scenes is typically considered as unknown and latents are often searched against all types of fingerprints in the database.

2.4.3 Ridge extraction

Since minutiae are special points on ridges, it is natural to first extract ridges and then detect the minutiae on ridges. Since ridges are darker than valleys, a straightforward method to detect ridges is to classify any pixel as a ridge pixel if its gray value is lower than a threshold (for example, the mean of its local neighborhood). However, for most fingerprint images, this method does not work well for the following reasons: (a) pores on ridges are brighter than the surrounding pixels; (b) ridges can be broken due to cuts or creases; (c) adjacent ridges may appear to be joined due to moist skin or pressure.

To deal with the above problems, fingerprint image enhancement is used to connect broken ridges and separate joined ridges. A successful fingerprint enhancement method is based on contextual filtering. Generally, this involves filtering the image with the real part of a 2D complex Gabor filter whose orientation and frequency are tuned to the local ridge orientation and frequency. Figure 2.21 shows the real part of 2D Gabor filters at three different scales and eight different orientations. Figure 2.22(b) shows the enhanced image of the fingerprint in Figure 2.22(a).

The enhanced image can be converted to a binary image by using either a global threshold (for example, using the mean pixel value of the enhanced image) or thresholds that are locally computed. A morphological operation, called thinning, is used to reduce the ridge width to one pixel. Thinning is a common technique in image

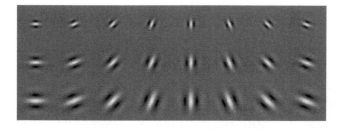

Fig. 2.21 Real parts of Gabor filters with eight different orientations (along the rows) and three different scales (along the columns).

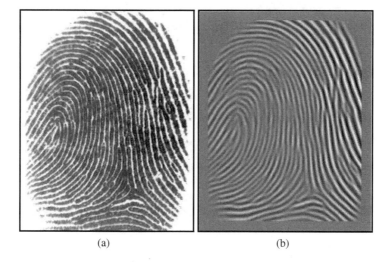

(a)   (b)

Fig. 2.22 Ridge enhancement by Gabor filtering. (a) Input fingerprint image and (b) enhanced image.

processing, which involves iteratively removing outer ridge pixels. Figure 2.23 gives the results of binarization and thinning steps.

2.4.4 Minutiae extraction

Once the thinned ridge image is available, the ridge pixels with three ridge pixel neighbors are identified as ridge bifurcations and those with only one ridge pixel neighbor are identified as ridge endings (see Figure 2.24). The direction of ridge ending is computed in the following way. Starting from the ending x, we trace the associated ridge to a fixed distance (say 10 pixels) and reach a point, say a. The direction xa is used as the minutia direction. For a bifurcation, there are three as-

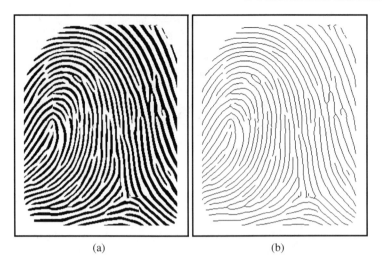

(a)   (b)

Fig. 2.23 Binarization and thinning results of the fingerprint image in Figure 2.22. (a) Binarized ridge image and (b) thinned ridge image.

sociated ridges, so we obtain three points by tracing the ridges to a fixed distance. The direction of the bifurcation is defined as the mean of the two directions whose difference is the smallest among the three ridges. Figure 2.25 shows the direction of minutiae marked on the ridge skeleton.

In practice, some of the minutiae detected using the above approach may be spurious due to artifacts in image processing and noise in the fingerprint image. To remove these spurious minutiae, a minutiae filtering algorithm is employed, which typically consists of a number of heuristic rules. For instance, minutiae satisfying any of the following conditions are deemed to be spurious minutiae and discarded:

1. minutiae that do not have an adjacent ridge on either side (mainly the endpoints of ridges along the finger border);
2. minutiae that are close in location and almost opposite in direction (namely, the difference between two minutiae directions is close to $180°$);
3. too many minutiae in a small neighborhood.

Figure 2.26 shows the effect of minutiae filtering.

2.5 Matching

Given the minutiae set $\{x_i^Q, y_i^Q, \theta_i^Q\}_{i=1}^M$ of a query fingerprint with M minutiae and the minutiae set $\{x_j^T, y_j^T, \theta_j^T\}_{j=1}^N$ of a template fingerprint with N minutiae, we now describe a simple matching algorithm which consists of three steps (see Figure 2.27):

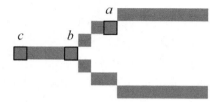

Fig. 2.24 Minutiae detection. Three different types of ridge pixels are marked: typical ridge pixel 'a', ridge bifurcation 'b', and ridge ending 'c'. Either a ridge bifurcation or a ridge ending defines a minutiae.

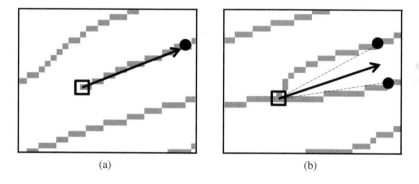

(a)   (b)

Fig. 2.25 Direction of a minutia. (a) Ridge ending and (b) ridge bifurcation.

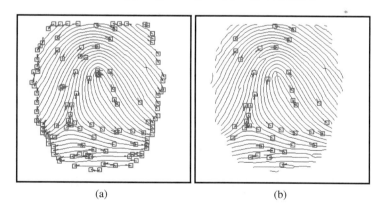

(a)   (b)

Fig. 2.26 Removing spurious minutiae. (a) Before minutiae filtering and (b) after minutiae filtering.

1. Alignment: Determine the geometric transformation between the two minutiae sets so that they are in the same coordinate system.
2. Correspondence: Form pairs of corresponding minutiae.
3. Score generation: Compute the match score based on the corresponding minutiae points.

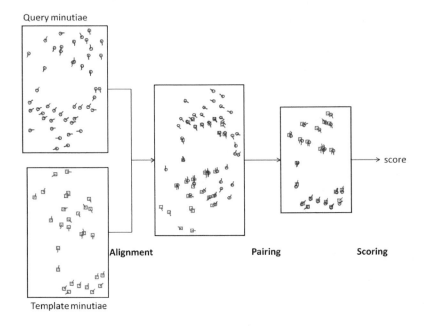

Fig. 2.27 Flowchart of a minutiae matching algorithm.

2.5.1 Alignment

Since two impressions of the same finger taken at different instances could differ due to different placement of the finger on the sensor, an alignment process is required to transform them to the same coordinate system. This process, also known as registration, transforms one image in such a way that it is geometrically aligned with the other. First, we need to specify a spatial transformation model. Generally, a rigid transformation is sufficient for fingerprint matching unless a severe nonlinear deformation is introduced during fingerprint acquisition. Generalized Hough transform is a well-known algorithm for estimating the spatial transformation between two point sets. The pseudo-code of the Generalized Hough transform algorithm is given in Algorithm 1.

---

input : Two minutiae sets $\{x_i^T, y_i^T, \theta_i^T\}_{i=1}^M$ and $\{x_j^Q, y_j^Q, \theta_j^Q\}_{j=1}^N$
output: Transformation parameters
Initialize accumulator array A to 0
for $i = 1, 2, \cdots, M$ **do**
 for $j = 1, 2, \cdots, N$ **do**
  $\Delta\theta = \theta_i^T - \theta_j^Q$
  $\Delta x = x_i^T - x_j^Q cos(\Delta\theta) - y_j^Q sin(\Delta\theta)$
  $\Delta y = y_i^T + x_j^Q sin(\Delta\theta) - y_j^Q cos(\Delta\theta)$
  $A[\Delta\theta][\Delta x][\Delta y] = A[\Delta\theta][\Delta x][\Delta y] + 1$
 end
end
return location of peak in A

Algorithm 1: Determining transformation parameters for aligning two sets of fingerprint minutiae using the Generalized Hough Transform Algorithm.

Figure 2.28 illustrates the Hough transform approach to alignment when only the translation (in x and y directions) between query and template minutiae sets is unknown.

Another popular fingerprint alignment algorithm is to first find a pair of matched minutiae, and then compute the rotation and translation parameters between two fingerprints based on this pair of minutiae. Since the basic properties of minutiae, namely location, direction and type, do not contain sufficient information for determining matched minutiae, additional information in the neighborhood of minutiae needs to be associated with each minutia to increase its distinctiveness. This additional information is termed as a minutia descriptor [15]. A widely used minutia descriptor is based on the set of minutiae in the neighborhood of the central minutia (namely, the minutia whose descriptor needs to be computed). The location and direction of neighboring minutiae are defined in the local minutia coordinate system using the central minutia as the origin and its direction as the x axis. This way, the descriptor is invariant with respect to the rigid transformation of fingerprints. The similarity between two minutiae descriptors is computed by (a) first a pairing of neighboring minutiae is established (using an algorithm similar to the algorithm described in the next subsection) and then (b) computing the product of the percentages of matched minutiae in the local region of each minutia as follows. Consider Figure 2.29, where three minutia descriptors shown; the central minutiae in Figures 2.29(a) and 2.29(b) are considered a match, while the central minutia in Figure 2.29(c) does not match with those in Figures 2.29(a) and 2.29(b). There are six matched minutiae (including the central one) between Figures 2.29(a) and 2.29(b), and three matched minutiae between Figures 2.29(a) and 2.29(c). Thus, the similarity between the minutiae in Figures 2.29(a) and 2.29(b) is $\frac{6}{8} \cdot \frac{6}{7}$, is greater than the similarity between the minutiae in Figures 2.29(a) and 2.29(c), which is $\frac{3}{8} \cdot \frac{3}{7}$. Since the descriptor-based alignment algorithm uses only a small neighborhood, it

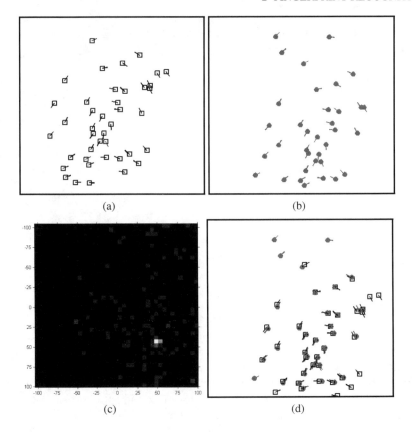

Fig. 2.28 Minutiae set alignment using the Hough transform. (a) query minutiae set, (b) template minutiae set, (c) accumulator array or the Hough space image, and (d) aligned minutiae sets. The "bright" spot in the Hough space in (c) indicates the cell that receives the most votes. The x and y translation corresponding to this cell is used for aligning the two minutiae sets.

usually outperforms the Generalized Hough transform algorithm when the common (overlapping) area between two fingerprints contains very few minutiae.

2.5.2 Pairing minutiae

After the two minutiae sets are aligned, the corresponding minutiae are paired. A minutia a in the template (reference) minutiae set is said to be in correspondence with minutia b in the query minutiae set if and only if their distance is within a predefined distance threshold (say, 15 pixels) and the angle between their directions is within another predefined angle threshold (say, 20 degrees). One minutia in the template fingerprint is allowed to match to at most one minutia in the query finger-

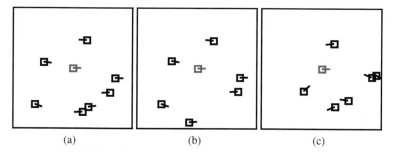

Fig. 2.29 Minutia descriptor. (a) Descriptor of a minutia (the central one) in a query fingerprint image, (b) descriptor of the mated minutia in a template fingerprint, and (c) descriptor of another minutia.

print and vice versa. The pseudo-code of a minutiae pairing algorithm is given in Algorithm 2.

---

input : Two minutiae sets $\{x_i^T, y_i^T, \theta_i^T\}_{i=1}^M$ and $\{x_j^Q, y_j^Q, \theta_j^Q\}_{j=1}^N$;
                Transformation parameters $(\Delta\theta, \Delta x, \Delta y)$
output: List of paired minutiae
Initialize: set flag arrays f^T, f^Q, and *count* as 0; *list* as empty
for $i = 1, 2, \cdots, M$ **do**
    for $j = 1, 2, \cdots, N$ **do**
        if $f^T[i] == 0$ & $f^Q[j] == 0$ & *distance between minutiae i and j* $< t_d$
        & *rotation between them* $< t_r$ **then**
            $f^T[i] = 1$
            $f^Q[j] = 1$
            $count = count + 1$
            $list[count] = \{i, j\}$
        end
    end
end
return *list*

Algorithm 2: Minutiae Pairing Algorithm.

2.5.3 Match score generation

In this final step, we need to compute a match score, which is then compared to a predefined threshold to classify the two fingerprints as a genuine match (they come from the same finger) or an impostor match (they come from two different fingers). This problem can be viewed as a two-class classification problem with genuine match as class-1 and impostor match as class-2. For this classification problem, several potential features for distinguishing genuine matches from impostor matches can be examined. The first feature is the number of paired minutiae. It is intuitive that genuine matches should have more paired minutiae than the impostor matches. The second useful feature is the percentage of matched minutiae in the overlapped area between the two fingerprints. Again, it is intuitive that this percentage be larger for genuine matches than for impostor matches. Given a set of minutiae, the fingerprint area can be approximated by the convex hull of its minutiae points. Figure 2.30 shows examples of a genuine match and an imposter match using a commercial matcher, Neurotechnology VeriFinger SDK 4.2.

(a) Match score = 614   (b) Match score = 7

Fig. 2.30 Fingerprint matching by a commercial matcher. (a) A genuine pair of fingerprints with 31 matched minutiae, and (b) an imposter pair with 6 matched minutiae. Corresponding minutiae between the two images are connected by lines. The match score is computed as some function of the number of matched minutiae and some other parameters that are proprietary to the commercial matcher.

2.5.4 Latent fingerprint matching

Latent fingerprint recognition is of critical importance to law enforcement agencies in identifying suspects and victims. Latent fingerprint matching is much more challenging than rolled or plain fingerprint matching due to typically poor image quality, small finger area, and large nonlinear distortion of most latents (see Figure 2.31). State-of-the-art feature extractors do not work well for many of the difficult latent images. Typically, minutiae in latents are manually marked by trained latent examiners in order to efficiently extract the limited information available. Figure 2.32 shows the manually marked minutiae in two typical latents.

Due to the limited number of minutiae in many latents, it is not possible to accurately match latents solely based on minutiae. As an example, latent fingerprints in a public domain latent fingerprint database, NIST SD27 [19], have 21 minutiae

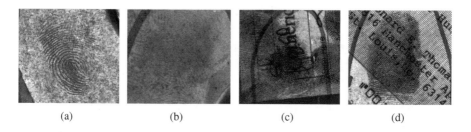

| | | | |
| (a) | (b) | (c) | (d) |

Fig. 2.31 Latent fingerprints with poor quality. (a) Partial fingerprint, (b) unclear ridge structure, (c) overlapped with other fingerprints, and (d) overlapped with complex background.

per fingerprint image, on average, (the minimum and maximum number of minutiae for latents in NIST SD27 are 5 and 82, respectively) while the corresponding (mated) rolled prints, on average, have 106 minutiae (the minimum and the maximum number of minutiae in the rolled prints in NIST SD27 are 48 and 193). One way to improve latent matching accuracy is to utilize a more complete feature set (namely, the extended feature set that includes Level 3 details) in matching. While some algorithms have been proposed for matching plain or rolled fingerprints using extended features, latent matching based on extended features is still an open problem. A main challenge is how to reliably encode and match Level 3 features in poor quality latents.

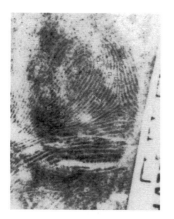 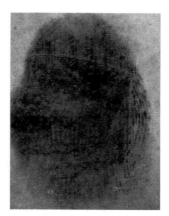

Fig. 2.32 Two latent fingerprints with manually marked minutiae.

2.5.5 Fingerprint individuality

Evidence based on fingerprints has been believed to be infallible and as such it has been accepted in U.S. courts of law for almost a century. However, the reliability of fingerprint evidence is being challenged under the Daubert standard, a set of criteria regarding the admissibility of scientific testimony largely derived from a 1993 Supreme Court case. The Daubert standard has two basic requirements for source of forensic evidence: the underlying scientific basis should be accepted widely, and its error rate should be known. It is the "known error rate" criterion of the Daubert rule that has been primarily used to question the scientific value of fingerprint evidence. Although many researchers have attempted to estimate the inherent individuality of fingerprints, the actual problem of estimating the error rate of latent fingerprint identification, which involves human factors in many stages (latent development, encoding, matching) is not yet solved. The only viable solution in the near term may be to keep improving the performance of automated fingerprint systems and ultimately replace human experts with automated systems.

2.5.6 Performance evaluation

The National Institute of Standards and Technology (NIST) has conducted several fingerprint technology evaluations (http://fingerprint.nist.gov), such as the Fingerprint Vendor Technology Evaluation (FpVTE), the Minutiae Interoperability Exchange Test (MINEX), Proprietary Fingerprint Template (PFT) testing, and the Evaluation of Latent Fingerprint Technologies (ELFT), which use operational data collected in forensic and government applications. The University of Bologna conducts FVC-onGoing (https://biolab.csr.unibo.it/fvcongoing/UI/Form/Home.aspx), which is an evolution of the international Fingerprint Verification Competitions (FVCs) organized between 2000 and 2006. Table 2.1 summarizes FpVTE 2003 Medium-Scale Test (MST), FVC2006, and ELFT 2008 (Phase II) results. It is important to note that system performance can vary widely depending on fingerprint data characteristics used in the evaluation. Further, while these evaluations are useful, the performance of different biometric systems cannot always be directly compared. In addition, technology evaluations like those conducted by NIST do not always reflect operational performance due to differences in data characteristics, operating environments, and user interactions with the fingerprint reader.

A fingerprint recognition system's operational performance is based on several factors, including sensor characteristics, the number of subjects and demographic distribution of the population enrolled in the system, and various environmental factors, including indoor versus outdoor, temperature, humidity, and so on. Moreover, the required FMR and FNMR values depend on the specific application. For example, Disney World's fingerprint-based entry system operates at a low FNMR, so as not to upset paying customers by rejecting them, at the expense of a higher FMR.

On the other hand, a high security fingerprint access control system may require low FMR at the risk of a higher FNMR.

In some cases, a fingerprint recognition system may not even successfully capture a user's fingerprint. These users may, for example, be in certain occupations that involve manual labor or the elderly with "worn-out" fingers. In practice, the Failure to Enroll (FTE) rate can be rather high (up to a few percentage points) depending on the target population, sensor characteristics, and the occupation of users in the population.

Table 2.1 Performance evaluation of fingerprint technology

Evaluation	Data	Best reported accuracies
NIST FpVTE 2003 (MST)	10,000 plain fingerprints	FNMR = 0.6% at FMR = 0.1%
FVC2006	140 fingers, 12 images per finger Electric field sensor (250 ppi)	FNMR = 15% at FMR = 0.1%
	Optical sensor (569 ppi)	FNMR = 0.02% at FMR = 0.1%
	Sweep sensor (500 ppi)	FNMR = 3% at FMR = 0.1%
NIST ELFT 2008 (Phase II)	835 latent prints, 100,000 rolled fingerprints	FNMR = 8% at FMR = 1%

2.6 Fingerprint Indexing

Besides alignment and matching, the minutiae points extracted from a fingerprint image can also be used to index fingerprints. Indexing is the process of assigning a numerical value (scalar or vector) to a fingerprint image based on the features extracted from it. Fingerprint indexing, like fingerprint classification, can be used to speed-up the fingerprint identification process by comparing the input probe image only against a small subset of images in the database (gallery) having comparable index values. Indexing based on minutiae points does not usually require explicit alignment of the fingerprints. Furthermore, unlike fingerprint classification schemes, the singular points need not be present in the image for indexing. This allows for the successful indexing of partial fingerprints. Note that partial capture of a fingerprint is one of the main sources of matching errors.

One of the most popular techniques for fingerprint indexing is based on triplets of minutiae (see Figure 2.33). In this technique, each minutiae triplet is described by a nine-dimensional feature vector consisting of the geometric properties of the triangle formed by the triplet. The features include the lengths of the sides of the triangle, the ridge count between each pair of vertices, and the orientation of the

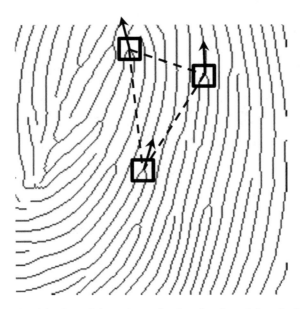

Fig. 2.33 A minutia triplet formed from three minutia points in a skeletonized fingerprint. The minutiae angles are computed from the directions of the ridges at the minutiae points (shown using arrowheads).

minutiae points at the vertices encoded with respect to the longest side. These features are invariant to rotation and translation. However, the lengths of the sides are highly sensitive to non-rigid distortions. Furthermore, the correct ordering of the features and the three angles depend on correctly identifying the longest side of the triangle, as shown in Figure 2.34. Unfortunately, the lengths of the triangle sides are not invariant to distortions. The actual indexing algorithm used, however, is based on geometric hashing in which the quantization procedure addresses the effects of non-rigid distortion to a certain extent.

In geometric hashing, all triangles extracted from a fingerprint are placed in a hash table where the feature vector pertaining to a triangle defines the key and the ID of the fingerprint that generated this feature vector defines the data value. During retrieval, each key of the input fingerprint is used to extract all IDs in the hash table stored under the same key. Finally, the number of times each ID is retrieved in the previous step is used as a similarity score between this ID and the input probe.

This technique can be improved by extracting a better set of features from the minutiae triplets that is more robust to non-rigid deformations. Here, the six-dimensional feature vector consists of the length of the longest side, the two smaller internal angles of the triangles (more robust to distortion compared to minutiae directions), the handedness of the triangle, its type, and its direction. The last two features depend on the type of minutiae points that form the triangle, i.e., a ridge bifurcation or a ridge ending. Although the process of determining the type of minutiae (ridge ending or bifurcation) is sensitive to noise, it is more robust to small

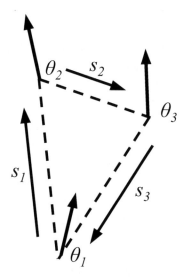

Fig. 2.34 Ordered feature set for a minutiae triplet. The longest side, S_1, appears first in the ordered set of features. Similarly, the transformed minutiae angles, θ_i, and the ridge counts are taken in specific order with respect to the longest side.

amounts of distortion. To be able to identify matching triangles in the presence of various sources of noise, several geometric constraints can also be applied.

During enrollment, the fingerprint features based on triplets are appropriately stored in a hash table. During retrieval, for each triplet in the input probe, multiple triangles are generated by applying a distortion function to the values of the angles. Each matching triangle found by this search must satisfactorily pass the geometric constraints imposed by the algorithm before being accepted as an actual match. After finding the matching triangles and the list of corresponding enrolled images, the retrieval proceeds by identifying the set of minutiae points $M = m_1, ..., m_r$ which are common between the input probe and an enrolled gallery image. For each of these minutiae points, m_i, the number of triangles in the enrolled image, I_d, which include m_i is counted. These counts are converted to posterior probabilities for the hypothesis that the image I_d belongs to the same identity as the probe given the common minutiae point m_i. Finally, an indexing score is computed for each I_d by summing its top n largest posterior probabilities. The retrieved images are sorted according to their indexing scores and the top N images from the database are output as possible hypotheses for matching.

2.7 Fingerprint Synthesis

Fingerprint synthesis refers to generating artificial fingerprint images that are similar to real fingerprint images. Fingerprint synthesis is mainly used for generating a large database of fingerprints for testing fingerprint recognition algorithms since collecting large databases of real fingerprint images is expensive both in terms of money and time. Another objective of fingerprint synthesis is to be able to model fingerprints and identify an appropriate set of parameters that characterize the fingerprints. The resulting model, in turn, can help in fingerprint feature extraction and matching. Here, we present a simple fingerprint synthesis algorithm consisting of two steps: Level 1 feature synthesis and Level 2 feature synthesis.

2.7.1 Level 1 feature synthesis

Level 1 features contain local ridge orientation and local ridge frequency. Since the variation in ridge frequency across a fingerprint is not large, it is typical to use a fixed ridge frequency (0.1 ridges per pixel). For the purpose of orientation field synthesis, it is desirable to have a parametric model of fingerprint orientation field, whose parameters can be adjusted to simulate various orientation fields. One such model is the Zero-pole model, whose parameters are the location and type of singular points:

$$RO(x,y) = \frac{1}{2} \sum_{i=1}^{M} t_i \arctan \left(\frac{y - y_i}{x - x_i} \right), \tag{2.15}$$

where M denotes the number of singular points, (x_i, y_i) denotes the coordinates of the ith singularity, and $t_i \in \{1, -1\}$ denotes its type (1 for loop and -1 for delta). The main limitation of the above model is that it cannot correctly model the arch-type fingerprints that do not have any singularity; the orientation field is assigned a value of 0 degree across the whole image plane.

A better model for arch-type orientation field is given by:

$$RO_{arch}(x,y) = \arctan \left(\max \left\{ 0, \left(k - 3\frac{y}{H} \right) \right\} \cdot \cos \left(\frac{x}{W} \pi \right) \right), \tag{2.16}$$

where H and W denote the height and width of the image and k ($2 < k < 5$) controls the curvature of arch. Figure 2.35 shows simulated orientation fields of three major finger pattern types, namely arch (using Eq. (2.16)), left loop, and whorl (using Eq. (2.15)).

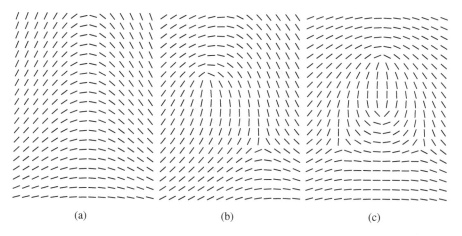

(a)   (b)   (c)

Fig. 2.35 Simulated fingerprint orientation fields. (a) Arch, (b) left loop, and (c) whorl.

2.7.2 Level 2 feature synthesis

Ridge pattern is generated by performing Gabor filtering on an image initialized with random noise (see Figure 2.36). Parameters of Gabor filters are the simulated orientation field and ridge frequency. The noise at each pixel follows uniform distribution in the range $[0, 255]$. Figure 2.37 shows several simulated fingerprint images of arch, left loop, and whorl.

Note that the synthesized images shown in Figure 2.37 appear different from real fingerprint images. As an example, there are no sweat pores on ridges and the ridge contours are too straight. For the evaluation of fingerprint matching algorithms, it is also necessary to simulate various intra-class variations related to (a) ridge thickness and image contrast due to factors like the wetness of skin; (b) finger pressure on sensor surface; and (c) finger placement on the sensor.

2.8 Palmprint

Friction ridge patterns on the palm of the hand and the sole of the foot (see Figure 2.38) have also been claimed to be unique and permanent and thus can be used for personal identification. But, it is understandable that palmprints and sole prints have fewer applications than fingerprints since it is not as convenient to capture them compared to fingerprints. In fact, sole prints are only used to register newborns in a hospital since it is easier to capture the sole print of newborns than fingerprints or palmprints (newborns tend to keep their fists closed!). Even there, only an inked impression of the sole print is stored in the file in case there is a dispute about baby swaps in the hospital. Palmprints are beginning to gain prominence in forensics for

Fig. 2.36 Noise image.

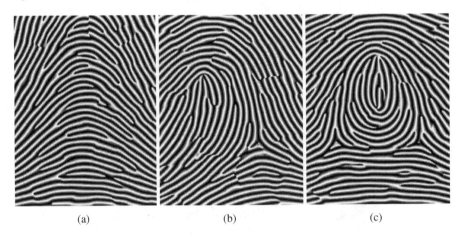

      (a)   (b)   (c)

Fig. 2.37 Simulated fingerprint images. (a) Arch, (b) left loop, and (c) whorl.

identifying crime suspects and may have potential value in civilian applications. However, law enforcement agencies do not yet have a large database of palmprints comparable in size to that of fingerprints. Under the FBI's Next Generation Identification (NGI) scenario, one of the major objectives is to include palmprint matching capability. But, as far as forensics application is concerned, the main benefit of using palmprints is in latent palmprint matching since it is estimated that about 30% of the latents found at crime scenes are those of palms.

    Understandably, matching palmprints is more complicated than matching fingerprints. First of all, in terms of image acquisition, it is more challenging to capture palmprints than fingerprints since the sensors are larger and more expensive and greater user cooperation is required to ensure a good quality palmprint image due to the concavity of the palm surface. Since palmprints, like fingerprints, are also friction ridge patterns, minutiae can also be used to match palmprints. However, the number of minutiae in a palmprint is an order of magnitude larger than the number of minutiae in a fingerprint (around 800 for palmprints vs. 80 for fingerprints). In this section, we first describe the main features observed in palmprints and then introduce palmprint recognition systems taking into account of above challenges for forensic and civilian applications, respectively.

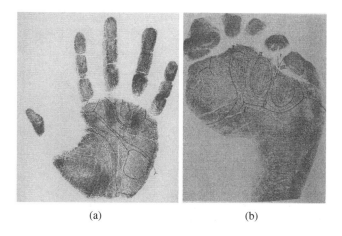

(a)   (b)

Fig. 2.38 Friction ridge patterns on palm and sole [11].

2.8.1 Palmprint features

Palmprints consist of two unique features, namely, the palmar friction ridges and the palmar flexion creases. Flexion creases are the firmer attachment areas to the basal skin structure. Flexion creases appear before the formation of friction ridges during the embryonic skin development stage, and both of these features are claimed to be immutable, permanent, and unique to an individual. The three major types of flexion creases that are most clearly visible in a palmprint are: distal transverse crease, proximal transverse crease, and radial transverse crease (see Figure 2.39). Various features in palmprints can be observed at different image resolutions. While major creases can be observed at less than 100 ppi, thin creases, ridges, and minutiae can be observed only at a resolution of at least 500 ppi; resolutions much greater than 500 ppi are needed to observe pores. These features are marked in the example palmprint in Figure 2.39.

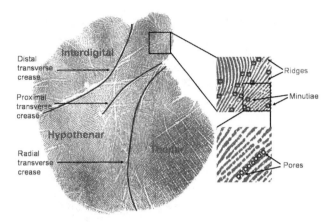

Fig. 2.39 Regions (interdigital, thenar and hypothenar), major creases (distal transverse crease, proximal transverse crease and radial transverse crease), ridges, minutiae and pores in a palmprint.

2.8.2 Palmprint recognition in forensics

Up to now, the main use of palmprint recognition has been to identify suspects by matching latent palmprints lifted from crime scenes against law enforcement palmprint databases. To achieve high accuracy, minutiae are the main features used in latent palmprint matching, which requires that palmprints be captured at 500 ppi or higher resolution. As indicated earlier, due to the large size of the palm area, the number of minutiae in a palmprint is approximately ten times the number of minutiae in a rolled fingerprint. It is due to this computational complexity that full palmprint to full palmprint matching is rarely performed, especially when ten (finger)print match provides sufficient accuracy in forensics, law enforcement, and border crossing applications.

Since the texture of a high resolution palmprint is very similar to a fingerprint, many minutiae extraction and matching techniques for fingerprints are directly applicable to palmprints. However, there is one major difference between palmprints and fingerprints, namely the presence of a large number of creases in palmprints. Due to these creases, ridge orientation field estimation algorithms for fingerprints do not perform very well. A modified orientation field estimation algorithm to handle the creases in palmprints consists of the following steps:

1. Detect a set of six strongest sinusoid waves in the Fourier transform of each local block (16×16 pixels) in a palmprint.
2. Cluster the strongest waves that are compatible with each other into a set of seed orientation fields. Two waves in adjacent blocks are said to be compatible if their orientation and frequency are similar.
3. Grow each seed orientation field by including adjacent and compatible waves.
4. Select the largest seed as the final orientation field.

After the orientation field is obtained, the fingerprint feature extraction steps, including Gabor filtering, binarization, thinning, and minutiae extraction, can be directly used for palmprint processing and matching. As shown in Figure 2.40, this modified orientation field estimation algorithm leads to a better ridge skeleton image compared to the ridge skeleton obtained from a state-of-the-art fingerprint feature extraction algorithm. Figure 2.41 shows an example of successful latent palmprint matching.

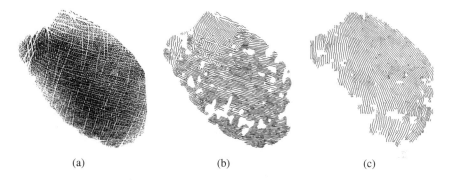

(a)   (b)   (c)

Fig. 2.40 Comparison of two feature extraction algorithms on palmprints. (a) A live-scan partial palmprint from the thenar region. (b) Ridge skeleton image of (a) obtained using a state-of-the-art fingerprint feature extraction algorithm. (c) Ridge skeleton image of (a) obtained using the palmprint feature extraction algorithm described earlier.

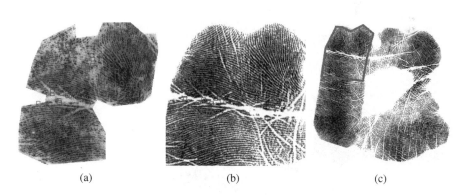

(a)   (b)   (c)

Fig. 2.41 Latent palmprint matching. (a) Latent palmprint with minutiae, (b) corresponding region in the mated palmprint, and (c) the mated full palmprint.

2.8.3 Palmprint recognition for access control

Palmprint recognition systems in forensics need high resolution images (at least 500 ppi), so they employ expensive scanners and have high computational complexity. To reduce computational complexity and the cost of palmprint scanners, which are critical issues in adopting biometrics technology in civilian applications (e.g., access control), some effort has been made to design real-time palmprint recognition systems that are based on low resolution (around 75 ppi) images. These systems capture palmprints directly using a commodity digital camera such as a webcam. Figure 2.42 shows a low resolution palmprint image. Note that ridges and minutiae are not clearly visible at this low resolution. Therefore, the low resolution palmprint matching systems are mainly based on flexion creases that are still visible. The low resolution palmprint recognition systems adopt a processing framework that includes (a) palmprint cropping and normalization based on detecting two finger gaps, (b) filtering the cropped image using 2D Gabor filter with predefined direction and frequency, and (c) binarizing the real and imaginary images. This palmprint encoding process is shown in Figure 2.43. To compute the similarity between two palmprints, the Hamming distance between the foreground (region of interest) real and imaginary binary filtered images of two palmprints is computed and divided by the number of foreground pixels. To account for small variance in the normalization step, the template image is typically rotated and translated to obtain its several different versions. The minimum distance between the query image and all the versions of the template image is chosen as the final distance. While the reported accuracies of the low resolution palmprint matching systems are impressive, they have not yet shown to be competitive with respect to fingerprint matching systems for access control or other civilian applications.

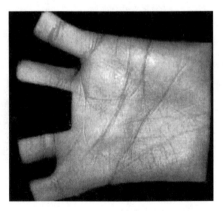

Fig. 2.42 A low resolution palmprint image (75 ppi) from PolyU palmprint database.

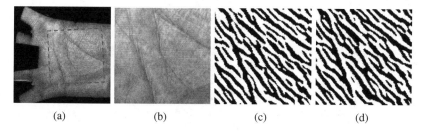

(a)   (b)   (c)   (d)

Fig. 2.43 Palmprint encoding. (a) Original palmprint image showing the region of interest and two finger gap positions used for normalization, (b) cropped image, (c) filtered and binarized image by the real part of Gabor filter, and (d) filtered and binarized image by the imaginary part of Gabor filter.

2.9 Summary

Fingerprint recognition is one of the most mature biometric technologies and it has been in use for over 100 years. Despite the maturity of fingerprint technology, its widespread adoption in a diverse set of applications has raised several new challenges that the scientific community is currently addressing.

1. While different types of fingerprint sensing technologies have been developed, capturing high quality fingerprint images from fingers under non-ideal conditions and unhabituated users is still problematic. One technology that shows promise is the acquisition of 3D fingerprints in a touchless mode. A major advantage of this modality is that it can capture rolled-equivalent fingerprint images much faster than the conventional rolling process. It may also avoid the skin distortion introduced by rolling and other pressure variations.
2. The wide deployment of fingerprint recognition systems in various applications has also resulted in some novel methods for circumvention. It has been reported that some individuals have successfully defeated positive recognition systems (e.g., physical access control systems) using spoof fingers and some individuals have successfully circumvented negative recognition systems (e.g., border control systems) by surgically altering their fingerprints. Further research is required to assure the integrity of fingerprints presented to the sensor.
3. Although fingerprint recognition is one of the earliest applications of pattern recognition, the accuracy of state-of-the-art fingerprint matching systems is still not comparable to human fingerprint experts in many situations, particularly latent print matching where image quality tends to be poor. State-of-the-art fingerprint identification systems require extensive manual intervention in latent encoding and in verifying a candidate list returned by the system. With the increase in latent matching transactions for civilian, law enforcement, and homeland security applications, automated latent processing and matching is a fruitful area of research.

4. The widespread use of fingerprint recognition systems in large-scale government and civilian applications has raised concerns about the fingerprint template's security and the resulting privacy of the user. Security and privacy are of particular concern in centralized databases, which can store millions of fingerprint templates. Privacy-enhancing technology, along with cancelable biometrics, is likely to raise the privacy and security levels of such critical personal information. However, more research is required to incorporate these schemes in an operational environment.

Bibliographical and Historical Remarks

The discovery of many archaeological artifacts having human fingerprint impressions on them indicates that ancient civilizations were aware of the fingerprints. However, this awareness did not appear to have resulted in any analysis of the fingerprint patterns and their individuality until the late seventeenth century [34, 40]. The first scientific study of fingerprint structures was reported in a publication by Nehemiah Grew in 1684 [34] and a detailed description of the anatomical formation of fingerprints was provided by Mayer in 1788 [40]. In 1823, Purkinje was the first to classify fingerprints into nine categories according to the ridge configurations [40]. Readers interested in knowing more about the early history of fingerprints are referred to [11, 40, 4, 34].

It was only in the late nineteenth century that the scientific community started contemplating the use of fingerprints as a tool for person identification. The foundation for modern fingerprint recognition was laid in 1880 by Henry Faulds [12] and Sir William Herschel [24], who independently suggested the individuality of fingerprints based on empirical observations. This was quickly followed by the work of Sir Francis Galton, who extensively studied the characteristics of fingerprints [18] and introduced the minutiae features for fingerprint matching [17]. The claim of uniqueness of fingerprints did not lead to an immediate demise of the anthropometric system of identification (introduced by Bertillon), which was in use at that time. This was due to the lack of an efficient scheme to index large fingerprint databases in such a way that human experts can quickly search for similar fingerprints and perform manual fingerprint identification. An important breakthrough was made by Edward Henry in 1899, who established the well-known "Henry system" of fingerprint classification [23].

In 1891, Argentine police officials initiated the fingerprinting of criminals and used fingerprints as evidence in a homicide case in 1892 [22]. This appears to be the first use of fingerprints in criminal proceedings. Soon, fingerprint recognition came to be formally accepted as a valid personal identification method and became a standard routine in forensics [34]. Fingerprint identification agencies were set up worldwide and fingerprint databases were established by law enforcement agencies. The Federal Bureau of Investigation (FBI) in the United States set up its fingerprint identification division in 1924 with a database of 810,000 fingerprint cards [13].

Various fingerprint recognition procedures, including techniques for latent finger-print acquisition [14] and standards for fingerprint matching were developed [33].

The initial success of fingerprint recognition led to its rapid expansion in law en-forcement and forensic applications. As a result, operational fingerprint databases became so huge that it was infeasible to perform manual fingerprint card searching even with the aid of "Henry system" of classification. This created a strong demand for automated fingerprint identification systems (AFIS). One of the first publica-tions on automated fingerprint matching was authored by Mitchell Trauring in 1963 [49]. The U.S. National Bureau of Standards (NBS), which later evolved into the National Institute of Standards and Technology(NIST), started the formal testing of automated fingerprint identification systems in 1970 [53] and the FBI installed its first prototype AFIS in 1972.

As rightly predicted by Trauring [49], the use of automated fingerprint recog-nition has not been limited to law enforcement and forensic applications. Today, automated fingerprint recognition technology is being used in a number of civilian applications for physical and logical access control and by government agencies for civil registry and border crossing. This has been made possible through technolog-ical advances in the following three main areas: live-scan fingerprint sensing, fin-gerprint image analysis and feature extraction, and fingerprint matching techniques. While the following paragraphs present a brief review of the evolution of automated fingerprint recognition technologies, the reader should consult [39, 10] for a more detailed description.

A good overview of the innovations in fingerprint sensing devices can be found in [39, 56]. The Frustrated Total Internal Reflection (FTIR) technique that is widely used for live-scan fingerprint acquisition was first proposed in 1984. While the con-cept of solid-state sensors was proposed in the 1980s, such sensors became com-mercially available only a decade later. In the last two decades, the focus has been on improving the sensing technology to reduce cost and make the sensors compact (e.g., sweep sensors), capture high resolution fingerprints, rapidly acquire impres-sions of all ten fingers, acquire fingerprints in a touchless manner, and detect spoof or fake fingers.

The most commonly used features used in automated fingerprint recognition are the minutiae, which are also known as Galton details [17]. With the advent of high resolution sensors, researchers have also been examining the use of more intri-cate details such as sweat pores and finer ridge structures for automated fingerprint recognition [28]. Several efforts have also been made to standardize the definition of minutiae [2, 26, 27] and other extended features in a fingerprint [3]. Attempts have also been made to quantify the uniqueness of different fingerprint features through statistical modeling [46, 42, 58]. The possibility of reconstructing a fingerprint from minutiae points has been established [44, 9], thereby challenging the previously held notion that a minutiae template does not divulge information about the actual fingerprint image.

Fingerprint image analysis and automated extraction of fingerprint features has been studied extensively over the last five decades. Most of the pre-processing steps in automated feature extraction such as computation of local image gradients [21], estimation of the fingerprint orientation field [31, 43, 5], regularization and modeling of the orientation field [45, 32, 51], estimation of the local ridge frequency [38, 25], segmentation of the fingerprint area from the background [43], and enhancement of the ridge-valley structure [41, 25] have been studied in detail. Several techniques have also been proposed for automated extraction of singular points (core and delta) that can facilitate easy alignment of fingerprint patterns [32, 54], minutiae detection either through binarization and thinning [43, 29] or through direct grayscale extraction [37], post-processing of extracted minutiae to filter out spurious ones and estimation of other features like ridge counts.

Numerous solutions have been proposed in the literature to tackle the problem of matching features from two fingerprint images to determine if they are from the same finger. These solutions include minutiae-based matchers [54, 29], and matchers based on other ridge and texture features [30]. While minutiae-based techniques are the most popular, there are a number of variations within this approach itself depending on how the minutia features are aligned, how the minutiae correspondences are determined, and how these correspondences are converted into similarity measures. The use of other features in addition to minutiae, such as orientation field [48], frequency map [50], and ridge skeleton [15] have also been considered. The problem of automatically classifying fingerprint images based on the "Henry system" of classification has also received wide attention due to its ability to speed-up the search in large-scale fingerprint identification systems [32, 7, 8]. Other indexing schemes that facilitate rapid search in large-scale systems without relying on the traditional fingerprint classes have been proposed [20, 6].

References

1. Fvc2006: the fourth international fingerprint verification competition. http://bias.csr.unibo.it/fvc2006/.
2. American National Standards Institute. Fingerprint Identification - Data Format for Information Exchange. Technical report, ANSI, 1986.
3. American National Standards Institute. Data Format for the Interchange of Extended Friction Ridge Features. Technical report, ANSI/NIST-ITL, 2010.
4. D. R. Ashbaugh. *Quantitative-Qualitative Friction Ridge Analysis: An Introduction to Basic and Advanced Ridgeology*. CRC Press, 1999.
5. A. M. Bazen and S. H. Gerez. Systematic Methods for the Computation of the Directional Fields and Singular Points of Fingerprints. *IEEE Transactions on Pattern Analysis and Machine Intelligence*, 24:905–919, July 2002.
6. B. Bhanu and X. Tan. Fingerprint indexing based on novel features of minutiae triplets. *IEEE Transactions on Pattern Analysis and Machine Intelligence*, 25(5):616–622, 2003.
7. G. T. Candela, P. J. Grother, C. I. Watson, R. A. Wilkinson, and C. L. Wilson. PCASYS: A Pattern-Level Classification Automation System for Fingerprints. NIST Tech. Report NISTIR 5647, August 1995.
8. R. Cappelli, A. Lumini, D. Maio, and D. Maltoni. Fingerprint Classification by Directional Image Partitioning. *IEEE Transactions on Pattern Analysis and Machine Intelligence*, 21(5):402–421, 1999.

9. R. Cappelli, A. Lumini, D. Maio, and D. Maltoni. Fingerprint Image Reconstruction From Standard Templates. *IEEE Transactions on Pattern Analysis and Machine Intelligence*, 29(9):1489–1503, September 2007.

10. C. Champod, C. Lennard, P. Margot, and M. Stoilovic. *Fingerprints and Other Ridge Skin Impressions*. CRC Press, 2004.

11. H. Cummins and M. Midlo. *Finger Prints, Palms and Soles: An Introduction to Dermatoglyphics*. Dover Publications, 1961.

12. H. Faulds. On the Skin Furrows of the Hand. *Nature*, 22:605, October 1880.

13. Federal Bureau of Investigation. *The Science of Fingerprints: Classification and Uses*. U.S. Government, 1984.

14. Federal Bureau of Investigation. *Processing Guide for Developing Latent Prints*. U.S. Government, 2000.

15. J. Feng. Combining minutiae descriptors for fingerprint matching. *Pattern Recognition*, 41(1):342–352, 2008.

16. J. Feng and A. K. Jain. Fingerprint reconstruction: From minutiae to phase. *IEEE Trans. on Pattern Analysis and Machine Intelligence*, 33(2):209–223, 2011.

17. F. Galton. Personal Identification and Description. *Nature*, 38:173–177, June 1888.

18. F. Galton. *Finger Prints*. McMillan, 1892.

19. M. D. Garris and R. M. McCabe. NIST Special Database 27: Fingerprint Minutiae from Latent and Matching Tenprint Images. NISTIR 6534, June 2000.

20. R. S. Germain, A. Califano, and S. Colville. Fingerprint matching using transformation parameter clustering. *IEEE Computational Science and Engineering*, 4(4):42–49, 1997.

21. R. C. Gonzlez and R. E. Woods. *Digital Image Processing*. Prentice Hall, 2008.

22. M. R. Hawthorne. *Fingerprints: Analysis and Understanding*. CRC Press, 2009.

23. E. R. Henry. *Classification and Uses of Finger Prints*. HM Stationery Office, London, 1900.

24. W. Herschel. Skin Furrows of the Hand. *Nature*, 23:76, November 1880.

25. L. Hong, Y. Wan, and A. K. Jain. Fingerprint Image Enhancement: Algorithm and Performance Evaluation. *IEEE Transactions on Pattern Analysis and Machine Intelligence*, 20(8):777–789, 1998.

26. International Committee for Information Technology Standards. ANSI/INCITS 378-2004: Information Technology - Finger Minutiae Format for Data Interchange. Technical report, ANSI/INCITS, 2004.

27. International Standards Organization. ISO/IEC 19794-2-2005: Information Technology – Biometric Data Interchange Formats – Part 2: Finger Minutiae Data. Technical report, ISO/IEC, 2005.

28. A. K. Jain, Y. Chen, and M. Demirkus. Pores and Ridges: High Resolution Fingerprint Matching Using Level 3 Features. *IEEE Transactions on Pattern Analysis and Machine Intelligence*, 29(1):15–27, January 2007.

29. A. K. Jain, L. Hong, and R. Bolle. On-line Fingerprint Verification. *IEEE Transactions on Pattern Analysis and Machine Intelligence*, 19(4):302–314, April 1997.

30. A. K. Jain, S. Prabhakar, L. Hong, and S. Pankanti. Filterbank-based Fingerprint Matching. *IEEE Transactions on Image Processing*, 9(5):846–859, May 2000.

31. M. Kass and A. Witkin. Analyzing Oriented Patterns. *Computer Vision, Graphics, and Image Processing*, 37:362–385, March 1987.

32. M. Kawagoe and A. Tojo. Fingerprint pattern classification. *Pattern Recognition*, 17:295–303, June 1984.

33. C. R. Kingston and P.L. Kirk. Historical Development and Evaluation of the '12 Point Rule' in Fingerprint Identification. *International Criminal Police Review*, 1965.

34. H. C. Lee and R. E. Gaensslen, editors. *Advances in Fingerprint Technology*. CRC Press, 2001.

35. M. Indovina *et al.* ELFT Phase II - an evaluation of automated latent fingerprint identification technologies. Technical report, NISTIR 7577, April 2009.

36. M. Kücken and A. C. Newell. Fingerprint formation. *Journal of Theoretical Biology*, 235(1):71–83, 2005.

37. D. Maio and D. Maltoni. Direct Gray-Scale Minutiae Detection In Fingerprints. *IEEE Transactions on Pattern Analysis and Machine Intelligence*, 19:27–40, January 1997.

38. D. Maio and D. Maltoni. Ridge-Line Density Estimation in Digital Images. In *Proceedings of the 14th International Conference on Pattern Recognition - Volume 1*, pages 534–538, 1998.

39. D. Maltoni, D. Maio, A. K. Jain, and S. Prabhakar. *Handbook of Fingerprint Recognition (2nd Edition)*. Springer Verlag, 2009.

40. A. A. Moenssens. *Fingerprint Techniques*. Chilton Book Company, 1971.

41. L. O'Gorman and J. V. Nickerson. An approach to fingerprint filter design. *Pattern Recognition*, 22:29–38, January 1989.

42. S. Pankanti, S. Prabhakar, and A.K. Jain. On the Individuality of Fingerprints. *IEEE Trans. Pattern Analysis and Machine Intelligence*, 24(8):1010–1025, 2002.

43. N. K. Ratha, S. Chen, and A. K. Jain. Adaptive flow orientation-based feature extraction in fingerprint images. *Pattern Recognition*, 28(11):1657–1672, 1995.

44. A. Ross, J. Shah, and A. K. Jain. From Template to Image: Reconstructing Fingerprints From Minutiae Points. *IEEE Transactions on Pattern Analysis and Machine Intelligence*, 29(4):544–560, April 2007.

45. B. G. Sherlock and D. M. Monro. A model for interpreting fingerprint topology. *Pattern Recognition*, 26(7):1047–1055, 1993.

46. David A. Stoney. Measurement of fingerprint individuality. In H. C. Lee and R. E. Gaensslen, editors, *Advances in Fingerprint Technology (2nd Edition)*, chapter 9, pages 327–388. CRC Press, 2001.

47. A. Sun, T. Tan, Y. Wang, and S. Z. Li. Ordinal palmprint representation for personal identification. In *Proc. IEEE Conf. Computer Vision and Pattern Recognition*, pages 279–284, 2005.

48. M. Tico and P. Kuosmanen. Fingerprint Matching Using an Orientation-based Minutia Descriptor. *IEEE Transactions on Pattern Analysis and Machine Intelligence*, 25(8):1009–1014, 2003.

49. M. Trauring. Automatic Comparison of Finger-ridge Patterns. *Nature*, 197:938–940, 1963.

50. D. Wan and J. Zhou. Fingerprint recognition using model-based density map. *IEEE Transactions on Image Processing*, 15(6):1690–1696, 2006.

51. Y. Wang, J. Hu, and D. Phillips. A Fingerprint Orientation Model Based on 2D Fourier Expansion (FOMFE) and Its Application to Singular-Point Detection and Fingerprint Indexing. *IEEE Transactions on Pattern Analysis and Machine Intelligence*, 29(4):573–585, 2007.

52. C. I. Watson. NIST Special Database 14: Mated Fingerprint Cards Pairs 2 Version 2, April 2001.

53. J. Wegstein. Automated fingerprint identification. Technical Report 538, U.S. National Bureau of Standards, August 1970.

54. J. H. Wegstein. An automated fingerprint identification system. Technical report, U.S. Department of Commerce, National Bureau of Standards, 1982.

55. C. Wilson. Fingerprint vendor technology evaluation 2003: Summary of results and analysis report. NISTIR 7123, http://fpvte.nist.gov/report/ir_7123analysis.pdf, June 2004.

56. X. Xia and L. O'Gorman. Innovations in fingerprint capture devices. *Pattern Recognition*, 36(2):361 – 369, 2003.

57. D. Zhang, W. K. Kong, J. You, and M. Wong. Online palmprint identification. *IEEE Trans. on Pattern Analysis and Machine Intelligence*, 25(9):1041–1050, 2003.

58. Y. Zhu, S. C. Dass, and Jain. Statistical Models for Assessing the Individuality of Fingerprints. *IEEE Transactions on Information Forensics and Security*, 2(3):391–401, September 2007.

Chapter 3
Face Recognition

"To ask how a human goes about face identification is probably an intractable question at present. But to ask how well and with what cues identification can occur is indeed a tractable question. So, too, is the matter of achieving effective machine identification and retrieval."

Goldstein, Harmon and Lesk, *Proceedings of the IEEE*, May 1971.

Human face images are useful not only for person recognition, but for also revealing other attributes like gender, age, ethnicity, and emotional state of a person. Therefore, face is an important biometric identifier in the law enforcement and human-computer interaction (HCI) communities. Detecting faces in a given image and recognizing persons based on their face images are classical object recognition problems that have received extensive attention in the computer vision literature. While humans are perceived to be good at recognizing familiar faces, the exact cognitive processes involved in this activity are not well-understood. Therefore, training a machine to recognize faces as humans do is an arduous task. However, general methods used in object recognition such as appearance-based, model-based, and texture-based approaches are also applicable to the specific problem of face detection and recognition. This chapter provides an overview of methods that have been developed for automated face recognition and discusses some of the challenges encountered by these systems.

3.1 Introduction

The face is the frontal portion of the human head, extending from the forehead to the chin and includes the mouth, nose, cheeks, and eyes. Being the foremost part in one's interactions with the outer world, the face houses most of the fundamental sensory organs necessary for perceiving the world around, namely, eyes for seeing, nose for smelling, mouth for tasting, and ears for hearing. The face is considered to be the most commonly used biometric trait by humans; we recognize each other and, in many cases, establish our identities based on faces. Hence, it has become a standard practice to incorporate face photographs in various tokens of authentication such as ID cards, passports, and driver's licenses.

Face recognition can be defined as the process of establishing a person's identity based on their facial characteristics. In its simplest form, the problem of face recognition involves comparing two face images and determining if they are of the same person. While humans seem to be adept in determining the similarity between two face images acquired under diverse conditions, the process of automated face recognition is beset with several challenges. Face images of a person may have variations in age, pose, illumination, and facial expressions (see Figure 3.1) as well as exhibit changes in appearance due to make-up, facial hair, or accessories (e.g., sunglasses). Training a machine to recognize face images exhibiting such unconstrained intra-user variations is a difficult task, especially since the exact cognitive and neural processes involved in humans for the task of face recognition (and recollection) is still not completely known. Moreover, there may be similarities between the face images of different persons (see Figure 3.2), especially if they are genetically related (e.g., identical twins, father and son, etc.). Such inter-class similarities further compound the difficulty of recognizing people based on their faces. Despite these challenges, significant progress has been made in the field of automated face recognition over the past two decades. Techniques for automated face recognition have been developed for the purpose of person recognition from still 2-dimensional (2D) images, video (a sequence of 2D images), and 3D range (depth) images.

The face modality has several advantages that make it preferable in many biometric applications. Firstly, unlike fingerprints, face can be captured at a longer stand-off distance using non-contact sensors. Hence, face is a suitable biometric identifier in surveillance applications. Secondly, the face conveys not only the identity, but also the emotions of a person (e.g., happiness or anger) as well as biographic information (e.g., gender, ethnicity, and age). The automated recognition of faces and associated emotions is necessary for designing interactive human-computer interfaces. Thirdly, there are large legacy face databases (e.g., U.S. driver's license repositories covers over 95% of the adult population), which enable large scale analysis of the face modality in terms of individuality or scalability. Finally, compared to other biometric traits like fingerprint and iris, people are generally more willing to share their face images in the public domain as evinced by the increasing interest in social media applications (e.g., Facebook) with functionalities like face tagging. Due to the above reasons, face recognition has a wide range of applications in law enforcement, civilian identification, surveillance systems, and entertainment/amusement systems. Figure 3.3 depicts some of these applications of face recognition.

3.1.1 Psychology of face recognition

Research in the fields of psychology and neuro-cognition indicates that certain parts of the brain are geared toward perceiving the face. Experiments have shown that humans find it difficult to detect or recognize faces that are inverted although they can perceive other inverted objects rather easily. Analysis of patients suffering from *prosopagnosia* (a disorder in which an individual loses his ability to recognize faces

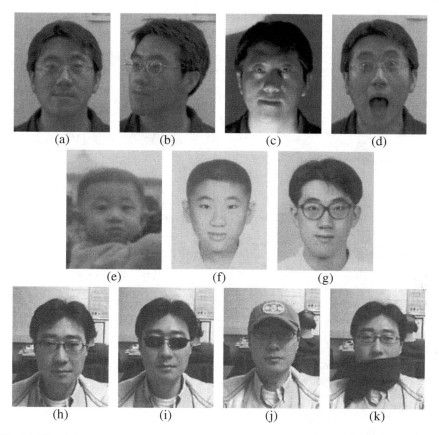

Fig. 3.1 The problem of intra-class (i.e., intra-user) variations is quite pronounced in the context of face recognition. The face image of an individual can exhibit a wide variety of changes that make automated face recognition a challenging task. For example, the face images in (b), (c), and (d) differ from the frontal face image of the person in (a) in terms of pose, illumination, and expression, respectively. The second row shows the variability introduced due to aging. Here, the images in (e), (f), and (g) were acquired when the person in (a) was 32, 21, and 15 years younger, respectively. The third row depicts the problem of occlusion of some facial features due to the person wearing accessories such as (h) prescription glasses, (i) sunglasses, (j) cap, and (k) scarf.

whilst retaining their ability to recognize other non-face objects) has shown that the loss in face recognition capability is caused by lesions in an area of the brain called the temporal cortex. This is also supported by a separate study that recorded an active response in the temporal cortex area of a monkey's brain when presented with images of faces.

The underlying mechanism of face perception in humans has been studied for two purposes: (a) to design machine recognition systems that can mimic the human ability to recognize faces and (b) to understand the neurological or psychological mechanism of brain functions for medical treatment. Because it is difficult to directly observe the brain functions related to face recognition, indirect observations

(b) Family[2]

(a) Twin[1]

[1] www.marykateandashley.com.
[2] news.bbc.co.uk/hi/english/in_depth/americas/2000/us_elections.

Fig. 3.2 The problem of inter-class similarity. The face images of some people (e.g., twins or families) exhibit similarities in appearance that can confound an automated face recognition system.

are commonly made to understand the mechanism supporting human face recognition. For example, based on the observations that human can recognize caricatures and cartoon faces, it is inferred that humans perceive the face based on certain higher-level characteristics. Studies using advanced brain imaging techniques such as functional magnetic resonance imaging (fMRI) are expected to reveal the precise face processing mechanism in the human brain.

3.1.2 Facial features

As indicated earlier, the face is composed of the forehead, eyebrows, eyes, nose, mouth, cheeks, and chin. Anthropometric studies have attempted to characterize the dimensions of the face based on a set of anatomically meaningful landmark or fiducial points. Figure 3.4 shows the representative landmark points used in several anthropometric studies. Anthropometric measurements have been used to study the growth patterns in humans as well as understand characteristics of the face as it pertains to gender and ethnicity. The forensic community has used these landmarks to identify face images. However, these measurements are not extensively used in automated face recognition systems due to their perceived lack of distinctiveness. Moreover, extracting these landmarks in poor quality face images may be challenging.

Similar to the case of fingerprints, the facial characteristics can be organized into the following three levels: (see Figure 3.5).

- **Level 1 details** consist of gross facial characteristics that are easily observable. Examples include the general geometry of the face and global skin color. Such features can be used to quickly discriminate between (a) a short round face and

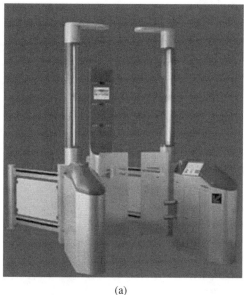

(a)

(b)

(c)

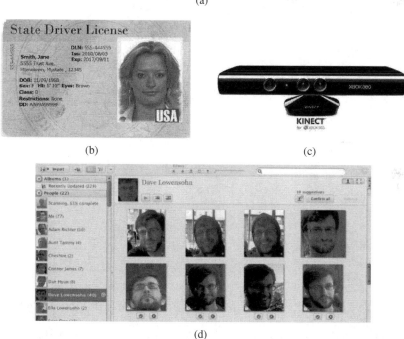

(d)

Fig. 3.3 Applications of automated face recognition: (a) Australia's SmartGate system that facilitates faster immigration clearance for registered travelers; (b) Morpho's driver license solution, where face recognition can be used to prevent a single person obtaining multiple licenses under different names; (c) Microsoft's Kinect device has face recognition capabilities for the purpose of personalizing the XBOX 360 gaming system based on the player's identity; and (d) Google's Picasa and other social network websites offer automated face tagging functionality for easy management of personal photo albums.

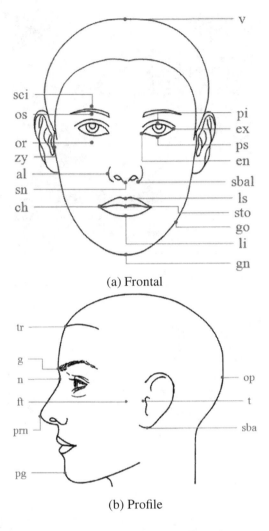

(a) Frontal

(b) Profile

Fig. 3.4 Anthropometric facial landmarks on (a) frontal and (b) profile views of a face (Adapted from the Anthropometry of the Head and Face, 1994).

an elongated thin face; (b) faces exhibiting predominantly male and female characteristics; or (c) faces from different races. These features can be extracted even from low resolution face images (< 30 interpupilary distance (IPD)[1]).

• **Level 2 details** consist of localized face information such as the structure of the face components (e.g., eyes), the relationship between facial components,

---

[1] IPD stands for Inter-Pupillary Distance, which represents the number of pixels between the centers of the two eyes in the given face image. IPD has been used to measure the image resolution in recent face recognition vendor tests.

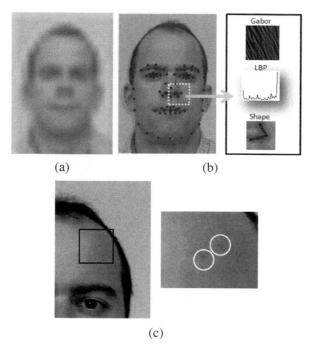

(a)   (b)

(c)

Fig. 3.5 Examples of the three levels of facial features. (a) Level 1 features contain appearance information that can be useful for determining ethnicity, gender, and the general shape of a face. (b) Level 2 features require detailed processing for face recognition. Information regarding the structure and the specific shape and texture of local regions in a face is used to make an accurate determination of the subject's identity. (c) Level 3 features include marks, moles, scars, and other irregular micro features of the face. This information is useful to resolve ambiguities when distinguishing identical twins, or to assist in forensic investigation scenarios.

and the precise shape of the face. These features are essential for accurate face recognition, and they require a higher resolution face image (30 to 75 IPD). The characteristics of local regions of the face can be represented using geometric or texture descriptors.

- **Level 3 details** consist of unstructured, micro level features on the face, which includes scars, freckles, skin discoloration, and moles. One challenging face recognition problem where Level 3 details may be critical is the discrimination of identical twins.

3.1.3 Design of a face recognition system

A typical face recognition system is composed of three modules: (a) image acquisition, (b) face detection, and (c) face matching (see Figure 3.6). The face image acquired from a sensor can be categorized based on (a) the spectral band (e.g., visible, infrared, and thermal) used to record the image and (b) the nature of the image rendering technique (e.g., 2D, 3D, and video). Since most of the automated face recognition systems make use of 2D images acquired in the visible spectrum, much of this chapter will discuss the processing of this type of images. Face detection (also known as face localization or segmentation) refers to the process by which the face is located in an image and its spatial extent is determined. This task can be significantly challenging when the face object is located in a cluttered background or when multiple face images at different scales are available within the same image. Due to the distinctive characteristic patterns of eyes, most commercial face recognition engines first detect the two eyes prior to localizing the spatial extent of the face. Face detection in 3D images is considered to be an easier problem compared to 2D images because of the availability of depth information. In video streams, face detection can be made robust by tracking the detected faces over a sequence of images. Face matching is usually carried out by comparing the features extracted from the probe and gallery images.

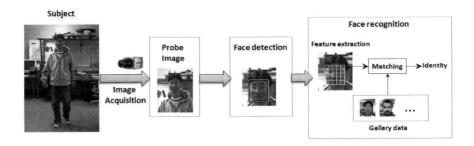

Fig. 3.6 Schematic of the face recognition process.

3.2 Image Acquisition

Automated face recognition requires the face data to be in a machine readable format. Conventional 2D photographs, 3D range or depth images, and videos are the three major types of image formats used in face recognition systems. Sensing technologies are continuously improving in order to increase the image resolution, capture more details by recording the face using multiple spectra (i.e., visible, infrared, and near-infrared), and facilitate real-time operation of 3D sensors.

3.2.1 2D Sensors

Until the development of sophisticated devices for capturing face information in 3D and invisible spectra, two-dimensional photographic images (also known as mug-shot or still images) were the only source used by automated face recognition systems. Therefore, a large number of sensors and face recognition techniques have been developed for acquiring and processing 2D face images pertaining to the visible spectrum. Figure 3.7 shows some of the 2D cameras in use today.

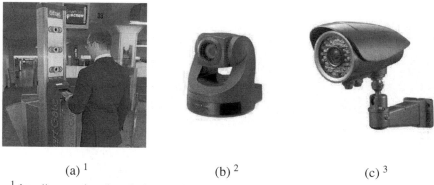

(a) [1]   (b) [2]   (c) [3]

[1] http://www.unisa.edu.au/unisanews/2005/June/biometrics.asp.
[2] http://ws.sel.sony.com/PIPWebServices/RetrievePublicAsset/StepID/SEL-asset-61461/
    370x251.
[3] http://electrocctv.com/index.php?main_page=product_info&cPath=5_15&products_id=21.

Fig. 3.7 Examples of 2D camera systems. (a) Multiple 2D cameras capturing face images at three different viewpoints, (b) Sony EVI-D70 Pan-Tilt-Zoom camera, and (c) Sony long range infrared camera.

Since the face is a 3-dimensional object, 2D images of a face may occlude some of the facial features. This phenomenon is referred to as self-occlusion. In general, the frontal view of a face contains more details than a profile view and hence, matching frontal views of a face can be expected to provide more accurate person recognition. Multi-camera configurations that capture face images at multiple pose angles have been used to address the pose variation problem. Recognition systems based on 2D face images are also greatly affected by variations in illumination and spatial resolution. To overcome these challenges, new sensors such as high resolution cameras, active pan-tilt-zoom (PTZ) cameras, and infrared cameras are being used. Figure 3.8 shows example images captured in the visible and near-infrared (NIR) spectral bands. A NIR camera can operate even under low illumination conditions because it uses a separate NIR illuminator. Since the NIR illumination is not visible to the human eye, such a camera can be used for covert face acquisition in a dark (e.g., night) environment.

Typical face acquisition systems have a short operating distance limited to approximately 1-2 meters. When the subjects are observed at longer distance, the face

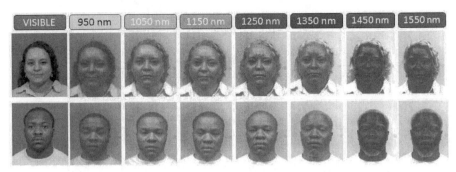

Fig. 3.8 Face images captured in the visible and near-infrared spectra at different wavelengths.

is captured at low resolution (see Figure 3.9), which may cause the face recognition process to fail. One approach to deal with the problem of low spatial resolution is to generate a higher resolution face image from the given low resolution image through a process called super-resolution. The other approach to improve the resolution of face images is to use high resolution cameras or PTZ cameras. A PTZ camera can dynamically zoom in or zoom out to obtain close-up images of objects of interest. However, the field of view of a PTZ camera is severely reduced when it zooms in to an object. Therefore, camera systems with paired static and PTZ cameras have emerged as a promising method to achieve zooming capability in a wide surveillance area. The static camera provides the wide field of view and then directs the PTZ camera to obtain high resolution images of target objects. Figure 3.10 shows an example face acquisition system with a pair of static and PTZ cameras and captured images from the static and PTZ cameras, respectively.

3.2.2 3D Sensors

The inherent pose, expression, and lighting variation problems in 2D face images stem from the 2D rendering of a 3D face object. Efforts in acquiring the face biometric in a 3D format have resulted in the development of 3D face capture systems. There are two types of 3D face capture systems: one is based on laser scanning and the other is based on stereographic reconstruction. It is generally regarded that laser scanners provide more accurate 3D face models, while stereographic cameras provide near real-time capture capability with slight loss in accuracy. Figure 3.11 shows some of the 3D sensors in use today.

The image captured by a 3D sensor typically covers about 120° of the human head and this image is referred to as a 2.5D scan. If a full 3D model of the face is required, it can be constructed by combining approximately three to five 2.5D scans captured from multiple views. 3D face models are usually represented as a polygonal mesh structure (e.g., triangular or rectangular) for computational efficiency (see

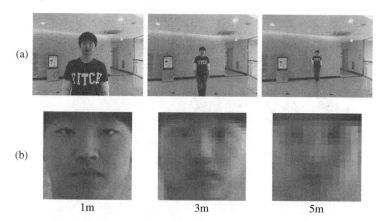

Fig. 3.9 Images recorded by a typical 2D camera with a resolution of 640 × 480 when the user is at three different distances from the camera (ranging from 1m to 5m). The first row (see (a)) shows the images as acquired by the camera, while the second row (see (b)) shows the face images obtained after face detection and resizing. The inter-pupillary distances (IPDs) are 35, 12, and 7 pixels for the face images obtained at 1m, 3m, and 5m, respectively. This example illustrates the steep decrease in the spatial resolution of the face images when the user is far away from the camera.

Figure 3.12). The 3D mesh structure changes depending on the preprocessing (e.g., smoothing, filling holes, etc.), mesh construction, and imaging process (scanning with laser sensor). Even though the 3D geometry of a face model changes depending on the pose, this change is very small and the model is generally regarded as being pose invariant. Further, the model is also robust to lighting variations. However, 3D face recognition is not invariant to changes in expression, aging, and occlusion. The drawbacks of 3D face acquisition include longer image acquisition time, the large data size of the 3D model (which requires higher computational resources during matching), and the relatively high price of 3D imaging sensors.

3.2.3 Video sequences

A video camera can continuously capture face images, thereby enabling the selection of a good quality face image (e.g., one with frontal pose and neutral expression) for recognition. The drop in price of video cameras has also made them a more viable solution for face recognition systems. Video-based sensors usually provide lower resolution images compared to still 2D sensors in order to handle the large amount of data streaming from the sensor to the storage or processing unit (30 frames per second in the National Television System Committee standard). Video compression techniques are also typically used to handle the large data stream, which can impact the quality of the images acquired in this mode.

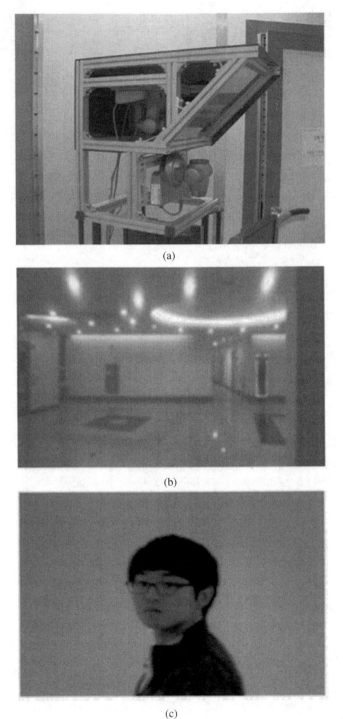

(a)

(b)

(c)

Fig. 3.10 An example of acquiring face images when the subject is far away from the camera. (a) A camera system consisting of a static and a Pan-Tilt-Zoom (PTZ) camera, (b) image of the person captured using the static camera as the person is walking into the room from the right, and (c) a close-up image of the person captured using the PTZ camera.

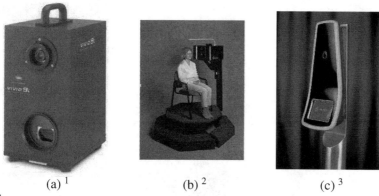

$$(a)\ ^1 \qquad\qquad (b)\ ^2 \qquad\qquad (c)\ ^3$$

[1] http://www.konicaminolta.com/instruments/about/index.html.
[2] http://www.alibaba.com/product-free/262924139/Head_Face_Color_3D_Scanner_
Model/showimage.html.
[3] http://www.gat-solutions.sk/en/3d-fastpass.

Fig. 3.11 Examples of 3D cameras. (a) Konica Minolta 3D Laser Scanner (VIVID 9i). (b) Cyberware Rapid 3D Scanner. (c) 3D FastPass^{TM} Face Reader from L-1 Identity solutions.

There is a significant interest in developing robust face recognition systems that will accept video streams as an input. Face recognition in video has attracted interest due to the widespread deployment of surveillance cameras. The ability to automatically recognize faces in real-time from video will facilitate, among other things, a covert method for human identification using an existing network of surveillance cameras. Two distinctive pieces of information are provided by a video stream: (a) multiple frames of the same subject and (b) temporal information pertaining to an individual's face. Multiple frames typically depict a variety of poses, allowing for the proper selection of a good quality frame (namely, a high quality face image in near-frontal pose) for superior recognition performance. The temporal information in video corresponds to the dynamic facial motion in the video. However, it is difficult to determine whether there are any identity-related details in facial motion (research in psychology has indicated that facial motion has some discriminatory information that may be useful in establishing identity).

3.3 Face Detection

Face detection is the first step in most face-related applications including face recognition, facial expression analysis, gender/ethnicity/age classification, and face modeling. Variations in pose and expression, diversities in gender and skin tone, and occlusions (e.g., due to glasses) are the typical challenges confounding face detection. While there are a number of approaches for detecting faces in a given image, state-of-the-art face detection methods are typically based on extracting local texture

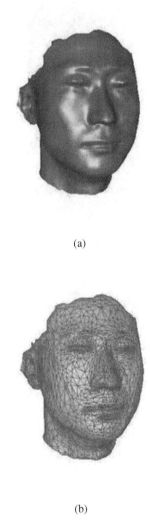

(a)

(b)

Fig. 3.12 (a) A full 3D model of the human face obtained using a 3D sensor. (b) The 3D face model represented using triangular meshes.

features from the given image and applying a binary (two-class) classifier to distinguish between a face and non-face. This approach follows the seminal work done by Viola and Jones in the field of real-time object detection. The face detection technique proposed by Viola and Jones has been widely used in various studies involving face processing because of its real-time capability, high accuracy, and availability as open-source software under the Open Computer Vision Library (OpenCV). However, the Viola-Jones face detector is not perfect and can produce both false positive and false negative errors as shown in Figure 3.13. A false positive error refers to the detection of a face where none exists, while a false negative error indicates that a face present in the image was not detected.

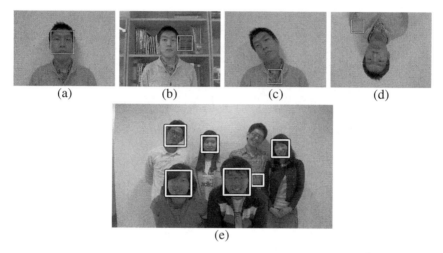

Fig. 3.13 The problem of face detection involves detecting a face in an image. Face detection algorithms have to be robust to variations in illumination, background, rotation, and image resolution. In this figure, the output of the Viola-Jones face detection algorithm, as implemented in the Open Computer Vision Library (OpenCV), is shown for different scenarios: (a) simple background, (b) cluttered background, (c) tilted face, (d) inverted face, and (e) multiple faces. Figures (b) through (e) have both false negatives (faces that are not detected) and false positives (non-face regions are wrongly categorized as faces).

3.3.1 Viola-Jones face detector

The Viola-Jones face detector scans through the input image with detection windows of different sizes and decides whether each window contains a face or not. Figure 3.14 shows the scanning process ranging from small to large windows. In each window, the existence of a face candidate is decided by applying a classifier to simple local features derived using rectangular filters. These rectangular filters can be grouped as two-rectangle, three-rectangle, and four-rectangle filters as shown in

Figure 3.15. Since these 2D rectangular filters are similar to the one-dimensional Haar wavelets used in the signal processing domain, they are also known as Haar-like filters. The feature values are obtained by computing the difference between the sum of the pixel intensities in the light and dark rectangular regions. For example, the three-rectangle filter can be used to detect the two eyes and the bridge of the nose. This is because the eyes typically have darker intensity values compared to the bridge of the nose and the application of the three-rectangle filter serves to further amplify these differences. The use of such low-level features rather than the raw pixel values allows faster face detection as well as provides robustness against changes in lighting and perspective.

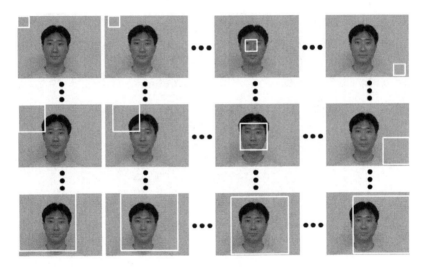

Fig. 3.14 The Viola-Jones method uses windows of different sizes to "scan" the entire image in order to determine the location of the face. In the above example, the window in the third column of the second row is likely to be detected as a face.

No single Haar-like filter can perform the face detection task with high accuracy. Therefore, a set of Haar-like filters of different sizes need to be applied to each window and the filter responses must be combined in an appropriate way in order to detect a face. As a result, the number of features in each detection window could be very large. For instance, more than $180,000$ different Haar-like features can be derived from a detection window of size 24×24 pixels. The computational burden involved in the computation of these features can be significantly reduced by pre-computing the integral image from the original image. An integral image S associated with the given image I can be computed as follows:

$$S(x,y) = \sum_{1 \leq x' \leq x, 1 \leq y' \leq y} I(x',y'), \qquad (3.1)$$

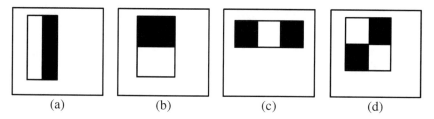

Fig. 3.15 The Viola-Jones method uses different types of Haar-like filters for face detection. These filters are applied to each window scanning the input image. When the combination of filter responses (features) in a certain window exceeds a threshold, a face is said to have been detected. Here, (a) and (b) are two-rectangle filters, (c) is a three-rectangle filter, and (d) is a four-rectangle filter. Note that the filters are shown relative to the detection window (outside rectangle).

where $I(x,y)$ is the intensity value of pixel (x,y) in the original image and $S(x,y)$ is the value of the corresponding pixel in the integral image. Thus, the integral image at location (x,y) contains the sum of all pixel intensities above and to the left of (x,y) in the original image. The integral image can be rapidly computed in a single pass over the original image. Once the integral image is available, the sum of pixel values within any arbitrary rectangular region in the original image can be computed based on just four array accesses as shown in Figure 3.16.

Though the integral image allows efficient computation of the feature values, it does not reduce the computational complexity to a level that is sufficient for real-time face detection. To achieve real-time detection, it is essential to determine a small subset of discriminative features from the complete set of features available within each window. By evaluating only this smaller subset of features and combining them using an appropriate function, a fast and effective face detector can be obtained. A variant of the Adaboost algorithm proposed in the pattern recognition literature can be used to select the discriminative features as well as to train the classifier function. The classifier function combines the feature values using appropriate weights and if the combined value is greater than a threshold, the window is classified as a face image.

The feature selection and classifier training algorithm works as follows. Let $f_j(w)$ be the feature value obtained by applying a filter f_j to the detection window w, $j = 1, 2, \cdots, L$, where L is the total number of filters. The detection window w is parameterized by its location and size. Each feature value can be used to construct a weak classifier that predicts whether the window w is a face image. Such a weak classifier can be defined as

$$h_j(w) = \begin{cases} 1 & \text{if } p_j f_j(w) \le p_j \theta_j \\ 0 & \text{otherwise,} \end{cases} \qquad (3.2)$$

where p_j is the sign (+ or -) determining the direction of the inequality, θ_j is the threshold, and $j = 1, 2, \cdots, L$. Given a training set of n example images that includes both faces and non-faces, the classifier can be trained as described in Algorithm 3. This algorithm selects the T most discriminative features among the L features and

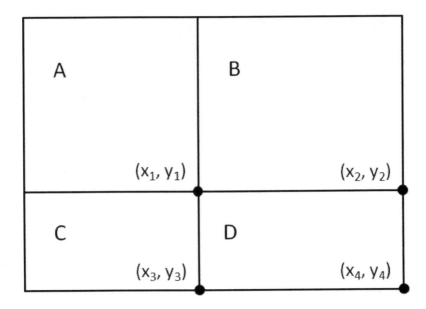

Fig. 3.16 The use of an integral image speeds up the feature computations in the Viola-Jones face detector. Let the value of the integral image at points $(x_1,y_1), (x_2,y_2), (x_3,y_3)$, and (x_4,y_4) be $S(x_1,y_1), S(x_2,y_2), S(x_3,y_3)$, and $S(x_4,y_4)$, respectively. Then, the sum of pixel values within the rectangle D can be calculated as $S(x_4,y_4) - S(x_2,y_2) - S(x_3,y_3) + S(x_1,y_1)$.

learns a linear classifier based on these features. Typically, the value of T is chosen to be much smaller (say in the order of few hundreds) than the value of L. The above training process can be carried out offline. During the actual face detection stage, only the T feature values need to be computed for each window and the outputs of the weak classifiers based on these features need to be combined using a linear function. This enables rapid categorization of each window into a face or a non-face. However, the original image must still be scanned with windows of different sizes to determine the location of the faces.

Figure 3.17 shows two most effective Haar-like features that are able to reject about 60% of non-faces. The first feature represents the fact that the eye region is typically darker than the cheek region. The second feature highlights the brighter nose bridge compared to the eye regions. Classifiers with a simple smaller set of filters can be first used to screen out a large number of non-face images in the early stage and then more powerful classifiers can be used in the later stage. A schematic of such a cascade classifier is shown in Figure 3.18.

Since the Viola-Jones face detection technique is a generic object detection approach, the same technique can be used to detect individual components within a detected face image. For example, an eye detector can be constructed by simply replacing the training set with examples of eye images and non-eye images. Fig-

Given n example image windows $(w_1, y_1), (w_2, y_2), \cdots, (w_n, y_n)$, where $y_i = 0, 1$ for non-face and face examples, respectively.
Let $l = \sum_{i=1}^{n} y_i$ be the number of face examples and $m = (n - l)$ be the number of non-face examples. Initialize weights $\tau_{1,i} = \frac{1}{2m}, \frac{1}{2l}$ for $y_i = 0, 1$ respectively.

for $t = 1, 2, \cdots, T$ **do**

Normalize the weights, $\tau_{t,i} \leftarrow \frac{\tau_{t,i}}{\sum_{k=1}^{n} \tau_{t,k}}$

For each weak classifier $h_j(w)$, compute the weighted error as
$\varepsilon_j \leftarrow \sum_{i=1}^{n} \tau_{t,i} |h_j(w_i) - y_i|$
Select the best weak classifier with respect to the weighted error, i.e.,
$h_t(w) \leftarrow h_q(w)$ and $\varepsilon_t \leftarrow \varepsilon_q$, where $q \leftarrow \arg\min_{j} \varepsilon_j$.

Update the weights: $\tau_{t+1,i} = \tau_{t,i} \beta_t^{1-e_i}$, where $e_i = 0$ if example w_i is classified correctly, $e_i = 1$ otherwise, and $\beta_t = \frac{\varepsilon_t}{1-\varepsilon_t}$.

end for

The final strong classifier is:

$$H(w) = \begin{cases} 1 & \text{if } \sum_{t=1}^{T} \alpha_t h_t(w) \geq \frac{1}{2} \sum_{t=1}^{T} \alpha_t \\ 0 & \text{otherwise,} \end{cases}$$

where $\alpha_t = \log \frac{1}{\beta_t}$.

Here, T features are selected in decreasing order of their discriminative power. The final classifier is a weighted linear combination of the T best weak classifiers based on the selected features, where the weights are proportional to the discriminative power of the features (inversely proportional to the training error rate).

Algorithm 3: The boosting algorithm for selecting the most discriminative Haar-like features and learning the classifier that categorizes each image window as a face or non-face.

ure 3.19 shows example face and eye detection results using the Viola-Jones face detector in OpenCV.

Even though the Viola-Jones face detector has demonstrated excellent performance in real-time applications, it still struggles when confronted with non-frontal facial poses, illumination changes, occlusion, etc. There have been a number of similar approaches proposed for more effective and efficient face detection. These schemes either use more robust features including Haar-like features with rotation variations, edges, motion cues, and Local Binary Patterns (LBP) or employ an improved learning algorithm compared to the Adaboost implementation shown in Algorithm 3.

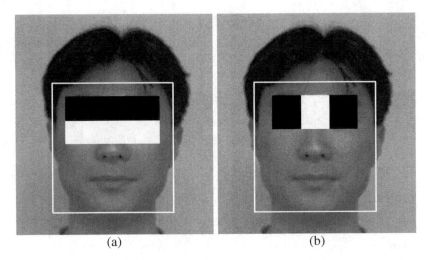

(a)   (b)

Fig. 3.17 Two most discriminative Haar-like features overlaid on an input image.

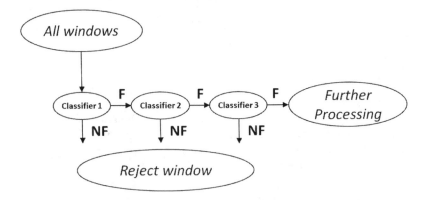

Fig. 3.18 Schematic of a cascaded classifier to speed-up the face detection process. The initial classifier uses only a few features and eliminates a large number of non-faces with minimal processing. Subsequent classifiers consider increasingly more features and further eliminate the remaining non-faces at the cost of additional processing. Here, F indicates that a classifier decides that the tested window contains a face candidate, while NF represents the classifier decision that there is no face candidate within the tested window.

3.4 Feature Extraction and Matching

There are three main approaches to match the detected face images (see Figure 3.20): appearance-based, model-based, and texture-based methods.

- *Appearance-based techniques* generate a compact representation of the entire face region in the acquired image by mapping the high-dimensional face image

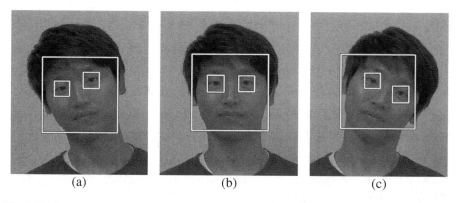

(a)   (b)   (c)

Fig. 3.19 Examples of face and eye detection using the Viola-Jones object detection approach.

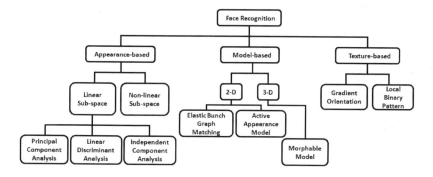

Fig. 3.20 Categorization of face recognition techniques.

into a lower dimensional sub-space. This sub-space is defined by a set of representative basis vectors, which are learned using a training set of images. Though the mapping can be either linear or non-linear, commonly used schemes such as Principal Component Analysis (PCA), Linear Discriminant Analysis (LDA), and Independent Component Analysis (ICA) involve linear projections.

- *Model-based techniques* attempt to build 2D or 3D face models that facilitate matching of face images in the presence of pose variations. While the Face Bunch Graphs (FBG) and Active Appearance Model (AAM) are examples of 2D face models, the morphable model is a 3D model.
- *Texture-based approaches* try to find robust local features that are invariant to pose or lighting variations. Examples of such features include gradient orientations and Local Binary Patterns (LBP).

More recently, schemes that make use of 3D models, video input, and micro level details (e.g., freckles, moles, scars) have been developed to improve the accuracy of face recognition systems. While this section describes some of the representative schemes for matching 2D still images, some of the recent developments are discussed in Section 3.5.

3.4.1 Appearance-based face recognition

Appearance-based schemes are based on the idea of representing the given face image as a function of different face images available in the training set, or as a function of a few basis faces. For example, the pixel value at location (x,y) in a face image can be expressed as a weighted sum of pixel values in all the training images at (x,y). The set of training images or basis faces forms a subspace and if the given face image is linearly projected onto this subspace, it is referred to as linear subspace analysis. The challenge here is to find a suitable low dimensional subspace that preserves the discriminatory information contained in the face images. In other words, the goal in linear subspace analysis is to find a small set of most representative basis faces. Any new face image can be represented as a weighted sum of the basis faces and two face images can be matched by directly comparing their vector of weights.

3.4.1.1 Principal Component Analysis

Principal Component Analysis (PCA) is one of the earliest automated methods proposed for face recognition. PCA uses the training data to learn a subspace that accounts for as much variability in the training data as possible. This is achieved by performing an Eigen value decomposition of the covariance matrix of the data. Specifically, PCA involves the following five steps.

1. Let $\mathbf{x}_1, \mathbf{x}_2, \cdots, \mathbf{x}_N$ be the training set, where each $\mathbf{x}_i$ represents a d-dimensional column vector. Compute the average of the training set as

$$\boldsymbol{\mu} = \frac{1}{N} \sum_{i=1}^{N} \mathbf{x}_i. \tag{3.3}$$

2. Define the data matrix $\mathbf{X}$ as follows: $\mathbf{X} = [(\mathbf{x}_1 - \boldsymbol{\mu})\,(\mathbf{x}_2 - \boldsymbol{\mu}) \cdots (\mathbf{x}_N - \boldsymbol{\mu})]$.
3. Calculate the data covariance matrix as

$$\mathbf{C} = \mathbf{X}\mathbf{X}^T, \tag{3.4}$$

where $\mathbf{X}^T$ is the transpose of matrix $\mathbf{X}$. Since $\mathbf{X}$ is a $d \times N$ dimensional matrix, the size of the covariance matrix $\mathbf{C}$ is $d \times d$.
4. Compute the Eigen vectors of the covariance matrix $\mathbf{C}$ by solving the following Eigen system.

$$\mathbf{C}\mathbf{E} = \lambda \mathbf{E}. \tag{3.5}$$

Here, $\mathbf{E} = [\mathbf{e}_1, \mathbf{e}_2, \cdots, \mathbf{e}_d]$, where $\mathbf{e}_1, \mathbf{e}_2, \cdots, \mathbf{e}_d$ are the d Eigen vectors of $\mathbf{C}$.

5. Any data vector $\mathbf{x}$ can be represented as a weighted sum of the Eigen vectors and these weights can be computed as $\boldsymbol{\omega} = \mathbf{E}^T \mathbf{x}$, where $\mathbf{E}^T$ is the transpose of $\mathbf{E}$. Note that $\boldsymbol{\omega} = [\omega_1, \omega_2, \cdots, \omega_d]^T$ is a d-dimensional column vector, where ω_j is the weight associated with Eigen vector $\mathbf{e}_j$, for $j = 1, 2, \cdots, d$. These weights are also known as Eigen coefficients.

A face image I of size $d_1 \times d_2$ pixels can be directly represented as a d-dimensional vector $\mathbf{x}$ containing all the pixel intensities in I, where $d = d_1 d_2$. Given a set of training face images $I_1, I_2, \cdots, I_N$, the above PCA steps can be applied to obtain the d Eigen vectors (also referred to as Eigenfaces). Instead of using the raw pixel values, it also possible to extract some features (e.g., gradient orientations) from the image and perform PCA on the resultant feature vectors. To perform face matching, the Eigen coefficients $\boldsymbol{\omega}^E$ and $\boldsymbol{\omega}^A$ corresponding to the gallery and probe face images, respectively, can be computed and the Euclidean distance between the two Eigen coefficients can be considered as a measure of dissimilarity between the two face images.

In the above PCA description, the dimensionality of the Eigen coefficients ($\boldsymbol{\omega}$) is the same as the dimensionality of the original data $\mathbf{x}$, which is d. It has already been pointed out that one of the goals of linear subspace analysis is to reduce the dimensionality. In PCA, this can be achieved by considering a lower dimensional subspace $\mathbf{E}'$, which is spanned by only d' ($d' < d$) Eigen vectors from $\mathbf{E}$ corresponding to the d' largest Eigen values. By projecting the data onto the subspace $\mathbf{E}'$, the dimensionality of Eigen coefficients becomes d', which is smaller than the original data dimension d. The Eigen vector corresponding to the largest Eigen value in PCA accounts for maximum variability in the data and is called the principal axis. Typically, it is possible to account for most of the variability in the data by selecting only a few Eigen vectors corresponding to the largest Eigen values in the descending order. Figure 3.21 shows the Eigenfaces corresponding to the seven largest Eigen values, which are obtained through training on face images contained in the ORL database.

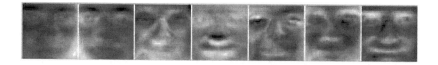

Fig. 3.21 Eigenfaces corresponding to the seven largest Eigen values derived from the ORL face database.

When the number of training samples (N) is smaller than the dimensionality of the data (d), there will be only ($N-1$) meaningful Eigen vectors and the remaining Eigen vectors will have associated Eigen values of zero. These ($N-1$) Eigen vectors can be computed quickly using the following trick. Define $\mathbf{C}^* = \mathbf{X}^T \mathbf{X}$. Since $\mathbf{C}^*$ is a $N \times N$ matrix and $N < d$, the Eigen decomposition of $\mathbf{C}^*$ can be computed more efficiently compared to that of $\mathbf{C}$. Let $\mathbf{E}^*$ be the matrix containing the Eigen vectors of $\mathbf{C}^*$. The matrix of meaningful Eigen vectors of $\mathbf{C}$ (associated with non-zero Eigen values) can be obtained as $\mathbf{V} = \mathbf{XE}^*$ and the Eigen coefficients corresponding to a data vector $\mathbf{x}$ can be computed as $\boldsymbol{\omega} = \mathbf{V}^T\mathbf{x}$.

A more generalized version of PCA is the Independent Component Analysis (ICA). PCA constrains the Eigen vectors to be orthogonal to each other and hence, the resulting Eigen coefficients are uncorrelated. However, the Eigen coefficients need not be independent[2]. On the other hand, ICA attempts to find a linear transformation that minimizes the statistical dependence between its components. Consequently, the ICA coefficients are independent or "the most independent possible". Moreover, unlike PCA, there is no relative order between the ICA coefficients. Figure 3.22 shows seven ICA components obtained through training on face images contained in the ORL database.

Fig. 3.22 Seven ICA components derived from the ORL face database. Note that there is no relative order between the ICA components.

3.4.1.2 Linear Discriminant Analysis

PCA can be referred to as an unsupervised learning method, because the class label (user identity information) is never used during the learning of the basis faces. Hence, the face recognition accuracy based on PCA cannot be expected to be very high. Linear Discriminant Analysis (LDA) explicitly uses the class label of the training data and conducts subspace analysis with the objective of minimizing intra-class variations and maximizing inter-class variations (see Figure 3.23). Therefore, LDA can generally be expected to provide more accurate face recognition when sufficient face image samples for each user are available during training.

The LDA coefficients can be computed as follows.

1. Let $(\mathbf{x}_1, y_1), (\mathbf{x}_2, y_2) \cdots, (\mathbf{x}_N, y_N)$ be the training set, where each $\mathbf{x}_i$ represents a d-dimensional column vector, $y_i \in \{1, 2, \cdots, c\}$ is the corresponding class label, and c is the number of classes. Compute the mean of each class as

$$\boldsymbol{\mu}_j = \frac{1}{N_j} \sum_{y_i = j} \mathbf{x}_i, \tag{3.6}$$

---

[2] If two random variables are independent, their correlation is zero. However, the reverse need not be always true.

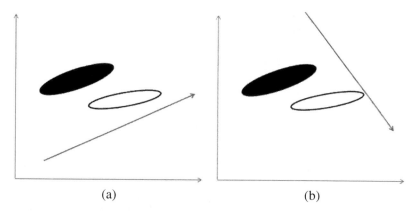

(a)　　　　　　　　　　　　　(b)

Fig. 3.23 Comparison of PCA and LDA for a two-class problem with two-dimensional data. Here, the data corresponding to the two classes are assumed to exist within two ellipses. (a) The principal axis in PCA is aligned such that when the data is projected onto this axis, the variance is maximized. (b) The principal axis in LDA is aligned such that when the data is projected onto this axis, the variance within each class is minimized and the separability between the two classes is maximized.

where N_j is the number of samples from class j and $j = 1, 2, \cdots, c$.

2. Define the within and between class scatter matrixes ($\mathbf{S}_w$ and $\mathbf{S}_b$, respectively) for the given training data as

$$\mathbf{S}_w = \sum_{j=1}^{c} \sum_{y_i=j} (\mathbf{x}_i - \boldsymbol{\mu}_j)(\mathbf{x}_i - \boldsymbol{\mu}_j)^T, \text{ and} \tag{3.7}$$

$$\mathbf{S}_b = \sum_{j=1}^{c} N_j (\boldsymbol{\mu}_j - \boldsymbol{\mu})(\boldsymbol{\mu}_i - \boldsymbol{\mu})^T, \tag{3.8}$$

where $\boldsymbol{\mu} = (1/N) \sum_{i=1}^{N} \mathbf{x}_i$.

3. The LDA subspace is constructed such that it minimizes $\mathbf{S}_w$ and maximizes $\mathbf{S}_b$, which is achieved simultaneously by maximizing $\mathbf{S}_w^{-1} \mathbf{S}_b$. The Eigen vectors maximizing $\mathbf{S}_w^{-1} \mathbf{S}_b$ can be calculated by following a similar approach as in PCA, i.e., by solving the following Eigen system.

$$\mathbf{S}_w^{-1} \mathbf{S}_b \mathbf{E} = \lambda \mathbf{E}. \tag{3.9}$$

4. Any data vector $\mathbf{x}$ can be represented as a weighted sum of the above Eigen vectors and these weights can be computed as $\boldsymbol{\omega} = \mathbf{E}^T \mathbf{x}$, where $\mathbf{E}^T$ is the transpose of $\mathbf{E}$.

Given a set of training face images $I_1, I_2, \cdots, I_N$, the above LDA steps can be applied to obtain the d Eigen vectors of $\mathbf{S}_w^{-1} \mathbf{S}_b$ (also referred to as Fisherfaces). To perform face matching, the LDA coefficients $\boldsymbol{\omega}^E$ and $\boldsymbol{\omega}^A$ corresponding to the gallery and probe face images, respectively, can be computed and the Euclidean distance between the two LDA coefficients can be considered as a measure of dissimilarity between the two face images.

When the size of the training data (N) is smaller than the dimensionality of the data (d), S_w^{-1} often becomes singular. To avoid this problem, one can first apply PCA to the training samples to reduce the data dimensionality and then apply LDA to the transformed data having lower dimensionality. Figure 3.24 shows seven Fisherfaces corresponding to the seven largest Eigen values that are obtained through training on face images contained in the ORL database.

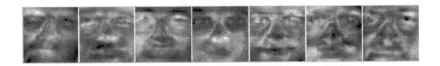

Fig. 3.24 Seven Fisherfaces corresponding to the seven largest Eigen values derived from the ORL face database.

3.4.2 Model-based face recognition

Model-based techniques try to derive a pose-independent representation of the face images that can enable matching of face image across different poses. These schemes typically require the detection of several fiducial or landmark points in the face (e.g., corners of eyes, tip of the nose, corners of the mouth, homogeneous regions of the face, and the chin), which leads to increased complexity compared to appearance-based techniques. Some of the model-based techniques can be used for face recognition as well as generating realistic face animation. Face Bunch Graph models will be discussed in this section, while the more advanced face modeling schemes will be discussed in Section 3.5.3.

3.4.2.1 Elastic Bunch Graph Matching

The Elastic Bunch Graph Matching (EBGM) scheme represents a face as a labeled image graph with each node being a fiducial or landmark point on the face. While each node of the graph is labeled with a set of Gabor coefficients (also called a jet) that characterizes the local texture information around the landmark point, the edge connecting any two nodes of the graph is labeled based on the distance between the corresponding fiducial points. The Gabor coefficient at a location in the image can be obtained by convolving the image with a complex 2D Gabor filter centered at that location. By varying the orientation and frequency of the Gabor filter, a set of coefficients or a Gabor jet can be obtained. The use of fiducial points enables plotting of partial graphs even if the face is tilted or occluded.

A Face Bunch Graph (FBG) model can be constructed in two stages from a training set of face images with a specific pose. In the first stage, the designer has to manually mark the desired fiducial points and define the geometric structure of the image graph for one (or a few) initial image(s). The image graphs for the remaining images in the training set can be obtained semi-automatically, by comparing the new images to model graphs (images that have been already marked) based on the extracted Gabor jets. During this process, manual intervention is required only if the fiducial points are identified incorrectly (see Figure 3.25). Since all the training images have the same pose, the graphs corresponding to these face images will have the same structure (i.e., the nodes refer to identical fiducial points). The same process can be repeated for different face poses (e.g., frontal view, half and full profile views), with each pose having a different graph structure.

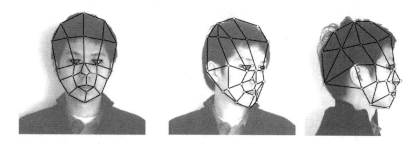

Fig. 3.25 Determining the image graphs for face images with different poses. The nodes are positioned automatically based on comparing the Gabor jets extracted from the given image to those in the model graphs. One can observe that, in general, the fitting process finds the fiducial points quite accurately. However, errors may occur as can be observed in the case of the middle face image above. In the middle image, the chin was not found accurately; further, the leftmost node and the node below it should ideally be located at the top and the bottom of the ear, respectively.

In the second stage, a FBG is obtained from the individual image graphs by combining a representative set of individual graphs in a stack-like structure. Thus, each node in the FBG is labeled by a set of Gabor jets that represent the local variations in the associated fiducial point among the population of users in the training set. A set of jets corresponding to the same fiducial point is called a bunch. For example, an eye bunch may include jets from open, closed, male and female eyes, etc. that cover the variations in the local structure of the eye. An edge between two nodes of the FBG is labeled based on the average distance between the corresponding nodes in the training set. Typically, a separate FBG is constructed for each pose and the correspondence between the nodes of bunch graphs belonging to different poses is specified manually.

Given a FBG, the fiducial points for a new face image are found by maximizing the similarity between a graph fitted to the given image and the FBG of identical pose. This process is known as Elastic Bunch Graph Matching (EBGM) and it consists of the following three steps:

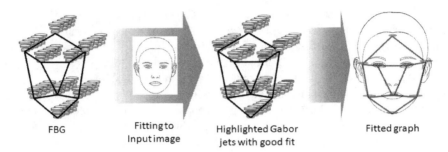

FBG   Fitting to Input image   Highlighted Gabor jets with good fit   Fitted graph

Fig. 3.26 The Face Bunch Graph (FBG) serves as a general representation of faces. Each stack of discs represents a jet. From a bunch of jets attached to each node, only the best fitting one is selected for computing the similarity and such jets are indicated by the gray shading.

- Find the approximate face position by coarsely scanning the input image with a condensed FGB (an average graph obtained by taking the mean Gabor jets at each bunch). This is achieved by extracting the Gabor jets at some discrete locations in the given image and comparing it to the jets in the condensed FBG, while taking into account the geometric structure of the FBG.
- Refine the position and size of the face by searching the image again with the full FBG, whose size and aspect ratio is systematically varied. When computing the similarity between a Gabor jet in the given image and a bunch of jets in the FBG, only the FBG jet that best matches with the given image jet is considered.
- Precisely locate the fiducial points by moving all the nodes locally and relative to each other to optimize the graph similarity further.

The result of the EBGM algorithm is an image graph that best represents the given image based on the available FBG model. Figure 3.26 shows a Face Bunch Graph with a stack of discs (jets) at each node and a schematic of fitting an image graph to an input image. In order to match two face images, say the probe and gallery images, image graphs are first computed from both these images. The graph corresponding to the gallery image is also sometimes referred to as model graph. The similarity between image graph from the probe image and the model graph is computed as the average similarity between the jets at the corresponding fiducial points. Since the fiducial points and their correspondence are known, the two graphs can be matched successfully even with some missing nodes. Consequently, the EBGM scheme is more robust to pose variations than the appearance-based approaches.

3.4.3 Texture-based face recognition

Appearance-based schemes typically make use of the raw pixel intensity values, which are quite sensitive to changes in ambient lighting and facial expressions. An alternative is to use more robust feature representation schemes that characterize

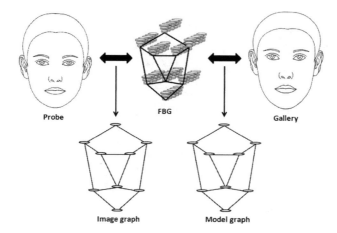

Probe   FBG   Gallery

Image graph   Model graph

Fig. 3.27 Schematic of generating image and model graphs from probe and gallery images using the Face Bunch Graph (FBG). Note that there are bunches (set of jets) at each node in FBG, but only one jet at each node in the image and model graphs.

the texture of an image using the distribution of local pixel values. Scale Invariant Feature Transformation (SIFT) and Local Binary Pattern (LBP) are two most well-known schemes for analysis of local textures.

3.4.3.1 Scale Invariant Feature Transform

Scale Invariant Feature Transform (SIFT) is one of the most popular local representation schemes used in object recognition. Computation of SIFT features consists of two stages: (a) key point extraction, and (b) descriptor calculation in a local neighborhood at each key point. Just like the fiducial points in the model-based approach, the key points can be used to achieve tolerance against pose variations. However, the number of key points in SIFT could be quite large (in the order of hundreds) and finding the correspondences between the key points from two different images is a challenging task. If we assume that the face images are roughly pre-aligned (for instance, using the eye locations), the key point detection process can be bypassed and the descriptor can be constructed directly from the entire face image. The descriptor is usually a histogram of gradient orientations within a local neighborhood. The face image is typically divided with multiple patches and the SIFT descriptor is constructed from each patch. The final descriptor is obtained by concatenating all the descriptors from all the patches. Figure 3.28 shows a schematic diagram of the above SIFT descriptor construction process.

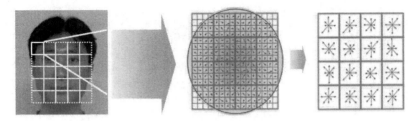

Fig. 3.28 Schematic diagram of SIFT descriptor construction. The key point detection process can be bypassed if the face images are pre-aligned.

3.4.3.2 Local Binary Pattern

Local Binary Pattern (LBP) has been successfully used as a local texture descriptor in general object recognition as well as in face recognition. LBP features are usually obtained from image pixels of a 3×3 neighborhood region (see Figure 3.29(a)). The basic LBP operator compares the 8 neighboring pixel intensity values to the intensity value of the central pixel in the region and represents the result as a 8-bit binary string. This binary code can be further converted into a decimal number by applying weights to each bit and computing the sum as shown in Figure 3.29(a).

Multiscale LBP (MLBP) is an extension of the basic LBP. As illustrated in Figure 3.29(b), MLBP introduces a radius parameter R, which means that the compared neighbors are R pixels away from the center pixel. There is also another parameter P, which is the number of sampling points along the circle of radius R. If a sampling point is off the pixel grid, bilinear interpolation of pixel values can be applied to obtain the intensity value of the sampling point. The MLBP operator with parameter R and P is often denoted as $LBP_{P,R}$. Generally, MLBP with larger value of P provides more detailed information about the local region. However, when P becomes larger, the dimension of the descriptor also increases. MLBP operators with different values of R encode different local image structures, ranging from micro to macro details as illustrated in Figure 3.30. Smaller values of R lead to detection of micro details, while larger values of R highlight the macro features.

After LBP encoding of each pixel, the face image is divided into several smaller windows and the histogram of local binary patterns in each window is computed. The number of bins in the histogram is 8 and 2^P for the basic LBP and MLBP, respectively. A global feature vector is then generated by concatenating histograms of all the individual windows and normalizing the final vector. Finally, two face images can be matched by computing the similarity (or distance) between their feature vectors.

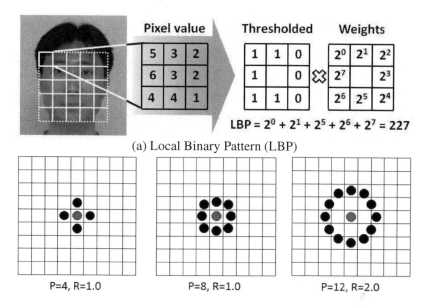

(a) Local Binary Pattern (LBP)

P=4, R=1.0   P=8, R=1.0   P=12, R=2.0

(b) Multiscale Local Binary Pattern (MLBP)

Fig. 3.29 Schematic diagram of (a) Local Binary Pattern (LBP) and (b) Multiscale LBP calculation. P and R represent the distance of the sampling points from the center pixel and the number of the sampling points to be used, respectively.

Fig. 3.30 Local Binary Pattern (LBP) images encoded at different scales.. From left to right: original image; images encoded using $LBP_{8,1}$, $LBP_{8,3}$, and $LBP_{8,5}$ operators, respectively.

3.4.4 Performance evaluation

There are a number of face image databases available in the public domain. Table 3.1 summarizes some of the representative public domain face image databases. Most of the face recognition studies used their own choice of databases and experimental setup. Even for the same database and same recognition algorithm, the recognition accuracy can vary due to factors like different evaluation protocols (e.g., division of probe and gallery set), different face detection and image normalization schemes, and different parameter selections (e.g., dimensionality of the subspace). Therefore, it is difficult to compare published experimental results.

Table 3.1 Face image databases.

Face DB	#subjects	#images	Variations included
ORL	40	400	i, e, t
Yale	15	165	p, e
AR	126	4,000	e, i, o
MIT	16	432	p, i, s
UMIST	20	564	p
CMU PIE	68	41,368	p, i, e
XM2VTS	295	1,180 (videos)	p, i, t
FERET	10,465	14,051	p, i, e, t
FRGC (v. 2.0)	568	36,818	i, e, t
MBGC	522	9,307	s, i, o
FG-NET	82	1002	p, i, e, t
MORPH	20,569	78,207	t

p: pose; i: illumination; e: expression; o: occlusion; s: scale; t: time interval (aging).

In an effort to compare the accuracy of different face recognition techniques on a common and large-scale face image database, a few face recognition competitions have been held. The Facial Recognition Technology (FERET) program that ran from 1993 through 1997 was the first effort to benchmark various face recognition techniques with participants from various universities. After FERET, the Face Recognition Vendor Test (FRVT) and Face Recognition Grand Challenge (FRGC) continued the benchmark tests with participants from both industry and academia. In FRVT 2002, the best algorithm achieved a rank-1 identification accuracy of around 70% under near frontal pose and normal lighting conditions on a large database (121,589 images from 37,437 subjects). The FRVT 2006 evaluations were performed for the verification scenario and the best face recognition systems had a False Reject Rate (FRR) of 0.01 at a False Accept Rate (FAR) of 0.001 for high resolution (approximately 400 pixels inter-pupillary distance (IPD)) 2D images and 3D images. Recent evaluations such as the Multiple Biometric Evaluation 2010 show that the performance of face recognition systems have improved in comparison to the earlier tests.

Figure 3.31 shows the improvement of face recognition performance from 1993 to 2006 in terms of False Reject Rate at a fixed False Accept Rate in verification mode.

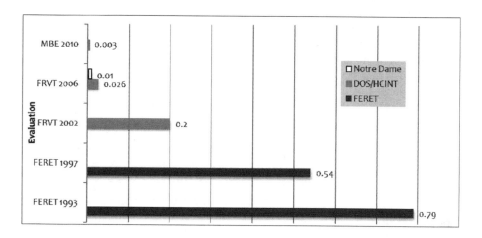

Fig. 3.31 Improvement in face recognition accuracy from 1993 to 2010 in terms of False Reject Rate at a fixed False Accept Rate in the verification mode. Note that Notre Dame and DOS/HCINT face image databases are not available in the public domain.

Recently, there have been efforts to collect a large number of face images from the Internet to evaluate face recognition performance. Labeled Faces in the Wild (LFW) and the collection of face images from Facebook are such examples. The LFW data set consists of more than 13,233 face images of 5,947 people; 1,680 subjects have two or more images that can be used to evaluate face recognition algorithms. Currently, 22 different algorithms have been evaluated on LFW data set and the evaluation results are posted on the official website[1].

3.5 Advanced Topics

3.5.1 Handling pose, illumination, and expression variations

Pose variation is one of the major sources of performance degradation in face recognition. The face is a 3D object that appears different depending on the direction from which the face is imaged. Thus, it is possible that images of the same subject taken from two different view points may appear more different (intra-user variation) than images of two different subjects taken from the same view point (inter-user variation).

---

[1] http://vis-www.cs.umass.edu/lfw/

Illumination or lighting variation is another source of performance degradation. Since the face is a 3D object, different lighting sources can generate various illumination conditions and shadings. There have been attempts to develop facial features that are invariant under illumination changes. Another alternative is to learn and compensate for the lighting variations using prior knowledge of lighting sources based on training data.

To overcome the aforementioned problems, face recognition systems based on 3D images has been developed. 3D face recognition methods use the surface geometry of the face. Unlike 2D face recognition, 3D face recognition is robust against pose and lighting variations due to the invariance of the 3D shape against these variations. The probe is usually a 2.5D image and the gallery can be either a 2.5D image or a 3D model. Identification can be performed between two range (depth) images or between a 2D image and the 3D face model.

Facial expression is an inherent phenomenon that causes large intra-class variations. There are some local-feature-based approaches and 3D-model-based approaches designed to handle the expression problem. On the other hand, the recognition of facial expressions itself is an active research area in the fields of human computer interaction and communications.

Another source of performance degradation in face recognition is occlusion. Face images often appears occluded by other objects or by the face itself (i.e., self-occlusion), especially in surveillance videos. Most of the commercial face recognition engines reject the images when the eyes cannot be detected. Local-feature-based methods have been proposed to overcome the occlusion problem.

3.5.2 Heterogeneous face recognition

Heterogeneous face recognition refers to matching face images across different image formats that have different image formation characteristics. Examples include matching 2D images to 3D models, images from the visible spectrum to infrared images, mug shots to forensic sketches, or scanned photos to images acquired using a regular digital camera. Figure 3.32 shows examples of heterogeneous images commonly encountered in face recognition. Since heterogeneity can increase the intra-class variability, special care needs to be taken in heterogeneous face recognition.

The most commonly encountered scenario in heterogeneous face recognition involves gallery databases with 2D still images from the visible spectrum and probe images from some alternate modality (e.g. infrared, sketch, or 3D). This is because of the existence of legacy face databases (e.g., driver's license photos, law enforcement mug shot records, the Department of State's Visa database) that contain photographs of a majority of the population in the U.S. as well as in most other developed nations. Unfortunately, there are many scenarios in which the probe images are not photographs. For example, in law enforcement, when no face image of the suspect is available, a forensic sketch may be developed through a verbal description

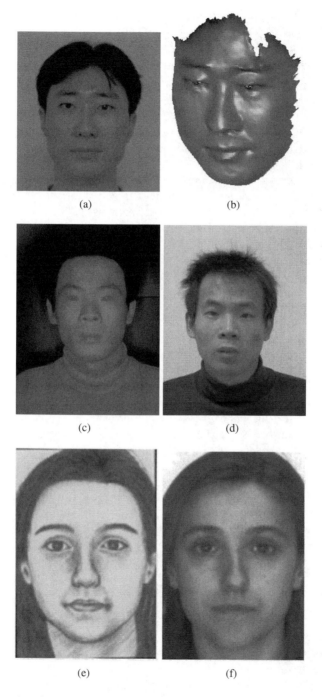

Fig. 3.32 Examples of matching heterogeneous face images. The top row corresponds to the scenario where a 2D mug-shot shown in (a) is matched against the 3D model shown in (b). The middle row is an example of matching a 2D image recorded in the near infra-red spectrum (figure (c)) against the 2D mug-shot recorded in the visible spectrum (figure (d)). The bottom row corresponds to matching a forensic sketch shown in (e) against the 2D mug-shot shown in (f).

of a suspect's appearance. In order to identify subjects in such scenarios, specialized algorithms for heterogeneous face recognition must be employed.

The collection of solutions to heterogeneous face recognition can be organized into three categories:

- **Synthesis methods**: Synthesis methods seek to generate a synthetic visible photograph from the alternate face image format that is available. Once a visible face image has been synthesized, it can be matched using standard face recognition algorithms. Synthesis solutions to heterogeneous face recognition are generative methods and they typically use techniques like local linear embedding or Markov random fields.
- **Feature-based methods**: Feature-based methods encode face images from both modalities using feature descriptors that are largely invariant to changes between the two domains. For example, local binary patterns and SIFT feature descriptors have been shown to be stable between the sketch and visible photographs, as well as near-infrared face images and visible photographs. Once face images from both image formats are represented using feature descriptors, feature extraction methods such as LDA can be used to improve the discriminative abilities of the representation. The matching stage of the feature-based methods is performed by measuring the distance or similarity between the feature vector representation of the two face images.
- **Prototype similarity methods**: Prototype similarity methods represent the face image as a vector of similarities to the images in a prototype database. Suppose that we need to match a probe image of format A with a gallery image of format B. The prototype database consists of a collection of subjects whose face images are available both in format A and format B. The prototypes are analogous to a training set - in this case they help approximate the distribution of faces. The probe image can be matched against the images of format A from the prototype database to generate a vector of similarities. Another vector of similarities can be obtained by matching the gallery image against the images of format B in the prototype database. These similarities could be measured using texture-based representations (e.g., LBP, SIFT) of the face images. The probe and gallery images can be matched by directly comparing the two similarity vectors. Linear discriminant analysis may also be applied on the similarity vectors to improve the recognition accuracy. An advantage of the prototype similarity approach is that the feature representation may be different for the probe and gallery image formats. This property is useful in scenarios such as 3D to 2D matching, where common feature descriptors do not exist between the two image formats.

3.5.3 Face modeling

The objective of face modeling is to encode the properties of a face image (e.g., shape, appearance, aging) using a compact set of parameters that allows interpretation of any new face image by generating synthetic images that are as similar as possible to the given image. Thus, the parametric representation not only allow comparison between different face images, but can also be used for generating realistic animations of the face. Active Appearance Model (AAM), Active Shape Model (ASM), and morphable models are the most popular face modeling techniques.

3.5.3.1 Active Appearance Model

Active Appearance Model (AAM) is a statistical model of the facial appearance generated by combining shape and texture variations. Given a set of training face images $I_1, I_2, \cdots, I_N$, the AAM can be constructed as follows. Let $\mathbf{p}_i$ represent a vector of fiducial points in image I_i. Exact correspondences of fiducial points are required across all the N training images. By applying PCA to the training set of fiducial points $\mathbf{p}_1, \mathbf{p}_2, \cdots, \mathbf{p}_N$, any $\mathbf{p}_j$ can be approximated as

$$\mathbf{p}_j = \mathbf{p}_\mu + \mathbf{E}_s \boldsymbol{\omega}_{s_j}, \qquad (3.10)$$

where $\mathbf{p}_\mu$ is the mean shape, $\mathbf{E}_s$ is the matrix of Eigen vectors (representing orthogonal modes of variation) obtained by applying PCA to the training set, and $\boldsymbol{\omega}_{s_j}$ is a set of shape parameters. To build a texture model, each training image is warped so that its fiducial points match the mean shape. Let $\mathbf{g}_i$ represent the face texture extracted from image I_i, i.e., the vector pixel intensities after warping I_i to match the mean shape. The texture model is defined similar to the shape model as

$$\mathbf{g}_j = \mathbf{g}_\mu + \mathbf{E}_g \boldsymbol{\omega}_{g_j}, \qquad (3.11)$$

where $\mathbf{g}_\mu$ is the mean texture, $\mathbf{E}_g$ is the matrix of Eigen vectors obtained by applying PCA to the training set $\mathbf{g}_1, \mathbf{g}_2, \cdots, \mathbf{g}_N$, and $\boldsymbol{\omega}_{g_j}$ is a set of texture parameters. The shape and texture parameters can be considered together and any face image I_j can be represented as $\boldsymbol{\omega}_j = (\boldsymbol{\omega}_{s_j}, \boldsymbol{\omega}_{g_j})$. Now the problem is to find the best shape and texture parameter vectors $\boldsymbol{\omega}_j$ that minimizes the difference between the given image I_j and a synthetic image I_j^m generated by the current model defined by $\boldsymbol{\omega}_j$. This is usually achieved through an appropriate optimization scheme. The model parameters $\boldsymbol{\omega}_j$ and $\boldsymbol{\omega}_k$ derived from two different face images I_j and I_k, respectively, can be directly matched to determine the similarity between I_j and I_k. Figure 3.33 shows an example of how the AAM technique splits the face image into shape and texture components as well as the model fitting process.

3.5.3.2 Morphable Model

Morphable Model (MM) uses 3D points (both location and depth information about the fiducial points) for representing the 3D face shape and color texture (pixel intensities in the red, green, and blue channels) for representing the facial appearance. In contrast, AAM typically uses only the location of the fiducial points and the gray scale pixel intensities. Therefore, morphable model can be considered as a 3D

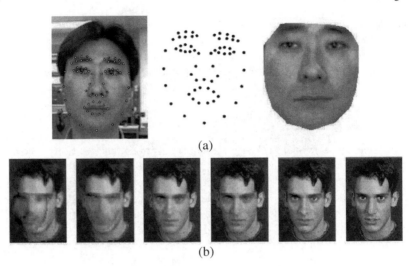

(a)

(b)

Fig. 3.33 AAM training and fitting examples. (a) The training image is split into shape and shape-normalized texture. (b) Examples of the AAM fitting iterations.

version of the AAM with color texture. Since the morphable model uses 3D information, the fitting procedure is more complicated than AAM with the added considerations of focal length, ambient light intensity, intensities and angles of directed light, color contrast, and gains and offsets of color channels. Figure 3.34 shows an example of fitting a morphable model to 2D images at various poses.

3.5.3.3 Facial Aging Model

Aging-related changes on the face manifest themselves in a number of different ways: (a) wrinkles and speckles, (b) weight loss and gain, and (c) change in shape of face primitives (e.g., sagged eyes, cheeks, or mouth). All these aging-related variations degrade face recognition performance. A simple way to handle aging variations is to update the face template in the database periodically. However, this is possible only in some controlled face verification applications. Though aging variations have a negative impact on face recognition accuracy, the problem of age-invariant face recognition has not been extensively studied because of two reasons. Firstly, pose and lighting variations are generally considered to be more critical factors that degrade face recognition performance. Secondly, until recently, no public domain databases were available for studying the effect of aging.

One of the successful approaches to age-invariant face recognition is to build a 2D or 3D generative model for face aging. The aging model can be used to compensate for the aging process in face matching or age estimation. These methods first transform the probe image to the same age as the gallery image using a trained aging model in order to compensate for the age effect. While model-based methods have

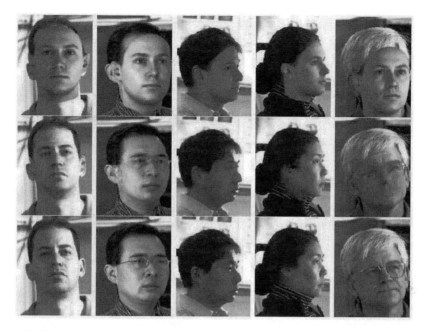

Fig. 3.34 Example of morphable model fitting. Top row: Initial parameters. Middle row: Results of fitting, rendered on top of the input images. Bottom row: Input images. The fifth column is an example of a poor fit. Images are from [4]. ©IEEE

been shown to be effective in age-invariant face recognition, they have some limitations. Firstly, construction of facial aging models is difficult and the constructed models may not represent the aging process very well. Since the facial aging process is rather complex and the number of training images is often very limited, constructing the aging model requires the use of strong parametric assumptions that are often unrealistic in real-world face recognition scenarios. Secondly, additional information in the form of true ages of the faces in the training set and the locations of landmark points on each face image are needed for constructing the aging model. This information is not always available. A further constraint on the training set is that the images should be captured under controlled conditions (e.g., frontal pose, normal illumination, neutral expression). Unfortunately, such constraints are not easy to satisfy in practice, especially in scenarios where the face images being compared are subject to significant changes not only in aging, but also in pose, illumination, and expression.

In order to overcome the limitations of the generative aging model, approaches based on discriminative models have also been proposed. In a discriminative aging model, the face images are represented by a set of robust features (e.g., MLBP), then projected on to some subspace where the aging variation is compensated. An example of a discriminative aging model is the use of gradient orientation pyramid for feature representation, combined with the use of support vector machines for verifying faces across age progression. Figure 3.35 shows some example face image pairs that can be successfully matched using the aforementioned generative or discriminative aging models.

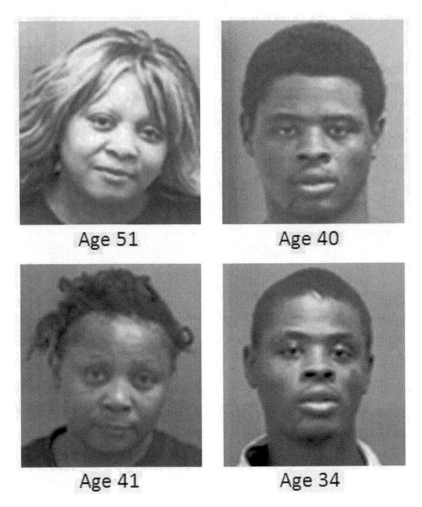

Fig. 3.35 Example face image pairs at different ages taken from two different subjects. A leading commercial matcher failed to match these pairs, but a generative or discriminative aging model were able to match these pairs. Top and bottom rows correspond to the probe and gallery images, respectively.

3.6 Summary

This chapter reviewed the various face recognition approaches with emphasis on matching 2D still images captured in the visible spectrum. Even though there have been steady improvements in face recognition performance over the past two decades, several challenges remain due to the large intra-class variations and small inter-class variations caused by pose and lighting variations, expression, occlusion, aging, and non-robust representation of face image data. While 3D face recognition systems have been developed to overcome pose and illumination problems, a number of factors (e.g., high cost and existence of large legacy face databases in the 2D domain) have hindered the practical deployment of 3D face recognition systems. Advanced sensing techniques to capture higher resolution images in multiple spectra, face detection techniques that can handle pose changes, and robust representation and matching schemes are crucial to further enhance the accuracy of face recognition systems.

Bibliographical and Historical Remarks

While face recognition has a long history in forensic applications, its use in the biometric domain is relatively recent. The first attempt to identify a subject by comparing a pair of facial photographs was reported in a British court in 1871 [24] and the first known systematic method for face recognition was developed by the French criminologist, Alphonse Bertillon in 1882 [3].

On the other hand, the automated face recognition scheme was not reported in the literature until 1966 [5]. Most of the early work in automated face recognition focused on the use of descriptive features such as the position, size, and spatial relationship between eyes, nose, mouth, and head contour. However, automatically extracting these features from poor quality images exhibiting variations in viewpoints is a difficult task.

Bledsoe et al. [5] worked on an automated face recognition project from 1964 to 1965. This project was called *man-machine* because a set of facial features were manually extracted from face photographs. These features were then fed to a computer to conduct the automatic matching process. Based on the set of manually annotated feature points a list of 20 distances was derived and used to compute the similarity between face images. This work was continued at Stanford Research Institute in 1966. Their system consistently outperformed humans on a database of over 2,000 photographs. Goldstein [10] also used 34 descriptive features (simple morphological descriptions about face, hair, eyebrows, etc.) to identify individuals based on face images. These features were provided to a set of trained jurors to perform identification tasks. He concluded that six different features were required to identify a person in a 255-subject database, and predicted that 14 features were required to identify a person in a database with 4 million subjects. This seems to have been the first attempt to describe the individuality aspect of the human face, although it did not account for variations in pose, illumination, and expression.

The first fully automated face identification system was developed by Kanade [11] using a set of facial parameters based on local histogram of gray scale pixel values. Following this system, many other automated face recognition systems were introduced [7]. The Principal Component Analysis (PCA) method was first applied on face images by Sirovich [26] for image compression, then by Turk and Pentland [27] for identification. The PCA-based approach greatly reduced the computational burden commonly associated with processing face images (at that time) and inspired more active research in face recognition. Another popular face recognition method is the Linear Discriminant Analysis (LDA) [2], which is based on the Fisher's Linear Discriminant Analysis. Some other well known methods include Elastic Bunch Graph Matching (EBGM) [29] and Local Binary Pattern (LBP) [19] based feature representation.

All face recognition schemes mentioned above rely on a reasonably accurate face detection procedure. The face detector proposed by Viola and Jones [28] was the first robust real-time face detector requiring limited computational resources during its operation. A number of similar face detection methods were designed following this scheme, thereby facilitating the development of fully automated real-time face recognition systems.

Since 1997, when the first systematic face recognition evaluation was conducted, the performance of automated face recognition systems have improved dramatically. This improvement is due to significant advancements made in computer vision and pattern recognition algorithms, as well as sensor technology. The use of 3D geometry and skin texture analysis on high resolution images resulted in the best identification accuracy in FRVT 2006 [23]. Current research in automatic face recognition focuses on robust recognition under unconstrained environments, developing more robust feature representations using distribution based descriptors, and utilizing multi-spectral information.

References

1. M.S. Bartlett, J.R. Movellan, and T.J. Sejnowski. Face recognition by independent component analysis. *IEEE Transactions on Neural Networks*, 13(6):1450–1464, 2002.
2. P. N. Belhumeur, J. P. Hespanha, and D. J. Kriegman. Eigenfaces vs. fsherfaces: recognition using class specific linear projection. *IEEE Transactions on Pattern Analysis and Machine Intelligence*, 19(7):711–720, 1997.
3. A. Bertillon. *Signaletic Instructions including the Theory and Practice of Anthropometrical Identification, R.W. McClaughry Translation*. The Werner Company, 1896.
4. V. Blanz and T. Vetter. Face recognition based on fitting a 3d morphable model. *IEEE Transactions on Pattern Analysis and Machine Intelligence*, 25(9):1063–1074, 2003.
5. W. W. Bledsoe. Man-machine facial recognition, 1966. Tech. Report. PRI: 22, Panoramic Res. Inc.
6. Kevin W. Bowyer, Kyong Chang, and Patrick J. Flynn. An evaluation of multimodal 2d+3d face biometrics. *IEEE Transactions on Pattern Analysis and Machine Intelligence*, 27(4):619–624, 2005.

7. R. Brunelli and T. Poggio. Face recognition: Features versus templates. *IEEE Transactions on Pattern Analysis and Machine Intelligence*, 15(10):1042–1052, 1993.

8. T. F. Cootes, G. J. Edwards, and C. J. Taylor. Active appearance models. *IEEE Transsctions on Pattern Analysis and Machine Intelligence*, 23(6):681–685, 2001.

9. Martin Paul Evison and Richard W. Vorder Brudgge. *Computer-Aided Forensic Facial Comparison*. CRC Press, Boca Raton, FL, 2010.

10. A. J. Goldstein and L. D. Harmon. Identification of human faces. *Proceedings of IEEE*, 59(5):748–760, 1971.

11. T. Kanade. Picture processing system by computer complex and recognition of human faces, 1973. PhD dissertation, Kyoto University.

12. B. Klare and A. K. Jain. On a taxonomy of facial features. In *Proc. IEEE International Conference on Biometrics: Theory, Applications, and Systems (BTAS)*, pages 1–8, 2010.

13. K.-C. Lee, J. Ho, M.-H. Yang, and D. Kriegman. Video-based face recognition using probabilistic appearance manifolds. *IEEE Computer Society Conference on Computer Vision and Pattern Recognition*, I:16–22, 2003.

14. S. Z. Li, R. Chu, S. Liao, and L. Zhang. Illumination invariant face recognition using near-infrared images. *IEEE Transactions on Pattern Analysis and Machine Intelligence*, 29(4):627–639, 2007.

15. S. Z Li and A. K. Jain. *Handbook of Face Recognition*. Springer-Verlag, Secaucus, NJ, 2005.

16. D. G. Lowe. Distinctive image features from scale invariant keypoints. *International Journal of Computer Vision*, 60(2):91–110, 2004.

17. J. Lu, K.N. Plataniotis, A.N. Venetsanopoulos, and S.Z. Li. Ensemble-based discriminant learning with boosting for face recognition. *IEEE Transactions on Neural Networks*, 17(1):166–178, 2006.

18. X. Lu and A. K. Jain. Deformation modeling for robust 3d face matching. *IEEE Transactions on Pattern Analysis and Machine Intelligence*, 30(8):1346–1356, 2008.

19. T. Ojala, M. Pietikainen, and T. Maenpaa. Multiresolution gray-scale and rotation invariant texture classification with local binary patterns. *IEEE Transactions on Pattern Analysis and Machine Intelligence*, 24(7):971–987, 2002.

20. A. J. O'Toole, P. J. Phillips, F. Jiang, J. Ayyad, N. Penard, and H. Abdi. Face recognition algorithms surpass humans matching faces over changes in illumination. *IEEE Transactions on Pattern Analysis and Machine Intelligence*, 29(9):1642–1646, 2007.

21. M. J. Jones P. A. Viola. Robust real-time face detection. *International Journal of Computer Vision*, 57(2):137–154, 2004.

22. Unsang Park, Yiying Tong, and Anil K. Jain. Age invariant face recognition. *IEEE Transactions on Pattern Anal. Mach. Intell.*, 32(5):947–954, 2010.

23. P. J. Phillips, W. T. Scruggs, A. J. O'Toole, P. J. Flynn, K. W. Bowyer, C. L. Schott, and M. Sharpe. Face Recognition Vendor Test 2006: FRVT 2006 and ICE 2006 Large-Scale Results, Tech. Report NISTIR 7408, NIST, 2007.

24. G. Porter and G. Doran. An anatomical and photographic technique for forensic facial identification. *Forensic Science International*, 114(2):97–105, 2000.

25. H. A. Rowley, S. Baluja, and T. Kanade. Neural network-based face detection. *IEEE Transactions on Pattern Analysis and Machine Intelligence*, 20(1):23–38, 1998.

26. L. Sirovich and M. Kirby. Low-dimensional procedure for the characterization of human faces. *Journal of Optical Society of America, A*, 4(3):519–524, 1987.

27. M. Turk and A. Pentland. Eigenfaces for recognition. *Cognitive Neuroscience*, 3:72–86, 1991.

28. P. A. Viola and M. J. Jones. Robust real-time face detection. In *International Conference on Computer Vision*, page 747, 2001.

29. L. Wiskott, J.-M. Fellous, N. Kruger, and C. von der Malsburg. Face recognition by elastic bunch graph matching. *IEEE Transactions on Pattern Analysis and Machine Intelligence*, 19(7):775–779, 1997.

30. S. Zhou, V. Krueger, and R. Chellappa. Probabilistic recognition of human faces from video. *Computer Vision and Image Understanding*, 91:214–245, 2003.

Chapter 4
Iris Recognition

"[The iris] consists of pectinate ligaments adhering into a tangled mesh revealing striations, ciliary processes, crypts, rings, furrows, a corona, sometimes freckles, vasculature, and other features."

John Daugman, in *Biometrics: Personal Identification in Networked Society (Jain et al.)*, 1999

The rich texture of the iris can be used as a biometric cue for person recognition. The richness and variability observed in the iris texture is due to the agglomeration of multiple anatomical entities composing its structure. Due to the presence of distinctive information at multiple scales, a wavelet-based signal processing approach is commonly used to extract features from the iris. One of the most popular approaches to iris recognition generates a binary code to represent and match pairs of irides. First, a segmentation routine is used to detect the iris region in the ocular image captured by the camera. Next, a geometric normalization method is used to transform the nearly annular iris region into a rectangular entity. Then, this rectangular entity is convolved with a Gabor filter resulting in a complex response, and the phase information of the ensuing response is quantized into a binary code, commonly referred to as the iris code. Finally, Hamming distance is used to compare two iris codes and generate a match score, which is used for biometric recognition. This chapter discusses the salient aspects of a typical iris recognition system.

4.1 Introduction

The use of the ocular region as a biometric trait has gained impetus, especially due to significant advancements made in iris recognition since 1993. The ocular region of the human face consists of the eyes and the surrounding structures such as facial skin, eyebrows, and nose bridge (Figure 4.1). While various components of the eye have been proposed as biometric indicators (viz., iris, retina, and conjunctival vasculature), it is the iris that has been extensively studied in the biometrics literature and used in large-scale biometric systems.

The iris is an internal organ of the eye that is located just behind the cornea and in front of the lens. The primary function of the iris is to regulate the amount of light entering the eye by dilating or contracting a small opening in it called the pupil. The iris contracts the pupil when the ambient illumination is high and dilates it when the

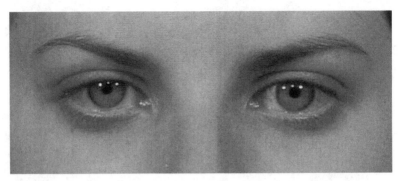

Fig. 4.1 The ocular region of the human face includes the eyes, eyebrows, nose bridge, and facial skin. The iris is the colored structure located in the annular region of the eye and is bounded by the pupil (the dark opening in the eye) and the sclera (the white of the eye). When viewed in detail, even the left iris and the right iris of an individual exhibit significant differences in their texture, although some global similarities may be observed. It must be noted that a typical iris recognition system does not use the color of the iris for human recognition.

illumination is low. The iris is a multilayered structure and a cross-section of the iris reveals the following layers:

- The posterior layer at the back, which is two cells thick, contains heavily pigmented epithelial cells, making it impenetrable to light.
- The muscle layer above it consists of the sphincter and dilator muscles that contract and dilate the pupil.
- The stromal layer, located above the muscles, is made up of collagenous connective tissue (arranged in an arch-like configuration) and blood vessels (arranged along the radial direction).
- The anterior border layer is the foremost layer and has an increased density of chromatophores (i.e., pigment containing cells) compared to the stromal layer.

The anterior portion of the iris - consisting collectively of the muscles, stroma, and the border layers - is the foremost visible portion of the iris. Therefore, it can be imaged by a camera and is the focus of all automated iris recognition systems. Figure 4.2 shows an image of the iris as viewed by a near-infrared camera. The iris, from this perspective, appears as an annular entity bound by the pupillary boundary (that separates it from the dark pupil) and the limbus boundary (that separates it from the white sclera).

The iris image is partitioned into two zones: the central pupillary zone and the surrounding ciliary zone. These two zones are divided by a circular zigzag ridgeline known as the collarette. Many pit-like irregular structures appear mainly in the region around the collarette. These structures are called crypts (Fuchs crypts) and they permit fluids to quickly enter and exit the iris during dilation and contraction of the pupil. Near the outer part of the ciliary zone, concentric lines can be seen, especially in case of darkly pigmented irides[1]. These lines become deeper as the pupil dilates and are called contraction furrows. In the pupillary zone, radial furrows are observed.

The agglomeration of the aforementioned structures imparts a rich texture to the iris. The term *texture* denotes the characteristics of an image in terms of its homogeneity, coarseness, regularity, directionality, etc. The biometric literature indicates that the iris exhibits substantial diversity in its texture across the population. The uniqueness of each iris is assumed to be a consequence of the random morphogenesis of its textural relief during prenatal growth. Even the irides of monozygotic twins exhibit differences in their texture, thereby suggesting that these patterns are determined epigenetically by random events during development that impact the morphogenesis of the tissue. Using the terminology developed in Chapter 1, the iris texture is predominantly a phenotypic trait with limited genetic penetrance.

The color of the iris is primarily defined by the pigmentation present in it. The pigmentation itself is controlled by the number of melanin granules - a genetically determined factor. However, other factors, such as the cellular density of the stroma, can also affect the color of the iris. As will be explained later, the color of the iris does *not* play a significant role in iris recognition systems. It is the texture detail present in the anterior portion of the iris that is useful for recognition.

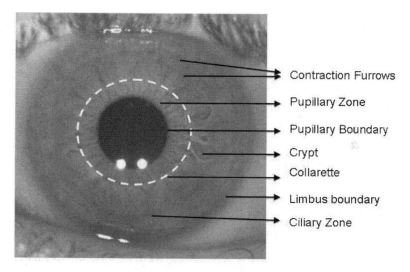

Fig. 4.2 Anatomy of the iris as observed by a near-infrared camera placed in front of the eye. The rich texture of the iris is due to its anterior portion consisting of the musculature, stroma, and the anterior border layers. When the anterior border layer recedes, the collarette becomes visible as a zig-zag line separating the ciliary zone from the pupillary zone. Crater-like irregular structures called crypts are often observed when the anterior layer thins out, thereby revealing the heavily pigmented and much darker posterior layer.

---

[1] The plural form of iris is *irides* although the term *irises* has also been extensively used in the biometric literature.

4.2 Design of an Iris Recognition System

An iris recognition system may be viewed as a pattern matching system whose goal is to compare two irides and generate a match score indicating their degree of similarity or dissimilarity. Thus, a typical iris recognition system has four different modules: the acquisition, segmentation, normalization, and encoding/matching modules. Figure 4.3 indicates the flow of information in a typical iris recognition system.

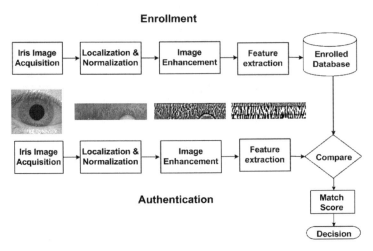

Fig. 4.3 The block diagram of an iris recognition system. The matching performance of an iris recognition system can be impacted by the accuracy of the segmentation module, which detects the iris and establishes its spatial extent in an image of the ocular region.

1. *Acquisition*: The role of the acquisition module is to obtain a 2D image of the eye using a monochrome CCD camera that is sensitive to the near-infrared (NIR) range of the electromagnetic spectrum. An external source of NIR light, often co-located with the acquisition system, is used to illuminate the iris. Most iris recognition systems require the participating individual to be cooperative and to place their eye in close proximity to the camera. The system typically captures a series of images of the eye and, based on a quality evaluation scheme, retains only a few images that are deemed to have sufficient iris texture information for further processing.

2. *Segmentation*: The segmentation module localizes the spatial extent of the iris in the image of the eye by isolating it from other structures present in its vicinity. These structures include the sclera, the pupil, the eyelids, and the eyelashes. Typically, segmentation is accomplished by detecting the inner and outer boundaries of the iris (commonly referred to as the pupillary boundary and the limbus boundary, respectively), and the eyelids and eyelashes that can interrupt the circular contour of the limbus boundary. The integro-differential operator, explained

later, is commonly used to detect the boundaries of the iris, although, more recently, the use of active contours has been proposed in order to account for the case when the boundaries cannot be represented as a simple conic section such as a circle or an ellipse. Iris segmentation is a critical component of any iris biometric system; inaccuracies in localizing the iris can severely impact the matching accuracy of the system, thereby undermining its utility.

3. *Normalization*: Once the inner and outer boundaries of the iris are estimated, a geometric normalization scheme is invoked to transform the iris texture within the annular region from cartesian coordinates to pseudo polar coordinates via a rubber sheet model. This process is often alluded to as the "unwrapping of the iris" and it results in a rectangular entity whose rows correspond to the angular direction in the original iris and whose columns correspond to its radial direction. The purpose of this exercise is three-fold: (a) it accounts for variations in pupil size that can impact the spatial extent of the iris; (b) since the size of the pupil can vary across the population, the normalization scheme ensures that the irides of different individuals are mapped into a common image domain; and (c) during the matching stage, two normalized irides can be registered by a simple translation operation that can account for the tilting of the head during the image acquisition process. Associated with each unwrapped iris is a binary mask that labels valid iris pixels with a "1", thereby separating them from pixels corresponding to the eyelids and eyelashes that are identified in the segmentation module and assigned a label "0". Geometric normalization is followed by some photometric transformations that enhance the textural structure of the unwrapped iris.

4. *Encoding and Matching*: While the unwrapped iris may be directly used to compare two irides (e.g., by using correlation filters), typically a feature extraction routine is used to encode its textural content. Most encoding algorithms perform a multi-resolution analysis of the iris by applying wavelet filters and examining the ensuing response. A commonly used encoding mechanism uses quadrature 2D Gabor Wavelets to extract the local phasor information of the iris texture. Each phasor response (the magnitude of the response is not used) is then encoded using two bits of information based on the quadrant of the complex plane in which it lies. The resulting 2D binary code is referred to as the iris code. Two such iris codes can be compared using the Hamming distance, which computes the number of corresponding bits that are different across them; the binary mask computed in the segmentation module is used to ensure that only bits corresponding to valid iris pixels are compared. Prior to computing the Hamming distance, a registration procedure may be necessary to align the two iris codes.

Each of these modules is described in detail in the subsequent sections of this chapter.

Figure 4.4 shows two important applications of an iris recognition system. The first application is the use of iris recognition at airports for recognizing passengers, employees, and flight crews where high accuracy as well as fast processing are crucial, especially when matching an individual against a watch list. The second application is the use of iris recognition in a coal mine. Note that the individuals working in a coal mine may not be able to provide good quality fingerprints or face images due to the working conditions.

4.3 Image Acquisition

An image of the eye is obtained using a sensor that is sensitive to the near-infrared (NIR) portion of the electromagnetic spectrum. This typically corresponds to the 700nm - 900nm range of the infra-red (IR) spectral band. The use of a NIR sensor has at least two distinct advantages:

- First, the textural nuances of dark-colored irides are not clearly resolved in the visible[2] portion of the electromagnetic spectrum due to the absorption characteristics of the melanin that is found in the iris. Therefore, color images of dark-colored irides do not clearly reveal the rich texture of the iris. Increasing the wavelength of the illuminant aids in the better penetration of the anterior portion of dark-colored irides, thereby divulging these complex patterns. The use of NIR illumination along with a NIR sensor is, therefore, preferred in order to elicit textural details on the surface of the iris. This is illustrated in Figure 4.5. The three rows in this figure correspond to three different irides acquired using a multispectral camera. This camera captures the red, green, blue, and NIR spectra of each iris. The top row depicts a dark brown iris, the middle row a green iris, and the bottom row a light-blue iris. As can be seen in this figure, the textural details of the dark-brown iris are more evident in the NIR channel than in the red, green, or blue channels.
- Second, NIR light cannot be perceived by the human eye. This ensures that the image acquisition process is non-intrusive, even when the eye is required to be in close proximity to the sensor and the NIR light source. Typically, the source of NIR illumination is in the proximity of the subject to ensure that the illumination power is not unduly large as this can be harmful to the eye.

Most systems acquire a series of NIR eye images from the subject and utilize quality measures to choose a subset of images (often just 1 image) for further processing. Most iris recognition systems expect 100 - 200 pixels across the iris in the radial direction for successful processing. Images of the iris can, however, be negatively impacted by several factors, including partially closed eyelids, intruding eyelashes, harsh or non-uniform illumination, low resolution, and extremely dilated or constricted pupil. By appropriately controlling the ambient illumination and requiring subjects to interact with the system in a co-operative manner, some of these conditions can be avoided. Figure 4.6 shows sample images of the eye taken from three publicly available iris databases.

---

[2] Regular digital cameras typically record images in the visible spectrum. Such images are referred to as *color* images or *RGB* images. RGB refers to Red, Green and Blue - three primary colors that can be mixed appropriately to generate other colors. Thus, a digital color image is composed of three different channels - RGB - that pertain to the visible portion of the electromagnetic spectrum.

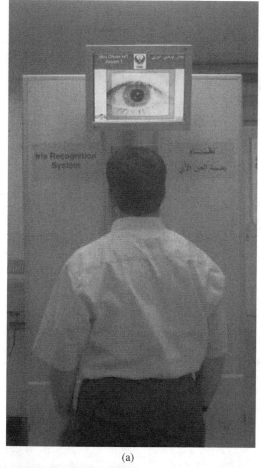

(a)

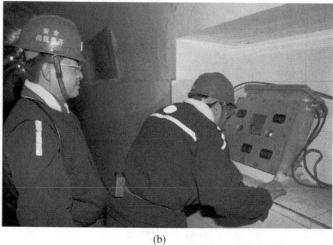

(b)

Fig. 4.4 Practical examples of iris recognition systems. (a) The iris recognition system used in UAE for identifying expellees attempting to re-enter the country. (b) An iris recognition system being used in a coal mine in China.

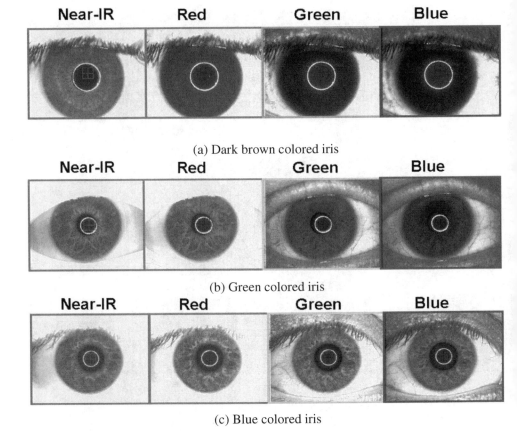

(a) Dark brown colored iris

(b) Green colored iris

(c) Blue colored iris

Fig. 4.5 The texture revealed in three different irides when they are observed in the NIR, red, green, and blue channels. (a) A dark brown colored iris, (b) a green colored iris, and (c) a blue colored iris. The color of the iris was visually assessed by a human. Notice that in (a), the texture of the iris is not clearly resolved in the red, green, and blue channels; however, it is better resolved in the NIR channel. On the contrary, in (c), the texture of the iris is reasonably resolved in all 4 channels. Thus, the use of the NIR channel for iris recognition is particularly beneficial for dark colored irides.

A number of commercial iris capture devices are currently available. Figure 4.7 lists a few examples. The Panasonic BM-ET 330 is a portable device weighing about 5 lbs and has a range between 11.8 and 15.7 inches. It can obtain images of both eyes simultaneously. The LG Iris Access 4000 has an auto-focus lens and is also able to acquire images of both eyes simultaneously. It can be wall-mounted and has an operating distance between 10.2 and 14.2 inches. The IRISPASS-M, which weighs about 11 lbs, can also be wall-mounted and has an operational range between 1-2 feet. MobileEyes is a hand-held tethered dual-eye capture device that weighs about 2.8 lbs. The IGH1000 is a hand-held iris device (however, it can be wall-mounted

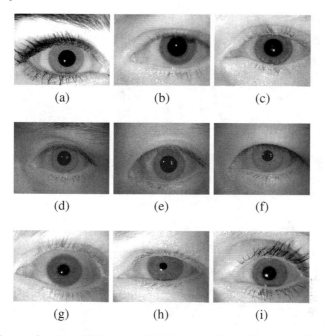

(a)   (b)   (c)

(d)   (e)   (f)

(g)   (h)   (i)

Fig. 4.6 Iris images from the ICE (top row), CASIA version 3 (middle row) and MBGC (bottom row) databases. All these images were acquired in the NIR spectrum. The ICE and MBGC images were obtained using the LG EOU 2200 camera, while the CASIA version 3 images were obtained using the OKI IRISPASS device.

as well) that weighs only 750 g. It has a focal distance between 4.7 and 11.8 inches, and captures the image of a single eye.

In all the above devices, the subject's eye has to be relatively stable and in close proximity to the camera. However, more recent research has explored the possibility of acquiring iris scans from moving subjects who are at a considerable distance from the acquisition device (see Figure 4.8). This represents a daunting task, since the iris is a slightly oscillating object (due to the hippus movements initiated by its muscles) within a moving object (the eye-ball), which is located within yet another moving object (the head)! Further, the device has to be equipped with lenses having a long focal length (e.g., 8 inches). An appropriately designed choke-point[3] can ensure that the subject's gaze is directed toward the iris camera while simultaneously activating the NIR illuminant present in the vicinity of the choke-point. The versatility of current iris recognition systems will be substantially enhanced if the iris image can be acquired from non-cooperative subjects in challenging environments characterized by harsh illumination and large stand-off distances.

---

[3] An example would be a portal that constrains the subject's gaze and regulates their walking speed

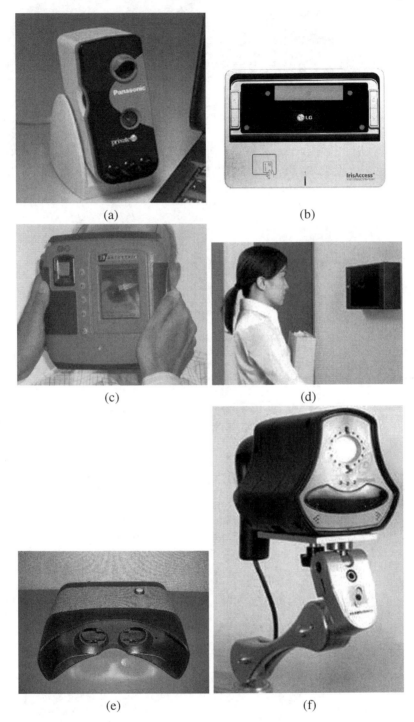

(a)   (b)

(c)   (d)

(e)   (f)

Fig. 4.7 Examples of commercialized iris image acquisition devices: (a) Panasonic BM-ET 330, (b) LG IrisAccess 4000, (c) Datastrip Easy Verify, (d) Oki IrisPass, (e) Retica MobileEyes, and (f) IrisGuard IGH1000. Most iris acquisition devices require the subject to be extremely cooperative and situated at a short distance from the camera. Specialized NIR lighting is necessary to illuminate the eye during image acquisition.

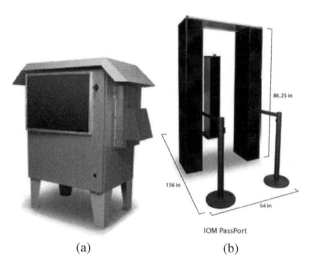

Fig. 4.8 Examples of Iris On the Move (IOM) systems: (a) Pass Thru, and (b) Passport Portal. IOM systems can potentially facilitate the covert acquisition of eye images for iris recognition.

4.4 Iris Segmentation

An iris camera captures an image of the eye that, besides the iris, includes the pupil, eyelids, eyelashes, and sclera. As seen in Figure 4.6, the iris is perceived to be located in the vicinity of these structures in a 2D image of the eye. The process of locating and isolating the iris from such an image is known as iris localization or segmentation. The primary task of segmentation is to determine pixels in the image that correspond to the iris region.

Iris segmentation is not an easy task for the following reasons:

- The iris texture exhibits a great degree of irregularity and its textural content varies substantially across eyes. Indeed, the iris could be viewed as a stochastic texture containing numerous "edge" like features that are randomly distributed on its anterior surface. Simple image models cannot be used to describe its content, thereby precluding the use of appearance-based schemes (i.e., schemes that model the iris texture based on its visual appearance) for iris localization.
- The iris is an annular-like structure bounded by the pupil in its internal perimeter, and the sclera and eyelids in its external perimeter. Incorrectly estimating these boundaries (contours) can result in the over-segmentation or under-segmentation of the iris entity. In some eye images, these boundaries (especially the limbus boundary) may not be very sharp, thereby affecting the accuracy of the boundary estimation process. Further, the boundary defined by the eyelids is irregularly shaped.
- The iris texture may be partially occluded by eyelashes. The eyelashes protruding into the iris image can generate spurious edges and affect the segmentation process.

The contrast in image intensity between the pupil and the iris offers a good cue for identifying the pupillary boundary[4]. Similarly, the contrast between the iris and the sclera can be used to detect the limbus boundary, although the magnitude of the intensity gradient across the limbus boundary may be stronger than that of the pupillary boundary in NIR images. One of the most commonly used methods in iris segmentation relies on the detection of these boundaries. It assumes that (a) both these boundaries can be approximated using circles, and (b) the magnitude of the edge pixels contributing to these boundaries is stronger than those pertaining to other circular contours in the image. The entire operation can be summarized using an integro-differential operator as described below.

4.4.1 Segmentation using the integro-differential operator

The integro-differential operator, qualified by the order statistic (max), is of the form

$$max(r, x_0, y_0) \left| G_\sigma(r) * \frac{\partial}{\partial r} \oint_{r, x_0, y_0} \frac{I(x, y)}{2\pi r} ds \right|. \tag{4.1}$$

Here, I is the input eye image and $I(x, y)$ is the pixel intensity of the image at location (x, y). According to Equation (4.1), the given image I is convolved with a radial Gaussian filter $G_\sigma(r)$ of scale σ and radius r. This is essential to ensure that sharp edges corresponding to crypts, freckles, and furrows are reasonably blurred. Next, using a circle of radius r and centered at (x_0, y_0) in the image, the intensity gradient of those pixels lying on the circumference of this circle is computed. For each pixel, the gradient is computed along the line connecting it to the center of the circle; this is denoted by the differential operator $\frac{\partial}{\partial r}$. The sum of these gradient values, along the perimeter of the circle and normalized by the factor $2\pi r$, is then computed. This is denoted by the integral operator $\oint_{r, x_0, y_0}$ in Equation (4.1). The parameters (r, x_0, y_0) that result in the maximum sum is assumed to define the circular contour of the pupillary boundary.

A similar procedure is used to detect the limbus boundary. However, in this case, the arc of integration is constrained to the near-vertical pixels on the circumference of the circle. This is necessary since the contour of the limbus may be interrupted by the upper and lower eyelids and, therefore, the effect of those pixels that do not belong to the limbus boundary has to be minimized. Figure 4.9 illustrates the output of this segmentation routine. In the eye image on the left, the limbus contour is not interrupted by the eyelids. Thus, the annular region defined by the two boundaries contains only those pixels corresponding to the iris. However, in the eye image on the right, both the pupillary and limbus contours are interrupted by the eyelids. Hence, a post-processing step is necessary to identify the eyelid boundaries and, subsequently, isolate those pixels within the annular region that correspond to the iris. It must be noted that the centers of the pupillary and limbus boundaries are typ-

---

[4] This contrast is relatively low for eyes afflicted with cataract.

ically different, i.e., the iris is not necessarily concentric with the pupil. In fact, the pupil center is nasal (i.e., shifted toward the nose bridge) and inferior to (i.e., below) the iris center.

The eyelids can be detected by searching for a parabolic edge within the region defined by the outer circle. Typically, a spline-fitting procedure is used to accomplish this. It is also possible to detect the eye-lashes infringing into the iris texture by searching for strong near-vertical edges in the segmented iris.

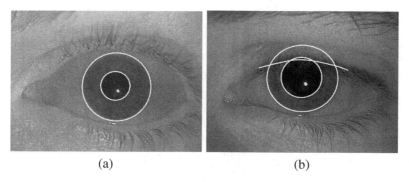

(a)   (b)

Fig. 4.9 Iris segmentation using the integro-differential operator. White lines are used to denote the output of the circle fitting algorithm. (a) An eye image in which the pupillary and limbus boundaries are not interrupted by the eyelids, and (b) an eye image in which the two boundaries are observed to be interrupted by the eyelids. In the case of (b), a post-processing scheme is required to detect the eyelids and extract the iris pixels from the annular region defined by the two circular contours.

4.4.2 Segmentation using Geodesic Active Contours (GAC)

The integro-differential operator described above (and its variants) assume that the outer boundary of the iris can be approximated using a circle or an ellipse. However, as noted earlier, the presence of eyelid boundaries and eyelashes in the image may necessitate the application of a post-processing scheme to detect these entities *after* using the integro-differential operator. Alternately, a single contour-fitting method that simultaneously demarcates the iris from the sclera as well as the eyelids/eyelashes can be used. This is possible by adopting active contour methods that can detect irregular boundaries. In this subsection, the use of Geodesic Active Contours (GAC) to detect the outer boundary of the iris will be described.

This approach is based on the relation between active contours and the computation of geodesics (minimal length curves). The strategy is to evolve an arbitrarily initialized curve from within the iris under the influence of geometric properties of the iris boundary. GACs combine the energy minimization approach of the classical "snakes" and the geometric active contours based on curve evolution.

Let $\gamma(t)$ be the curve, that has to gravitate toward the outer boundary of the iris, at a particular time t. The time t corresponds to the iteration number. Let ψ be a function measuring the signed distance from the curve $\gamma(t)$. That is, $\psi(x,y) =$ distance of point (x,y) to the curve $\gamma(t)$.

$$\psi(x,y) = \begin{cases} 0 & \text{if (x,y) is on the curve;} \\ < 0 & \text{if (x,y) is inside the curve;} \\ > 0 & \text{if (x,y) is outside the curve.} \end{cases} \quad (4.2)$$

Here, ψ is of the same dimension as that of the eye image $I(x,y)$. The curve $\gamma(t)$ is called the level set of the function ψ. Level sets are the set of all points in ψ where ψ is some constant. Thus $\psi = 0$ is the zeroth level set, $\psi = 1$ is the first level set, and so on. ψ is the implicit representation of the curve $\gamma(t)$ and is called the embedding function since it embeds the evolution of $\gamma(t)$. The embedding function evolves under the influence of image gradients and the region's characteristics so that the curve $\gamma(t)$ approaches the desired boundary of the iris. The initial curve $\gamma(t)$ is assumed to be a circle of radius r just beyond the pupillary boundary. Let the curve $\gamma(t)$ be the zeroth-level set of the embedding function. This implies that

$$\frac{d\psi}{dt} = 0.$$

By the chain rule,

$$\frac{d\psi}{dt} = \frac{\partial\psi}{\partial x}\frac{dx}{dt} + \frac{\partial\psi}{\partial y}\frac{dy}{dt} + \frac{\partial\psi}{\partial t},$$

i.e.,

$$\frac{\partial\psi}{\partial t} = -\nabla\psi.\gamma\prime(t),$$

where ∇ is the gradient operator. Splitting the $\gamma\prime(t)$ in the normal $(N(t))$ and tangential $(T(t))$ directions,

$$\frac{\partial\psi}{\partial t} = -\nabla\psi.(v_N N(t) + v_T T(t)).$$

Now, since $\nabla\psi$ is perpendicular to the tangent to $\gamma(t)$,

$$\frac{\partial\psi}{\partial t} = -\nabla\psi.(v_N N(t)). \quad (4.3)$$

The normal component is given by

$$N = \frac{\nabla\psi}{\|\nabla\psi\|}.$$

Substituting this in Equation (4.3),

$$\frac{\partial \psi}{\partial t} = -v_N \|\nabla \psi\|.$$

Let v_N be a function of the curvature of the curve κ, stopping function K (to stop the evolution of the curve) and the inflation force c (to evolve the curve in the outward direction) such that,

$$\frac{\partial \psi}{\partial t} = -(div(K\frac{\nabla \psi}{\|\nabla \psi\|}) + cK)\|\nabla \psi\|.$$

Thus, the evolution equation for $\psi_t{}^5$ such that $\gamma(t)$ remains the zeroth level set is given by

$$\psi_t = -K(c + \varepsilon \kappa)\|\nabla \psi\| + \nabla \psi . \nabla K, \qquad (4.4)$$

where, K, the stopping term for the evolution, is an image dependant force and is used to decelerate the evolution near the boundary; c is the velocity of the evolution; ε indicates the degree of smoothness of the level sets; and κ is the curvature of the level sets computed as

$$\kappa = -\frac{\psi_{xx}\psi_y^2 - 2\psi_x\psi_y\psi_{xy} + \psi_{yy}\psi_x^2}{(\psi_x^2 + \psi_y^2)^{\frac{3}{2}}}.$$

Here, ψ_x is the gradient of the image in the x direction; ψ_y is the gradient in the y direction; ψ_{xx} is the 2nd order gradient in the x direction; ψ_{yy} is the 2nd order gradient in the y direction; and ψ_{xy} is the 2nd order gradient, first in the x direction and then in the y direction. Equation (4.4) is the level set representation of the geodesic active contour model. This means that the level-set C of ψ is evolving according to

$$C_t = K(c + \varepsilon \kappa)\mathbf{N} - (\nabla K.\mathbf{N})\mathbf{N} \qquad (4.5)$$

where N is the normal to the curve. The term $\kappa \mathbf{N}$ provides the smoothing constraints on the level sets by reducing their total curvature. The term $c\mathbf{N}$ acts like a balloon force and it pushes the curve outward towards the object boundary. The goal of the stopping function is to slow down the evolution when it reaches the boundary. However, the evolution of the curve will terminate only when $K = 0$, i.e., near an ideal edge. In most images, the gradient values will be different along the edge, thus requiring the use of different K values. In order to circumvent this issue, the third geodesic term $((\nabla K.\mathbf{N}))$ is necessary so that the curve is attracted toward the boundary (∇K points toward the middle of the boundary). This term makes it possible to terminate the evolution process even if (a) the stopping function has different values along the edges, and (b) gaps are present in the stopping function.

The stopping term used for the evolution of level sets is given by

$$K(x,y) = \frac{1}{1 + (\frac{\|\nabla(G(x,y)\star I(x,y))\|}{k})\alpha} \qquad (4.6)$$

---

[5] The subscript t denotes the iteration number

where $I(x,y)$ is the image to be segmented, $G(x,y)$ is a Gaussian filter, and k and α are constants. As can be seen, $K(x,y)$ is not a function of t.

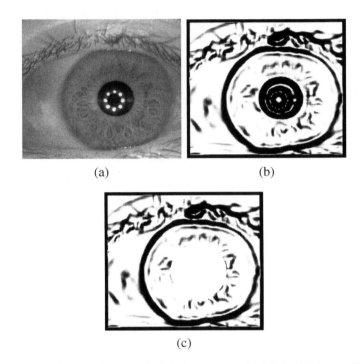

(a)   (b)

(c)

Fig. 4.10 Stopping function for the geodesic active contours. (a) Original iris image, (b) stopping function K, and (c) modified stopping function K'.

Consider an iris image to be segmented as shown in Figure 4.10 (a). The stopping function K obtained from this image is shown in Figure 4.10 (b) (for $k = 2.8$ and $\alpha = 8$). Assuming that the inner iris boundary (i.e., the pupillary boundary) has already been detected, the stopping function K is modified by deleting the circular edges corresponding to the pupillary boundary, resulting in a new stopping function K'. This ensures that the evolving level set is not terminated by the edges of the pupillary boundary (Figure 4.10 (c)).

A contour is first initialized near the pupil (Figure 4.11 (a)). The embedding function ψ is initialized as a signed distance function to $\gamma(t = 0)$ which looks like a cone (Figure 4.11 (b)). Discretizing equation 4.4 leads to the following equation:

$$\frac{\psi_{i,j}^{t+1} - \psi_{i,j}^{t}}{\Delta t} = -cK'_{i,j}\|\nabla \psi^t\| - K'_{i,j}(\varepsilon \kappa_{i,j}^t\|\nabla \psi^t\|) + \nabla \psi_{i,j}^t.\nabla K_{i,j}^{'t}, \qquad (4.7)$$

where Δt is the time step (e.g., Δt can be set to 0.05). The first term $(cK'_{i,j}\|\nabla \psi^t\|)$ on the right hand side of the above equation is the velocity term (advection term) and, in the case of iris segmentation, acts as an inflation force. This term can lead to

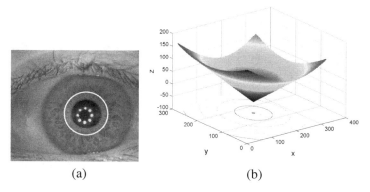

Fig. 4.11 Contour initialization for iris segmentation using GAC. (a) Zeroth level set (initial contour), (b) mesh plot denoting the signed distance function ψ.

singularities and hence is discretized using upwind finite differences. The upwind scheme for approximating $\|\nabla\psi\|$ is given by

$$\|\nabla\psi\| = \sqrt{A},$$
$$A = min(D_x^- \ \psi_{i,j},0)^2 + max(D_x^+ \ \psi_{i,j},0)^2 +$$
$$min(D_y^- \ \psi_{i,j},0)^2 + min(D_y^+ \ \psi_{i,j},0)^2.$$

$D_x^- \ \psi$ is the first order backward difference of ψ in the x-direction; $D_x^+ \ \psi$ is the first order forward difference of ψ in the x-direction; $D_y^- \ \psi$ is the first order backward difference of ψ in the y-direction; and $D_y^+ \ \psi$ is the first order forward difference of ψ in the y-direction. The second term $(K_{i,j}'(\varepsilon\kappa_{i,j}^t\|\nabla\psi^t\|))$ is a curvature based smoothing term and can be discretized using central differences. In our implementation, $c = 0.65$ and $\varepsilon = 1$ for all iris images. The third geodesic term $(\nabla\psi_{i,j}^t.\nabla K_{i,j}'^t)$ is also discretized using the central differences.

After evolving the embedding function ψ according to Equation (4.7), the curve begins to grow until it satisfies the stopping criterion defined by the stopping function K'. But at times, the contour continues to evolve in a local region of the image where the stopping criterion is not strong. This leads to over-evolution of the contour. This can be avoided by minimizing the thin plate spline energy of the contour. By computing the difference in energy between two successive contours, the evolution scheme can be regulated. If the difference between the contours is less than a threshold (indicating that the contour evolution has stopped at most places), then the contour evolution process is terminated. The evolution of the curve and the corresponding embedding functions are illustrated in Figure 4.12.

Since the radial fibers may be thick in certain portions of the iris, or the crypts present in the ciliary region may be unusually dark, this can lead to prominent edges in the stopping function. If the segmentation technique is based on parametric

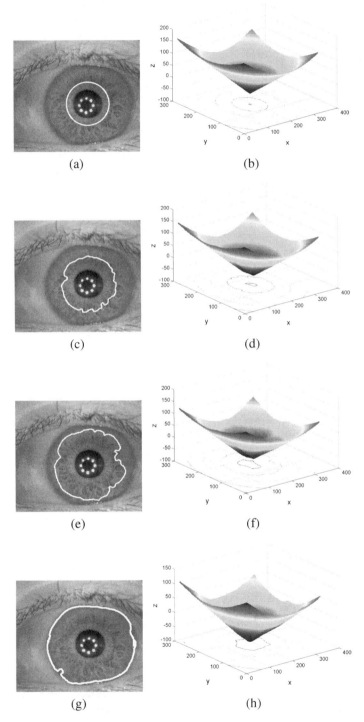

Fig. 4.12 Evolution of the geodesic active contour during iris segmentation. (a) Iris image with initial contour, (b) embedding function ψ (X and Y axes correspond to the spatial extent of the eye image and the Z axis represents different level sets), (c,d,e,f) contours after 600 and 1400 iterations, and their corresponding embedding functions, and (g,h) Final contour after 1800 iterations (contours shown in white).

curves, then the evolution of the curve might terminate at these local minima. However, geodesic active contours are able to split at such local minima and merge again. Thus, they are able to effectively deal with the problems of local minima, thereby ensuring that the final contour corresponds to the true limbus boundary (Figure 4.13).

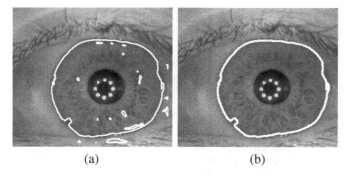

(a)   (b)

Fig. 4.13 The final contour obtained when segmenting the iris using the GAC scheme. (a) Example of a geodesic contour splitting at various local minima, (b) final contour (contours shown in white).

4.4.3 Generating iris masks

The localized iris could potentially be occluded due to other noisy regions such as the eyelashes, shadows, or specular reflections. Thus, a noise mask is generated, which records the locations of such undesired iris occlusions.

4.5 Iris Normalization

The amount of iris texture (i.e., its spatial extent) that is revealed in an image can be impacted by a number of factors. Chief among them is the dilation and contraction of the pupil in response to ambient illumination. The size of the iris (i.e., the number of valid iris pixels) increases when the pupil contracts in response to bright light and decreases when the pupil dilates in low light. Apart from this, factors such as the resolution of the sensor and the imaging distance also impact the number of iris pixels that can be gleaned from an image of the eye. Further, the size of the pupil can vary across individuals. To address these variations in size, the segmented iris is unwrapped and converted from cartesian coordinates to a normalized pseudo-polar coordinate system. This normalization operation is performed by representing the segmented iris as a rectangular image, the rows of which correspond to concentric regions of the iris. This transformation is called Daugmans rubber sheet model and it re-maps every point in the annular region between the two circular boundaries (viz., the pupillary and limbus boundaries) to pseudo-polar coordinates (r, θ), where $r \in [0,1]$ and $\theta \in [0,2\pi]$, as shown in Figure 4.14.

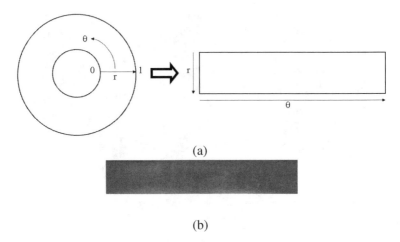

(a)

(b)

Fig. 4.14 Iris normalization. (a) Daugman's rubber sheet model is used for iris normalization. The normalization routine converts the pixel coordinates in the annular region between the pupillary and limbus boundaries to polar coordinates. This addresses the problem of variations in pupil size across multiple images. (b) Example of a normalized iris.

The re-mapping of the iris region I from cartesian (x,y) coordinates to the normalized polar coordinates (r, θ) is expressed as:

$$I(x(r,\theta),y(r,\theta)) \rightarrow I(r,\theta), \tag{4.8}$$

with

$$x(r,\theta) = (1-r)x_p(\theta) + rx_l(\theta), \tag{4.9}$$

and

$$y(r,\theta) = (1-r)y_p(\theta) + ry_l(\theta), \tag{4.10}$$

where x_p, y_p and x_l, y_l are the coordinates of points sampled from the pupillary and limbus boundaries, respectively. Along with the localized iris, the noise masks are also unwrapped to facilitate faster matching.

In order to account for the irregularity and effect of eyelids/eyelashes on the limbus boundary extracted using the GAC scheme, only those points on the contour lying on the boundary of the iris and sclera (as opposed to that of the iris and the eyelids) are used to estimate the radius and center of the iris. Specifically, six points at angles of $[-30^0, 0^0, 30^0, 150^0, 180^0, 210^0]$ with respect to the horizontal axis are selected from the extracted contour and their mean distance from the center of the pupil is used as the approximate radius of the iris (R). A circle is next fitted through all the points on the contour that are within a distance of R pixels from the center of the pupil. This circle estimates the actual limbus boundary of the iris. Figure 4.15 denotes this procedure.

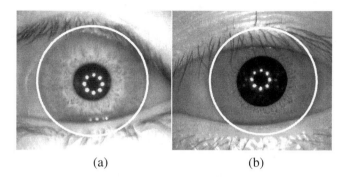

(a)   (b)

Fig. 4.15 When GAC is used to localize the outer iris boundary, then an additional step is needed to facilitate normalization. Thus, the irregular boundary deduced using active contours is converted to a circular boundary as shown in the image above. Those pixels that are included within the circular boundary, but excluded by the irregular boundary are considered to be non-iris pixels and excluded by the mask.

4.6 Iris Encoding and Matching

The process of extracting a numerical feature set from the iris is called iris encoding. This corresponds to the feature extraction stage indicated in Chapter 1. To encode the normalized iris texture pattern, a two dimensional Gabor wavelet is usually convolved with the unwrapped iris image. A 2D Gabor wavelet, over an image domain (x,y), is given by:

$$G(x,y) = e^{-\pi[(x-x_0)^2/\alpha^2+(y-y_0)^2/\beta^2]}e^{-2\pi i[(u_0(x-x_0)+v_0(y-y_0)]}, \qquad (4.11)$$

where (x_0,y_0) denote the position in the image, (α,β) denote the effective width and length, and (u_0,v_0) ascertain the wave direction with a spatial frequency $\omega_0 = \sqrt{u_0^2 + v_0^2}$.

The real and imaginary components of this wavelet can be separated as:

$$\Re\{G(x,y)\} = e^{-\pi[(x-x_0)^2/\alpha^2+(y-y_0)^2/\beta^2]}\cos(-2\pi[(u_0(x-x_0)+v_0(y-y_0)]), \qquad (4.12)$$

and

$$\mathfrak{I}\{G(x,y)\} = e^{-\pi[(x-x_0)^2/\alpha^2+(y-y_0)^2/\beta^2]}\sin(-2\pi[(u_0(x-x_0)+v_0(y-y_0)]),$$
$$(4.13)$$

respectively. The real and imaginary outputs obtained by convolving a 2D Gabor wavelet with a normalized iris image are shown in Figure 4.16.

(a)   (b)

Fig. 4.16 Real and imaginary outputs of convolving an image with a 2D Gabor wavelet.

The output of the Gabor wavelets is demodulated to compress the data. This is performed by quantizing the phase information into four different levels, one for each quadrant of the complex plane. As the normalization is earlier performed in the polar coordinates, the wavelet in polar coordinates can be expressed as:

$$H(r,\theta) = e^{-i\omega(\theta-\theta_0)}e^{-(r-r_0)^2/\alpha^2}e^{-i(\theta-\theta_0)^2/\beta^2}, \qquad (4.14)$$

where (r_0,θ_0) denote the center frequency of the wavelet, while all other variables denote the same parameters as in Equation (4.11).

Given the normalized iris image $I(\rho,\phi)$ in the polar coordinate system, the demodulation and phase quantization process can be written as:

$$h_{Re,Im} = sign_{Re,Im}\int_\rho\int_\phi I(\rho,\phi)e^{-i\omega(\theta_0-\phi)}e^{-(r_0-\rho)^2/\alpha^2}e^{-(\theta_0-\phi)^2/\beta^2}\rho d\rho d\phi, \quad (4.15)$$

where $h_{Re,Im}$ is the complex valued bit whose real and imaginary components are dependent on the sign of the integral. This is illustrated in Figure 4.17. The response of this operation is a binary output referred to as *iris code*. The dimension (or length) of the iris code depends upon the size of the normalized iris image, which in turn depends upon the resolution along the r and θ axes. A dimension of 2048 is commonly used.

The normalized Hamming Distance (HD) between two iris codes is used as a measure of dissimilarity between two irides. This value is computed by masking every iris code with its respective mask to disregard noisy regions. The Hamming Distance between two iris codes is computed as

$$HD = \frac{\|(IrisCodeA \oplus IrisCodeB) \cap MaskA \cap MaskB\|}{\|MaskA \cap MaskB\|} \qquad (4.16)$$

The XOR operator ($\oplus$) detects the bits that disagree between the two iris codes, while the AND operator ($\cap$) masks the noisy regions. The denominator helps in normalizing the total number of bits that disagree in the interval $[0,1]$. A perfect match between two iris codes will result in a HD value of 0. See Figure 4.18.

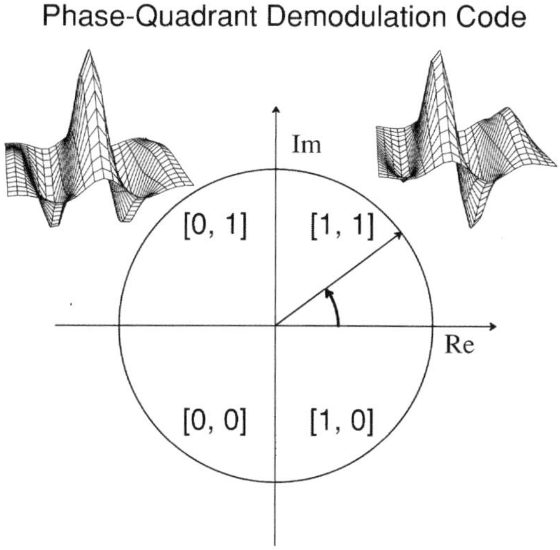

Phase-Quadrant Demodulation Code

Fig. 4.17 An illustration of the phase demodulation and quantization process used to encode the iris. The phasor response at each pixel in the normalized iris is quantized into two bits of information.

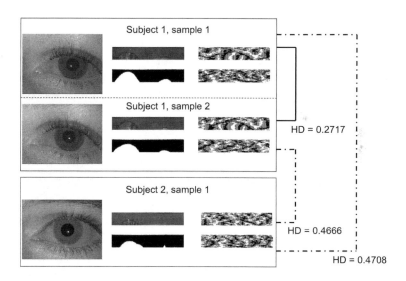

Fig. 4.18 The process of matching a pair of irides. Here, three images of the eye belonging to two different subjects are shown. Each image is subjected to a segmentation routine in order to extract the iris, which is converted to a rectangular entity via Daugman's rubber sheet model. The segmentation routine results in a binary mask, where a 1 indicates an iris pixel and a 0 indicates a non-iris pixel. The normalized iris is processed using Gabor wavelets and the resulting phasor response is quantized into an iris code. The Hamming Distance (HD) between two iris codes of the same iris is expected to be smaller than that corresponding to two different irides.

4.7 Iris Quality

Depending on the field of view of the iris sensor, an iris image usually includes the upper and lower eyelashes and eyelids, and some regions of the eyebrow as shown in Figure 4.19. However, only the rich textual information of the iris between the pupillary and limbus boundaries is used for recognition. Thus, for a given iris image (or a video frame), quality evaluation is typically based on factors that degrade or reduce the size of the iris region.

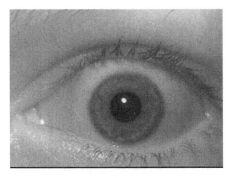

Fig. 4.19 A sample NIR iris image captured from a cooperative user under near ideal conditions.

Some of the factors that can significantly reduce the quality of an iris image include (a) occlusion, (b) defocus, or out-of-focus, (c) motion blur, (d) non-uniform illumination, (e) low resolution, or large imaging distance, (f) iris dilation, (g) off-angled imaging, and (h) the presence of accessories such as fake or printed contact lenses. Examples are shown in Figure 4.20.

4.7.1 Quality assessment techniques

While most quality evaluation schemes consider only a single or a pair of factors, newer techniques consider a wider range of factors for quality assessment. Some of these are described here.

- Examining the sharpness of a portion between the pupil and iris: Sharpness of an image is usually an indicator of the proper focusing of the object being imaged and thus is usually used in determining the quality of an iris image. Here, sharpness is essentially computed as the normalized magnitude of the intensity gradient near the pupillary boundary. Let (X_p, Y_p) and r_p denote the center and the radius of the pupil, respectively, and r_i denote the radius of the iris. A region of interest is selected such that all the pixels (x, y) lying within the region satisfy the following conditions:

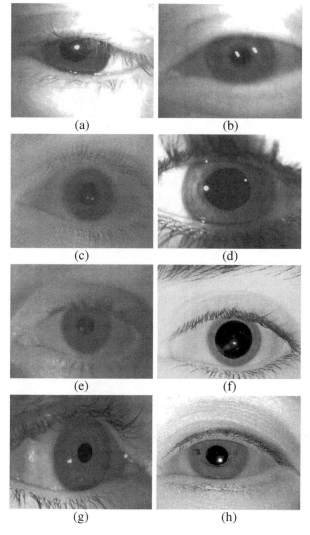

Fig. 4.20 Poor quality iris images caused by (a) occlusion, (b) defocus, (c) motion blur, (d) non-uniform illumination, (e) low resolution sensor, (f) iris dilation, (g) off-angled imaging, and (h) the presence of a printed contact lens.

$$(y_p - 0.8r_p) < y < (y_p + 0.8r_p) \qquad\qquad (4.17)$$

and

$$-\sqrt{r_p^2 - (y-y_p)^2} + 0.1r_i < x - x_p < -\sqrt{r_p^2 - (y-y_p)^2} + 0.2r_i$$
$$(4.18)$$

Figure 4.21 illustrates the region of interest that is specified by the above conditions.

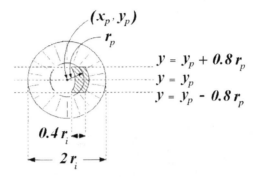

Fig. 4.21 Region of interest selected for estimating the sharpness of the iris.

From the selected region of interest, the median values of the pixels falling in the pupil region, M_p, and the iris region, M_i, are computed. Then, for all the pixels in the selected region whose intensity values lie between M_p and M_i, the absolute values of their horizontal gradients are gathered in a set. From this set, the average of the top 20 values are computed, and denoted by the variable S. The sharpness measure of a given iris image, $\frac{1}{w}$, is then computed by the following equation:

$$\frac{1}{w} = \frac{S}{H}, \tag{4.19}$$

where $H = (M_i - M_p)$, denotes the step size. If the sharpness measure is above a threshold value of 0.5, the image is considered to be well focused and, therefore, of good quality.

- Quantifying the energy of high spatial frequencies over the entire image: This method determines the sharpness over the whole image using 2D Fourier analysis in order to eliminate optically defocused images.

For a given image represented as a 2D function of the real plane $I(x,y)$, its 2D Fourier transform $F(\mu,v)$ is defined by:

$$F(\mu,v) = \frac{1}{(2\pi)^2} \int\int I(x,y) \exp(-i(\mu x + vy)) dx dy. \tag{4.20}$$

The defocused image, $D_\sigma(\mu,v)$, is related to the 2D Fourier transform of the corresponding in-focus image, $F(\mu,v)$, by the following model:

$$D_\sigma(\mu,v) = \exp\left(-\frac{\mu^2 + v^2}{\sigma^2}\right) F(\mu,v). \tag{4.21}$$

Defocusing primarily attenuates the highest frequencies in the image, while the lower frequency components are virtually unaffected. This is because the exponential term in the above equation approaches to unity as the frequencies (μ, v) become small. Thus, an effective method of identifying a defocused image would be to simply measure its total power in the 2D Fourier domain at higher spatial frequencies (as they are most attenuated by defocus). To make this quality measure independent of the image content, the ratio of power of the higher frequency bands may be compared to that of the lower frequency bands.

- Analyzing the Fourier spectra of local iris regions: This can be used to detect poor quality images caused by factors such as (a) out-of-focus blur, (b) motion blur, and (c) occlusion due to the eyelashes, and/or eyelids. The Fourier analysis of a given iris image yields a significant amount of information, which can be used to isolate poor quality images from a given set of images. For an out-of-focus image, the Fourier spectrum is supposed to be largely dominated by the low frequency components. On the other hand, an iris image with occlusions contains significant middle and high frequency components that are caused by the eyelashes. The Fourier spectrum of a motion blurred image lacks middle and high frequency components, and has frequency distribution similar to that of an out-of-focus image.

The descriptor used for estimating the quality of an iris image can then be defined as:

$$D = \left[(F_1 + F_2 + F_3); \frac{F_2}{F_1 + F_3} \right], \qquad (4.22)$$

where

$$F_i = \int\int_{\Omega \,=\, \{(u,v)|f_1^i \,<\, \sqrt{u^2+v^2} \,<=\, f_2^i\}} |F(u,v)| \, du dv \quad i = 1, 2, 3, \qquad (4.23)$$

and $F(u,v)$ is the 2D Fourier spectrum of the iris region, while F_1, F_2, and F_3 denote the power of the low, middle, and high frequency components, respectively. Frequencies f_1^i and f_2^i are the radial frequency pair, that form the extrema of the corresponding frequency components.

The quality descriptor D consists of two discriminating frequency features. The first feature is the total spectrum power of the iris region that can effectively discriminate severely occluded iris images from high quality images. The second feature is a ratio of the middle frequency power to the other frequency powers. For a clearly focused image, this ratio is high, when compared to out-of-focus or motion blurred images.

For a given iris image, I, two 64×64 regions are selected as shown in Figure 4.22, and the quality descriptor values are computed. The mean of the resulting two local quality descriptors is regarded as an appropriate quality measure of the iris image.

- Measuring the energy from 2D wavelets at local concentric bands of iris: This approach evaluates the quality of a given iris image using 2D wavelets on local concentric bands of a segmented iris. The local quality measure is then used as a

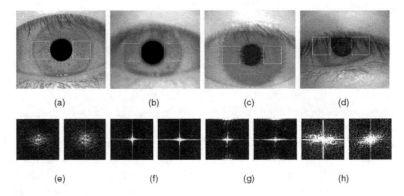

Fig. 4.22 (a) An iris image of good quality. Poor quality iris images, caused by (b) out-of-focus, (c) motion blur, and (d) occlusion. The images (e), (f), (g), and (h) show the Fourier spectra of the selected two local iris regions of size 64 × 64 (highlighted by the white boxes), corresponding to images (a), (b), (c), and (d), respectively. Image reproduced from [23]. ©IEEE.

weighting scheme in the matching process to yield improved results. The analysis is performed on local regions since the quality can vary from region to region. Thus, the method uses higher weights for inner regions of the iris that are more stable compared to the outer regions that are more prone to occlusions.

Given an image $I(x, y) \in R^2$, its Continuous Wavelet Transform (CWT), defined as the convolution with a series of wavelet functions, is given by the following equation:

$$w(s, x_0, y_0) = \frac{1}{\sqrt{s}} \int \int_{R^2} I(x, y) \phi \left(\frac{x - x_0}{s}, \frac{y - y_0}{s} \right) dx dy, \qquad (4.24)$$

where s is the dilation (scale) factor, and (a, b) denotes the translation (shift) factor. The wavelet ϕ is considered to be a Mexican hat wavelet, which is essentially a band pass filter for edge detection at scales s. The choice of the wavelet is due to its high sensitivity to features exhibiting sharp variations (e.g., pits, freckles, etc.) and non-linearity (e.g., collarette, furrows, etc.). First, in order to capture various features at multiple scales, the product responses are obtained, given by the following equation:

$$w^{mul}(s_1, s_2, s_3) = w(s_1) \times w(s_2) \times w(s_3). \qquad (4.25)$$

Here, s_1, s_2, s_3 are three considered scales. To perform quality evaluation of an iris image, the iris is segmented to obtain the boundaries of the pupil and iris. The segmented iris is then partitioned into multiple concentric bands of fixed width, which are centered at the pupil center.

To obtain the local quality measure, the energy E_t of the t-th band ($t = 1, 2, ...T$), where T denotes the total number of bands, is computed by the following equation:

$$E_t = \frac{1}{N_t} \sum_{i=1}^{i=N_t} | w_{t,i}^{mul} |^2, \tag{4.26}$$

where $w_{t,i}^{mul}$ represents the i-th product based wavelet coefficient in the t-th band, and N_t is the total number of wavelet coefficients in the t-th band. The energy, E_t, is considered as a good indicator of the distinctiveness of the iris features, and is therefore a reliable measure of the local quality. A high value of E_t suggests a good quality image.

The quality index of the entire iris image, Q, is defined as the weighted average of the band-wise local quality values, and is given by:

$$Q = \frac{1}{T} \sum_{t=1}^{T} (m_t \times \log(E_t)), \tag{4.27}$$

where T represents the total number of bands and m_t is the weight, given by $m_t = \exp\{-\| l_t - l_c \|^2 /(2q)\}$. The variable l_c denotes the center of the pupil, and l_t denotes the mean radius of the t-th band with respect to l_c.

To incorporate local quality measures into the matching scheme, Daugman's Hamming distance matching algorithm is modified as:

$$HD_w = \frac{1}{B} \frac{\sum_{i=1}^{B} \sqrt{E_{g(i)}^X \times E_{g(i)}^Y} \times (X_i \otimes Y_i)}{\sum_{i=1}^{B} \sqrt{E_{g(i)}^X \times E_{g(i)}^Y}}, \tag{4.28}$$

where X_i and Y_i represent the i-th bit of the iris code sequences X and Y, respectively, and N is the total number of bits in the sequence. $g(i)$ is the index of the band that contains the i-th bit of the IrisCode, and $E_{g(i)}^X$ and $E_{g(i)}^Y$ are the local quality measures of the $g(i)$-th band in X and Y, respectively. The symbol $\oplus$ represents the logical XOR operation.

Iris image quality assessment is an area of continuing research. While initial research has shown the benefits of incorporating iris quality, its assessment and use in a real-time environment is still an open challenge.

4.8 Performance Evaluation

According to the biometric literature, the structural texture in the iris is substantially diverse across the population. As stated before, even the irides of monozygotic twins exhibit structural differences. Large-scale testing has confirmed the potential of iris patterns to identify individuals in a large database of subjects. Experiments conducted by Daugman on a database of 632,500 iris images (316,250 persons spanning 152 nationalities) suggest the possibility of a decision policy that could yield zero error rates. However, this rate is predicated on the quality of the iris image, which must be strictly monitored to ensure reasonable textural clarity. Tests conducted in

2006 by the National Institute of Standards and Technology involving a broad range
of image quality suggest that the false nonmatch rate of the best performing iris
recognition algorithms can vary between 1.1 to 1.4 percent at a false match rate of
0.1 percent.

4.9 Summary

The tremendous progress in iris recognition systems has resulted in several challenges and new opportunities, which have been the focus of recent research efforts.
We conclude this chapter by listing some of these challenges.

- The iris is a moving object with a small surface area, residing within an eyeball
  that can move independently of the iris. The eyeball in turn is within the head,
  another moving object. The formidable challenge, therefore, is to reliably locate
  the eyeball and localize the iris's position in images obtained at a distance from
  unconstrained human subjects. Because acquisition modules typically image the
  iris in the NIR spectrum, appropriate invisible lighting is required to illuminate
  the iris while acquiring the image. These factors confound the system's ability
  to operate successfully when the subject is more than a few meters away from
  the camera. Recent efforts have successfully designed and developed iris-on-the-
  move and iris-at-a-distance recognition systems. Other efforts are investigating
  technologies such as wavefront-coded imaging to increase the camera's depth of
  field.
- Nonideal irides can result from motion blur, camera diffusion, transmission
  noise, out-of-focus imaging, occlusion from eyelids and eyelashes, head rotation,
  off-axis gaze or camera angle, specular reflection, poor contrast, and natural lu-
  minosity - factors that can lead to a higher false nonmatch rate. Robust image
  restoration schemes are needed to enhance the quality of such iris images before the system processes them. Recent research has attempted to deal with the
  problem of off-axis iris images by designing suitable calibration and geometric
  correction models.
- A common assumption is that the textural relief of an iris is unique because of
  its random morphogenesis, and large-scale empirical evaluations have confirmed
  this notion across a large segment of the population. However, no effective theoretical models exist for quantifying the iris's individuality. Although researchers
  have used match-score distributions and IrisCode statistics to infer the iris biometric's degrees of freedom, no one has yet directly used the iris's biological
  underpinnings to ascertain its individuality. This interesting problem has implications for using iris recognition in a court of law in accordance with Daubert's
  admissibility criteria and Federal Rules of Evidence.
- By combining the iris with other ocular features such as conjunctival vasculature, researchers might be able to develop robust ocular-based multibiometric
  systems that can operate in environments characterized by harsh lighting, moving subjects, and large stand-off distances. Explicitly combining ocular features

with local facial attributes such as skin texture and facial marks in the periocular region (the region around the eye) can enhance the performance of face-based biometric systems. Using the iris in a multimodal framework can enhance matching accuracy and reduce constraints on the depth of field by allowing the use of low-resolution iris images.

- The use of biometric systems in large-scale government and civilian applications has raised concerns about the iris template's security and the retention of its owner's privacy. Security and privacy are of particular concern in centralized databases, which can store millions of iris templates. Privacy-enhancing technology, along with cancelable biometrics (see Chapter 7, Security of Biometric Systems), is likely to raise the privacy and security levels of such personal information. However, more research is required to incorporate these schemes in an operational environment.

Despite its challenges, iris recognition is gaining popularity as a robust and reliable biometric technology. The iris's complex texture and its apparent stability hold tremendous promise for leveraging iris recognition in diverse application scenarios, such as border control, forensic investigations, and cryptosystems. The use of other ocular features and facial attributes along with the iris modality could enable biometric recognition at a distance with excellent matching accuracy. The future of iris-based recognition looks bright, particularly in military applications that demand the rapid identification of individuals in dynamic environments.

Bibliographical and Historical Remarks

The possibility of using the iris[6] as a cue for human recognition or categorization was suggested by various individuals, including French police officer Alphonse Bertillon in 1885 [2], American ophthalmologist Frank Burch in 1936 and British ophthalmologist James Doggart in 1949 [14]. In 1987, American Ophthalmologists Leonard Flom and Aran Safir were issued a patent for designing a conceptual framework for automated iris recognition [15]. However, their patent did not include a specific procedure for feature extraction and matching and was, therefore, a broad generalization of the process for automated iris recognition. A few years later, at the suggestion of Flom and Safir, renowned computer vision scientist John Daugman actually designed and evaluated a method for automated iris recognition [11, 6]. To this day, many of the algorithms originally designed by Daugman are still being used in commercial iris recognition systems.

Daugman employed the integro-differential operator for localizing the inner and outer contours of the iris. He introduced the rubber sheet model to transform the iris from an annular structure to a normalized fixed-size rectangular entity; this was an elegant way of accommodating variations in iris diameter and head tilt whilst ensuring ease of matching. He used 2-D Gabor filters [10] for examining the texture

---

[6] The word *iris* is derived from the Greek word $\iota\rho\iota\varsigma$ meaning "rainbow"

of the normalized iris image. The term "iris code", that refers to the binarized phasor response obtained when the normalized iris image is convolved with a Gabor filter, is also due to Daugman [11]. A rigorous treatment of iris codes can be found in [12, 22]. The work in [20] established that some bits in the iris code are more consistent than the others. The use of iris codes in designing biometric cryptosystems and indexing schemes has also been demonstrated [17, 18].

In 1994, Wildes et al. [36] suggested the use of the Generalized Hough Transform for iris segmentation. The proposed technique relied on the use of gradient-based edge detectors to process the input eye image prior to invoking the Hough-based voting scheme for detecting the pupillary boundary, the limbus boundary and the eyelid contours. Feature extraction was performed on the segmented iris image using a four-band Laplacian-of-Gaussian filter, and the normalized cross-correlation values between corresponding bands were used to compare two irides [37].

Apart from the integro-differential operator and the Hough Transform method, other approaches to iris segmentation include those based on Fourier Series [13], Geodesic Active Contours [33], Fuzzy Clustering [29], and Elastic Models [19]. The use of alternate feature encoding and matching schemes, other than the classical wavelet-based methods, have also been investigated. Examples include those based on Ordinal Features [34], Scale Invariant Feature Transforms [1] and Correlation Filters [35]. A survey of other approaches to iris recognition can be found in [3].

Methods for processing off-axis iris images, in which the eye gaze is directed away from the camera, have been discussed in [32]. While iris processing has been traditionally done in the near-infrared spectrum, recent work has explored the possibility of acquiring and processing iris images in the visible spectrum and the shortwave infrared spectrum [4, 27, 31, 24]. The benefits of multispectral iris analysis are likely to be realized in future iris recognition systems.

The issue of image quality is of paramount importance due to its impact on both iris segmentation and feature encoding. A detailed reading list is available in the NIST Biometrics Quality Homepage currently hosted at http://www. nist.gov/itl/iad/ig/bio_quality.cfm. Evaluation of iris recognition algorithms have been conducted as part of *Independent Testing of Iris Recognition Technology* (ITIRT [21]), *Iris Challenge Evaluation* (ICE [25, 26]), *Multibiometric Grand Challenge* (MBGC), *Iris Exchange Evaluation* (IREX [16]) and *Noisy Iris Challenge Evaluation* (NICE [28]).

References

1. C. Belcher and Y. Du. Region-based sift approach to iris recognition. *Optics and Lasers in Engineering*, 47(1):139–147, 2009.
2. A. Bertillon. La couleur de l'iris. *Revue Scientifique*, 1885.
3. K. Bowyer, K. Hollingsworth, and P Flynn. Image understanding for iris biometrics: a survey. *Computer Vision and Image Understanding*, 110(2):281–307, 2008.
4. C. Boyce, A. Ross, M. Monaco, L. Hornak, and X. Li. Multispectral iris analysis: A preliminary study. In *Proc. of IEEE Computer Society Workshop on Biometrics at the Computer Vision and Pattern Recognition (CVPR) Conference*, New York, USA, June 2006.

5. Y. Chen, S. Dass, and A. K. Jain. Localized iris quality using 2-d wavelets. In *Advances in Biometrics*, pages 373–381. Springer, 2005.
6. J. Daugman. Biometric personal identification system based on iris analysis. United States Patent 5291560, March 1994.
7. J. Daugman. How iris recognition works. *IEEE Transactions on Circuits and Systems for Video Technology*, 14(1):21–30, January 2004.
8. J. Daugman. Probing the uniqueness and randomness of iriscodes: Results from 200 billion iris pair comparisons. *Proceedings of IEEE*, 94(11):1927–1935, 2006.
9. J. Daugman and C. Downing. Epigenetic randomness, complexity, and singularity of human iris patterns. *Proceedings of Royal Society Biological Sciences*, B(268):1737–1740, 2001.
10. J. G. Daugman. Two-dimensional spectral analysis of cortical receptive field profiles. *Vision Research*, 20(10):847–856, 1980.
11. J. G. Daugman. High confidence visual recognition of persons by a test of statistical independence. *IEEE Transactions on Pattern Analysis and Machine Intelligence*, 15(11):1148–1160, November 1993.
12. J. G. Daugman. The importance of being random: Statistical principles of iris recognition. *Pattern Recognition*, 36(2):279–291, 2003.
13. J. G. Daugman. New methods in iris recognition. *IEEE Trans. on System, Man, and Cybernetics, Part B*, 37(5):1167–1175, 2007.
14. J. H. Doggart. *Ocular Signs in Slit-lamp Microscopy*. Kimpton, London, 1949.
15. L. Flom and A. Safir. Iris recognition system. United States Patent 4641349, February 1987.
16. P. Grother, E. Tabassi, G. W. Quinn, and W. Salamon. IREX I: Performance of iris recognition algorithms on standard images. Technical Report NISTIR 7629, National Institute of Standards and Technology, October 2009.
17. F. Hao, R. Anderson, and J. Daugman. Combining crypto with biometrics effectively. *IEEE Transactions on Computers*, 55:1081–1088, September 2006.
18. F. Hao, J. Daugman, and P. Zielinski. A fast search algorithm for a large fuzzy database. *IEEE Transactions on Information Forensics and Security*, 3(2):203–212, June 2008.
19. Z. He, T. Tan, Z. Sun, and X. Qiu. Towards accurate and fast iris segmentation for iris biometrics. *IEEE Transactions on Pattern Analysis and Machine Intelligence*, 31(9):1670–1684, September 2009.
20. K. P. Hollingsworth, K. W. Bowyer, and P. J. Flynn. The best bits in an iris code. *IEEE Transactions on Pattern Analysis and Machine Intelligence*, 31(6):964–973, June 2009.
21. International Biometric Group. Independent testing of iris recognition technology. Technical report, 2005.
22. A. W. K. Kong, D. Zhang, and M. .S. Kamel. An analysis of iriscode. *IEEE Transactions on Image Processing*, 19(2):522–532, February 2010.
23. L. Ma, T. Tan, Y. Wang, and D. Zhang. Personal identification based on iris texture analysis. *IEEE Transactions on Pattern Analysis and Machine Intelligence*, 25(12):1519–1533, December 2003.
24. H.T. Ngo, R.W. Ives, J.R. Matey, J. Dormo, M. Rhoads, and D. Choi. Design and implementation of a multispectral iris capture system. In *Forty-Third Asilomar Conference onSignals, Systems and Computers*, pages 380 –384, November 2009.
25. P. J. Phillips, K. W. Bowyer, P. J. Flynn, X. Liu, and W. T. Scruggs. The iris challenge evaluation 2005. In *IEEE Second International Conference on Biometrics: Theory, Applications and Systems*, Crystal City, USA, September/October 2008.
26. P. J. Phillips, W. T. Scruggs, A. J. OToole, P. J. Flynn, K. W. Bowyer, C. L. Schott, and M. Sharpe. FRVT 2006 and ICE 2006 large-scale results. Technical Report NISTIR 7408, National Institute of Standards and Technology, March 2007.
27. H. Proença. Iris recognition: On the segmentation of degraded images acquired in the visible wavelength. *IEEE Transactions on Pattern Analysis and Machine Intelligence*, 32(8):1502 – 1516, August 2010.
28. H. Proença and L. A. Alexandre. The NICE I: Noisy iris challenge evaluation - part I. In *IEEE International Conference on Biometrics: Theory, Applications, and Systems*, Washington DC, USA, September 2007.

29. H. Proença and L.A. Alexandre. Iris segmentation methodology for non-cooperative recogni-
    tion. *IEE Proceedings - Vision, Image, and Signal Processing*, 153(2):199–205, 2006.
30. A. Ross. Iris recognition: The path forward. *IEEE Computer*, pages 30–35, February 2010.
31. A. Ross, R. Pasula, and L. Hornak. Exploring multispectral iris recognition beyond 900nm. In
    Proc. of 3rd IEEE International Conference on Biometrics: Theory, Applications and Systems,
    Washington DC, USA, September 2009.
32. S. Schuckers, N. Schmid, A. Abhyankar, V. Dorairaj, C. Boyce, and L. Hornak. On tech-
    niques for angle compensation in nonideal iris recognition. *IEEE Trans. on System, Man, and
    Cybernetics, Part B*, 37(5):1176–1190, 2007.
33. S. Shah and A. Ross. Iris segmentation using geodesic active contours. *IEEE Transactions on
    Information Forensics and Security*, 4(4):824–836, 2009.
34. Zhenan Sun and Tieniu Tan. Ordinal measures for iris recognition. *IEEE Transactions on
    Pattern Analysis and Machine Intelligence*, 31(12):2211–2226, December 2009.
35. J. Thornton, M. Savvides, and B. V. K. Vijaya Kumar. Robust iris recognition using advanced
    correlation techniques. In *Second International Conference on Image Analysis and Recog-
    nition (ICIAR)*, volume 3656, pages 1098–1105, Toronto, Canada, September 2005. Springer
    Berlin / Heidelberg.
36. R. Wildes, J. Asmuth, G. Green, S. Hsu, R. Kolczynski, J. Matey, and S. Mcbride. A system
    for automated iris recognition. In *Proceedings of the Second IEEE Workshop on Applications
    of Computer Vision*, pages 121–128, 1994.
37. R. P. Wildes. Iris recognition: An emerging biometric technology. *Proceedings of the IEEE*,
    85(9):1348–1363, September 1997.
38. G. Zhang and M Salganicoff. Method of measuring the focus of close-up image of eyes.
    United States Patent 5953440, 1999.

Chapter 5
Additional Biometric Traits

> Every biometric system relies on one or more biometric modalities. The choice of modality is a key driver of how the system is architected, how it is presented to the user, and how match vs. nonmatch decisions are made. Understanding particular modalities and how best to use the modalities is critical to overall system effectiveness.

Whither Biometrics Committee, National Research Council, 2010

Earlier chapters in this book focused exclusively on three specific biometric modalities - fingerprint, face, and iris. These traits have been extensively studied in the literature and have been incorporated in several government, military, and civilian biometric systems around the world. However, apart from these traits, several other biometric attributes have also been studied in the context of applications ranging from border control systems to surveillance to forensic analysis. Examples of such attributes include hand geometry, ear, speech, signature, gait, DNA, and teeth. Further, soft biometric attributes (i.e., attributes that provide some information about the individual, but lack the distinctiveness and permanence to sufficiently differentiate any two individuals) such as scars, marks, and tattoos (SMT), periocular region, and human metrology have also been studied in the biometric literature. This chapter will introduce a few of these traits in order to convey the breadth of work being conducted in the field of biometrics.

5.1 Introduction

As stated in Chapter 1, a wide variety of biometric traits have been proposed and studied in the literature. In some cases, academic curiosity about the uniqueness and permanence of certain biological traits has spurred exploratory research (e.g., iris); in other cases, new application domains have resulted in the exploration of novel biometric traits (e.g., periocular biometrics). Furthermore, certain biometric traits are uniquely suited for some applications and scenarios. For example, voice may be more practical in tele-commerce applications; the ear may be useful in surveillance applications where only the side-profile of the human face is available; gait patterns may be relevant in identification-at-a-distance scenarios; hand geometry may be appropriate for use in systems requiring the verification (as opposed to identification) of a few enrolled identities thereby mitigating some of the concerns associated with using a strong biometric cue such as fingerprint; and the iris or fingerprint may be chosen in applications where the subject is cooperative and in close proximity to the sensor.

Apart from the aforementioned traits, ancillary information such as gender, ethnicity, age, height, and eye color can also be used to improve the matching accuracy of a biometric system. For example, if a female subject (probe) is matched incorrectly against a male subject (in the gallery), then the gender information can be used by the biometric system to reject the match. Ancillary attributes provide additional information about the individual, but lack the distinctiveness and permanence to sufficiently differentiate two individuals. However, they can be used to narrow the search space of potential matches in an identification system (e.g., if the input probe is deemed to be an "Asian Male", then an identification system can constrain its search only to "Asian Male" identities in the database) or when other biometrics traits are not readily available (e.g., using the periocular information when the iris is deemed to be of poor quality). Such traits are commonly referred to as *soft biometrics* in the literature. Unlike some other attributes such as fingerprint and iris, soft biometric traits are not necessarily "unique" to an individual. They can be shared across a significant fraction of the population (e.g., gender) and may lack permanence (e.g., scars, marks, and tattoos, abbreviated as SMT).

Given the diversity of biometric traits discussed in the literature, in the interest of being concise, we restrict our discussion to the following four biometric traits in this chapter: ear, gait, hand geometry, and soft biometrics.

5.2 Ear

The appearance, structure, and morphology of the human ear has been studied as a biometric cue for a number of years. While most face recognition systems extract the attributes of the human face from frontal images, the visibility of the ear in non-frontal poses of the face (e.g., side view) makes it a viable biometric in many scenarios. The human ear is observed to exhibit variations across individuals as assessed by the curves, surfaces, and geometric measurements pertaining to the visible portion of the ear, commonly referred to as the pinna. The structure of the pinna depicting various anatomical features can be seen in Figure 5.1.

As a biometric trait, the ear offers several advantages: (a) the structure of the ear has been observed to be stable despite aging, and ear growth is almost linear after the age of four; (b) the ear, unlike other facial features, is minimally impacted by changes in facial expression; and (c) image acquisition does not involve explicit contact with the sensor.

A typical ear recognition system consists of the following components: (a) an ear detection module (also known as segmentation) that localizes the position and spatial extent of the ear in an image; (b) a feature extraction module that extracts discriminative features from the ear; (c) a matching module that compares the fea-

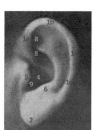

(1) Helix Rim
(2) Lobule
(3) Antihelix
(4) Concha
(5) Tragus
(6) Antitragus
(7) Crus of Helix
(8) Triangular Fossa
(9) Incisure Intertragica

Fig. 5.1 External anatomy of the ear. The visible flap is often referred to as the *pinna*. The intricate structure of the pinna coupled with its morphology is believed to be unique to an individual, although large-scale evaluation of automated ear recognition systems has not been conducted.

tures extracted from two ear images and generates a match score; and (d) a decision module that processes the match score(s) and establishes the identity of the subject.

5.2.1 Ear detection

A number of techniques have been proposed in order to locate the ear in a given image. These approaches can be categorized into the following groups.

1. Template Matching:
   In a template matching scheme, a template of a typical ear is constructed and is matched with each location in the query image. The location giving the highest score is considered as the region containing the ear. The template may consist of an edge image of the ear or a set of descriptors extracted from the ear such as the response to a set of filters or a histogram of shape curvatures in case a 3D image of the ear is being used for recognition. Detection based on response to a set of pre-selected filters, known as the Viola and Jones technique, is also commonly used for detecting faces in an image.
2. Model-based Detection:
   A model-based detection technique assumes certain characteristics of the shape of the ear and tries to find regions that manifest such characteristics. The shape of the helix, for example, is usually elliptical so a generalized Hough transform tuned for detecting ellipses can be used to locate the ear in an edge image. Features extracted using chain codes[1] can also be used to classify each curve obtained from an image to be a curve associated with the ear, such as a helix or an anti-helix.
3. Morphological-operator-based Detection:
   Since the structure of the ear is usually more intricate than the structure of the remaining region in a profile face image, morphological transformations such

---

[1] A chain code typically measures the local orientations along the length of the curve.

as the Top-hat transformation can be used. A Top-hat transformation essentially subtracts a morphologically smoothened version of an image from itself, thereby highlighting finer details.

4. Face-geometry-based Detection:
   Since in a profile image the nose can be easily detected as the point with high curvature, it is possible to constrain the search for the ear in an appropriate location relative to the nose.

Ear detection performance can be improved by utilizing a two-stage processing, where the skin region is segmented from the profile image in the first stage and the ear is detected in this reduced search space during the second stage.

5.2.2 Ear recognition

1. Subspace analysis-based techniques:
   Similar to recognizing face images, projecting the ear image onto a set of principal directions is an effective way to obtain a salient and compact representation of an ear. Subspace projection techniques such as PCA, ICA, and LDA have been successfully used in literature for matching ear images. Furthermore, manifold learning based techniques such as Locally Linear Embedding (LLE) and Kernel PCA have also been used to perform ear recognition.

2. Sparse representation-based techniques:
   Optimization techniques that minimize L-1 norm of the distance vector between the transformed query and all the transformed templates in a database have been shown to provide high recognition accuracy in object recognition studies. This technique has also been successfully used for ear recognition.

3. Point set matching-based techniques:
   Elastic bunch graph matching is an effective technique to recognize faces based on responses to a bank of Gabor filters at some fiducial points on the face. This technique has also been successfully used for matching ear images where a number of landmark points can be easily detected, thanks to its complex structure.
   Scale Invariant Feature Transform (SIFT) is a well known technique for matching two images where a set of salient points can be reliably and repeatably extracted from them. In order to match two images using SIFT features, corner points are detected from two images and matched based on image gradient-based features extracted from the neighborhood region of each point. See Figure 5.2 for an example of SIFT points being matched between two ear images.

4. Image filtering-based techniques:
   In certain techniques, the ear image is first enhanced to highlight the discriminative features and suppress the noise. Two common techniques that use this basic procedure are force field transformation and local binary patterns.

   a. Force field transformation:
      A force field transformation essentially obtains the intensity of the forces at

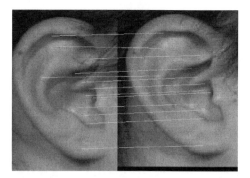

Fig. 5.2 Comparing two ear images by using the SIFT key points matching scheme. Here, the SIFT keypoints are first extracted from each image prior to comparing them.

each location in the image where each pixel is considered as a source of the force with intensity proportional to its value. Force field transformation has been shown to effectively remove the noise in the ear image leading to significant improvement in recognition accuracy. Further, a set of lines indicating the gradients of this force field can be extracted and used for matching. See Figure 5.3 for a depiction of force field extracted from an ear image with the force field lines marked.

b. Local binary patterns:

Local binary patterns essentially characterize each pixel based on variation of intensity of that pixel along a set of directions. The variation along each direction is encoded as a single bit indicating whether the intensity is increasing or decreasing, and the set of bits associated with each direction is used to obtain an integer value for each pixel. Such a transformation effectively reduces the effect of illumination variations and other sources of noise, thereby generating an enhanced image which can be used for robust matching.

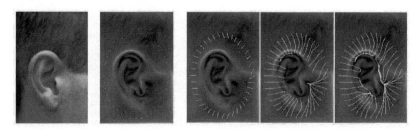

Fig. 5.3 Extraction of force field lines from an ear image using an iterative approach.

5. Geometric measurements-based techniques:

Features obtained by measuring certain geometric characteristics of the ear can also be used as a set of discriminative features. As an example, the centroid of an ear image obtained from its edge image can be used as a center to draw concentric circles with pre-specified radii. Various measurements, such as number of points on a circle intersecting the edge image or distance between two consecutive intersections, can be used as a feature vector. Characteristics of different curves present in the edge image such as the coordinates of endings and bifurcations can also be used as additional features.

6. Transformation-based techniques:

   Various image transformation techniques such as Fourier transform or wavelet transform can also be applied to extract discriminative features from an ear image. Fourier transform can also be applied in order to obtain a rotation and translation invariant representation of the ear - for example, by using a polar coordinate system and extracting only the magnitude of the Fourier transform.

7. 3D techniques:

   In some scenarios, acquiring a 3D rendition of the ear entity may be possible. 3D images offer depth information that can be used in conjunction with the 2D texture information to improve the recognition accuracy. In the case of 3D ear images, local histograms of shape curvature values can be used to match two ear images. The Iterative Closest Point (ICP) algorithm is commonly used to register and match 3D ears. In the ICP technique, each point in the input ear image is used to obtain a corresponding point in the template image and the input is then rotated and translated in order to minimize the distances between corresponding points. This procedure is iteratively applied until convergence, and the resultant set of distances is used to compute the matching score.

5.2.3 Challenges in ear recognition

Although several algorithms for ear detection and matching have been proposed in the literature, large-scale public evaluation of ear recognition algorithms has not been conducted. Further, there are no commercial biometric systems at this time that explicitly utilize features of the ear for human recognition. But the performances of ear recognition algorithms have been tested on some standard ear datasets. Experiments suggest that ear images obtained under controlled conditions can result in good recognition accuracy. However, the performance of ear recognition methods on non-ideal images obtained under varying illumination and occlusion conditions is yet to be established. Several challenges have to be overcome to make this possible.

1. Ear Occlusion:

   One of the main challenges faced by an ear recognition system is occlusion due to the subject's hair. One way to address such occlusion is by capturing the thermogram along with the visible light image. In a thermogram, the hair can be easily detected (and possibly isolated) as its temperature is usually lower than that of the skin.

2. Earprint Identification:

Earprints, or earmarks, are marks left by secretions as a result of pressing the ear against a flat surface. These marks mainly consist of impressions of the helix, anti-helix, tragus, and anti-tragus. Other features include the earlobe and the crus of helix, but they are less frequently observed. Earprints can be compared based on details such as the notches and angles in imprinted samples, the positions of moles, folds, and wrinkles, and the position of pressure points. Figure 5.4 provides a set of example earprints lifted from crime scenes.

Earprints are known to be available in approximately 15% of the crime cases and have also been considered in some court cases as a source of forensic evidence. However, due to significant variations among the multiple impressions of an ear, individualization based on earprint is frequently disputed. The main reasons confounding the individualization of earprint include (a) variable deformations caused by the force applied by the ear to the surface, (b) the duration of the ear's contact with the surface (c) ornamental modifications to the ear, such as piercing, and (d) changes in the shape and size of the ear due to aging.

Earprint identification is usually manually performed by identifying and matching a set of geometric features from the earprint such as the intersection points of ear curves with a regular grid or locations of certain other landmark points. Fully automated systems utilizing SIFT features have also been designed to match two earprints, but their performances has not been extensively evaluated in operational environments.

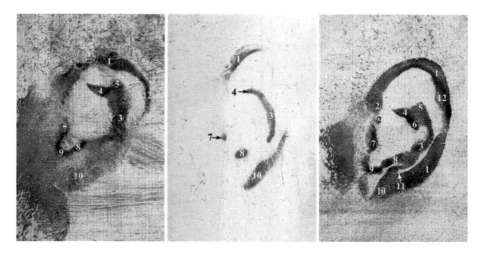

Fig. 5.4 Examples of earprints in which various anatomical features are indicated. This image is reproduced from [21]. The labels in this image are as follows: 1. helix; 2. crus of helix; 3-6. parts of anti-helix; 7. tragus; 8. antitragus; 9. incisure intertragic; 10. lobe.

5.3 Gait

The demand for human identification at a distance has gained considerable traction, particularly due to the need for covertly recognizing individuals in unconstrained environments with uncooperative subjects. In such environments, the person of interest may not be interacting with the biometric system in a concerted manner. Further, the individual might be moving in this environment characterized by variable illumination and a non-uniform background. Biometric modalities such as fingerprint and iris cannot be easily acquired at large stand-off distances.[2] On the contrary, the face and gait modalities can easily be acquired at a distance, although the smaller spatial resolution of the face at long distances can degrade accuracy of face recognition systems. As a result, gait-based human recognition has received some interest for biometric recognition at a distance. *Gait* is defined as the pattern of locomotion in animals. Human gait, therefore, is the manner in which people walk. While the formal definition of gait refers to human *motion*, practical algorithms for gait recognition include both dynamic and static features (such as body shape) of the moving human body. It can be viewed as a behavioral trait that is impacted by the musculo-skeletal structure of the human body.

Gait recognition is perceived as an attractive solution for distance-based identification for a number of reasons. First and most importantly, human gait has been observed to have some person-specific characteristics. Psychological studies by Cutting and Kozlowski showed that humans are capable of deducing gender and recognizing known individuals based on gait. Second, the gait biometric can be acquired passively and, therefore, explicit subject interaction is not required for data acquisition. Passive collection is beneficial in an environment where subjects are being observed covertly. Finally, discriminatory features of human gait can be extracted in low resolution images. This suggests that expensive camera systems may not be required for gait recognition.

Typically, an algorithm for gait recognition begins with a silhouette extraction process. This component aims to isolate (i.e., segment or localize) the contour of the human body from a video sequence. A simple method for accomplishing this is through background subtraction, on a frame-by-frame basis, although more sophisticated methods based on Gaussian Mixture Models and Hidden Markov Measure Field exist as well. Once the silhouette is determined, features can be extracted for further processing. Methods for feature extraction are typically *model-based* or *model-free*.

Model-based approaches incorporate structural information of the human body either based on *a priori* information or through models of the human body deduced from training data. A wide variety of biped models[3] are commonly used, although they vary in terms of complexity and information extracted. The benefit of a model-based approach is that a good model allows for robust and consistent feature extraction. Since features are obtained from structural information, distortion in silhouette

---

[2] The distance between the subject and the acquisition device is referred to as *stand-off distance*.

[3] Biped models are two-legged models.

shape is less likely to induce error. Model-free approaches, on the other hand, generally aim to extract features based on the movement of the silhouette through time. The primary advantage of a model-free approach is computational simplicity, as many algorithms of this class can be executed rapidly. However, a commonly cited concern of model-free algorithms is their inability to adapt to silhouette distortions arising from variations in camera viewpoint and clothing, or errors in segmentation. In the following section, two popular algorithms for feature extraction will be briefly discussed.

5.3.1 Feature extraction and matching

5.3.1.1 Model-based approach

An example of a model-based approach is a five-link biped model that is used to represent human locomotion. This model is designed for representing gait across the saggital plane (side profile) and is demonstrated in Figure 5.5.

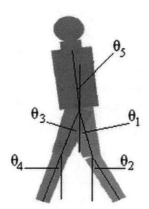

Fig. 5.5 A five-link biped model used for modeling the human body for gait recognition.

Including the coordinates of the centroid, (x,y), the model consists of 7 parameters. Each of the five angles are denoted as sagittal plane elevation angles (SEAs) and defined as the angle between the main axis of the body part and the y axis. Each component of the model is also defined by a height (ℓ), and length component of the top and bottom bases (t and b). Using $\alpha = t/l$ and $\beta = b/l$, each part p_i, $i = 1,\ldots,5$ is represented as $p_i = \{\alpha_i, \beta_i, \ell_i\}$. These part heights are further normalized with respect to the trunk (ℓ_5) to obtain scale invariance. The complete model is defined as follows:

$$H = \{K, R, M\} \tag{5.1}$$

$$K = \{\alpha_1, \beta_1, \alpha_2, \beta_2, \ldots, \alpha_5, \beta_5\} \qquad (5.2)$$

$$R = \{r_1, r_2, \ldots, r_5\}, \; r_i = \ell_i/\ell_5 \qquad (5.3)$$

$$M = \{x, y, \theta_1, \theta_2, \theta_3, \theta_4, \theta_5\} \qquad (5.4)$$

Using the above parameters, space domain features are computed for recognition. These include ankle elevation (s_1), knee elevation (s_2), ankle stride width (s_3), and knee stride width (s_4). The Discrete Fourier Transform is computed for each of these features and then used as the primary feature vector for recognition. An illustration of these features is provided in Figure 5.6.

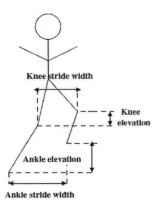

Fig. 5.6 The space domain features extracted from the five-link biped model.

5.3.1.2 Model-free approach

Perhaps the most popular model-free approach is the Gait Energy Image (GEI) algorithm. While it does not result in superior matching performance, this algorithm is often cited as a benchmark for comparison due to its ease of implementation. GEI aims to quantify the gait dynamics of an individual via a single image-based representation. Given N binary silhouette images, $\{S_t(x,y)\}$, at various time instances denoted by t, the gait energy image is defined as:

$$G(x,y) = \frac{1}{N} \sum_{t=1}^{N} S_t(x,y) \qquad (5.5)$$

In short, Equation (5.5) represents the averaged silhouette intensity over N frames. Prior to averaging, the images must be normalized such that the height of each silhouette is the same. In addition, the images must be aligned according to the horizontal centroid. Horizontal alignment allows for the moving shape dynamics to be visualized in the final image. An example is provided in Figure 5.7. Here, the rightmost image in each row represents the gait energy image.

Fig. 5.7 An example showing the normalized silhouette frames along with the gait energy image (GEI). The two rows correspond to two different subjects. In each row, 7 frames are used to derive the GEI which is the rightmost image.

For each gait energy image, gait dynamics is captured in terms of pixel intensity. The energy images are transformed to feature vectors and used for gait recognition.

5.3.1.3 Feature matching

The resulting feature vectors constructed using the methods outlined above often result in large dimensionality, which is difficult to classify, especially when the number of training samples is small. Typically, a combination of Principal Component Analysis (PCA) and Linear Discriminant Analysis (LDA) are used for dimensionality reduction and subspace optimization. The reduced feature vectors are then compared using the Euclidean distance metric.

5.3.2 Challenges in gait recognition

The matching performance of gait recognition algorithms is impacted by factors such as clothing, footwear, walking surface, walking speed, walking direction (with respect to the camera), etc. Further, the gait pattern of an individual can change over time, especially with variations in body mass The impact of these factors is difficult to mitigate and, therefore, evaluation of gait recognition algorithms has been predominantly conducted in controlled environments. This has prevented the incorporation of gait recognition in commercial biometric systems.

5.4 Hand Geometry

Hand geometry, as the name suggests, refers to the geometric structure of the hand. This structure includes width of the fingers at various locations, width of the palm, thickness of the palm, length of the fingers, contour of the palm, etc. Although these metrics do not vary significantly across the population, they can still be used to verify the identity of an individual. Hand geometry measurement is non-intrusive and the verification involves a simple processing of the resulting features. Unlike palmprint, this method does not involve extraction of detailed features of the hand (for example, wrinkles on the skin).

Hand geometry-based verification systems have been commercially available since the early 1970s. The earliest literature on the hand geometry biometric is in the form of patents or application-oriented description. Sidlauskas introduced a 3D hand profile identification apparatus that was successfully used for hand geometry recognition. Hand geometry systems have been deployed in several nuclear power plants across the United States. Also, hand geometry kiosks are present at Ben Gurion airport (Tel Aviv, Israel) for rapid verification of frequent travelers.

A typical hand geometry system consists of four main components: image acquisition, hand segmentation and alignment, feature extraction, and feature matching.

5.4.1 Image capture

Most hand geometry systems acquire an image of the back of the human hand. This image is often referred to as the dorsal aspect of the hand. Thus, most commercial systems require the subject to place their hand on a platen with the palm facing downward. A suitably positioned camera above the hand is then used to acquire an image of the dorsal aspect. Different types of imaging configurations have been discussed in the hand geometry literature as described below.

1. Contact-based vs Contactless: A typical system requires the user to place her hand on a flat surface prior to capturing. Such systems are contact-based and require explicit cooperation of the subject being identified. However, hygiene is an issue of concern to some users in such systems. Furthermore, the large size of the hand (compared to, say, fingers) limits the use of a hand geometry system on smaller devices (e.g., mobile phones). To address these issues, contactless recognition systems have been proposed. However, such systems are required to address the intra-class variability in the captured images due to the articulation of the hand in all three dimensions.
2. Dorsal vs Palmar: Traditionally, an image of the hand is acquired by placing the hand on a flat surface and imaging the back of the hand with a CCD camera. However, there has been interest in capturing the ridge patterns present on the palm and fingers along with the hand shape by imaging the palmar aspect of the hand (that includes the inner palm). See Figure 5.8 (b) for an example. One

drawback of such a system is that it is rather inconvenient for a user to place the hand on a platen with the palm facing upward.

3. Peg-based vs Pegless: In order to guide the positioning of the hand on the platen for imaging purposes (e.g., to prevent the fingers from touching each other), a few pegs are usually placed on the sensor platen. See Figure 5.8 (a). The user is expected to move his hand forward till one of the pegs touches the webbings between a pair of fingers. Although the use of pegs obviates the need for image alignment, it adds to the complexity of using the system and, thus, greater inconvenience to users. See Figure 5.9 for an example where the user has incorrectly placed his fingers around the pegs.

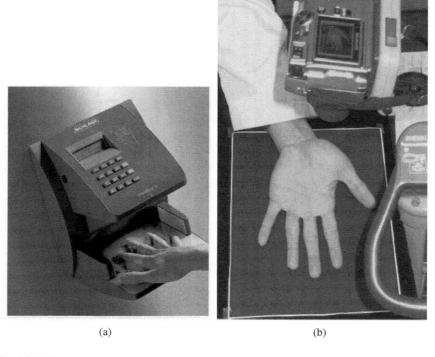

(a)   (b)

Fig. 5.8 Different imaging configurations for acquiring a sample of the human hand. a) A constrained hand capture scenario. b) An unconstrained capture scenario.

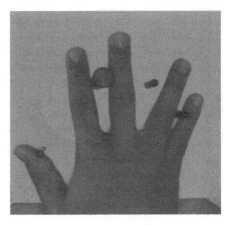

Fig. 5.9 Example showing incorrect placement of the hand in a peg-based system..

5.4.2 Hand segmentation

After the hand image is captured, the hand boundary must be extracted in order to determine the region of interest. To accomplish this, typically, the image is thresholded in order to deduce the region associated with the hand. This is followed by certain morphological operators (e.g., dilation and erosion followed by a connected region analysis) to extract the silhouette of the hand. If the image is very noisy (e.g., due to variable illumination and shadows), then more complex segmentation techniques such as the mean shift algorithm may be needed.

The segmented hand may still contain some artifacts such as the pegs on the platen, rings worn by the user, clothing that covers certain parts of the hand, and discontinuous contours due to non-uniform lighting. These artifacts are removed using specialized image processing techniques that are tailored to specific artifacts. Once a reliable hand shape is obtained, a hand contour is extracted and is used for further processing.

Due to variations in the way in which the users place their hand, the silhouettes extracted from multiple captures of the same hand may not be precisely aligned. It is important to account for these variations before extracting features, especially if the features are not invariant to such geometric transformations. A typical set of transformations include the rotation and translation of the hand, and the movement of individual fingers. It is easier to take into account the global affine transformations such as translation or rotation of the entire hand, while accommodating the movement of a single finger automatically is relatively difficult. To remedy this situation, the segmented hand may be further divided to obtain smaller segments corresponding to individual fingers. Features can then be extracted separately from each of these segments.

5.4.3 Feature Extraction

Typically, two kinds of features are extracted from a hand or a finger silhouette: one-dimensional geometric measurements and two-dimensional shape-based features. The geometric measurements include length and width of fingers, length and width of the palm, and thickness of the fingers. See Figure 5.10 for an example of geometric measurements obtained from a hand image.

It is also possible to use the set of points along the contours of the silhouette (or the segmented image itself) as features. The dimensionality of these features can be reduced in order to obtain a more discriminative and compact representation of the hand. Such shape-based features are expected to be more discriminative than the geometric features due to the fact that they model the structure of the entire hand, rather than portions of the hand, thereby exploiting more information.

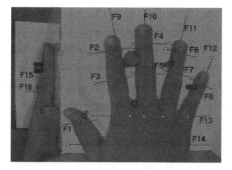

Fig. 5.10 This figure illustrates the axes along which the geometric measurements of the hand image are extracted. As can be seen here, the geometric measurements include the lengths of the fingers, widths of the fingers, width of the palm and the depth of the hand. While individual measurements may not be discriminative enough for biometric recognition, an agglomeration of these measurements results in a feature vector that can effectively be used for biometric verification.

5.4.4 Feature matching

The features extracted from a segmented hand image can often be denoted as a feature vector in the Euclidean space. Consequently, common distance measures such as Euclidean and Manhattan distances can be effectively used to compare two hand images. In case a sufficient amount of training data is available, more sophisticated distance measures such as the Mahalanobis distance[4] can also be used for robust matching. If the sampling of points on the silhouette are directly used for matching,

---

[4] Mahalanobis distance essentially weights the different dimensions of the feature vector based on variation of the features along that dimension. For example, if there is a large variation of fea-

then distance measures such as the Hausdorff distance[5] can be used to obtain the matching scores. It is also possible to use machine learning schemes to design classifiers such as multi-class Support Vector Machines (SVM) that can map the input feature set into one of many identities.

5.4.5 Challenges in hand geometry recognition

Hand geometry systems have been successfully deployed in several applications including nuclear power plants, border control systems, recreational centers and time-and-attendance systems. In these applications, the biometric system typically operates in the *verification* mode. Since the hand geometry of subsets of individuals can be similar, the *identification* accuracy due to this biometric modality can be low. Further, the shape of an individual's hand can change with time - a factor that is especially pronounced in young children. More recent research has explored the use of hand geometry in conjunction with fingerprints and low-resolution palmprints in a multibiometric configuration for improved accuracy.

5.5 Soft Biometrics

There are many situations where primary biometric traits (i.e., face, fingerprint and iris) are either corrupted or unavailable, and the soft biometric information is the only available clue to solving a crime. For example, while a surveillance video may not capture the complete face of a suspect, the face image in the video may reveal the suspect's gender and ethnicity, or the presence of a mark or tattoo may provide additional valuable clues. We will discuss some of the soft biometric traits (i.e., periocular, facial marks, and tattoos) below. The periocular biometric is gaining increasing attention since it offers a trade-off between using the entire face image and the iris portion only. Facial marks and tattoos are also gaining widespread attention since they offer complementary information that can be exploited along with primary biometric traits.

---

ture values across one dimension, differences along that dimension are assigned a smaller weight compared to those dimensions along which the variation is small.

[5] Hausdorff distance between two set of points A and B is given by $H(A,B) = \max\{h(A,B), h(B,A)\}$ where $h(A,B) = \max_{a \in A}\{\min_{b \in B} d(a,b)\}$ and d is a measure of distance between two points such as the Euclidean distance. Essentially, Hausdorff distance is the distance between a point in one set that is farthest away from all points in the other set, to its closest point in the other set.

5.5.1 Periocular

The periocular region represents the region around the eyes. It predominantly consists of the skin, eyebrow, and eye. The use of the periocular region as a biometric cue represents a good trade-off between using the entire face region or using only the iris for recognition. When the entire face is imaged from a distance, the iris information is typically of low resolution; this means the matching performance due to the iris modality will be poor. On the other hand, when the iris is imaged at small standoff (typically, 1 meter), the entire face may not be available, thereby forcing the recognition system to rely only on the iris. However, the periocular biometric can be used for a wide range of distances. Figure 5.11 shows sample periocular images collected from two different subjects. Periocular images can also be captured in the NIR spectrum to minimize illumination variation compared to visible spectrum. The key steps in preprocessing, feature extraction, and matching visible band periocular images are described below.

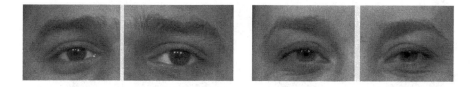

Fig. 5.11 Example of periocular images from two different subjects.

5.5.1.1 Preprocessing

Periocular images contain common components across images (i.e., iris, sclera, and eyelids) that can be represented in a common coordinate system. Once a common area of interest is localized, a global feature representation scheme can be used. A global representation scheme is holistic in that it characterizes the entire periocular region rather than only the local regions. The iris or eyelids are good candidates for the alignment process. While iris detection can be performed fairly well due to the approximately circular geometry of the iris and a good contrast between the iris and the sclera, accurately detecting the eyelids is more difficult. The inner and outer corners of the eye can also be considered as reference points, but there can be multiple candidates as shown in Figure 5.12. Therefore, we will discuss an iris-based image alignment method in this section. The iris can be used for translation and scale normalization of the image, but not for rotation normalization. However, small rotation variations can be overcome by using a rotation tolerant feature representation in the feature extraction stage.

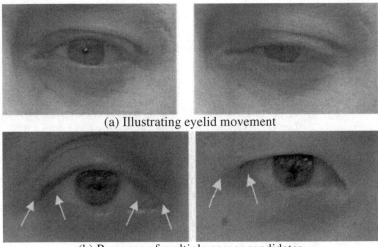

(a) Illustrating eyelid movement

(b) Presence of multiple corner candidates

Fig. 5.12 Example images showing difficulties in periocular image alignment.

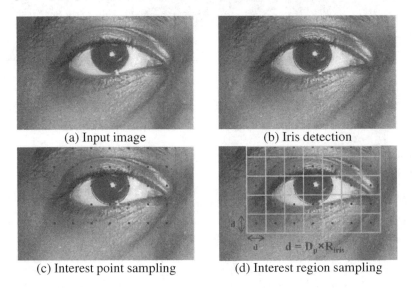

(a) Input image   (b) Iris detection

(c) Interest point sampling   (d) Interest region sampling

Fig. 5.13 Schematic of image alignment and feature extraction processes for periocular images.

5.5.1.2 Feature extraction

The features can be extracted using all the pixel values in the region of interest that is defined with respect to the iris. From the center, C_{iris}, and the radius, R_{iris}, of the iris, multiple ($=n_{pi}$) interest points $p_1, p_2, \ldots, p_{n_{pi}}$ are selected within a rectangular window defined around C_{iris} with a width of $6 \times R_{iris}$ and a height of $4 \times R_{iris}$ as shown

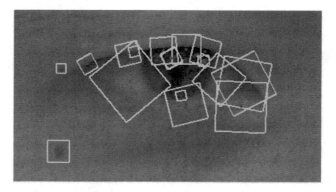

Fig. 5.14 Examples of local features and bounding boxes for descriptor construction using SIFT operator. Each bounding box is rotated with respect to the major orientation or gradient.

in Figure 5.13. The number of interest points is decided based on the sampling frequency ($1/D_p$), which is inversely proportional to the distance between interest points, $D_p \times R_{iris}$. For each interest point p_i, a rectangular region r_i is defined. The dimension of each rectangle (r_i) in the ROI is of size ($D_p \times R_{iris}$) by ($D_p \times R_{iris}$). When $D_p=1$, the size of the rectangle becomes $R_{iris} \times R_{iris}$ (see Figure 5.13 (d)).

For the construction of the descriptor in each region, r_i, some of the distribution-based descriptors such as gradient orientation (GO) histogram and local binary pattern (LBP) can be used. The responses of GO and LBP are quantized into 8 distinct values to build an eight bin histogram in each sub-region. The eight bin histogram is constructed from a partitioned sub-region and concatenated across the various sub-regions to construct a feature vector. A Gaussian blurring with a standard deviation, σ, can be applied prior to extracting features using the GO and LBP methods in order to smooth out variations across local pixel values.

Alternatively, a set of salient key points can be detected in scale space following the Scale Invariant Feature Transformation (SIFT) method. Features are extracted from the bounding boxes for each key point based on the gradient magnitude and orientation. The size of the bounding box is proportional to the scale (i.e., the standard deviation of the Gaussian kernel in scale space construction). Figure 5.14 shows the detected key points and the surrounding boxes on a periocular image. While the GO and LBP features are extracted only around the eye, the SIFT features are extracted from all salient regions. Therefore, the SIFT approach is expected to provide more distinctiveness across subjects.

5.5.1.3 Feature matching

For the GO and LBP features, the Euclidean distance is used to calculate the match scores. The distance ratio-based matching scheme is used for the SIFT as described below.

Given an image I_i, a set of SIFT key points $K_i = \{k_{i1}, k_{i2}, \cdots, k_{in}\}$ is detected. In matching a pair of images I_i and I_j, all the keypoints K_i from I_i and K_j from I_j are compared to determine how many keypoints are successfully matched. The Euclidean distances from k_{ia} to all the key points in K_j are calculated to obtain the closest distance d_1 and the second closest distance d_2. When the ratio d_1/d_2 is sufficiently small (less than a threshold th_{ratio}), k_{ia} is considered to have a matching key point in K_j. By using the ratio of d_1 and d_2, both the similarity and the uniqueness of point pairs are considered.

Recent studies on person identification using periocular biometric traits, both in visible and NIR spectra, show high identification accuracies (over 80%). However, such an accuracy is possible only when the images are of good quality and exhibit low intra-class variations. It has also been shown that the periocular biometric can assist person identification when the face is occluded. Figure 5.15 shows examples of automated face and periocular region detection for (a) a full face and (b) an occluded face. Figure 5.16 shows example matching results of periocular images.

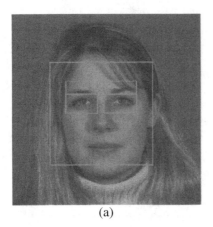 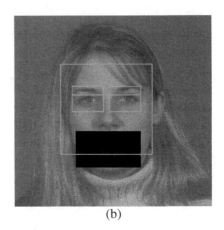

(a)   (b)

Fig. 5.15 Examples of automated face and periocular region detection on (a) a full face and (b) an occluded face. Face recognition performance degrades with the occluded face, but the periocular biometric still shows good identification performance. Images are from the FRGC 2.0 database.

5.5.2 Face marks

Advances in sensing technology have made it easy to capture high resolution face images. From these high resolution face images, it is possible to extract details of skin irregularities, also known as facial marks. This has opened new possibilities in face representation and matching schemes. These skin details are mostly ignored and considered as noise in a typical face recognition system. However, facial marks can be used to (a) supplement existing facial matchers to improve the identification

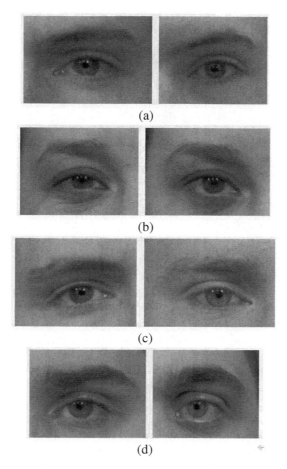

(a)

(b)

(c)

(d)

Fig. 5.16 Example matching results with four different pairs of periocular images from four different subjects. Image pairs in (a) and (b) are successfully matched whereas image pairs in (c) and (d) failed to match. The reasons for failure are due to intra-class variations caused by pose and illumination changes and movements of eyebrow and eyelids.

accuracy, (b) facilitate fast face image retrieval, (c) enable matching or retrieval with partial or off-frontal face images, and (d) provide more descriptive evidence about the similarity or dissimilarity between face images, which can be used as evidence in legal proceedings. Figure 5.17 shows some representative facial mark types.

5.5.2.1 Preprocessing

To represent the face marks in a common coordinate system, primary facial features such as eyes, eye brows, nose, mouth, and face boundary (Figure 5.19) are detected by using an Active Appearance Model (AAM) or Active Shape Model

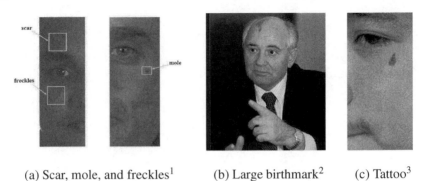

(a) Scar, mole, and freckles[1]   (b) Large birthmark[2]   (c) Tattoo[3]

[1] FERET database.
[2] http://www.wnd.com/index.php?fa=PAGE.view&pageId=63558.
[3] http://blog.case.edu/colin.mulholland/2007/09/20/a_way_of_expression.

Fig. 5.17 Examples of facial marks.

(ASM). These primary facial features will be disregarded in the subsequent facial mark detection process. Example landmarks detected in face images are shown in Figure 5.19.

Using the detected landmarks, the face image is mapped to the mean shape to simplify the mark detection, matching, and retrieval. Let S_i, $i = 1, ..., N$ represent the shape of each of the N face images in the database (gallery) based on the set of landmarks. Then, the mean shape is simply defined as $S_\mu = \sum_{i=1}^{N} S_i$. Each face image, S_i, is mapped to the mean shape, S_μ, by using the Barycentric coordinate based texture mapping process. First, both S_i and S_μ are subdivided into a set of triangles. Given a triangle T in S_i, its corresponding triangle T' is found in S_μ. Let r_1, r_2, and r_3 (r'_1, r'_2, and r'_3) be the three vertices of T (T'). Then, any point, p, inside T is expressed as $p = \alpha r_1 + \beta r_2 + \gamma r_3$ and the corresponding point p' in T' is similarly expressed as $p' = \alpha r'_1 + \beta r'_2 + \gamma r'_3$, where $\alpha + \beta + \gamma = 1$. This way, the pixel value at p is mapped to p'. Figure 5.18 shows the schematic of the Barycentric mapping process. By repeating this mapping process for all the points inside all triangles, the texture in S_i is mapped to S_μ.

After this mapping process, all face images are normalized in terms of scale and rotation and this allows for the representation of each facial mark in a face-centered common coordinate system. Figure 5.19 shows the schematic of mean face construction.

A blob detection operator is applied to the face image mapped into the mean shape. To suppress false positives in the blob detection process caused by the presence of primary facial features, a generic mask, denoted by M_g, is constructed from the mean shape S_μ. However, the generic mask does not cover user-specific facial features such as a beard or small wrinkles around the eyes or mouth that are likely to increase the false positives. Therefore, a user specific mask, M_s, is also built using the edge image. The edge image is obtained by using the conventional Sobel operator. The user specific mask M_s, constructed as a sum of M_g and edges that are

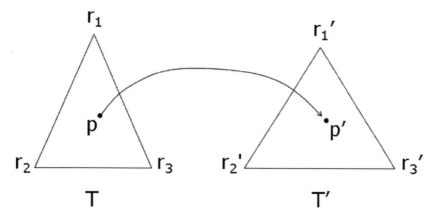

Fig. 5.18 Schematic of texture mapping process using the triangular Barycentric coordinate system.

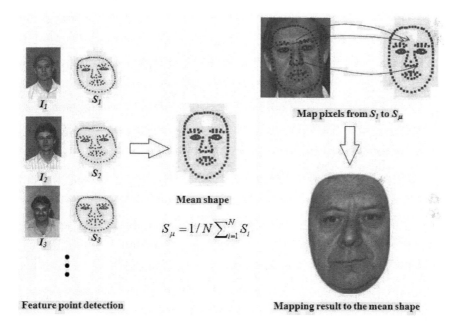

$$S_\mu = 1/N \sum_{i=1}^{N} S_i$$

Map pixels from S_1 to S_μ

Mean shape

Feature point detection   **Mapping result to the mean shape**

Fig. 5.19 Schematic showing the construction of the mean face image.

connected to M_g, helps in removing most of the false positives appearing around the beard or small wrinkles around the eyes or mouth.

5.5.2.2 Mark detection and classification

Lindeberg proposed that local maxima over multiple image scales of normalized Gaussian derivatives (i.e., $\sigma^2 \nabla^2 G$) reflects the characteristic size of a local structure . This allows for a blob detection with automatic scale selection, which is invariant with image scale. Motivated by this, we detect facial marks via scale space analysis. The scale space extrema detection starts by constructing a normalized multiscale representation of the face image by convolving the input images, $I(x,y)$, with a Laplacian of Gaussian (LoG) filter with a sequence of σ_k as

$$D(x,y,\sigma_k) = \sigma_k^2 \nabla^2 G(x,y,\sigma_k) * I(x,y), \quad k = 1,2,\cdots,n, \tag{5.6}$$

where $\sigma_k^2 \nabla^2 G$ is the scale-normalized Laplacian of Gaussian operator, and $\sigma_k = k\sigma_0, k = 1,2,\cdots,n$, with σ_0 being a constant value ($=\sqrt{2}$) for the initial scale.

Next, the local extrema over both spatial and scale space in every $3 \times 3 \times 3$ image block is detected . The detected candidate mark locations have the following characteristics:

- The detected location contains candidate facial marks.
- The detected scale (σ_k) indicates the size of the corresponding facial mark.
- The absolute value of $D(x,y,\sigma)$ reflects the strength of the response. This strength may be used as the confidence value to select stable marks.
- The sign of $D(x,y,\sigma)$ helps in assessing the pixel intensity of the facial mark. A positive (negative) sign represents a dark (bright) facial mark with brighter (darker) surrounding skin.

The overall mark detection process is shown in Figure 5.20.

For each detected local extrema, a local bounding box, whose size is proportional to the associated scale, is determined. Pixels in the bounding box are binarized with a threshold value selected as the mean of the surrounding pixels. A local extrema is darker or brighter than its surrounding region, so the average value of the surrounding area can serve to effectively segment the blob in the bounding box. Next, the blobs are classified in a hierarchical fashion: 'linear' versus 'all' followed by 'circular' versus 'irregular'. For determining linearity, two eigenvalues λ_1 and λ_2 are obtained through the eigen decomposition of the spatial coordinates of the blob pixels. When λ_1 is significantly larger than λ_2, the mark is classified as being a linear blob. For circularity detection, the following observation is used: a circle, with radius M_2 will enclose most of the blob pixels if they are circularly distributed. Therefore, a decision of 'circular' or 'irregular' can be made based on the ratio of the number of pixels within and outside of this circle. The pixel intensity of the blob can be deduced based on the sign of $D(x,y,\sigma)$, as stated earlier. The schematic for blob classification is shown in Figure 5.21.

Figure 5.22 illustrates five examples of facial detection results using the proposed mark detection and classification method. It can be observed that the proposed method is robust to noise and provides good estimates of the size and class of the marks.

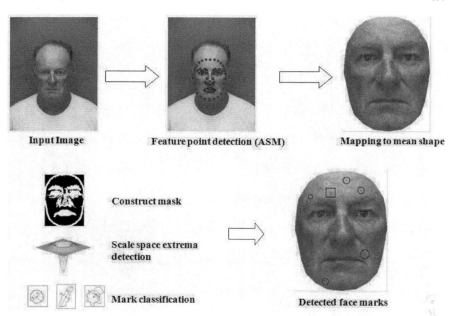

Fig. 5.20 Schematic of the mark detection process.

Fig. 5.21 Schematic of the mark classification scheme. Left: The eigenvalues λ_1 and λ_2 are computed based on the the spatial coordinates of the blob pixels. In this example, the largest eigenvalue, λ_1, is significantly larger than the smallest eigenvalue, λ_2, thereby suggesting linearity. Middle: The circular nature of the mark can be deduced after fitting a circle to the blob pixels. Here, a circle of radius M_2 is used to enclose the pixels inside the blob. Since the ratio of the number of blob pixels within the circle to the number of blob pixels outside the circle is large, this mark may be labeled as being 'circular'. Right: The sign of the difference in pixel intensities between the interior (e_{in}) and exterior (e_{out}) of the blob can help assess whether the mark is bright or dark.

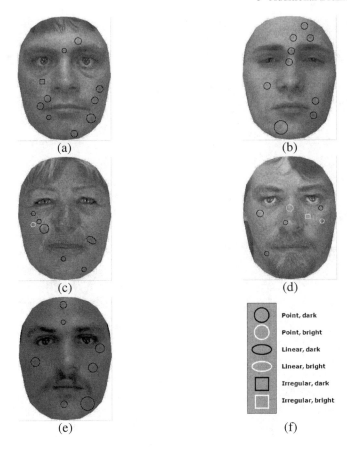

Fig. 5.22 Example mark detection and classification results. (a), (b), (c), (d), (e) are example images with detected marks. (f) Symbols used to denote six different mark classes.

5.5.2.3 Mark matching

The detected facial marks are encoded into a 48-bin histogram representing the morphology, color, and location of facial marks. To encode the location information of facial marks, the face image in the mean shape space is subdivided into eight different regions as shown in Figure 5.23. Each mark is encoded by a six digit binary number representing its morphology and color. When there is more than one mark in the same region, a bit by bit summation is performed. The six bin values are concatenated for the eight different regions in the order as shown in Figure 5.23 to generate the 48-bin histogram. If a mark is observed on the borderline of the face segments, it is included into both the regions. Given the indices obtained from face images, the histogram intersection method is used to calculate the matching scores. Let $H^1(i)$ and $H^2(j)$ be the two histograms representing the mark indices, then the histogram intersection is calculated as $\sum_{k=1}^{48} \left(H^1(k) \& H^2(k) \right)$, where $\&$ represents the logical *and* operation. The score range of the mark index based matching is [0,48].

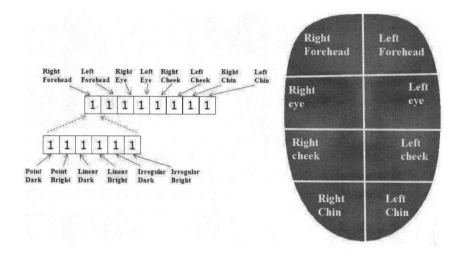

Fig. 5.23 Schematic of the mark-based indexing scheme.

Figure 5.24 shows example mark detection and matching results with an identical twin database collected by the University of Notre Dame. In all the four pairs of identical twins shown in this figure, facial marks help in differentiating identical twins when combined with a leading commercial face recognition engine.

5.5.3 Tattoo

The use of tattoos imprinted on human body in suspect identification started with the Bertillon system. Since then, images of tattoos on the human body have been routinely collected and used by law enforcement agencies to assist in suspect and victim identification. When the primary biometric traits are unavailable or corrupted, tattoos can be used to identify victims or suspects. Figure 5.25 shows examples of tattoo images used in victim and suspect identifications.

Tattoos provide more discriminative information than the traditional demographic indicators such as age, height, race, and gender for person identification. Many individuals acquire tattoos in order to display their personality, or to indicate their their membership in a group. Therefore, recognition of tattoos can provide a better understanding of an individuals' background and membership in various organizations, especially criminal gangs. Figure 5.26 shows example tattoo images showing membership in Mexikanemi Mafia gang.

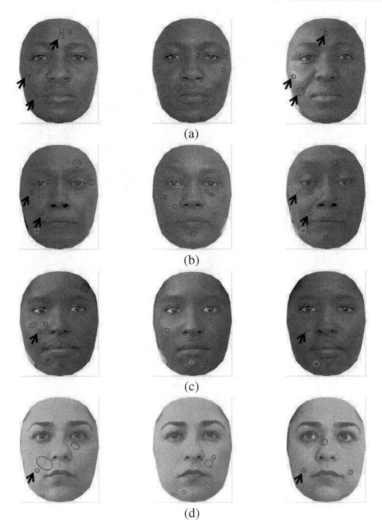

(a)

(b)

(c)

(d)

Fig. 5.24 Example matching results with four different identical twins. Images in the first and third columns belong to the same subject and images in the second column are the twins. The first, second, and third columns correspond to the probe, incorrect match using FaceVACS only, and correctly matched true mates using FaceVACS and mark index, respectively. Black arrows in each row show the facial marks correctly detected and classified that contribute to individualize the identical twins.

The current practice of matching tattoos is based on a set of predefined keywords. Assigning keywords to individual tattoo images is both tedious and subjective. A content-based image retrieval system for tattoo image retrieval can overcome many of the limitations of the keyword-based tattoo retrieval. We will briefly describe a system that extracts local image features based on the Scale Invariant Feature

Transform (SIFT). Contextual or side information, i.e., location of tattoo on the body and keyword (class) assigned to the tattoo, is utilized to improve both the retrieval time and retrieval accuracy. Geometrical constraints are also introduced in SIFT keypoint matching to reduce false retrievals.

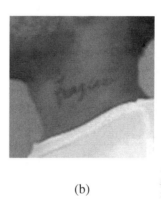

(a)	(b)

Fig. 5.25 Example tattoo images used in identifying (a) an Asian Tsunami (2004) victim in Indonesia and (b) a suspect.

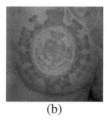

(a)	(b)	(c)	(d)

Fig. 5.26 Example gang tattoo images indicating the membership in the Mexikanemi Mafia gang in Texas.

5.5.3.1 Tattoo classes and body location

The ANSI/NIST-ITL1-2011 standard defines eight major classes (i.e. human, animal, plant, flag, object, abstract, symbol, and other) and a total of 70 subclasses (e.g. male face, cat, narcotics, American flag, fire, figure, national symbols, and wording) for categorizing tattoos. A search of a tattoo image database involves matching the class label of a query tattoo with the labels of the tattoos in the database. This tattoo matching procedure based on manually assigned ANSI/NIST class labels has the following limitations: (a) class label does not capture the semantic information contained in tattoo images; (b) labeling millions of tattoo images maintained by law enforcement agencies is both subjective and time consuming; (c) tattoos often contain multiple objects and cannot be adequately classified into a single ANSI/NIST classes; (d) tattoo images have large intra-class variability; and (e) ANSI/NIST classes are not complete for describing new tattoo designs.

Tattoo location on the body is a useful piece of information because it can be tagged precisely and objectively. Hence, searching for similar images at the same body location can significantly reduce the matching time without any loss of matching accuracy. The National Crime Information Center (NCIC) has defined 31 major categories (e.g., arm, calf, and finger), and 71 sub categories (e.g., left upper arm, right calf, and left hand finger) for denoting body location of tattoos.

5.5.3.2 Feature extraction

Scale Invariant Feature Transform (SIFT) is a well known and robust local feature based approach used for object recognition. It has been shown that SIFT features provide better performance than low-level image attributes, (e.g., color, texture, and shape) for tattoo image matching and retrieval. SIFT extracts repeatable characteristic feature points from an image and generates descriptors representing the texture around the feature points. These feature points are invariant to image scale and rotation, and are shown to provide robust matching across a range of affine distortion, change in 3D viewpoints, additive noise, and change in illumination.

5.5.3.3 Feature Matching

In addition to the conventional SIFT matching process as described in section 5.5.1.3, a set of local geometric constraints can be applied to reduce the number of false matching points. Let M_{ij} represent the set of matching keypoints between two images I_i and I_j. Then, M_{ij} can be expressed in terms of two different subsets $M_{ij} = M_{ij,T} \cup M_{ij,F}$, where $M_{ij,T}$ represents the set of true matching points and $M_{ij,F}$ represents the set of false matching points. It is expected that removing the false matching points will increase the retrieval accuracy. The number of false matchings in the presence of viewpoint variations or blurring in the image is likely to be large. When a key point belongs to $M_{ij,F}$, it is likely to match to many other key points. On the other hand, a keypoint in $M_{ij,T}$ is likely to match to either one or a very small number of other key points. Given a query image I, it is matched with all the images in the gallery database D and the number of matching points is obtained for each gallery image. Let L_m, $m = 1, 2, 3, \ldots$, represent the set of key points in the query image that are matched into the same key point in D. Let the size of the area covered by L_m be A_m. Then, L_m is regarded as belonging to $M_{ij,F}$ if A_m is larger than a threshold t ($t = 0.2$). All the matching keypoints not in $M_{ij,F}$ are regarded as true matching points. Finally, the number of key points that belong to $M_{ij,T}$ is used to retrieve the top-N candidate images from the tattoo image database. Figure 5.27 shows example matching results on a duplicate and non-duplicate tattoo image pairs. The number of matching keypoints for a duplicate pair is observed to be much larger than that for a non-duplicate pair.

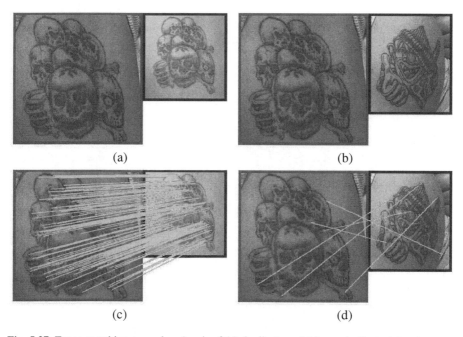

(a)   (b)

(c)   (d)

Fig. 5.27 Tattoo matching examples. A pair of (a) duplicate and (b) non-duplicate tattoo images and their SIFT matching results. There are 129 and 12 matching keypoints in the (c) duplicate and (d) non-duplicate pairs, respectively. Number of octaves and scales are selected as 3 and 4, respectively. The feature vector associated with each keypoint has 128 dimensions.

Figure 5.28 shows example tattoo images retrieval results based on the SIFT matcher, body location, and ANSI/NIST class label for three different queries. For query 1, three different duplicate images from the database were successfully retrieved at rank 1, 2 and 6. The corresponding match scores for these three retrieved images are: 163, 157 and 26. The low score for the third retrieved image at rank 6 is possibly due to low contrast (fading) of the tattoo. Two duplicate tattoos were retrieved, at ranks 1 and 2, for query 2 and one duplicate image was retrieved for query 3 at rank 6. Note that due to the small size of the tattoo in query 3, the number of SIFT keypoints extracted is small and hence all the match scores for the retrieved images are low as well.

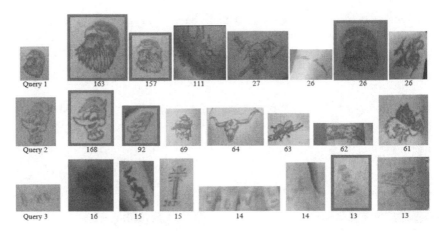

Fig. 5.28 Retrieval examples. Each row shows a query and its top-7 retrieved images along with the associated match scores.

5.6 Summary

A wide variety of biometric traits have been studied in the literature. Given the growing application domain for biometrics, it is likely that the use of soft biometric[6] traits such as ear, gait, hand geometry, and soft biometrics will become prevalent as well as necessary in some contexts. This would allow for the design of effective biometric systems that utilize the most appropriate set of biometric traits based on factors such as the application scenario, nature of the target population, availability of biometric traits, computational resources available, etc. Thus, investigating new biometric modalities for potential use especially in unconstrained and uncooperative user scenarios has its benefits.

At the same time, one needs to establish the distinctiveness of a biometric trait, its permanence and susceptibility to spoofing. But this can be a rather tedious and long-winding exercise. For example, although fingerprint matching has been used for over 100 years in forensics, the uniqueness or individuality of the fingerprint is still an ongoing area of research. Similarly, modeling of the aging process of the face and its effect on face matching accuracy is an active area of research. In the case of iris, there is a lack of longitudinal data to even begin to investigate the aging phenomena. Thus, as new biometric traits are studied, the onus is on researchers to analyze the advantages and disadvantages of each trait and determine the value added.

---

[6] Scars, marks, and tattoos (SMT) are an integral part of the FBI's Next Generation Identification (NGI) system.

References

1. ANSI/NIST-ITL 1-2011, Data Format for the Interchange of Fingerprint, Facial, & Scar, Mark & Tattoo (SMT).

2. A. Bertillon (R.W. McClaughry Translation). *Signaletic Instructions including the theory and practice of Anthropometrical Identification.* The Werner Company, 1896.

3. G. Amayeh, G. Bebis, A. Erol, and M. Nicolescu. Peg-free hand shape verification using high order zernike moments. In *Proceedings of the IEEE Workshop on Biometrics at CVPR*, New York, 2006.

4. B. Bhanu and H. Chen. *Human Ear Recognition by Computer.* Springer, 1st edition edition, 2008.

5. M. Burge and W. Burger. Ear biometrics in computer vision. In *Proc. of the 15th International Conference on Pattern Recognition ICPR*, pages 826–830, Barcelona, Spain, 2000.

6. J. Bustard and M. Nixon. Robust 2D ear registration and recognition based on SIFT point matching. In *Proc. of the Biometrics: Theory, Applications, and Systems BTAS*, Washington, DC, USA, 2008.

7. K. Chang, K. Bowyer, S. Sarkar, and B. Victor. Comparison and combination of ear and face images in appearance-based biometrics. *IEEE Transactions on Pattern Analysis and Machine Intelligence*, 25:1160–1165, 2003.

8. J. Cutting and L. Kozlowski. Recognizing friends by their walk. *Bulletin of the Psychonomic Society*, 9(5):353–356, 1977.

9. N. Duta. A survey of biometric technology based on hand shape. *Pattern Recognition*, 42:2797–2806, 2009.

10. H. Dutagaci, B. Sankur, and E. Yoruk. A comparative analysis of global hand appearance-based person recognition. *Journal of Electronic Imaging*, 17(1), 2008.

11. R. H. Ernst. Hand ID system. United States Patent Number US 3576537, 1971.

12. J. Han and B. Bhanu. Individual recognition using gait energy image. *IEEE Transactions on Patter*, 28(2):316–322, 2006.

13. D. Hurley, M. Nixon, and J. Carter. Force field feature extraction for ear biometrics. *Computer Vision and Image Understanding*, 98(3):491–512, 2005.

14. I. H. Jacoby, A. J. Giordano, and W. H. Fioretti. Personnel identification apparatus. United States Patent Number US 3648240, 1972.

15. A. K. Jain, A. Ross, and S. Pankanti. A prototype hand geometry-based verification system. In *2nd International Conference on Audio- and Video-based Biometric Person Authentication (AVBPA)*, pages 166–171, Washington D.C., March 1999.

16. L. Kozlowski and J. Cutting. Recognizing the sex of a walker from a dynamic point light display. *Perception and Psycophysics*, 21:575–580, 1977.

17. A. Kumar, D. C. M. Wong, H. C. Shen, and A. K. Jain. Personal authentication using hand images. *Pattern Recognition Letters*, 27:1478–1486, 2007.

18. J-E. Lee, A. K. Jain, and R. Jin. Scars, Marks and Tattoos (SMT): Soft Biometric for Suspect and Victim Identification. In *Proceedings of Biometrics Symposium at the Biometric Consortium Conference*, Florida, USA, September 2008.

19. T. Lindeberg. Feature detection with automatic scale selection. *International Journal of Computer Vision*, 30(2):79–116, 1998.

20. D. G. Lowe. Distinctive image features from scale invariant keypoints. *International Journal of Computer Vision*, 60(2):91–110, 2004.

21. L. Meijerman, A. Thean, C. van der Lugt, R. van Munster, G. van Antwerpen, and G. Maat. Individualization of earprints: Variation in prints of monozygotic twins. *Forensic Science, Medicine, and Pathology*, 2(1):39–49, 2006.

22. R. P. Miller. Finger dimension comparison identification system. United States Patent Number US 3576538, 1971.

23. M. Nixon, T. Tan, and R. Chellappa. *Human Identification Based on Gait.* Springer, 2006.

24. U. Park and A. K. Jain. Face matching and retrieval using soft biometrics. *IEEE Transactions on Information Forensics and Security*, 5(3):406–415, 2010.

25. R. K. Rowe, U. Uludag, M. Demirkus, S. Parthasaradhi, and A. K. Jain. A Multispectral Whole-hand Biometric Authentication System. In *Proceedings of Biometric Symposium, Biometric Consortium Conference*, Baltimore, USA, September 2007.
26. D. P. Sidlauskas. 3d hand profile identification apparatus. United States Patent Number US 4736203, 1988.
27. R. Zhang, C. Vogler, and D. Metaxas. Human gait recognition. *Proceedings of the IEEE International Workshop on Computer Vision and Pattern Recognition*, 2004.

Chapter 6
MULTIBIOMETRICS

"It is time to stop arguing over which type of pattern classification technique is best because that depends on our context and goal. Instead we should work at a higher level of organization and discover how to build managerial systems to exploit the different virtues and evade the different limitations of each of these ways of comparing things."

Minsky, 1991.

Person recognition systems that consolidate evidence from multiple sources of biometric information in order to determine the identity of an individual are known as multibiometric systems. For example, face and iris traits, or fingerprints from all ten fingers of an individual, may be used together to accurately and robustly resolve the identity of the person. Multibiometric systems can overcome many of the limitations of unibiometric systems because the different biometric sources usually compensate for the inherent limitations of one another. Hence, multibiometric systems are generally expected to be more reliable and accurate than unibiometric systems, as well as provide a wider population coverage (reduce the failure to enroll rate). The process of consolidating the information or evidence presented by multiple biometric sources is known as information fusion, which is the main focus of this chapter. More specifically, this chapter introduces the different sources and types of biometric information that can be fused and the various fusion methodologies.

6.1 Introduction

Person recognition systems based on individual biometric traits like fingerprint, face, and iris have been the focus of this book thus far. Most of these biometric systems can be labeled as unibiometric systems because they rely on a single biometric source for recognition. Any piece of evidence that can be independently used to recognize a person is called a *source* of biometric information. Unibiometric systems have some limitations. What if the biometric source becomes unreliable due to sensor or software malfunction, poor quality of specific biometric trait of the user, or deliberate manipulation? Furthermore, high-security applications and large-scale civilian identification systems place stringent accuracy requirements that cannot be met by existing unibiometric systems. Examples of such applications include the

US-VISIT program and the Unique Identification (UID) system in India, where identities of a very large number of individuals (hundreds of millions) need to be resolved. To address the requirements of such applications, there is a need to move beyond the traditional paradigm of biometric recognition based on a single source of biometric information and consider systems that consolidate evidence from multiple biometric sources for recognition (see Figure 6.1).

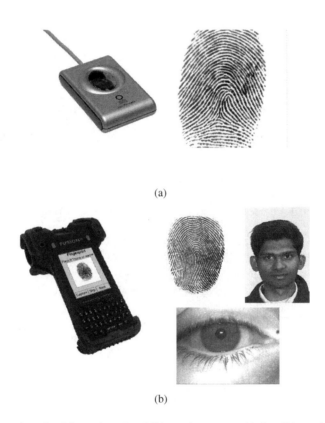

(a)

(b)

Fig. 6.1 Illustration of unibiometric and multibiometric systems. (a) A unibiometric system recognizes the user based on a single biometric source (e.g., a single fingerprint impression captured using a fingerprint sensor), (b) a multibiometric system identifies the user based on multiple biometric sources; the *Fusion* multibiometric system developed by Cogent Systems, which is capable of capturing fingerprint, face, and iris images of a person is shown in (b).

Humans recognize one another based on the evidence presented by multiple biometric characteristics (e.g., face, gait, and voice) in addition to contextual details (e.g., prior knowledge about the presence of a person at a particular time and location). The recognition process itself may be viewed as the reconciliation of evidence pertaining to these multiple information sources. Each source on its own cannot always be reliably used to perform recognition. However, the consolidation of information presented by these multiple cues can result in a more accurate determination or verification of identity. Similarly, biometric systems can also be designed to recognize a person based on information acquired from multiple biometric sources. Such systems, known as *multibiometric systems*, are expected to be more accurate compared to unibiometric systems that rely on a single piece of biometric evidence. Multibiometric systems are not new. In fact, the first biometric system developed by Bertillon (see Chapter 1), can be considered a multibiometric system because it combines evidence from different measurements of the human body. Similarly, Automated Fingerprint Identification Systems (AFIS) used by law enforcement agencies around the world routinely capture all ten fingers and then combine the decisions made based on individual fingers to obtain a more reliable identity decision on a subject.

Accuracy improvement, which is the primary motivation for using multibiometric systems, happens due to two reasons. Firstly, the fusion of multiple biometric sources effectively increases the dimensionality of the feature space and reduces the overlap between the feature distributions of different individuals. In other words, a combination of multiple biometric sources is *more unique* to an individual than a single biometric sample. Secondly, noise, imprecision, or inherent drift (caused by factors like aging) in a subset of the biometric sources can be compensated by the discriminatory information provided by the remaining sources. Thus, availability of multiple biometric sources provides redundancy and fault-tolerance in the sense that the recognition system continues to operate even when certain biometric acquisition modules fail. Apart from enhancing the recognition accuracy, multibiometric systems may also offer the following advantages over unibiometric systems.

1. Alleviate the non-universality problem and reduce the failure to enroll errors. For example, if a person cannot be enrolled in a fingerprint system due to worn-out ridge details or missing fingers (see Figure 1.13), he can still be identified using his other traits like face or iris.
2. Provide a degree of flexibility in user authentication. Suppose a user enrolls into the system using several different traits. Later, at the time of authentication, only a subset of these traits may be acquired based on the nature of the application under consideration and the convenience of the user. Multibiometric systems may also be helpful in the *continuous* monitoring or tracking of an individual in situations when a single trait is not sufficient or available at all times.
3. Enable the search of a large biometric database in a computationally efficient manner. This can be achieved by first using a relatively simple but less accurate modality to prune the database before using the more complex and accurate modality on the remaining data to perform the final identification task, thereby improving the throughput of a biometric identification system.
4. Increase the resistance to spoof attacks. This is because it becomes increasingly difficult to circumvent multiple biometric sources simultaneously. Furthermore, by asking the user to present a random subset of traits at the point of acquisition, a multibiometric system can facilitate a challenge-response mechanism that verifies the presence of a *live* user. As an example, a person could be enrolled with

all ten fingerprints, but at the time of authentication, the system could ask him to present only three fingers in a particular sequence (left index, followed by right index, followed by left middle finger).

While multibiometric systems do offer a number of advantages, they are usually more expensive than unibiometric systems due to the need for additional hardware (computational or storage resources) and larger enrollment and recognition times. Hence, it is essential to carefully analyze the tradeoff between the added cost and the benefits accrued when making a business case for the use of multibiometrics in a specific application (see Figure 6.2). Despite these limitations, multibiometric systems are being increasingly deployed in many large-scale identification systems involving millions of users (e.g., border control or national identity systems) because of their ability to achieve high recognition accuracy based on existing technologies, which far outweighs the additional cost in such applications.

In designing a multibiometric system, we need to address the following four design issues.

1. Information sources: What are the various sources of biometric information that should be used in a multibiometric system?
2. Mode of operation: Should the data corresponding to multiple biometric sources be acquired simultaneously in a parallel mode or in a sequence? Similarly, should the information acquired be processed sequentially or simultaneously?
3. Level of fusion: What type of information (i.e., raw data, features, match scores, or decisions) is to be fused?
4. Fusion approach: What fusion scheme should be employed to combine the information presented by multiple biometric sources?

The subsequent sections consider each of these questions in turn. But, one should bear in mind that these questions are not completely independent. For example, the choice of biometric sources may dictate the acquisition strategy or the type of information to be fused (see Table 6.1).

6.2 Sources of Multiple Evidence

There are five possible scenarios that can provide multiple sources of biometric information as shown in Figure 6.2. Based on the sources of evidence, multibiometric systems can be classified into multi-sensor, multi-algorithm, multi-instance, multi-sample, and multimodal systems. In the first four scenarios, multiple pieces of evidences are derived from a single biometric trait (e.g., fingerprint *or* iris), while in the fifth scenario (also called multimodal biometric system) multiple biometric traits (e.g., fingerprint *and* iris) are used. It is also possible for a multibiometric system to utilize a combination of two or more of the five scenarios discussed below (Table 6.1). For example, since the UID system in India uses all ten fingers and two irides, it is both multi-instance and multimodal. Such systems are called *hybrid* multibiometric systems.

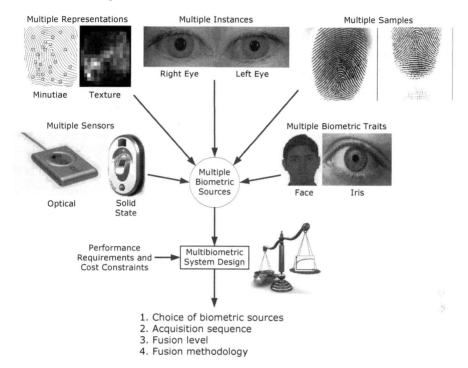

1. Choice of biometric sources
2. Acquisition sequence
3. Fusion level
4. Fusion methodology

Fig. 6.2 Multibiometric systems utilize information from multiple biometric sources to establish an identity. Based on the information sources used, multibiometric systems can be classified into multi-sensor, multi-algorithm, multi-instance, multi-sample, and multimodal systems. In the first four scenarios, a single biometric trait provides multiple sources of evidence. In the fifth scenario, different biometric traits are used as sources of evidence. While in principle, a large number of sources can be combined to improve the identification accuracy, practical factors such as cost of deployment, small training sample size, accuracy requirements, throughput time, and user acceptance will limit the number of sources used in a particular application.

6.2.1 Multi-sensor systems

In these systems, a single biometric trait is imaged or captured using multiple sensors in order to extract diverse information. For example, a system may record the two-dimensional texture content of a person's face using a CCD camera and the three-dimensional surface shape (also called the depth or range image) of the face using a range sensor in order to perform authentication (see Figure 6.3). The introduction of a new sensor (in this case, the range sensor) to measure the facial surface variation increases the cost of the multibiometric system. However, the availability of multi-sensor data pertaining to a single trait can not only improve the matching accuracy of the overall recognition system, but also assist in the intermediate processing stages of the individual component systems like image segmentation and registration.

Table 6.1 Dependencies between the design choices in a multibiometric system. While a check mark (✓) indicates that the two design choices are compatible, a cross mark (×) indicates that the two choices are not compatible.

Multibiome-tric sources	Type of information fused				Acquisition architecture		Processing architecture	
	Raw data	Features	Scores	Decisions	Serial	Parallel	Serial	Parallel
Multiple sensors	✓	✓	✓	✓	✓	✓	✓	✓
Multiple representa-tions	×	✓	✓	✓	×	✓	✓	✓
Multiple matchers	×	×	✓	✓	×	✓	✓	✓
Multiple instances	×	✓	✓	✓	✓	✓	✓	✓
Multiple samples	✓	✓	✓	✓	✓	×	✓	✓
Multiple traits	×	✓	✓	✓	✓	✓	✓	✓

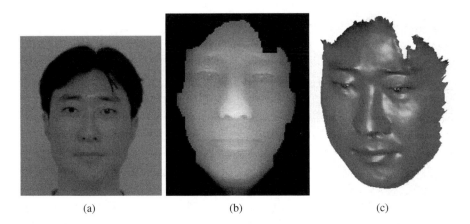

(a)   (b)   (c)

Fig. 6.3 Constructing a 3D face texture by combining the evidence presented by a 2D texture image and a 3D range image. (a) The 2D face texture of a person, (b) the corresponding 3D range (depth) image (here, blue represents farther distance from the camera while red represents a closer distance), and (c) the 3D surface after mapping the 2D texture information from (a).

Another example of multi-sensor fusion is the use of both a thermal infrared camera and a visible light camera for face recognition. Spatial registration between the data obtained from the multiple sensors is usually one of the fundamental issues in designing a multi-sensor system. However, this may not be always the case and there are multi-sensor systems in which registration is either "built in" to the sensor or registration may not be needed. The range sensor that acquires the 2D texture and 3D range images in Figure 6.3 is an example of the first category. If an optical and a capacitive fingerprint sensor are used to capture fingerprints, the two fingerprint images can be processed independently without spatially registering them. However, in this scenario, the user is required to interact with the sensors one at a time, leading to larger enrollment and verification times.

6.2.2 Multi-algorithm systems

In these systems, the same biometric data is processed using multiple algorithms. For example, a texture-based algorithm and a minutiae-based algorithm can operate on the same fingerprint image in order to extract diverse feature sets that can improve the performance of the system (see Figure 6.4). This kind of system does not require the use of new sensors and, hence, is cost-effective. Furthermore, since the user is not required to interact with multiple sensors, there is no additional inconvenience. However, it does require the introduction of new feature extractor and/or matcher modules, which may increase the computational requirements of the system. The main limitation of multi-algorithm systems is that since the different sources of evidence are obtained from the same raw data (e.g., right index fingerprint image), the multiple sources tend to be correlated. This usually limits the possible improvement in the matching accuracy. For example, if the acquired fingerprint image is noisy, it will affect both the texture-based and minutiae-based algorithms but to different extents. Figure 6.5 shows an example where fusion of multiple algorithms improves the accuracy.

A multi-algorithm system can use multiple feature sets (i.e., multiple representations) extracted from the same biometric data or multiple matching schemes operating on a single feature set. The combination of a texture-based algorithm and a minutiae-based fingerprint matching algorithm (shown in Figure 6.4) is an example of the first category, while fusion of results from multiple minutiae matchers like Hough transform, one-dimensional string matching and two-dimensional dynamic programming is an illustration of the latter. Another example of a system using multiple feature sets is a face recognition system that employs different feature extraction schemes like Principal Component Analysis (PCA), Independent Component Analysis (ICA), and Linear Discriminant Analysis (LDA) to encode (i.e., represent) a single face image.

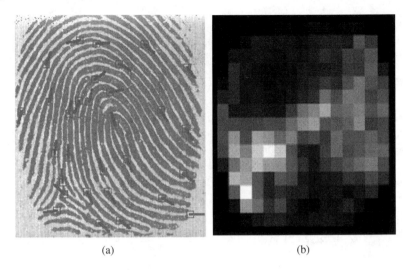

(a)   (b)

Fig. 6.4 Extracting different sets of features from the same fingerprint image. (a) Minutia features extracted from a fingerprint image, (b) texture features extracted from the fingerprint image in (a).

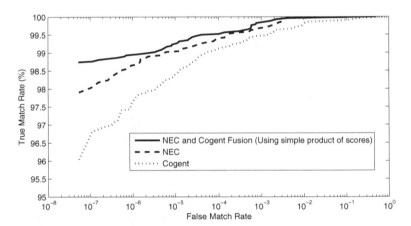

Fig. 6.5 Accuracy improvement in a multi-algorithm fingerprint verification system. This example is extracted from the Fingerprint Vendor Technology Evaluation (FpVTE) [37] conducted by the National Institute of Standards and Technology (NIST) in 2003. Fusion of evidence from the two most accurate matchers in FpVTE 2003, namely, NEC and Cogent Systems, leads to marginal improvement in the True Accept Rate (also known as Genuine Accept Rate) as compared to the individual matchers.

6.2.3 Multi-instance systems

These systems use multiple instances of the same body trait and are also sometimes referred to as multi-unit systems. For example, the left and right index fingers, or the left and right irides of an individual may be used to verify an individual's identity. These systems generally do not necessitate the introduction of new sensors nor do they entail the development of new feature extraction and matching algorithms and are, therefore, easier to implement. However, in some cases, a new sensor arrangement might be necessary in order to facilitate the simultaneous capture of the various units/instances. Automated Fingerprint Identification Systems (AFIS), that obtain tenprint information from a subject, can benefit from sensors that are able to rapidly acquire impressions of all ten fingers in three stages as shown in Figure 6.6.

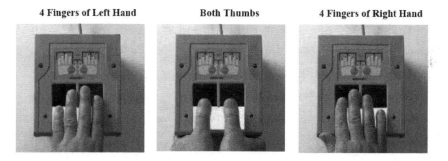

Fig. 6.6 A fingerprint sensor developed by Identix that allows rapid acquisition of all ten fingers in three steps. (Source: Nationwide Solutions)

Multi-instance systems are especially beneficial for users whose biometric traits cannot be reliably captured due to inherent problems. For example, a single finger may not be a sufficient discriminator for a person with dry finger skin. However, the integration of evidence across multiple fingers may serve as a good discriminator in this case. Similarly, an iris system may not be able to image significant portions of a person's iris due to drooping eyelids. The consideration of both the irides will result in the availability of additional texture information that can be used to reliably establish the individual's identity. Multi-instance systems are often necessary in applications where the size of the system database (i.e., the number of enrolled individuals) is very large (the FBI's IAFIS database currently has more than 60 million ten-print images) and all ten fingers provide additional discriminatory information that is required for high search accuracy (see Figure 6.7). Due to this reason, the Department of Homeland Security (DHS) in the United States, which originally collected only the two index fingers for its US-VISIT border control program, is now collecting all ten fingerprints.

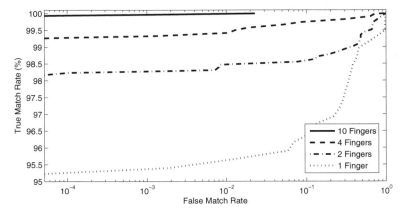

Fig. 6.7 Accuracy improvement in a multi-instance fingerprint verification system. This example extracted from FpVTE 2003 [37] shows that fusion of evidence from the multiple fingers leads to significant improvement in the accuracy.

6.2.4 Multi-sample systems

A single sensor may be used to acquire multiple samples of the same biometric trait in order to account for the variations that can occur in the trait, or to obtain a more complete representation of the underlying trait. A face system, for example, may capture (and store) the left and right profile images along with the frontal image of a person's face in order to account for variations in the facial pose. Similarly, a fingerprint system equipped with a sensor with a small sensing area may acquire multiple dab prints of an individual's finger in order to capture various regions of the fingerprint. These fingerprint images can be fused together to form a complete fingerprint, which will provide a large number of minutiae as shown in Figure 6.16.

One of the key issues in a multi-sample system is determining the *number* of samples that need to be acquired from a biometric trait. It is important that the procured samples represent the *variability* as well as the *typicality* of the individual's biometric data. To achieve this objective, an appropriate sample collection protocol that takes into account the variability of the samples has to be established beforehand. For example, a face recognition system utilizing both the frontal and side-profile images[1] of an individual may stipulate that the side-profile image should be a three-quarter view of the face. Alternately, given a set of biometric samples, the system should be able to automatically select the "optimal" subset that would best represent the individual's variability.

---

[1] Note that if the different facial profiles of a user are captured simultaneously using multiple cameras, it would be considered as a multi-sensor system and not as a multi-sample system.

6.2.5 *Multimodal systems*

Multimodal systems combine the evidence presented by different body traits for establishing identity. Some of the earliest multimodal biometric systems utilized face and voice features to establish the identity of an individual. Since the different biometric traits of an individual are expected to be uncorrelated (e.g., fingerprint and iris), use of multimodal biometric systems generally leads to greater improvement in performance compared to other types of multibiometric systems. However, some combinations of biometric traits (e.g., voice and lip movement) could exhibit significant correlation, and employing such combinations may not provide a significant performance improvement.

The cost of deploying multimodal biometric systems is substantially more due to the requirement of multiple sensors and, consequently, the development of appropriate user interfaces (see Figure 6.8 for examples of interfaces that can capture multimodal biometric data). Although the identification accuracy can be significantly improved by utilizing an increasing number of traits, this number is generally restricted by practical considerations such as the cost of deployment, enrollment time, throughput, expected error rate, user habituation issues, etc. Furthermore, there is a diminishing return after strong biometric traits (e.g., fingerprint and iris) have already been fused. In fact, depending on the fusion scheme, there may even be a performance degradation if many biometric traits with lower accuracy are added.

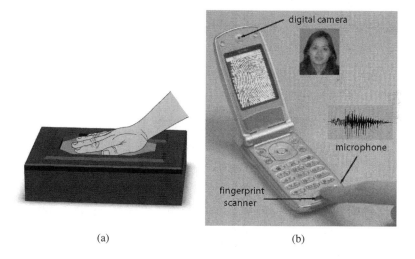

(a) (b)

Fig. 6.8 Examples of interfaces that can record multibiometric data. (a) Concept diagram of a whole-hand scanner that can simultaneously acquire palmprint, fingerprints from all five fingers of a hand, and hand-shape (Source: Lumidigm Inc.), (b) a mobile phone that can acquire multiple modalities like fingerprint, face, and voice. Preliminary efforts have also been made to modify the camera on the phone to capture iris image as well.

While the five types of multibiometric systems mentioned above have their own pros and cons, multi-instance and multimodal biometric systems are more popular than the other three types, because they offer a greater scope for enhancing the recognition accuracy and increasing the population coverage (see Figure 6.9). Many large-scale biometric identification systems deployed in practical applications including the FBI-IAFIS, US-VISIT, and the Unique Identification (UID) project in India use multiple instances or multiple traits or a combination of both (see Figure 6.10 and Figure 6.8(a)). Besides the above five scenarios, it is also possible to use biometric traits in conjunction with non-biometric authenticators like tokens or password. When more than one identification factor (among passwords, tokens, and biometric traits) is used, the scenario is referred to as *multi-factor authentication*.

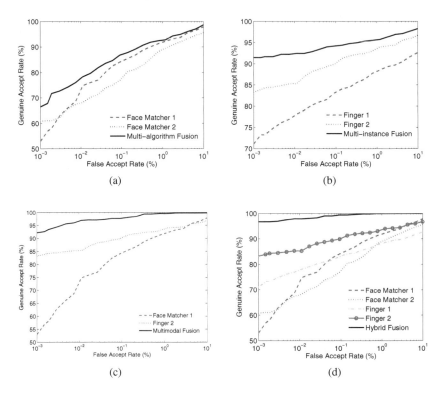

Fig. 6.9 Comparison of accuracy improvements in different types of multibiometric systems based on the NIST-Biometric Score Set Release 1 (BSSR1) database. (a) A multi-algorithm system, where evidence is fused from two different face matchers operating on the same face image, (b) a multi-instance system, where information from two different fingers are combined, and (c) a multimodal system, where evidence is accumulated from a single finger and face. (d) A hybrid multibiometric system, where the sources of information include two fingers and two face matchers.

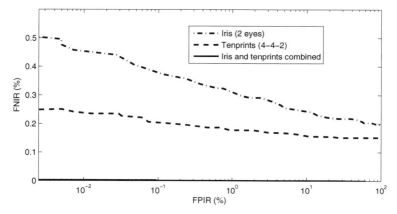

Fig. 6.10 Accuracy improvement in a multi-instance and multimodal biometric identification system with fingerprint and iris modalities (Source: UID Authority of India). Note that in applications such as UID, where de-duplication of hundreds of millions of identities needs to performed, a very low False Positive Identification Rate (FPIR) as well as a very low False Negative Identification Rate (FNIR) are required. This level of accuracy can be achieved only when all ten fingers and both irides are fused. Note that the fusion of 10 fingerprints and 2 irides on this database of 20,000 subjects gives almost zero FNIR and zero FPIR.

6.3 Acquisition and Processing Architecture

One of the key considerations while designing a biometric system is its usability. It is important to design ergonomic and convenient user interfaces, which can efficiently capture good quality biometric images, leading to a lower failure to enroll rate. This is particularly true in the case of multibiometric systems, because multiple pieces of evidence pertaining to an individual's identity must be reliably acquired whilst causing minimum inconvenience to the user. The order or sequence of biometric data acquisition has a bearing on the convenience imparted to the user. Furthermore, the sequence in which the procured biometric data is processed can significantly impact the throughput time in large-scale identification systems (involving millions of enrolled users) since it may be possible to arrive at an identification decision rapidly with a relatively small number of traits.

6.3.1 Acquisition sequence

The acquisition sequence in a multibiometric system refers to the order in which the various sources of evidence are acquired from an individual (in the case of multi-algorithm systems, only a single biometric sample is required and, therefore, the acquisition methodology is not an issue). The acquisition sequence could be either *serial* or *parallel*. Typically, multibiometric systems employ the serial acquisition approach, where the evidence is gathered sequentially, i.e., each source is independently obtained with a short time interval between successive acquisitions. In some cases, the evidence may be acquired simultaneously (in parallel fashion). For example, the face and iris information of a user may be obtained nearly simultaneously by utilizing two cameras housed in the same unit. Similarly, the face, voice, and lip movements of a user may be acquired simultaneously by capturing a video, and multiple fingerprints can be captured in parallel using a multi-finger slap scanner (shown in Figure 6.6). While serial acquisition does not require any special sensor arrangement and typically has a lower installation cost, parallel acquisition can decrease enrollment and authentication times and improve the usability of multibiometric systems.

6.3.2 Processing sequence

The processing sequence adopted by a multibiometric system refers to the order in which the acquired information is processed to render a decision which could be independent of the order in which the information is acquired. Thus, information may be *acquired sequentially* but *processed simultaneously* and vice versa.

In the serial or cascade mode, the processing of information takes place sequentially. In Figure 6.11, the fingerprint information of the user is first processed; if the fingerprint sub-system is unable to determine the user's identity, then the data corresponding to the face biometric is processed. In such an arrangement, the processing time can be effectively reduced if a decision is made without waiting for the outputs of all the unibiometric systems. The user can also be allowed to choose which of his biometric traits should be captured first, leading to even greater convenience. In addition to improving user convenience, the cascading scheme also allows fast and efficient searches in large scale identification tasks (also called database indexing or filtering). The matching result obtained using each modality can be used to successively prune the database, thereby making the search faster and more efficient. However, robust algorithms are essential to efficiently handle the various sequence of events that are possible in a cascaded multibiometric system.

In the parallel mode, each unibiometric system processes its information independently at the same time and the processed information is combined using an appropriate fusion scheme (see Figure 6.12). A multibiometric system designed to operate in the parallel mode generally has a higher accuracy because it utilizes more evidence about the user for recognition. Most practical multibiometric systems have a parallel architecture because the primary goal of multibiometric system designers has been to reduce the error rates of biometric systems and not necessarily the throughput and/or processing time. However, a decision on the optimal number of biometrics sources to use still needs to be made and may involve studying the trade-off between accuracy and other factors like system cost and throughput.

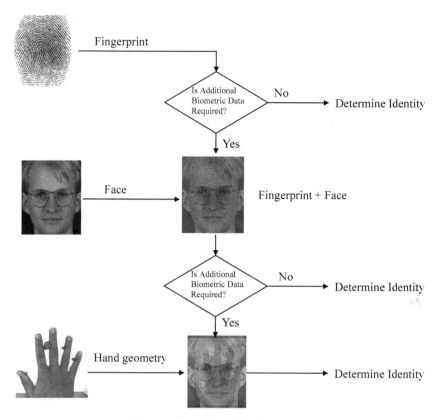

Fig. 6.11 In the cascade (or serial) mode of operation, evidence is incrementally processed in order to establish the user's identity. This scheme is also known as sequential pattern recognition. It enhances user convenience while reducing the average processing time since a decision can be made without having to acquire all the biometric traits.

Besides the two modes of operation discussed above, it is also possible to have a hierarchical (tree-like) architecture to combine the advantages of both cascade and parallel architectures. In such a scheme, a subset of the acquired modalities may be combined in parallel, while the remaining modalities may be combined in a serial fashion. Such an architecture can be dynamically determined based on the quality of the individual biometric samples as well as when encountering missing biometric data.

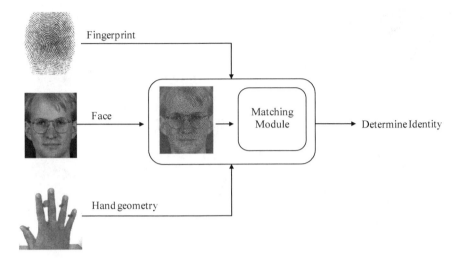

Fingerprint

Face

Matching
Module

Determine Identity

Hand geometry

Fig. 6.12 In the parallel mode of operation, the evidence acquired from multiple sources is simultaneously processed in order to establish user's identity. Note that the evidence pertaining to the multiple sources may be acquired in a sequential fashion.

6.4 Fusion Levels

A fundamental issue in the design of a multibiometric system is to determine the *type* of information that should be consolidated by the fusion module. In a typical biometric system, the amount of information available to the system gets compressed as one proceeds from the sensor module to the decision module (see Figure 6.13). The raw biometric data (e.g., image or video) is the richest in information content and subsequent processing (e.g., feature extraction) reduces the amount of information that is available to the system. It must be noted, however, that use of feature-level representation for fusion has certain advantages over the sensor-level (i.e, raw data-level) representation. Firstly, feature extraction is expected to provide an *invariant* representation of the biometric pattern under consideration. Secondly, the effect of noise is expected to decrease after feature extraction, which typically involves enhancement operations to suppress the inherent noise in the biometric data. However, the enhancement procedure itself may add some spurious information to the original raw data. Thus, there is an interplay between the amount of useful information that is available at any stage in a biometric system and the degree of noise corrupting this information.

In a multibiometric system, fusion can be accomplished by utilizing the information available in any of the four biometric modules (sensor, feature extractor, matcher, and decision modules). Figure 6.14 shows the various levels of fusion possible in a multibiometric system. Biometric fusion can be broadly classified into (a) fusion prior to matching, and (b) fusion after matching. This distinction is made be-

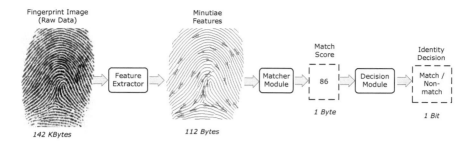

Fig. 6.13 The amount of information available for fusion gets reduced as one progresses along the various processing modules of a biometric system. The raw data represents the richest source of information, while the final decision (in a verification scenario) contains just a single bit of information. However, the raw data is corrupted by noise and may have large intra-class variability, which is typically reduced in the subsequent modules of the system.

cause once the matcher is invoked, the amount of information available to the fusion system drastically decreases. Moreover, fusion prior to matching can be applied during enrollment and/or authentication. On the other hand, fusion after matching can be applied only during authentication. Prior to matching, integration of information from multiple biometric sources can take place either at the sensor level or at the feature level. Schemes for integration of information after the classification/matcher stage can be further divided into three categories: fusion at the decision level, fusion at the rank level, and fusion at the match score level.

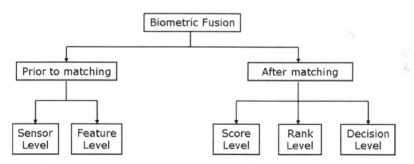

Fig. 6.14 Fusion can be accomplished at various levels in a biometric system. Most multibiometric systems fuse information at the score level or the decision level. Fusion at the rank level is applicable only to biometric systems operating in the identification mode.

Biometric systems that integrate information at an early stage of processing are believed to be more effective than those systems that perform integration at a later stage. Since the feature set contains richer information about the input biometric pattern than the match score or the decision label, integration at the feature level is expected to provide better recognition results than score or decision level fusion.

However, in practice this is not always true since (a) the fusion process has to reckon with the presence of noise in constituent feature sets, and (b) a new matching algorithm may be necessary to compare two fused feature sets. Developing efficient matching algorithms is often the most challenging aspect in the design of a biometric system and, thus, fusion at the sensor or feature levels introduces additional processing complexities.

6.4.1 Sensor-level fusion

Sensor-level fusion entails the consolidation of evidence presented by multiple sources of raw data *before* they are subjected to feature extraction. In the image processing literature, this is referred to as image-level or pixel-level fusion. The phrase "sensor-level fusion" is used in order to accommodate other types of raw data also such as voice, video, etc. The flow of information in a multibiometric system that employs sensor-level fusion is shown in Figure 6.15. While Figure 6.15 shows that sensor-level fusion is performed during both enrollment and authentication, this need not be the case always. It is possible to design a multibiometric system where fusion is applied only during enrollment or during authentication. In general, a sensor-level fusion function $\mathbf{f}_S(.)$ converts a collection of M biometric samples $B = \{\mathbf{B}_1, \mathbf{B}_2, \cdots, \mathbf{B}_M\}$ into a single fused sample $\mathbf{B}_f$, i.e.,

$$\mathbf{B}_f = \mathbf{f}_S(\mathbf{B}_1, \mathbf{B}_2, \cdots, \mathbf{B}_M). \tag{6.1}$$

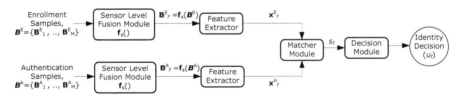

Fig. 6.15 Information flow in multibiometric system that employs sensor-level fusion.

Sensor-level fusion is applicable only for multi-sensor and multi-sample systems. For example, a small fingerprint sensor may capture two or more impressions of a person's fingerprint and create a composite fingerprint image that reveals a more complete ridge structure (see Figure 6.16). This process, known as *mosaicing*, is particularly useful in sweep-sensors in which each image slice represents only a small portion of the fingerprint and, hence, an appropriate stitching algorithm is required to integrate the various slices to form the complete fingerprint image.

Mosaicing can also be performed in face recognition where multiple 2D images representing different poses can be stitched to generate a single image. It is also possible to combine the 2D texture of a person's face with the corresponding 3D scan (i.e., the range image) in order to create a 3D texture model. The availability of this model permits the generation of new (previously unseen) 2D images of a person's face (e.g., at different poses, illumination, head-tilt, etc.) without actually employing a scanner to capture such images.

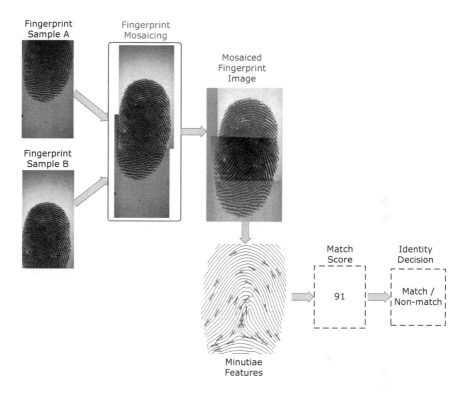

Fig. 6.16 Illustration of a sensor-level fusion scheme where multiple impressions of the same finger are stitched together using a process called mosaicing to generate a composite fingerprint image.

6.4.2 Feature-level fusion

Feature or representation-level fusion involves consolidating the evidence presented by two different biometric feature sets of the same individual. Figure 6.17 shows the typical information flow in a multibiometric system using feature-level fusion. Mathematically, a feature-level fusion function $\mathbf{f}_R(.)$ converts a collection of M biometric feature sets $X = \{\mathbf{x}_1, \mathbf{x}_2, \cdots, \mathbf{x}_M\}$ into a single fused feature set $\mathbf{x}_f$, i.e.,

$$\mathbf{x}_f = \mathbf{f}_R(\mathbf{x}_1, \mathbf{x}_2, \cdots, \mathbf{x}_M). \tag{6.2}$$

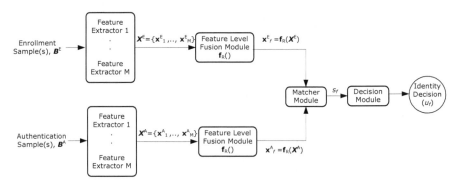

Fig. 6.17 Typical information flow in a multibiometric system that employs feature-level fusion.

Feature-level fusion schemes can be categorized into two broad classes, namely, homogeneous and heterogeneous. A homogeneous feature fusion scheme is used when the feature sets to be combined are obtained by applying the same feature extraction algorithm to multiple samples of the same biometric trait (e.g., minutia sets from two impressions of the same finger). This approach is applicable to multi-sample and multi-sensor systems. Heterogeneous feature fusion techniques are required if the component feature sets originate from different feature extraction algorithms or from samples of different biometric traits (or different instances of the same trait).

6.4.2.1 Homogeneous feature fusion

Homogeneous feature fusion can be used for template update or template improvement as discussed below.

- **Template update**: A template in the database can be updated based on the evidence presented by the current feature set in order to reflect (possibly) permanent changes in a person's biometric. Hand geometry systems use this process to update the geometric measurements stored in the database in order to account for changes in an individual's hand over a period of time. Usually, the template is updated after every successful authentication. Therefore, the information flow in such a system does not follow the typical flow shown in Figure 6.17. A simple template update scheme is shown in equation (6.3). Here, the average of the current template ($\mathbf{x}^E$) and the new feature vector obtained during authentication ($\mathbf{x}^A$) is computed and stored as the new template ($\hat{\mathbf{x}}^E$), provided the authentication is successful.

$$\hat{\mathbf{x}}^E = \begin{cases} \frac{\mathbf{x}^E + \mathbf{x}^A}{2}, & \text{if } \mathscr{M}\left(\mathbf{x}^E, \mathbf{x}^A\right) \geq \tau, \\ \mathbf{x}^E, & \text{otherwise}, \end{cases} \tag{6.3}$$

where $\mathscr{M}(.,.)$ is the matching function that computes the similarity between two feature vectors and τ is the decision threshold.

- **Template improvement**: In the case of fingerprints, the minutiae information available in two impressions can be combined by appropriately aligning the two prints and then removing duplicate minutia, thereby generating a larger minutia set (see Figure 6.18). This process, known as template improvement, can also be used to remove spurious minutiae points that may be present in a feature set. While template update is used to accommodate temporal changes in a person's biometric, the purpose of template improvement is to increase the number of features (*and* decrease the number of spurious features) whilst retaining its integrity.

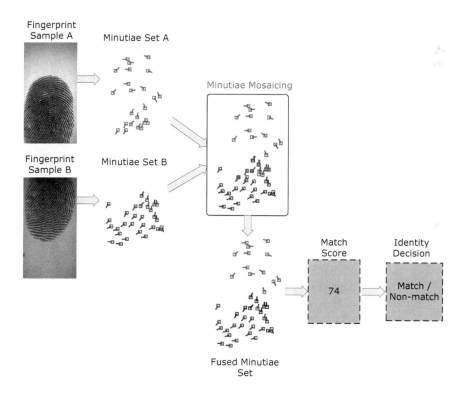

Fig. 6.18 Illustration of a homogeneous feature fusion (template improvement) scheme where minutia sets extracted from multiple impressions of the same finger are reconciled to generate a larger minutia set.

6.4.2.2 Heterogeneous feature fusion

How does one consolidate feature sets originating from different algorithms and different biometric modalities? Feature level fusion is difficult to achieve in such cases because of the following reasons:

1. The relationship between the feature spaces of different biometric systems may not be known.
2. The feature sets of multiple modalities may be incompatible. For example, the minutiae set of fingerprints and the eigen-coefficients of face have different representation schemes. One is a variable length feature set (i.e., it varies across fingerprint images) whose individual values parameterize a minutia point; the other is a fixed length feature set (i.e., face images are represented by a fixed number of eigen-coefficients) whose individual values are scalar entities.
3. If the two feature sets are fixed length feature vectors, then one could consider augmenting them to generate a new larger feature set. However, concatenating two feature vectors might lead to the curse-of-dimensionality problem, where increasing the number of features might actually degrade the system performance especially in the presence of small number of training samples. Although the curse-of-dimensionality is a well known problem in pattern recognition, it is particularly pronounced in biometric applications because of the time, effort, and cost required to collect large amounts of biometric (training) data.
4. Most commercial biometric systems do not provide access to the feature sets used in their products due to proprietary reasons. Hence, very few biometric researchers have focused on heterogeneous feature fusion and most of them generally prefer fusion schemes that use match scores or decision labels.

If the length of each of the two feature vectors to be consolidated is fixed across all users, then a feature concatenation scheme followed by a dimensionality reduction procedure may be adopted for feature-level fusion. Consider a multibiometric system where fixed-length feature vectors from two biometric sources are available, i.e., $X = \{\mathbf{x}_1, \mathbf{x}_2\}$, where $\mathbf{x}_1 \in \mathbb{R}^{d_1}$ and $\mathbf{x}_2 \in \mathbb{R}^{d_2}$. The objective is to fuse these two feature sets in order to yield a new feature vector, $\mathbf{x}_f$, that would better represent the biometric sample of an individual. The vector $\mathbf{x}_f$ of dimensionality d, $d < (d_1 + d_2)$, can be generated by first concatenating vectors $\mathbf{x}_1$ and $\mathbf{x}_2$, and then performing feature selection or feature transformation on the resultant feature vector in order to reduce its dimensionality (see Figure 6.19). The key stages of such an approach are described below.

Feature Normalization: The individual feature values of vectors $\mathbf{x}_1 = [x_1^1, x_1^2, \cdots, x_1^{d_1}]$ and $\mathbf{x}_2 = [x_2^1, x_2^2, \cdots, x_2^{d_2}]$ may exhibit significant differences in their range as well as form (i.e., distribution). Augmenting such diverse feature values will not be appropriate in many cases. For example, if the x_1^i's are in the range $[0, 100]$ while the x_2^i's are in the range $[0, 1]$, then the distance between two augmented feature vectors will be more sensitive to the x_1^i's than the x_2^i's.

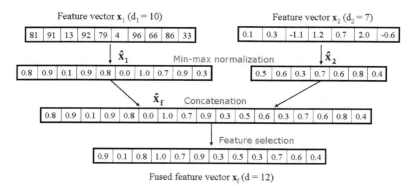

Fig. 6.19 A simple scheme for the fusion of two heterogeneous feature vectors whose lengths are fixed across all users. In this example, min-max normalization is performed based on the assumption that the ranges of feature values are $[0, 100]$ and $[-3, 3]$ for the first and second feature vectors, respectively.

The goal of feature normalization is to modify the location (mean) and scale (variance) of the features values via a transformation function in order to map them into a common domain. Adopting an appropriate normalization scheme also helps address the problem of outliers in feature values. Feature normalization may not be necessary in cases where the feature values pertaining to multiple sources are already comparable.

A simple normalization scheme that is often used in practice is the min-max normalization scheme, which transforms the features values such that they fall in the range $[0, 1]$, irrespective of their original values. Let x and $\hat{x}$ denote a feature value before and after normalization, respectively. The min-max technique computes $\hat{x}$ as

$$\hat{x} = \frac{x - \min(h_x)}{\max(h_x) - \min(h_x)}, \qquad (6.4)$$

where h_x is the function that generates x, and $\min(h_x)$ and $\max(h_x)$ represent the minimum and maximum of all possible x values that will be observed, respectively. The min-max technique is effective when the minimum and the maximum values of the component feature values are known beforehand. In cases where such information is not available, an estimate of these parameters has to be obtained from the available set of training data. Normalizing the feature values using the min-max normalization techniques results in modified feature vectors $\hat{\mathbf{x}}_1 = \left[\hat{x}_1^1, \hat{x}_1^2, \cdots, \hat{x}_1^{d_1} \right]$ and $\hat{\mathbf{x}}_2 = \left[\hat{x}_2^1, \hat{x}_2^2, \cdots, \hat{x}_2^{d_2} \right]$.

One of the limitations of the min-max normalization technique is its sensitivity to outliers in the training data. The presence of a single outlier, i.e., a feature having a very high or very low value can lead to an incorrect estimate of the maximum or minimum parameter, respectively. A number of normalization techniques have been proposed to effectively handle outliers. Some of these techniques will be discussed in section 6.4.3.2 in the context of score level fusion.

Feature Selection or Transformation: Augmenting the two normalized feature vectors, $\hat{\mathbf{x}}_1$ and $\hat{\mathbf{x}}_2$, results in a new feature vector, $\hat{\mathbf{x}}_f = \left[\hat{x}_1^1, \hat{x}_1^2, \cdots, \hat{x}_1^{d_1}, \hat{x}_2^1, \hat{x}_2^2, \cdots, \hat{x}_2^{d_2} \right]$, $\hat{\mathbf{x}}_f \in \mathbb{R}^{d_1 + d_2}$. The curse-of-dimensionality dictates that the augmented vector of dimensionality $(d_1 + d_2)$ need not necessarily result in an improved matching performance compared to that obtained by $\hat{\mathbf{x}}_1$ and $\hat{\mathbf{x}}_2$ alone. In order to avoid this problem, a feature selection process is applied. Feature selection is a dimensionality reduction scheme that entails choosing a minimal feature set of size d, $d < (d_1 + d_2)$, such that a criterion (objective) function applied to the training set of feature vectors is optimized.

Examples of feature selection algorithms include sequential forward selection (SFS), sequential backward selection (SBS), sequential forward floating search (SFFS), sequential backward floating search (SBFS), "plus l take away r", and branch-and-bound search . These feature selection techniques rely on an appropriately formulated criterion function to elicit nearly optimal subset of features from a larger feature set. In the case of a biometric system, this criterion function could be the Equal Error Rate (EER), the total error rate, the d-prime measure, the area under the ROC curve, or the average GAR at pre-determined FAR values corresponding to the training set.

Dimensionality reduction may also be accomplished using feature *transformation* methods where the vector $\hat{\mathbf{x}}_f$ is subjected to a linear or a non-linear mapping that projects it to a lower dimensional subspace. Examples of such transformations include the use of principal component analysis (PCA), independent component analysis (ICA), multidimensional scaling (MDS), and Kohonen Maps. The application of a feature selection or feature transformation procedure results in a new feature vector $\mathbf{x}_f = [x^1, x^2, \cdots, x^d]$, which can now be used to represent the biometric sample(s) of an individual.

6.4.3 Score-level fusion

When match scores output by different biometric matchers are consolidated in order to arrive at a final recognition decision, fusion is said to be done at the score level. This is also known as fusion at the measurement level or confidence level. After the raw data and feature vectors representations, the next level of fusion is based on match scores. It is relatively easy to access and combine the scores generated by different biometric matchers. Consequently, score-level fusion is the most commonly used approach in multibiometric systems.

The general flow of information in a multibiometric verification system using score-level fusion is shown in Figure 6.20. Score-level fusion is a challenging problem when the match scores generated by the individual matchers are not homogeneous. Non-homogeneity could be due to the following two reasons:

1. One matcher may output a distance or dissimilarity measure (a smaller distance indicates a better match) while another may output a similarity measure (a larger similarity value indicates a better match). Furthermore, the outputs of the individual matchers need not be on the same numerical scale (range).
2. The match scores may follow different probability distributions due to different characteristics of the individual matchers.

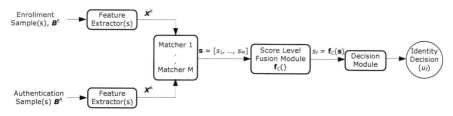

Fig. 6.20 Flow of information in a match score-level fusion scheme.

Score-level fusion methodologies will vary depending on whether the multibiometric system operates in the verification or identification mode. Score fusion in a multibiometric verification system can be considered as a two-class pattern classification problem, where the goal is to determine whether the query corresponds to a "genuine" user or an "impostor". Let $\mathbf{s} = [s_1, s_2, \cdots, s_M]$ be the match score vector obtained by comparing the query biometric features X^A to the enrolled template X^E using M different matchers. Here, s_m represents the match score output by the mth matcher. Based on the training set of match scores from the genuine and impostor classes, a classifier learns a decision boundary between the two classes. Figure 6.21 shows an example of a linear decision boundary learned by a classifier based on the genuine and impostor match scores from two different matchers. During authentication, any match score vector that falls in the genuine region (to the right of the decision boundary in Figure 6.21) is classified as "genuine". In general, the decision boundary can be quite complex depending on the nature of the classifier.

Depending on the model used for classification, the score fusion techniques can be further classified into three broad categories, namely, likelihood-ratio-based fusion, transformation-based fusion, and fusion based on other classification approaches (see Figure 6.22). However, this categorization is not rigid and some score fusion techniques may be categorized under multiple approaches or may involve more than one basic approach.

6.4.3.1 Likelihood-ratio-based score fusion

This approach is based on the Bayesian decision theory and the Neyman-Pearson approach to statistical hypothesis testing. For the sake of simplicity, let ω_0 and ω_1

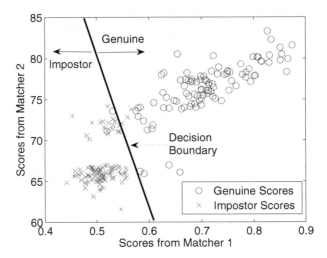

Fig. 6.21 Example of a linear decision boundary learned in a 2-dimensional ($M = 2$) feature space. During verification, any match score vector that falls in the region marked as 'Genuine' (to the right of the decision boundary) is classified as a "genuine" user. On the other hand, any match score vector that falls in the region marked as 'Impostor' (to the left of the decision boundary) is classified as "impostor".

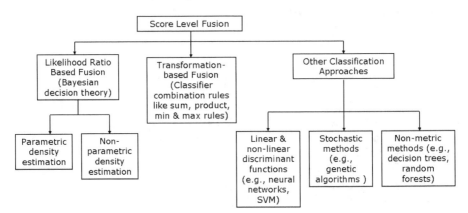

Fig. 6.22 Taxonomy of classification approaches that can be used for score level fusion in a multi-biometric verification system. Note that the above categorization is not strict and some score fusion techniques may be categorized under multiple approaches or may involve more than one basic approach.

denote the impostor and genuine classes, respectively. Let $P(\omega_0)$ and $P(\omega_1)$ be the prior probabilities of observing the impostor and genuine classes, respectively. Further, let the conditional density function for the genuine match scores be denoted as $p(s|\omega_1)$ and the corresponding density function for the impostor scores be denoted as $p(s|\omega_0)$. The posterior probability $P(\omega_j|s)$ can be computed from $p(s|\omega_j)$ using the Bayes formula:

$$P(\omega_j|s) = \frac{p(s|\omega_j)P(\omega_j)}{p(s)}, \tag{6.5}$$

where $j = 0, 1$ and $p(s) = \sum_{j=0}^{1} p(s|\omega_j)P(\omega_j)$.

The objective is to decide between the genuine and impostor classes based on the observed match score vector s. To minimize the average probability of error, one should select the class ω_j that has the highest posterior probability. In other words, the decision rule for minimum error rate is:

$$\text{Decide } \omega_1 \text{ if } P(\omega_1|s) > P(\omega_0|s). \tag{6.6}$$

The minimum error rate Bayes decision rule is obtained by substituting equation (6.5) in equation (6.6), which can be expressed as

$$\text{Decide } \omega_1 \text{ if } P(\omega_1)p(s|\omega_1) > P(\omega_0)p(s|\omega_0). \tag{6.7}$$

If the prior probabilities of the two classes are assumed to be equal, i.e., if $P(\omega_0) = P(\omega_1) = 0.5$, the minimum error rate decision rule can be simplified as follows:

$$\text{Decide } \omega_1 \text{ if } \frac{p(s|\omega_1)}{p(s|\omega_0)} > 1. \tag{6.8}$$

The statistic $p(s|\omega_1)/p(s|\omega_0)$ is known as the *likelihood ratio*. While the decision rule in equation (6.8) minimizes the total error rate, it is not widely used in biometric systems because it assumes that both false accept and false reject errors are equally costly. In a practical biometric system, it is often desirable to have an upper bound on the false accept rate. In other words, it is required that the false accept rate of the biometric system is less than, say 0.1%. This can be achieved by modifying the decision rule in equation (6.8) based on the Neyman-Pearson criterion.

Let Ψ be a statistical test for testing the null hypothesis H_0: *s corresponds to an impostor* against the alternative hypothesis H_1: *s corresponds to a genuine user*. Let $\Psi(s) = j$ imply a decision in favor of H_j, where $j = 0, 1$. The probability of correctly rejecting H_0 when H_1 is true is known as the *genuine accept rate* or the *power* of the test. The probability of rejecting H_0 when H_0 is true is known as the *false accept rate* or *level* of the test denoted by α. The Neyman-Pearson theorem states that

1. For testing H_0 against H_1, there exists a test Ψ and a constant η such that

$$P(\Psi(s) = 1|H_0) = \alpha \tag{6.9}$$

and

$$\Psi(\mathbf{s}) = \begin{cases} 1, & \text{when } \frac{p(\mathbf{S}|\omega_1)}{p(\mathbf{S}|\omega_0)} \geq \eta, \\ 0, & \text{when } \frac{p(\mathbf{S}|\omega_1)}{p(\mathbf{S}|\omega_0)} < \eta. \end{cases} \qquad (6.10)$$

2. If a test satisfies equations (6.9) and (6.10) for some η, then it is the most powerful test for testing H_0 against H_1 at level α.

According to the Neyman-Pearson theorem, given the false accept rate (FAR) α, the *optimal* test for deciding whether a match score vector $\mathbf{s}$ corresponds to a genuine user or an impostor is the likelihood-ratio test. The decision rule based on the likelihood-ratio test can be expressed as

$$\text{Decide } \omega_1 \text{ if } \frac{p(\mathbf{s}|\omega_1)}{p(\mathbf{s}|\omega_0)} \geq \eta. \qquad (6.11)$$

For a specified FAR, one can select a threshold η such that the above decision rule maximizes the genuine accept rate (GAR) and there does not exist any other decision rule with a higher GAR. However, this optimality of the likelihood-ratio test is guaranteed only when the underlying match score densities, namely, $p(\mathbf{s}|\omega_1)$ and $p(\mathbf{s}|\omega_0)$ are known. In practice, only a finite set of genuine and impostor match scores are available for training, so the densities $p(\mathbf{s}|\omega_1)$ and $p(\mathbf{s}|\omega_0)$ must be reliably estimated from this training data before applying the likelihood-ratio test.

Density estimation is a well-studied problem in statistics. In parametric density estimation, the form of the density function (e.g., Gaussian) is assumed to be known and only the parameters of this density function (e.g., mean and standard deviation) are estimated from the training data. For example, if the density function is assumed to be Gaussian, only the mean and the standard deviation parameters that characterize this density are estimated during training. Figure 6.23 shows the decision boundary of a likelihood-ratio-based fusion scheme in the case of a two-dimensional score vector whose conditional densities are assumed to be Gaussian.

In the context of biometric systems, it is very difficult to choose a specific parametric form for the density of genuine and impostor match scores. This is because the genuine and impostor match score distributions generally have a large tail and may have more than one mode (see Figure 6.24). Moreover, if the parametric form for the score densities is not selected carefully, it may lead to anomalies like disconnected decision regions. This is because the resulting likelihood-ratio may not be monotonic[2] with respect to the match scores. For example, in Figure 6.23, the query would be classified as belonging to the genuine class if the two match scores have large positive values (decision region R_0 to the top left of R_1) as well as large negative values (decision region R_0 to the bottom right of R_1).

Non-parametric density estimation techniques such as density histogram, k-Nearest Neighbor, and kernel density estimator (also known as Parzen window

---

[2] A higher similarity score indicates that there is a larger likelihood that the query belongs to the genuine class. Therefore, the relationship between the match score and likelihood-ratio is usually monotonic.

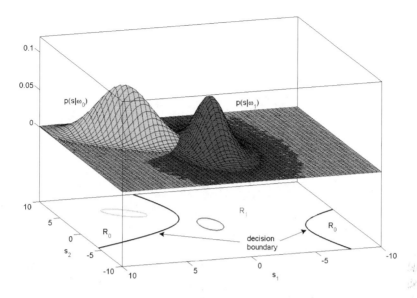

Fig. 6.23 Decision boundary of a likelihood-ratio-based fusion scheme when the conditional densities of the two-dimensional score vector $\mathbf{s} = [s_1, s_2]$ are assumed to be Gaussian. Here, $p(\mathbf{s}|\omega_1)$ and $p(\mathbf{s}|\omega_0)$ represent the genuine and impostor match score densities, respectively. In this example, the decision boundary consists of a hyperbola, and thus the decision region R_0 (corresponding to the genuine class) is not connected. This is because the likelihood-ratio is not monotonic with respect to the match scores. The ellipses indicate contours of constant density, where the density value is $1/e$ times that at the peak of the distribution.

method) do not assume any standard form for the density function and are essentially data-driven. A mixture of densities whose functional forms are known (e.g., mixture of Gaussians) can also be used for density estimation. This mixture method can be categorized as either parametric or semi-parametric depending on whether the number of mixture components is fixed *a priori* or is allowed to vary based on the observed data. Although the non-parametric and semi-parametric approaches can model any distribution, the reliability of the obtained estimate depends significantly on the number of samples that are available for learning the densities, especially if the dimensionality of the match score vector (M) is large. In practice, there is only a limited availability of training data, particularly for the genuine class. Therefore, it is important to carefully choose the appropriate density estimation method.

The density estimation process can be simplified greatly if the match scores output by the M matchers are assumed to be statistically independent under both the hypotheses H_0 and H_1. Under this assumption, the conditional joint density $p(\mathbf{s}|\omega_j)$ can be expressed as the product of the marginal conditional densities, i.e.,

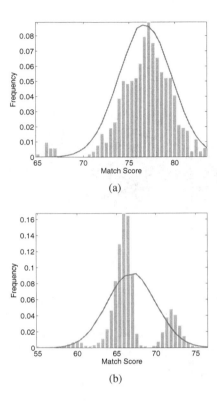

Fig. 6.24 Histograms of match scores and the corresponding Gaussian density estimates for the Face-G matcher in the NIST BSSR1 database. (a) Genuine scores and (b) Impostor scores. Note that the Gaussian density does not account well for the tail in the genuine score distribution and the multiple modes in the impostor score distribution.

$$p(\mathbf{s}|\omega_j) = p(s_1, s_2, \cdots, s_M|\omega_j) = \prod_{m=1}^{M} p(s_m|\omega_j), \ j = 0, 1. \qquad (6.12)$$

The likelihood-ratio-based decision rule under the assumption of statistical independence between matchers is given by

$$\text{Decide } \omega_1 \text{ if } \prod_{m=1}^{M} \frac{p(s_m|\omega_1)}{p(s_m|\omega_0)} \geq \eta. \qquad (6.13)$$

In a multimodal biometric system, each one of the M matchers uses features from a different biometric trait (e.g., face, fingerprint, and hand geometry), which generally tend to be mutually independent. Hence, the underlying assumption in Equation (6.12) is reasonable in most multimodal biometric systems. On the other hand, the independence assumption may not be true for a multi-sample biometric system since the different samples of the same biometric trait usually tend to be correlated. However, unless the correlation between matchers is very high (say, over 0.9), degradation in accuracy as a result of independence assumption is not severe. Since such extreme scenarios are rarely encountered in practical multibiometric systems, it is appropriate to use the independence assumption as a rule of thumb.

6.4.3.2 Transformation-based score fusion

Transformation-based score fusion schemes are usually approximations of the general minimum error rate Bayes decision rule presented in equation (6.7). To apply the Bayes decision rule, estimates of the posterior probabilities $P(\omega_0|\mathbf{s})$ and $P(\omega_1|\mathbf{s})$ are required, which in turn requires the computation of the conditional joint densities $p(\mathbf{s}|\omega_0)$ and $p(\mathbf{s}|\omega_1)$. As mentioned earlier, estimating M-dimensional joint densities is a challenging problem, especially when the number of training samples is limited and M is large. Approximations to $P(\omega_j|\mathbf{s})$ can take place at two levels.

1. Firstly, an estimate of $P(\omega_j|\mathbf{s})$ can be obtained using the marginal posterior probabilities $P(\omega_j|s_m)$, $m = 1, 2, \cdots, M$. This can be achieved using different classifier combination rules shown in Table 6.2. All these combination rules have the following general form: $P(\omega_j|\mathbf{s}) \approx h(P(\omega_j|s_1), P(\omega_j|s_2), \cdots, P(\omega_j|s_M))$ and are based on two fundamental assumptions: (a) the match scores of different matchers are statistically independent, i.e., equation (6.12) is true, and (b) the prior probabilities of the genuine and impostor classes are equal, i.e., $P(\omega_1) = P(\omega_0) = (1/2)$. Approximating the posterior probabilities in the minimum error rate decision rule (equation (6.6)) using the classifier combination techniques leads to the following decision rule:

Decide ω_1 if

$$h(P(\omega_1|s_1), P(\omega_1|s_2), \cdots, P(\omega_1|s_M)) > h(P(\omega_0|s_1), P(\omega_0|s_2), \cdots, P(\omega_0|s_M)).$$
(6.14)

Among the classifier combination rules, the product rule is a direct implication of the assumptions that the match scores output by the M matchers are statistically independent and the classes have equal priors. However, a key limitation of the product rule is its sensitivity to errors in the estimation of the posterior probabilities. Even if one of the classifiers outputs a probability close to zero, the product of the M posterior probabilities is rather small and this often leads to an incorrect classification decision. The sum rule is generally more effective than the product rule, especially when the estimates of the marginal posterior probabilities are unreliable. The sum rule can be derived from the product rule by assuming that the posterior probabilities do not deviate dramatically from the prior probabilities for each class. Since the sum decision rule is robust to errors in the estimation of the posterior probabilities, it usually works quite well in practice and is commonly used in multibiometric systems. The max, min, and median rules can also be obtained by various approximations of the product and sum rules.

Table 6.2 Classifier combination rules approximate the joint posterior probabilities $P(\omega_j|\mathbf{s} = [s_1, s_2, \cdots, s_M])$ using the marginal posterior probabilities $P(\omega_j|s_m)$, $j = 0, 1$, $m = 1, 2, \cdots, M$. These rules have the following general form: $P(\omega_j|\mathbf{s}) \approx h(P(\omega_j|s_1), P(\omega_j|s_2), \cdots, P(\omega_j|s_M))$. All these combination rules are based on two assumptions: (a) the match scores of different matchers are statistically independent, and (b) the prior probabilities of the genuine and impostor classes are equal, i.e., $P(\omega_1) = P(\omega_0) = (1/2)$.

Combination Rule	$h(P(\omega_j|s_1), P(\omega_j|s_2), \cdots, P(\omega_j|s_M)) =$
Product	$\prod_{m=1}^{M} P(\omega_j|s_m)$
Sum	$\sum_{m=1}^{M} P(\omega_j|s_m)$
Max	$\max_{m=1}^{M} P(\omega_j|s_m)$
Min	$\min_{m=1}^{M} P(\omega_j|s_m)$
Median	$median_{m=1}^{M} P(\omega_j|s_m)$

2. The classifier combination rules can be applied only if the output of each biometric matcher is of the form $P(\omega_j|s_m)$, i.e., the posterior probability of class ω_j given the match score output by the mth matcher. Converting a match score into marginal posterior probabilities again requires the estimation of the marginal genuine and impostor match score densities. Rather than computing the marginal score densities for each matcher, one may transform the match scores obtained from different matchers into a common domain and directly apply the classifier combination rules on the transformed scores. This approach is based on the assumption that the match score and posterior probability for the genuine class are related as follows.

$$P(\omega_1|s_m) \propto g_m(s_m), \qquad (6.15)$$

where g_m is a monotonic function and $m = 1, 2, \cdots, M$. This transform g_m is usually referred to as the *score normalization* function and $g_m(s_m)$ is called the normalized match score. Once the match scores from different matchers are normalized, classifier combination rules such as the sum, max, and min rules can be applied to obtain the fused match scores. The corresponding combination rules are referred to as *sum of scores*, *max score*, and *min score* fusion rules, respectively, because the normalized match scores may not have any direct probabilistic interpretation (normalized scores may not even lie in the interval $[0,1]$). Due to the same reason, the product rule is generally not applicable to normalized scores. In general, the transformation based score fusion rules can be expressed as

$$\text{Decide } \omega_1 \text{ if } h(g_1(s_1), g_2(s_2), \cdots, g_M(s_M)) > \tau, \qquad (6.16)$$

where τ is the decision threshold set by the system administrator.

Formally, score normalization is defined as the process of changing the location and scale parameters of the match score distributions, so that the match scores of different matchers are transformed into a common domain. The location and scale parameters of a match score distribution are usually estimated from the training data. While the effect of the location parameter is to translate the score distribution along the horizontal direction, the effect of the scale parameter is to stretch out the distribution. If a transformation function alters the location and scale parameters without changing the basic shape of the distribution, such a transformation is said to preserve the score distribution. Some of the well-known score normalization schemes are summarized in Table 6.3. No normalization scheme has been shown to be optimal for all kinds of match score data. In practice, it is recommended that a number of normalization techniques be evaluated to determine the one that gives the best performance on the given data.

Table 6.3 Summary of commonly used score normalization techniques. The function ψ in tanh normalization is known as the Hampel influence function, and it reduces the influence of the scores at the tails of the distribution during the estimation of location and scale parameters. In this table, it is assumed that the location and scale parameters of a distribution can be estimated from a given set of training scores $\{\hat{s}_m^i\}$, for $m = 1, 2, \cdots, M$ and $i = 1, 2, \cdots, L_1, (L_1 + 1), (L_1 + 2), \cdots, (L_1 + L_0)$. Here, $\hat{s}_m^i$ represents the ith score in the training set corresponding to the mth matcher. It is also assumed that the first L_1 scores in the training set correspond to the genuine class, the subsequent L_0 scores correspond to the impostor class, and the total number of training samples is L, i.e., $L = L_1 + L_0$.

Normalization scheme	Normalization function $g(s_m)$	Location parameter (μ_m)	Scale parameter (σ_m)
Min-max	$\frac{s_m - \mu_m}{\sigma_m}$	$\min_{i=1}^{L} \hat{s}_m^i$	$\left(\max_{i=1}^{L} \hat{s}_m^i\right) - \mu_m$
Z-score	$\frac{s_m - \mu_m}{\sigma_m}$	$\frac{1}{L}\sum_{i=1}^{L} \hat{s}_m^i$	$\frac{1}{L}\sum_{i=1}^{L}\left(\hat{s}_m^i - \mu_m\right)^2$
Median	$\frac{s_m - \mu_m}{\sigma_m}$	$median_{i=1}^{L}\hat{s}_m^i$	$median_{i=1}^{L}\left|\hat{s}_m^i - \mu_m\right|$
Tanh	$\frac{1}{2}\left\{\tanh\left(0.01\left(\frac{s_m - \mu_m}{\sigma_m}\right)\right) + 1\right\}$	$\frac{1}{L_1}\sum_{i=1}^{L_1}\psi(\hat{s}_m^i)$	$\frac{1}{L_1}\sum_{i=1}^{L_1}\left(\psi(\hat{s}_m^i) - \mu_m\right)^2$

The simplest normalization technique is the *min-max* normalization. Min-max normalization is best suited for the case where the bounds (maximum and minimum values) of the scores produced by a matcher are known. In this case, one can easily transform the minimum and maximum scores to 0 and 1, respectively. However, even if the match scores are not bounded, the min-max normalization can be applied based on the minimum and maximum values estimated from the given set of training match scores. But this method is very sensitive to outliers in the training data. Min-max normalization retains the original shape of the score distribution except for a scaling factor and transforms all the scores into a common range $[0, 1]$. Distance scores can be transformed into similarity scores by subtracting the normalized score from 1.

Another commonly used score normalization technique is the *z-score* normalization that uses the arithmetic mean and standard deviation of the training data. Again, both mean and standard deviation statistics are sensitive to outliers in the training data. Z-score normalization does not guarantee a common numerical range for the normalized scores of the different matchers.

The *median* and *median absolute deviation* (MAD) statistics are insensitive to outliers as well as points in the extreme tails of the distribution. However, when the score distribution is not Gaussian, median and MAD are poor estimates of the location and scale parameters. Therefore, this normalization technique does not transform the scores into a common numerical range.

The tanh normalization uses the mean and standard deviation estimates of only the genuine scores as given by Hampel estimators. Hampel estimators are based on the following influence (ψ)-function:

$$\psi(u) = \begin{cases} u & 0 \leq |u| < a, \\ a * sign(u) & a \leq |u| < b, \\ a * sign(u) * \left(\frac{c - |u|}{c - b}\right) & b \leq |u| < c, \\ 0 & |u| \geq c, \end{cases} \quad (6.17)$$

where

$$sign\{u\} = \begin{cases} +1, & \text{if } u \geq 0, \\ -1, & \text{otherwise.} \end{cases}$$

A plot of the Hampel influence function is shown in Figure 6.25. The Hampel influence function reduces the influence of the scores at the tails of the distribution (identified by a, b, and c) during the estimation of the location and scale parameters. Hence, this method is not sensitive to outliers. However, if many of the points that constitute the tail of the distributions are discarded, the estimate may not be accurate. Therefore, the parameters a, b, and c must be carefully chosen depending on the amount of noise in the available training data.

Among the various transformation-based score fusion techniques available, the sum of scores decision rule is the most commonly used technique in multibiometric systems. This decision rule is often used in conjunction with min-max or z-score normalization techniques. While the sum of scores rule is simple, it is also quite robust to variations in the scores of the individual matchers, and this is the reason for its widespread usage. A modification of the sum of scores rule is the weighted sum of scores rule (or simply, weighted sum rule), where the combined match score is computed as a weighted sum of the normalized scores of the individual matchers. The rationale behind the weighted sum rule is that due to differences in the score distributions of the individual matchers, the proportionality constant in equation (6.15) may not be equal for all $m = 1, 2, \cdots, M$. Weights are assigned to scores of the individual matchers to alleviate this problem and these weights are often selected so as to optimize some criteria like the equal error rate or area under the ROC curve.

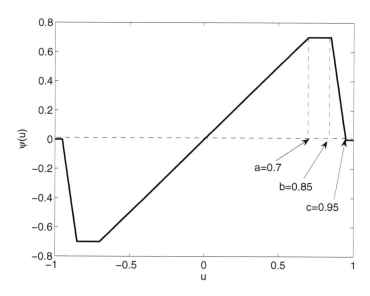

Fig. 6.25 An example of a Hampel influence function with $a = 0.7$, $b = 0.85$, and $c = 0.95$.

6.4.3.3 Score fusion based on other classification approaches

A number of other classification approaches can be used to indirectly learn the decision boundary between the genuine and impostor scores. Some examples include support vector machines (SVM), neural networks, k-nearest neighbor classifier, linear discriminant analysis, decision trees, and random forests. A detailed analysis of the various discriminative models is beyond the scope of this book. However, in the context of biometric systems, it is important to consider the following two issues while selecting the appropriate discriminative model:

- Unbalanced training set: The number of genuine match scores available for training is $O(N)$, but the number of impostor scores is $O(N^2)$, where N is the number of users in the training database. For example, if a multibiometric training database has N users and if each user provides t biometric samples, then the maximum number of genuine scores that can be obtained from this database is $Nt(t - 1)/2$. On the other hand, $(N(N - 1)t^2)/2$ impostor matches can be performed using the same database. Suppose that $N = 100$ and $t = 4$, the number of genuine scores available for training is only 600, while the number of impostor scores is 79,200.
- Cost of misclassification: Depending on the biometric application, the cost of accepting an impostor may be very different from the cost of rejecting a genuine user. For example, a biometric system deployed in a security application may be required to have a false accept rate (FAR) of less than 0.1%. Therefore, the fusion

strategy needs to minimize the false reject rate (FRR) at the specified FAR values rather than minimizing the total error rate (sum of FAR and FRR).

6.4.3.4 Score fusion in identification mode

The key difference between score fusion in the verification and identification modes is the structure of the match score data and the output decision. In a verification system, the score data is in the form of a vector $\mathbf{s} = [s_1, s_2, \cdots, s_M]$, where s_m represents the match score output by the mth matcher and it corresponds to a single claimed identity. The goal is to determine whether the identity claim comes from a "genuine" user or an "impostor" based on $\mathbf{s}$. On the other hand, the score data in an identification system is in the form of a $N \times M$ matrix $\mathbf{S} = [s_{n,m}]$, where $s_{n,m}$ is the match score output by the mth matcher corresponding to the nth identity. In this case, the objective is to assign an identity I_k to the user based on the score matrix $\mathbf{S}$.

With minor modifications, many of the decision rules designed for the verification scenario can also be extended to the identification mode. However, it is not straightforward to apply fusion schemes based on other discriminative models to the identification scenario. This is because multibiometric identification is a multi-class pattern classification problem, where the number of classes (N) can be very large.

Firstly, the minimum error rate decision rule for the identification mode is:

$$\text{Decide identity } I_k \text{ if } P(I_k|\mathbf{S}) > P(I_n|\mathbf{S}), \ \forall \, n = 1, 2, \cdots, N, k \neq n, \qquad (6.18)$$

where $P(I_n|\mathbf{S})$ is the posterior probability that the identity of the user is I_n given the score matrix $\mathbf{S}$. By applying the Bayes formula, the minimum error rate Bayes decision rule can be obtained as

$$\text{Decide identity } I_k \text{ if } P(I_k)p(\mathbf{S}|I_k) > P(I_n)p(\mathbf{S}|I_n), \ \forall \, n = 1, 2, \cdots, N, k \neq n, \quad (6.19)$$

where $p(\mathbf{S}|I_n)$ is the likelihood of observing the score matrix $\mathbf{S}$ given that the true identity is I_n and $P(I_n)$ is the prior probability of observing the identity I_n. If the prior probabilities for all the users are assumed to be equal, i.e., if $P(I_n) = (1/N)$, $\forall \, n = 1, 2, \cdots, N$, the minimum error rate decision rule can be simplified as follows:

$$\text{Decide identity } I_k \text{ if } p(\mathbf{S}|I_k) > p(\mathbf{S}|I_n), \ \forall \, n = 1, 2, \cdots, N, k \neq n. \qquad (6.20)$$

Ideally, the conditional density of $\mathbf{S}$ must be estimated individually for each user because it captures the complete information about dependencies between the scores assigned to the different users and the user-specific characteristics of the match scores. However, directly estimating the conditional density of $\mathbf{S}$ is not practical due to the following two reasons: (a) since $\mathbf{S}$ is a $N \times M$ dimensional matrix and N is usually quite large in identification scenarios (of the order of tens of millions), estimating the density of $\mathbf{S}$ requires a large number of training samples for each user, which is not feasible; and (b) the density of $\mathbf{S}$ needs to be re-estimated frequently due to changes in the list of enrollees.

If the match scores for different persons are assumed to be statistically independent, the likelihood $p(\mathbf{S}|I_n)$ can be simplified as

$$p(\mathbf{S}|I_n) = \prod_{j=1}^{N} p(\mathbf{s}_{j,.}|I_n) = p(\mathbf{s}_{n,.}|I_n) \prod_{j=1,j\neq n}^{N} p(\mathbf{s}_{j,.}|I_n). \qquad (6.21)$$

Here, $\mathbf{s}_{n,.}$ represents the nth row of the score matrix $\mathbf{S}$, $p(\mathbf{s}_{n,.}|I_n)$ is the density of genuine match scores corresponding to user I_n and $p(\mathbf{s}_{j,.}|I_n), j \neq n$ are the densities of the impostor scores when the claimed identity is I_n. However, when the genuine (impostor) match scores of all users are assumed to be identically distributed, $p(\mathbf{s}_{n,.}|I_n) = p(\mathbf{s}|\omega_1)$ and $p(\mathbf{s}_{j,.}|I_n) = p(\mathbf{s}|\omega_0), j = 1,2,\cdots,N$, and $j \neq n$. Under this assumption, equation (6.21) can be further simplified as

$$p(\mathbf{S}|I_n) = p(\mathbf{s}_{n,.}|\omega_1) \prod_{j=1,j\neq n}^{N} p(\mathbf{s}_{j,.}|\omega_0) = \frac{p(\mathbf{s}_{n,.}|\omega_1)}{p(\mathbf{s}_{n,.}|\omega_0)} \prod_{j=1}^{N} p(\mathbf{s}_{j,.}|\omega_1). \qquad (6.22)$$

Now, the likelihood of observing the score matrix $\mathbf{S}$ given that the true identity is I_n is proportional to the likelihood ratio used in the verification scenario. Hence, the minimum error rate decision rule can be simplified as

$$\text{Decide identity } I_k \text{ if } \frac{p(\mathbf{s}_{k,.}|\omega_1)}{p(\mathbf{s}_{k,.}|\omega_0)} > \frac{p(\mathbf{s}_{n,.}|\omega_1)}{p(\mathbf{s}_{n,.}|\omega_0)}, \ \forall\, n = 1,2,\cdots,N. \qquad (6.23)$$

Furthermore, if the scores of different matchers are assumed to be conditionally independent, one can estimate the joint density of the genuine (impostor) match scores by the product of the marginal densities. Hence, the decision rule in equation (6.23) can be restated as

$$\text{Decide identity } I_k \text{ if } \prod_{m=1}^{M} \frac{p(s_{k,m}|\omega_1)}{p(s_{k,m}|\omega_0)} > \prod_{m=1}^{M} \frac{p(s_{n,m}|\omega_1)}{p(s_{n,m}|\omega_0)}, \ \forall\, n = 1,2,\cdots,N. \qquad (6.24)$$

Equations (6.23) and (6.24) can be considered as the likelihood-ratio-based decision rules for the identification scenario. Similarly, it is also possible to extend the transformation based score fusion schemes for identification. For example, the sum of scores decision rule for multibiometric identification can be stated as follows:

$$\text{Decide identity } I_k \text{ if } \sum_{m=1}^{M} g_m(s_{k,m}) > \sum_{m=1}^{M} g_m(s_{n,m}), \ \forall\, n = 1,2,\cdots,N. \qquad (6.25)$$

6.4.3.5 Quality-based score fusion

The quality of acquired biometric data directly affects the ability of a biometric matcher to perform the matching process effectively. Estimating the quality of a biometric sample and predicting the performance of a biometric matcher based on the estimated quality can be very useful in building robust multibiometric systems. This will allow dynamic assignment of weights to the individual biometric matchers based on the quality of the input sample to be verified. For example, consider a bimodal biometric system with iris and fingerprint as the two modalities. Suppose that during a particular access attempt by the user, the iris image is of poor quality but the fingerprint image quality is sufficiently good. In this case, a higher weight can be assigned to the fingerprint match score and a lower weight to the iris match score.

One method to perform quality-based fusion is to incorporate sample quality into the likelihood-ratio-based score fusion framework. Since a poor quality sample will be difficult to classify as genuine or impostor (see Figure 6.26), the likelihood ratio for such a sample will be close to 1. On the other hand, for good quality samples, the likelihood ratio will be greater than 1 for genuine users and less than 1 for impostors. Hence, the likelihood ratios resulting from the use of joint density of the match score and the associated quality will be implicity weighted by the respective sample quality.

If the M biometric matchers are assumed to be independent, the quality-based likelihood ratio fusion rule can be expressed as follows:

$$\text{Decide } \omega_1 \text{ if } \prod_{m=1}^{M} \frac{p(s_m, q_m | \omega_1)}{p(s_m, q_m | \omega_0)} \geq \eta, \tag{6.26}$$

where q_m is the quality of the match provided by the mth matcher, for $m = 1, \ldots, M$, $p(s_m, q_m | \omega_1)$ and $p(s_m, q_m | \omega_0)$ are the joint densities of the match score and the quality estimated from the genuine and impostor training scores, respectively, of the mth matcher.

Quality information can also be incorporated into transformation-based fusion schemes and methods based on other discriminative models. For example, the quality data can be used to dynamically modify the weights assigned to the different matchers in the weighted sum rule. Similarly, the quality values can be used to alter the cost of misclassification errors while training a support vector machine (SVM) classifier.

6.4.4 Rank-level fusion

When a biometric system operates in the identification mode, the output of the system can be viewed as a ranking of the enrolled identities. In this case, the output indicates the set of possible matching identities sorted in decreasing order of con-

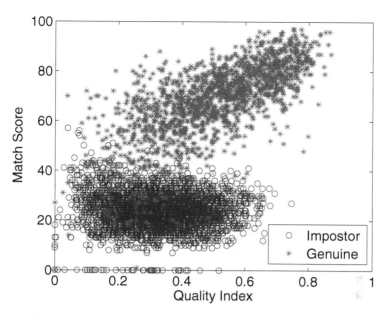

Fig. 6.26 Variations in match scores with respect to image quality for the fingerprint modality (adapted from [22]). Note that the genuine and impostor match scores are well-separated only for good quality (with quality index > 0.5) samples. The observed score distributions may be different if a different fingerprint matcher or quality index is used.

fidence. The goal of rank-level fusion schemes is to consolidate all the ranks output by the individual biometric subsystems in order to derive a consensus rank for each identity. Ranks provide more insight into the decision-making process of the matcher compared to just the identity of the best match, but they reveal less information than match scores. However, unlike match scores, the rankings output by multiple biometric systems are comparable. As a result, no normalization is needed and this makes the rank-level fusion schemes simpler to implement compared to the score-level fusion techniques.

Let $\mathbf{R} = [r_{n,m}]$ be the rank matrix in a multibiometric system, where $r_{n,m}$ is the rank assigned to identity I_n by the mth matcher, $m = 1, \cdots, M$ and $n = 1, \cdots, N$. Let $\hat{r}_n$ be a statistic computed for user I_n such that the user with the lowest value of $\hat{r}$ is assigned the highest consensus (or reordered) rank. The following three well-known methods can be used to compute the statistic $\hat{r}$.

Highest Rank Method: In the highest rank method, each user is assigned the highest rank (minimum r value) as computed by different matchers, i.e., the statistic for user I_n is

$$\hat{r}_n = \min_{m=1}^{M} r_{n,m}. \tag{6.27}$$

Ties are broken randomly to arrive at a strict ranking order. This method is useful only when the number of users is large compared to the number of matchers, which is usually the case in biometric identification systems. If this condition is not satisfied, most of the users will have ties rendering the final ranking uninformative. An advantage of the highest rank method is that it can utilize the strength of each matcher effectively. Even if only one matcher assigns a high rank to the correct user, it is still very likely that the correct user will receive a high rank after reordering.

Borda Count Method: The Borda count method uses the sum of the ranks assigned by the individual matchers to calculate the value of $\hat{r}$, i.e., the statistic for user I_n is

$$\hat{r}_n = \sum_{m=1}^{M} r_{n,m}. \tag{6.28}$$

The magnitude of the Borda count for each user is a measure of the degree of agreement among the different matchers on whether the input belongs to that user. The Borda count method assumes that the ranks assigned to the users by the matchers are statistically independent and all the matchers perform equally well.

Logistic Regression Method: The logistic regression method is a generalization of the Borda count method where a weighted sum of the individual ranks is calculated, i.e., the statistic for user I_n is

$$\hat{r}_k = \sum_{m=1}^{M} w_m r_{n,m}. \tag{6.29}$$

The weight, w_m, to be assigned to the mth matcher, $m = 1, \ldots, M$, is determined by logistic regression. The logistic regression method is useful when the different biometric matchers have significant differences in their accuracies. One limitation of this method is that it requires a training phase to determine the weights.

Figure 6.27 presents a simple example to illustrate the three rank level fusion techniques discussed above. For a given query face image, two face recognition algorithms rank the four users in the database based on their similarity. The fused score column in Figure 6.27 represents the value of $\hat{r}_n$. When the highest rank method is used, there is a tie for rank 1 between users "Alice" and "Bob". In this example, the reordered ranks were obtained by breaking the ties randomly. Since the highest rank and Borda count methods assume that both face matchers perform equally well, the reordered ranks tend to be a mixture of the ranks assigned individually by the two matchers. On the other hand, the logistic regression method assigns a higher weight to the ranks provided by the more accurate matcher. As a result, the reordered ranks can be expected to be similar to the ones provided by the matcher with a higher accuracy. In the example shown in Figure 6.27, the matcher 1 is more accurate than matcher 2. Therefore, a weight of 0.8 is assigned to it and due to this significant difference in the weights, the reordered ranks in the logistic regression case are exactly the same as the ranks assigned by the matcher 1.

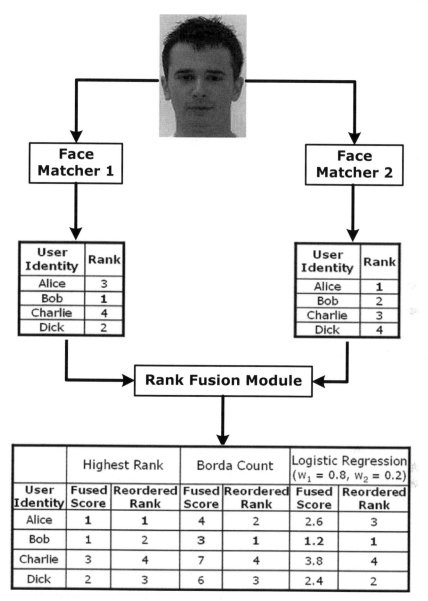

Fig. 6.27 An illustration of rank-level fusion as performed by the highest rank method, Borda count, and logistic regression. In this example, the three fusion schemes assign different consensus ranks to the individual identities.

6.4.5 Decision-level fusion

In a multibiometric system, fusion is carried out at the *abstract* or *decision* level when only the decisions output by the individual biometric matchers are available. For example, many commercial off-the-shelf (COTS) biometric matchers provide access only to the final recognition decision. When such COTS matchers are used to build a multibiometric system, only decision-level fusion is feasible. Methods proposed in the literature for decision-level fusion include "AND" and "OR" rules, majority voting, weighted majority voting, Bayesian decision fusion, the Dempster-Shafer theory of evidence, and behavior knowledge space.

"AND" and "OR" Rules: In a multibiometric verification system, the simplest method of combining decisions output by the different matchers is to use the AND and OR rules. The output of the AND rule is a "match" only when all the M biometric matchers agree that the input sample matches with the template. On the contrary, the OR rule outputs a "match" decision as long as at least one of the M matchers decides that the input sample matches with the template. The limitation of these two rules is their tendency to result in extreme operating points. When the AND rule is applied, the False Accept Rate (FAR) of the multibiometric system is extremely low (lower than the FAR of the individual matchers) while the False Reject Rate (FRR) is high (greater than the FRR of the individual matchers). Similarly, the OR rule leads to higher FAR and lower FRR than the individual matchers. When one biometric matcher has a substantially higher equal error rate compared to the other matcher, the combination of the two matchers using AND and OR rules may actually degrade the overall performance. Due to this phenomenon, the AND and OR decision fusion rules are rarely used in practical multibiometric systems.

Majority Voting: The most common approach for decision-level fusion is majority voting where the input biometric sample is assigned to that class ("genuine" or "impostor" for verification systems and identity I_k for identification systems) on which a majority of the matchers agree. If there are M biometric matchers, the input sample is assigned to a class if at least $\hat{m}$ of the matchers agree on that class, where

$$\hat{m} = \begin{cases} \frac{M}{2} + 1 & \text{if } M \text{ is even,} \\ \frac{M+1}{2} & \text{otherwise.} \end{cases} \quad (6.30)$$

When none of the classes is supported by $\hat{m}$ matchers, a "reject" decision is output by the system. Majority voting assumes that all the matchers perform equally well. The advantages of majority voting are: (a) no apriori knowledge about the matchers is needed, and (b) no training is required to come up with the final decision. The example shown in Figure 6.28 is a simple illustration of the majority voting scheme, where three face recognition matchers are used. In the identification mode, two of the three matchers identify the user as "Bob". Therefore, the final identity decision after fusion is also "Bob". Similarly, in the verification mode, since two of

the three matchers decide that the input face image matches with the template of the
claimed identity, namely "Bob", the final decision after fusion is "genuine".

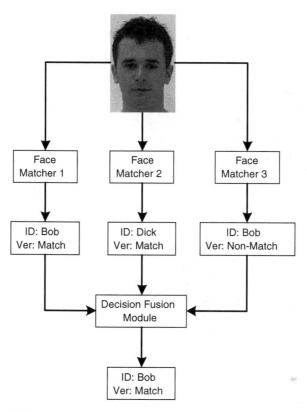

Fig. 6.28 Flow of information when decisions provided by multiple biometric matchers are combined using the majority vote fusion scheme. Here "ID" and "Ver" represent the identification and verification modes of recognition operation, respectively. For the verification mode, the claimed identity is Bob.

Weighted Majority Voting: When the matchers used in a multibiometric system do not have similar recognition accuracy, it is reasonable to assign higher weights to the decisions made by the more accurate matchers. In order to facilitate this weighting, the labels output by the individual matchers are converted into degrees of support as follows.

$$\tilde{s}_{n,m} = \begin{cases} 1, & \text{if output of the } m^{th} \text{ matcher is class } n, \\ 0, & \text{otherwise,} \end{cases} \qquad (6.31)$$

where $m = 1, \ldots, M$ and $n = 0, 1$ for verification or $n = 1, 2, \cdots, N$ for identification. The decision rule based on weighted voting can be stated as

$$\text{Decide in favor of class } k \text{ if } \sum_{m=1}^{M} w_m \tilde{s}_{k,m} > \sum_{m=1}^{M} w_m \tilde{s}_{n,m}, \ \forall \ n, \ k \neq n, \qquad (6.32)$$

where w_m is the weight assigned to the mth matcher.

Bayesian Decision Fusion: The Bayesian decision fusion scheme relies on transforming the discrete decision labels output by the individual matchers into continuous probability values. The first step in the transformation is the generation of the confusion matrix for each matcher by applying the matcher to a training set D. Consider a multibiometric verification system. Let C^m be the 2×2 confusion matrix for the mth matcher. The (j,k)th element of the matrix C^m (denoted as $c_{j,k}^{m}$) is the number of instances in the training data set where a pattern whose true class label is ω_j is assigned to the class ω_k by the mth matcher, where $j, k = 0, 1$. Let the total number of samples in D be L and the number of elements that belong to class ω_j be L_j.

Let $u_m \in \{0, 1\}$ be the class label assigned to the test sample by the mth matcher. The value $c_{j,u_m}^m / L_j$ can be considered as an estimate of the conditional probability $P(u_m | \omega_j)$ and L_j / L can be treated as an estimate of the prior probability of class ω_j. Given the vector of decisions made by M matchers $\mathbf{u} = [u_1, u_2, \cdots, u_M]$, the posterior probability of class ω_j, i.e., $P(\omega_j | \mathbf{u})$ can be calculated according to the Bayes rule as follows:

$$P(\omega_j | \mathbf{u}) = \frac{P(\mathbf{u} | \omega_j) P(\omega_j)}{P(\mathbf{u})}, \qquad (6.33)$$

where $j = 0, 1$ and $P(\mathbf{u}) = \sum_{j=0}^{1} P(\mathbf{u} | \omega_j) P(\omega_j)$. Therefore, the minimum error rate Bayes decision rule can be stated as

$$\text{Decide } \omega_1 \text{ if } P(\mathbf{u} | \omega_1) P(\omega_1) > P(\mathbf{u} | \omega_0) P(\omega_0). \qquad (6.34)$$

To simplify the computation of $P(\mathbf{u} | \omega_j)$, one can assume statistical independence between the different matchers. Under this assumption, $P(\mathbf{u} | \omega_j)$ is the product of the marginal probabilities, i.e.,

$$P(\mathbf{u} | \omega_j) = P(u_1, u_2, \cdots, u_M | \omega_j) = \prod_{m=1}^{M} P(u_m | \omega_j). \qquad (6.35)$$

Under the independence assumption, the decision rule is known as naive Bayes rule, which can be expressed as

$$\text{Decide } \omega_1 \text{ if } P(\omega_1) \prod_{m=1}^{M} P(u_m | \omega_1) > P(\omega_0) \prod_{m=1}^{M} P(u_m | \omega_0). \qquad (6.36)$$

Note that by changing the matching threshold τ_m for the mth biometric matcher, it is possible to vary the probabilities $P(u_m|\omega_j)$ of that specific matcher. However, in a multibiometric system the goal is to minimize the global error rate (the overall error rate of the multibiometric system after the fusion of decisions from the individual biometric matchers). Therefore, one must find an optimal solution for the local thresholds $\{\tau_1, \tau_2 \cdots, \tau_M\}$ such that the global error rate is minimized.

6.5 Summary

Multibiometric systems are expected to alleviate some of the limitations of unibiometric systems by consolidating the evidence presented by several different biometric sources. The integration of evidence in a multibiometric system is known as information fusion and, if appropriately implemented, can enhance the matching accuracy of a biometric recognition system. Apart from improving the matching accuracy, a properly designed multibiometric system can also increase population coverage (namely, reduce the failure to enroll rate), provide flexibility, and deter spoofing activities.

The design of a multibiometric system is governed by several factors, including the available sources of information, the acquisition and processing sequence to be adopted, the type of information to be combined, and the fusion strategy to be employed. Multibiometric systems can exploit the complementary strengths of different biometric sources such as multiple sensors, multiple representation schemes or features and matching algorithms, multiple instances or samples of the same biometric trait, and multiple traits. Generally, it is difficult to predict the optimal sources of biometric information relevant for a particular application and the appropriate fusion methodology based on recognition performance alone. Factors such as cost of system deployment, throughput time, user convenience, scalability, etc. also play a large role in selecting the sources of biometric information and adopting a particular fusion strategy.

Information fusion in biometrics can be accomplished at several levels. In this chapter, several fusion strategies pertaining to the sensor, feature set, match score, rank, and decision levels were introduced. Typically, early integration strategies (e.g., sensor or feature-level) are expected to result in better performance than late integration (e.g., score-level) strategies. However, it is difficult to predict the performance gain due to each of these strategies prior to invoking the specific fusion methodology. Fusion at the score level usually offers the best tradeoff between information content and ease of fusion. Hence, score-level fusion has been adopted by several practical multibiometric systems. A wide variety of score-level fusion techniques have been proposed in the literature and the performance of each scheme depends on the amount and quality of the available training data.

While the *availability* of multiple sources of biometric information (pertaining either to a single trait or to multiple traits) may present a compelling case for fusion, the *correlation* between the sources needs to be examined before determining their suitability for fusion. Combining uncorrelated or negatively correlated sources that make complementary errors is expected to result in a better improvement in matching performance than combining positively correlated sources. Apart from the dependence between the sources, the performance disparity between individual sources of information also impacts the matching accuracy of the fusion scheme. If the performance disparity between component matchers is large and if the fusion scheme fails to account for this disparity, then the performance of the "stronger" matcher *may* be diluted by the "weaker" one. This may also have an impact on the security of the biometric system because it may be possible to circumvent the system by spoofing just the "weaker" modality.

Finally, the development of a robust human computer interface (HCI) is necessary to permit the efficient acquisition of multibiometric data from individuals. A HCI that is easy to use can result in rapid user habituation and promote the acquisition of high quality biometric data, thereby reducing the error rates. With the increased use of biometrics in authentication applications and ever increasing demand for higher matching accuracies, multibiometric systems are now being considered as the next-generation biometric solution in a variety of government, military, and commercial person recognition systems.

Bibliographical and Historical Remarks

Multibiometric systems have a long history of usage in person recognition applications. In fact, the first person identification system advocated by Alphonse Bertillon in the late 19th century can be considered as a multibiometric system because it relies on accumulating evidence from several anthropometric measurements of the human body. Fingerprint identification systems have also been using prints from all the 10 fingers for more than 100 years. The problem of information fusion and the theory of multi-classifier systems have been rigorously studied for a fairly long time [17, 7]. However, the formal study of various intricacies involved in the design of multibiometric systems has been actively pursued only in the last two decades, coinciding with the growing popularity of biometric systems in a number of civilian and government applications.

Some of the earliest multimodal biometric systems utilized face and voice features (together called "talking heads") to establish the identity of an individual [2]. Another interesting multimodal combination is the fusion of fingerprint and face [33] because of its application in biometric passports. Some of the other multimodal combinations that have received attention in the literature include (a) fingerprint and hand-geometry, (b) fingerprint, palmprint and hand-geometry [32], (c) fingerprint and voice [35], (d) face and iris [36], (e) face and gait [13], and (f) face and ear. One of the reasons for considering these specific combinations could be that it is possible to design sensors that can capture these multiple traits simultaneously.

Multi-sensor systems have been quite popular in the face recognition domain. The early multi-sensor face recognition systems used visible and infrared cameras to capture the 2-dimensional (2D) representation of the face [34] for the purpose of tackling illumination variations. Later systems employed a 2D camera as well as range scanner to record the 3-dimensional (3D) texture pattern of the face [3]. The use of all the three sensors, namely, 2D camera, infrared camera, and range sensor has also been attempted [4]. Fusion of facial information from the red, green, and blue channels of a camera is also possible [15]. Among the other biometric traits, capture of fingerprints using both optical and capacitive sensor technologies has been proposed [20].

Numerous multi-algorithm systems have been designed for different multibiometric traits. For example, minutiae and texture features have been used for fingerprint recognition [30]. Similarly, a combination of features extracted using different subspace analysis techniques like PCA and LDA can be used for recognizing faces [29]. Different combinations of features extracted from the human voice and different matching algorithms have been utilized in the field of speaker recognition [27]. Fusion of multiple representations including geometry, line, appearance, and texture-based features have been attempted in the case of palmprints [16].

Most modern large-scale AFIS systems, including the FBI-IAFIS and DHS-IDENT systems use fingerprint information from multiple fingers for identification. Mosaicing of multiple fingerprint impressions at the image and feature levels has also been studied [21]. Accumulation of identity information over a sequence of face images contained in a video [40] is also an example of multi-sample system.

The taxonomy of multibiometric systems in terms of the levels of fusion has its origin in the early literature on distributed sensor systems [10], and was later adapted in the context of multibiometrics. Feature-level fusion is a relatively less explored topic, with limited work being done on both homogeneous [21] and heterogeneous feature fusion [39]. On the other hand, there is a huge volume of literature on score- and decision-level fusion.

Both the formalism of Bayesian decision theory and the hypothesis testing framework [19] of Neyman-Pearson have been in use for a long time in the area of statistical pattern recognition [5]. The likelihood-ratio-based score fusion scheme has been employed by various researchers with different density estimation techniques that fall under the parametric, semi-parametric [22, 23], and non-parametric [25] approaches. Kittler et al. [14] pioneered the work on classifier combination rules. The effects of various score normalization schemes have also been elaborately studied [11]. A number of other discriminative models have been proposed for score-level fusion in multibiometric systems. The work on quality-based fusion includes likelihood-ratio-based techniques [22], transformation-based schemes [1], and methods based on other discriminative models [6].

The work of Ho et al. [8] stands out in the case of rank-level fusion. Literature on decision-level fusion includes AND and OR rules, majority voting [18], weighted majority voting [17], Bayesian decision fusion [38], Dempster-Shafer theory of evidence [28], and behavior knowledge space [9]. An analysis of the effect of dependence between classifiers/matchers on fusion performance can be found in [24]. Readers who wish to read a comprehensive review and in-depth analysis of multibiometric systems should consult the *Handbook of Multibiometrics* [31].

Table 6.4 List of multimodal biometric databases available in the public domain.

Database Name	Available Modalities	Number of Subjects
BT-DAVID	Face, voice, and lip movement	100
M2VTS	Face, voice, and lip movement	37
XM2VTS	Face, voice, and lip movement	295
BANCA	Face and voice	208
BIOMET	Face, voice, fingerprint, hand shape, and online signature	91-130
MCYT	Face, all 10 fingers, signature	330
UND	Face (2D and 3D) and ear	80-350
NIST-BSSR1	Face and 2 fingers (only match scores are available)	517

The performance metrics of a biometric system such as accuracy, throughput, and scalability can be estimated with a high degree of confidence only when the system is tested on a large representative database. However, current multimodal biometric systems have been tested only on small databases containing fewer than 1,000 individuals. This is mainly due to the absence of legacy multimodal databases and the cost and effort involved in collecting a large multimodal biometric database. Some of the multimodal biometric databases that are available in the public domain are summarized in Table 6.4. To overcome the non-availability of large multimodal databases, researchers often use "virtual" multimodal databases, which are created by consistently pairing a user from one unimodal database (e.g., face) with a user from another database (e.g., fingerprint). The creation of such virtual users is based on the assumption that different biometric traits of the same person are independent. Apart from the eight multimodal biometric databases described in Table 6.4, several unimodal biometric databases are also available in the public domain. Some of the commonly used unimodal biometric databases are the Fingerprint Verification Competition (FVC) databases, the Carnegie Mellon University Pose, Illumination, and Expression (CMU-PIE) face database, the FERET face database and the Chinese Academy of Sciences - Institute of Automation (CASIA) iris image database. These unimodal biometric databases can be used for evaluating multi-sensor, multi-instance, multi-sample, and multi-algorithm biometric systems.

References

1. E. S. Bigun, J. Bigun, B. Duc, and S. Fischer. Expert Conciliation for Multimodal Person Authentication Systems using Bayesian Statistics. In *Proceedings of First International Conference on Audio- and Video-Based Biometric Person Authentication (AVBPA)*, pages 291–300, Crans-Montana, Switzerland, March 1997.

2. R. Brunelli and D. Falavigna. Person Identification Using Multiple Cues. *IEEE Transactions on Pattern Analysis and Machine Intelligence*, 17(10):955–966, October 1995.

3. K. I. Chang, K. W. Bowyer, and P. J. Flynn. An Evaluation of Multimodal 2D+3D Face Biometrics. *IEEE Transactions on Pattern Analysis and Machine Intelligence*, 27(4):619–624, April 2005.

4. K. I. Chang, K. W. Bowyer, P. J. Flynn, and X. Chen. Multibiometrics Using Facial Appearance, Shape and Temperature. In *Sixth IEEE International Conference on Automatic Face and Gesture Recognition*, pages 43–48, Seoul, Korea, May 2004.

5. R. O. Duda, P. E. Hart, and D. G. Stork. *Pattern Classification*. John Wiley & Sons, 2001.

6. J. Fierrez-Aguilar, J. Ortega-Garcia, J. Gonzalez-Rodriguez, and J. Bigun. Discriminative Multimodal Biometric Authentication based on Quality Measures. *Pattern Recognition*, 38(5):777–779, May 2005.

7. T. K. Ho. Multiple Classifier Combination: Lessons and Next Steps. In H. Bunke and A. Kandel, editors, *Hybrid Methods in Pattern Recognition*, volume 47 of *Machine Perception and Artificial Intelligence*, pages 171–198. World Scientific, 2002.

8. T. K. Ho, J. J. Hull, and S. N. Srihari. Decision Combination in Multiple Classifier Systems. *IEEE Transactions on Pattern Analysis and Machine Intelligence*, 16(1):66–75, January 1994.

9. Y. S. Huang and C. Y. Suen. Method of Combining Multiple Experts for the Recognition of Unconstrained Handwritten Numerals. *IEEE Transactions on Pattern Analysis and Machine Intelligence*, 17(1):90–94, January 1995.

10. S. S. Iyengar, L. Prasad, and H. Min. *Advances in Distributed Sensor Technology*. Prentice Hall, 1995.

11. A. K. Jain, K. Nandakumar, and A. Ross. Score Normalization in Multimodal Biometric Systems. *Pattern Recognition*, 38(12):2270–2285, December 2005.

12. A. K. Jain and D. Zongker. Feature Selection: Evaluation, Application, and Small Sample Performance. *IEEE Transactions on Pattern Analysis and Machine Intelligence*, 19(2):153–158, February 1997.

13. A. Kale, A. K. RoyChowdhury, and R. Chellappa. Fusion of Gait and Face for Human Identification. In *IEEE International Conference on Acoustics, Speech, and Signal Processing (ICASSP)*, volume 5, pages 901–904, Montreal, Canada, May 2004.

14. J. Kittler, M. Hatef, R. P. Duin, and J. G. Matas. On Combining Classifiers. *IEEE Transactions on Pattern Analysis and Machine Intelligence*, 20(3):226–239, March 1998.

15. J. Kittler and M. Sadeghi. Physics-based Decorrelation of Image Data for Decision Level Fusion in Face Verification. In *Fifth International Workshop on Multiple Classifier Systems*, pages 354–363, Cagliari, Italy, June 2004.

16. A. Kumar and D. Zhang. Personal Authentication using Multiple Palmprint Representation. *Pattern Recognition*, 38(10):1695–1704, October 2005.

17. L. I. Kuncheva. *Combining Pattern Classifiers - Methods and Algorithms*. Wiley, 2004.

18. L. Lam and C. Y. Suen. Application of Majority Voting to Pattern Recognition: An Analysis of its Behavior and Performance. *IEEE Transactions on Systems, Man, and Cybernetics, Part A: Systems and Humans*, 27(5):553–568, 1997.

19. E. L. Lehmann and J. P. Romano. *Testing Statistical Hypotheses*. Springer, 2005.

20. G. L. Marcialis and F. Roli. Fingerprint Verification by Fusion of Optical and Capacitive Sensors. *Pattern Recognition Letters*, 25(11):1315–1322, August 2004.

21. Y. S. Moon, H. W. Yeung, K. C. Chan, and S. O. Chan. Template Synthesis and Image Mosaicking for Fingerprint Registration: An Experimental Study. In *IEEE International Conference on Acoustics, Speech, and Signal Processing (ICASSP)*, volume 5, pages 409–412, Montreal, Canada, May 2004.

22. K. Nandakumar, Y. Chen, S. C. Dass, and A. K. Jain. Likelihood Ratio Based Biometric Score Fusion. *IEEE Transactions on Pattern Analysis and Machine Intelligence*, 30(2):342–347, February 2008.

23. N. Poh and S. Bengio. A Score-Level Fusion Benchmark Database for Biometric Authentication. In *Fifth International Conference on Audio- and Video-based Biometric Person Authentication (AVBPA)*, pages 1059–1070, Rye Brook, USA, July 2005.

24. N. Poh and S. Bengio. How Do Correlation and Variance of Base-Experts Affect Fusion in Biometric Authentication Tasks? *IEEE Transactions on Signal Processing*, 53(11):4384–4396, November 2005.

25. S. Prabhakar and A. K. Jain. Decision-level Fusion in Fingerprint Verification. *Pattern Recognition*, 35(4):861–874, April 2002.

26. National Institute of Standards and Technology. NIST Biometric Scores Set. Available at `http://http://www.itl.nist.gov/iad/894.03/biometricscores`, 2004.

27. D. Reynolds, W. Andrews, J. Campbell, J. Navratil, B. Peskin, A. Adami, Q. Jin, D. Klusacek, J. Abramson, R. Mihaescu, J. Godfrey, D. Jones, and B. Xiang. The SuperSID Project: Exploiting High-level Information for High-accuracy Speaker Recognition. In *IEEE International Conference on Acoustics, Speech, and Signal Processing (ICASSP)*, pages 784–787, Hong Kong, China, April 2003.

28. G. Rogova. Combining the results of several neural network classifiers. *Neural Networks*, 7(5):777–781, 1994.

29. A. Ross and R. Govindarajan. Feature Level Fusion Using Hand and Face Biometrics. In *Proceedings of SPIE Conference on Biometric Technology for Human Identification II*, volume 5779, pages 196–204, Orlando, USA, March 2005.

30. A. Ross, A. K. Jain, and J. Reisman. A Hybrid Fingerprint Matcher. *Pattern Recognition*, 36(7):1661–1673, July 2003.

31. A. Ross, K. Nandakumar, and A. K. Jain. *Handbook of Multibiometrics*. Springer, 2006.

32. R. K. Rowe, U. Uludag, M. Demirkus, S. Parthasaradhi, and A. K. Jain. A Multispectral Whole-hand Biometric Authentication System. In *Proceedings of Biometric Symposium, Biometric Consortium Conference*, Baltimore, USA, September 2007.

33. R. Snelick, U. Uludag, A. Mink, M. Indovina, and A. K. Jain. Large Scale Evaluation of Multimodal Biometric Authentication Using State-of-the-Art Systems. *IEEE Transactions on Pattern Analysis and Machine Intelligence*, 27(3):450–455, March 2005.

34. D. A. Socolinsky, A. Selinger, and J. D. Neuheisel. Face Recognition with Visible and Thermal Infrared Imagery. *Computer Vision and Image Understanding*, 91(1-2):72–114, July-August 2003.

35. K.-A. Toh, X. Jiang, and W.-Y. Yau. Exploiting Global and Local Decisions for Multimodal Biometrics Verification. *IEEE Transactions on Signal Processing, (Supplement on Secure Media)*, 52(10):3059–3072, October 2004.

36. Y. Wang, T. Tan, and A. K. Jain. Combining Face and Iris Biometrics for Identity Verification. In *Fourth International Conference on Audio- and Video-based Biometric Person Authentication (AVBPA)*, pages 805–813, Guildford, UK, June 2003.

37. C. Wilson, A. R. Hicklin, M. Bone, H. Korves, P. Grother, B. Ulery, R. Micheals, M. Zoepfl, S. Otto, and C. Watson. Fingerprint Vendor Technology Evaluation 2003: Summary of Results and Analysis Report. Technical Report NISTIR 7123, NIST, June 2004.

38. L. Xu, A. Krzyzak, and C. Y. Suen. Methods for Combining Multiple Classifiers and their Applications to Handwriting Recognition. *IEEE Transactions on Systems, Man, and Cybernetics*, 22(3):418–435, 1992.

39. J. Yang, J.-Y. Yang, D. Zhang, and J.-F. Lu. Feature Fusion: Parallel Strategy vs. Serial Strategy. *Pattern Recognition*, 38(6):1369–1381, June 2003.

40. S. Zhou, V. Krueger, and R. Chellappa. Probabilistic Recognition of Human Faces from Video. *Computer Vision and Image Understanding*, 91(1-2):214–245, July-August 2003.

Chapter 7
SECURITY OF BIOMETRIC SYSTEMS

"Security is, I would say, our top priority because for all the exciting things you will be able to do with computers.. organizing your lives, staying in touch with people, being creative.. if we don't solve these security problems, then people will hold back. Businesses will be afraid to put their critical information on it because it will be exposed."

Bill Gates (2005)

The primary reasons for using biometric recognition are to apprehend criminals, curtail financial fraud, secure national borders, or control access to physical facilities and logical resources. When the biometric system fails to meet these objectives, the security of the system is said to be breached. This breach of security can be in the form of denial-of-service to legitimate users, intrusion by unauthorized users, repudiation claims by authorized users, or misuse of the biometric data for unintended purposes. Security failures can occur either due to intrinsic limitations of the biometric system or due to explicit attacks by adversaries, who may be insiders (e.g., administrators and legitimate users) or external attackers. The objective of this chapter is to outline the common attacks against biometric systems and discuss techniques that can be employed to counter them. In particular, this chapter will focus on two of the most well-known attacks that are specific to biometric systems, namely, spoofing of biometric traits and leakage of biometric data. Liveness detection and biometric template security algorithms that can mitigate the above two threats will be discussed in detail.

7.1 Introduction

A natural question that arises in biometric recognition is which biometric system is "best" suited for a particular application. Of course, the answer to this question depends not only on technical merits and limitations of the biometric system (e.g., matching accuracy and throughput), but also on other socio-economic factors like user acceptability and system cost. However, given that all other factors are equal, one would obviously prefer a biometric system that has the least probability of failure. But what exactly constitutes a biometric system failure? Recall that in most applications, the primary purpose of using biometrics is to provide non-repudiable authentication. Authentication implies that (a) only legitimate or authorized users are able to access the physical or logical resources protected by the biometric system and (b) impostors are prevented from accessing the protected facilities or information. Non-repudiation ensures that an individual who accesses a certain resource cannot later deny using it. Thus, the *integrity* of a biometric system is determined by its ability to guarantee non-repudiable authentication.

From the perspective of the users, there are two additional requirements that a biometric system must meet. Firstly, the legitimate users must have timely and reliable access to the protected resource/service. This is referred to as the *availability* of the biometric system. Secondly, the biometric system and the personal data stored in it must be used only for the intended functionality, which is to control access to a specific resource and not for other unintended purposes. This is known as the *confidentiality* requirement. When one or more of the above three expectations (integrity, availability, and confidentiality) are not met, the biometric system is deemed to have failed.

Failure of a biometric system generally leads to a breach of security in applications or facilities that it is designed to protect. A security threat in a biometric system refers to the possibility of system failure. Depending on the type of failure, these security threats can be classified into four major classes (see Figure 7.1).

- **Denial-of-service (DoS)**: Legitimate users are prevented from obtaining access to the system or resource that they are entitled to, thereby causing inconvenience to genuine users. This violates the availability requirement. Frequent denial-of-service is likely to eventually drive the users towards abandoning the biometric system altogether.

- **Intrusion**: An unauthorized user gains illegitimate access to the system. Since intrusion affects the basic integrity of a biometric system, it is generally considered the most serious security threat.

- **Repudiation**: A legitimate user denies using the system after having accessed it. Corrupt users may deny their actions by claiming that illegitimate users could have intruded the system using their identity.

- **Function creep**: An adversary exploits the biometric system designed to provide access control to a certain resource to serve another application, which the system was never intended to perform. For example, a fingerprint template obtained from a bank's database may be used to search for that person's health records in a medical database. This violates the confidentiality requirement. Although the problem of function creep has been posed primarily as a security threat, it is also widely perceived as a major threat to user privacy.

Public confidence and acceptance of biometric technology will depend on the ability of system designers to guard against all possible security threats. However, no system is likely to be absolutely secure and foolproof. Given the right circumstances and plenty of time and resources, any security system can be broken. Even though

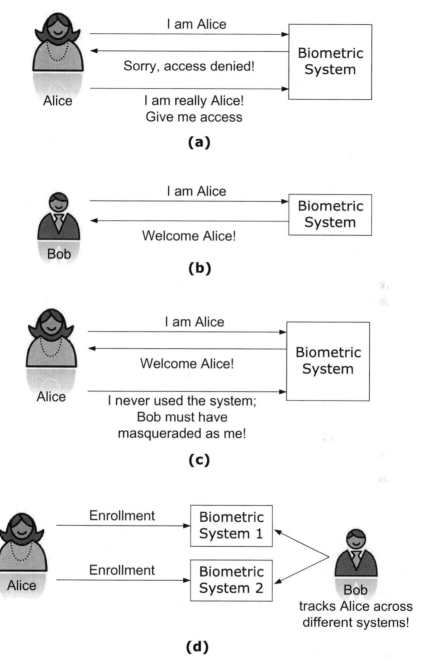

Fig. 7.1 Four major classes of security threats in a biometric system. (a) Denial of service, (b) Intrusion, (c) Repudiation, and (d) Function creep.

biometric system designers must strive to plug as many loopholes as possible, the reality is that the level of security ensured is generally based on the requirements of the application. In other words, the level of security in biometric systems used for critical applications like border control can be expected to be much higher than that of a biometric system used for logging in to a personal computer.

The first step in analyzing the security of biometric systems is to define a threat model, which identifies the various threat agents and attacks. In general, a *threat agent* can be defined as a person or a thing that can, or has the power to subvert the intended operation of a system. In the context of biometric systems, there are two kinds of threat agents.

- **Intrinsic limitations**: Even in the absence of any external attacks, a biometric system may fail due to its intrinsic limitations. As discussed in Chapter 1, all biometric systems are prone to two types of errors, namely, false match and false non-match. Moreover, a biometric device may also fail to capture or acquire a sample of the biometric identifier presented to it by the user, leading to failure to enroll and failure to capture errors. Since these errors are caused due to intrinsic limitations of various modules in a biometric system like sensor, feature extractor, and matcher, and not by any deliberate attack, the resultant failure or security breach is known as a *zero-effort attack*.

- **Adversaries**: A biometric system may also fail due to manipulation by adversaries, who could either be insiders or external entities. An insider is an authorized user of a biometric system, which includes both system administrators (super-users) and any other person enrolled in the biometric system. External entities can be classified as impostors and attackers. While the term impostor refers to any individual who intentionally or inadvertently tries to impersonate another enrolled person, an attacker is one who attempts to subvert the operation of a biometric system.

An *attack* refers to the actual mechanism or path that can be used to circumvent a biometric system. A taxonomy of attacks that can be mounted against a biometric system is shown in Figure 7.2. Based on the threat agent used in the attack, the attack mechanisms can be broadly categorized as those caused by intrinsic limitations (zero-effort attacks) and the ones caused by adversaries.

The consequences of a zero-effort attack will depend on the application. For instance, in a biometric verification system, a false non-match error will lead to denial-of-service and inconvenience to genuine users. On the other hand, in a negative recognition application such as screening, a false non-match will lead to intrusion and a false match will lead to denial-of-service. Since failure to enroll and failure to capture errors necessitate the operators to fall back on traditional (possibly unreliable) authentication mechanisms like ID cards, the effect of these errors is similar to that of a false non-match. The intrinsic limitations of a biometric system also make it hard to defend against repudiation claims.

The probability of success of a zero-effort attack is related to the recognition performance of a biometric system. Various metrics for measuring the recognition

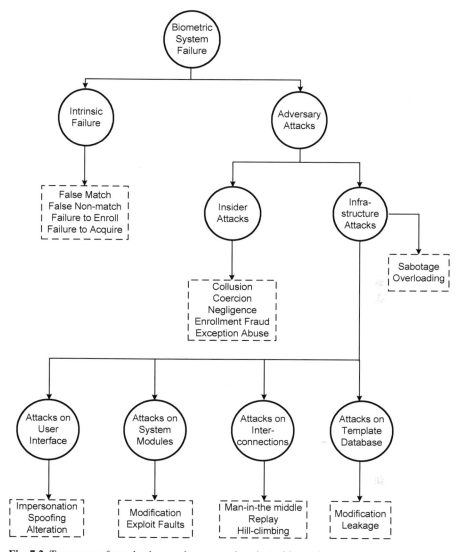

Fig. 7.2 Taxonomy of attacks that can be mounted against a biometric system.

performance of a biometric system have already been discussed in Chapter 1. These metrics include false match rate (FMR), false non-match rate (FNMR), failure to enrol rate (FTER), failure to capture rate (FTCR), false positive identification rate (FPIR), and false negative identification rate (FNIR). The recognition performances of various biometric systems have also been discussed in detail in chapters 2-6. Since the recognition performance is absolutely critical to public acceptance of a biometric system, there has been a constant push in the research community to develop new sensors, robust representation, and effective matching schemes to improve the recognition performance of biometric systems.

In this chapter, the focus will be on attacks that can be carried out by adversaries. Unlike the case of zero-effort attacks, the probability of success of an adversary attack depends on a number of tangible as well as intangible factors. This includes implementation and operational details of the biometric system, how the biometric system is integrated with the overall application (e.g., how does the biometric authentication interact with other modules in a physical access control application), the resourcefulness of the adversary (e.g., available time and computational power), and the behavior of users interacting with the biometric system. Therefore, it is relatively difficult to predict in advance all the possible ways in which the biometric system can be attacked. Only the commonly encountered attack mechanisms and the various countermeasures that can be applied to protect the biometric system against the resulting security threats are considered in the sections below.

7.2 Adversary Attacks

An adversary who intends to subvert a biometric system can make use of vulnerabilities either in the human element or in the system infrastructure. Accordingly, adversary attacks can be categorized as *insider attacks* and *infrastructure attacks* as shown in Figure 7.2. It is important to emphasize that the term "insider attacks" not only covers cases where an authorized user himself turns malicious and intentionally subverts a biometric system, but also includes cases where an external adversary circumvents the biometric system through direct or indirect involvement of an insider.

7.2.1 Insider attacks

Biometric systems require human interaction at a number of stages. For example, a human administrator is usually required to carry out the enrollment and de-enrollment of users. In addition, the administrator may also be involved in adjusting the security parameters controlling the performance of a biometric system such as threshold on the match scores and minimum limits on the quality of the acquired biometric sample. In attended applications, the administrator also appoints the operators to supervise the proper functioning of the biometric system and to guide the users. The operators are also typically responsible for operation of the fall-back system that will be used in the case of non-availability of the biometric system or when there is a failure to enroll/capture error. Finally, there are regular users who access applications or resources after authenticating themselves using the biometric system. These human interactions can be exploited in the following five ways to breach the security of a biometric system.

- **Collusion**: This refers to the scenario where an authorized user willingly turns malicious and attacks the biometric system either individually or in collaboration with external adversaries (possibly in return for monetary gain). Such an attack may lead to serious security breaches, especially if the attacker is a system administrator. Since the administrator typically has the status of a super-user with powers to modify or control most modules of the biometric system, it could be extremely difficult to guard against this attack. Even normal users can collude with adversaries to breach the security. For example, a malicious user could facilitate illegitimate access (e.g., prop the door open in a physical access control application) to an attacker by presenting his/her own biometric trait. The only safeguard against such an attack is to enforce responsible behavior among authorized users through proper training, rigorous monitoring, and auditing of all authentication transactions in order to detect any unusual pattern of activity, and penalizing those who do not conform to the rules.

- **Coercion**: A coercion attack is similar to collusion, the only difference being that a coerced user does not carry out the attack willingly. Rather the authorized user is forced to turn malicious, possibly through a physical threat (e.g., at gunpoint) or blackmail. It is desirable to reliably detect instances of coercion without putting the genuine users at a greater risk from the adversaries.

- **Negligence**: External attackers can also exploit the negligence of authorized users in order to circumvent the biometric system. A typical example is the failure of authorized users to properly log out of the system after completing their transaction. Propping a door open or permitting tailgating in physical access control scenarios can also be considered as negligence, if the intent of the authorized user is not malicious. Negligence can be minimized by periodically training the authorized users and constantly reminding them about the guidelines to be followed.

- **Enrollment Fraud**: The adversary may enroll himself into the biometric system illegally (under a false identity) by producing his biometric traits along with false credentials (e.g., fake passports and birth certificates). The reason for including this vulnerability under insider attack is that it is primarily caused by a flaw in the biometric system design, namely an over-reliance on existing (legacy) identity management systems for enrollment. In some biometric applications, such as verifying a ticket holder, the person's true identity does not matter as long as he/she is the one who paid for the ticket. However, in many government applications, such as distribution of welfare funds, fraudulent enrollment could be a serious issue.

    The solution to prevent enrollment fraud is to match the biometric traits of a new user against the traits of all enrolled users in order to detect a duplicate identity even before the new user is added to the system. This process is called *de-duplication*, which is a challenging problem because the number of enrolled users can be extremely large. For example, there are over 75 million travelers enrolled in the US-VISIT system and approximately 600 million people are expected to be enrolled under India's Unique Identity project over a span of the next five years. De-duplication in such large-scale applications requires huge computational resources as well as biometric systems with very low false positive and false negative identification rates (FRIR and FNIR). If de-duplication is ignored due to practical considerations such as the need to instantly switch from a legacy identity management system to a biometrics-based system, it is bound to affect the integrity of the resulting biometric system.

- **Exception Abuse**: Most biometric systems are equipped with a fall-back mechanism in order to permit handling of exceptional situations that may cause denial-of-service to legitimate users. Examples of exceptional scenarios may include processing users with no fingers in a fingerprint-based recognition system and failure of some hardware/software components of the biometric system. In such cases, the system administrator has the ability to bypass the recognition system and make decisions based on other credentials like secrets and tokens. This provides the motivation for the attacker to trigger the exception processing procedures (e.g., by purposely degrading the quality of his biometric trait) and attempt to exploit the loopholes in the fall-back mechanism. The problem can be minimized by improving the reliability of the biometric system and using multiple biometric modalities to enlarge the population coverage.

7.2.2 Infrastructure attacks

A generic biometric system consists of functional modules such as sensor, feature extractor, template database, matcher, and decision module. These functional modules are in turn composed of hardware and software components, and together with the communication channels interlinking them, they constitute the infrastructure of a biometric system. However, it is important to realize that there is a large diversity in the physical configuration of a biometric system. For example, it is possible to place all the functional modules and the interfaces between them on a single smart card (or more generally a secure processor). In such systems, known as system-on-card or match-on-card technology, the biometric information never leaves the card (or the chip) and only the recognition results (match or non-match) are transmitted to the application. On the other extreme, consider an Automated Fingerprint Identification System (AFIS) used in forensic applications. In the AFIS scenario, the modules of the biometric system are typically distributed across different physical locations (e.g. sensor may be at the crime scene, feature extractor and decision module may be at the regional investigation office, and matcher and database at a regional or national center). Other intermediate configurations where the sensor and feature extractor may reside together at a remote location (e.g., a mobile phone), while the matcher and database reside on the server are also possible.

There are a number of ways in which an adversary can manipulate the biometric infrastructure leading to security breaches. Attacks that are common to any security system such as *sabotage* and *overloading* can also be mounted against a biometric system. Sabotage usually involves physical damage to one or more components of the infrastructure such that the whole biometric system is rendered useless. Examples of sabotage include disabling the power supply, damaging the sensor surface or introducing excessive noise (interference) that prevents the normal operation of the system. Overloading is an attempt to defeat the system by overwhelming it with authentication requests. The motivation for these attacks is typically to deny access to genuine users. But it may also be used as a ploy to force the operator to rely on a fall-back mechanism that may be easier to circumvent.

Other infrastructure attacks can be systematically studied by categorizing them (see Figure 7.3) based on both the point of attack and the nature of attacks. The following four categories can be identified: (a) attacks at the interface between the user and the biometric system, (b) attacks on the system modules (sensor, feature extractor, matcher, and decision module), (c) attacks at the interconnection between the modules, and (d) attacks on the template database.

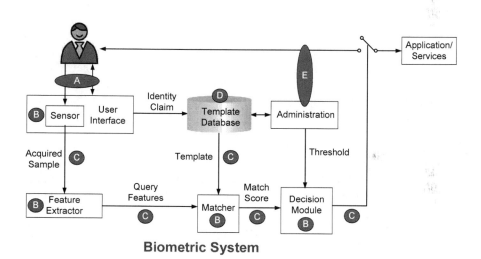

Fig. 7.3 Types of adversary attacks in a biometric system. The five major areas of vulnerability are: (A) user-biometric system interface, (B) biometric system modules, (C) interconnections between biometric modules, (D) template database, and (E) attacks through insiders (administrators or enrolled users).

7.3 Attacks at the User Interface

In general, any attempt by an attacker to break into the system by presenting a biometric trait can be considered as an attack at the user interface level. At this level, the following attacks and countermeasures are possible.

7.3.1 Impersonation

This refers to the situation where an impostor attempts to intrude the system by posing himself as another authorized user. The impersonation could be either casual or targeted. In *casual impersonation*, the identity to be attacked is chosen randomly and the impostor does not modify his/her own biometric identifiers in any way. The probability of success in such an attack is usually measured by the false match rate (FMR) of the biometric system. This attack can be countered by selecting a very low value of FMR and by restricting the number of failure attempts allowed within a time-frame.

Targeted impersonation occurs when the impostor attacks a specific identity enrolled in the biometric system, which is known to be easier to impersonate (also known as a "lamb" in the Doddington's Zoo). This attack exploits the fact that FMR is not uniform across all users. The impostor may also target an identity whose biometric characteristics are known to be similar to his traits (also known as "Evil Twin" attack). The same countermeasures used against casual impersonation may be employed to limit the success of this type of attack.

Finally, the impostor may also be able to modify his biometric characteristics to match that of the identity under attack. A common name for such an attack is *mimicry*. Examples of this attack include changing one's voice, forging a signature (see Figure 7.4), or mimicking a gait pattern. This threat is more common in systems using behavioral biometric traits and in applications with unattended mode of operation. Countering this attack requires biometric systems that have low false match rate (FMR) under skilled forgery.

(a)   (b)

Fig. 7.4 Example of a mimicry attack. (a) Genuine signature samples of a person, (b) skilled forgeries of the signature in (a) created by impostors. (Source: BioSecure Association)

7.3.2 Obfuscation

Any deliberate attempt by an attacker to change his biometric characteristic in order to avoid detection by the biometric system is called obfuscation. Thus, the key difference between mimicry and obfuscation is the motivation behind the attack. Obfuscation is mainly applicable in negative recognition applications, where the attacker wants to hide his true identity. However, it may also be applicable in verification systems that employ a fall-back mechanism to handle false rejects. In this scenario, the adversary may attempt to bypass the biometric system by forcing a false reject decision and then exploit the loopholes in the fall-back mechanism, which may be easier to circumvent.

Obfuscation can be done in a number of different ways. One possibility is to intentionally present a poor quality image or noisy biometric sample (e.g., face with non-neutral expression or a partially open eye) that may not be matched to his/her template in the database. In the case of face recognition, use of makeup, facial hair, and glasses can also lead to a false non-match. Fingerprints can be obliterated through techniques like abrasion, cutting, and burning, or may even be surgically altered or distorted (see Figure 7.5). Similarly, face can be altered using plastic surgery and iris transplants have been depicted in popular science fiction (e.g., in the movie Minority Report). Knowledge of the details of biometric processing algorithms can further facilitate such attacks. For example, if the attacker knows that a particular face recognition system is not robust to pose variations, he can easily circumvent it by presenting only a profile view of the face.

The most effective solution against obfuscation is to improve the robustness of biometric algorithms to intra-user variations in order to achieve a very low false non-match rate (FNMR). It may also be possible to automatically detect some of the alterations such as a non-frontal face or surgically modified fingerprint and subject such users to secondary inspection.

7.3.3 Spoofing

This is the most well-known attack at the user interface level, and it involves the presentation of a spoof biometric trait. A spoof is defined as any counterfeit biometric that is not obtained from a live person (see Figure 7.6). Spoofing includes the presentation of fake or artificial traits (e.g., gummy finger, thin film on top of a finger, photograph or mask of a face, recorded voice, etc.) and things as sinister as dismembered body parts (e.g., a dismembered finger) belonging to a legitimate user to the recognition system. If the sensor is unable to distinguish between spoofed and genuine biometric traits, the adversary can easily intrude the system under a false identity.

This attack requires knowledge of the biometric trait corresponding to the identity to be attacked. This knowledge could be obtained in one of the following four ways: (a) directly colluding with or coercing an authorized user, (b) covert acqui-

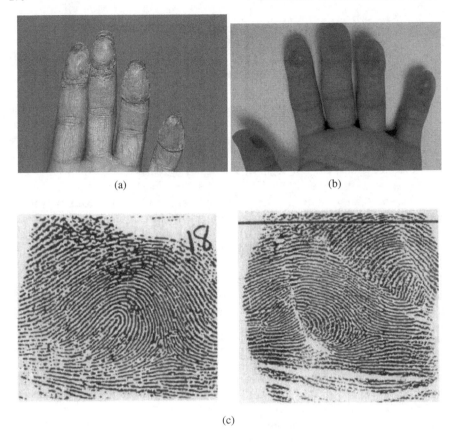

(a)   (b)

(c)

Fig. 7.5 Examples of fingerprint alteration. (a) Transplanted fingerprints from the friction ridge patterns found on the sole of the feet (http://www.clpex.com/images/FeetMutilation/L4.JPG), (b) fingerprints obliterated by biting off the finger skin, and (c) fingerprints altered by making a Z shaped cut on the fingertip, lifting and switching the two triangles, and stitching them back; left image shows the original fingerprint and the altered fingerprint is shown on the right. The alteration shown in (c) involved a man using the name Alexander Guzman, who was arrested by Florida officials in 1995 for possessing a false passport and found to have mutilated fingerprints. After a two-week search based on manually reconstructing the altered fingerprints and searching the FBI database, the reconstructed fingerprints of Alexander Guzman were linked to the fingerprints of Jose Izquiredo, who was an absconding drug criminal. This example illustrates both the usefulness of a biometric system as well as the desperate measures that criminals often take to circumvent a biometric system.

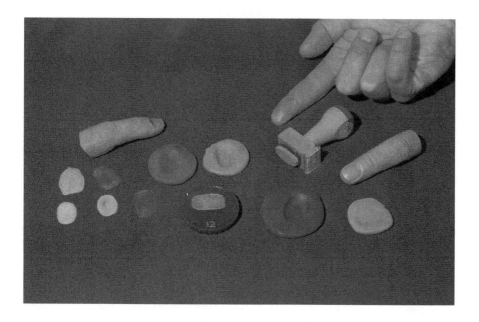

(a)

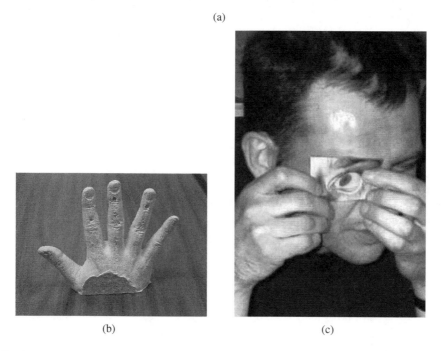

(b)   (c)

Fig. 7.6 Examples of spoofed biometric traits. (a) Fake fingerprints made from glue and dismembered fingers (Source: Lumidigm, Inc.), (b) a fake hand made of plaster, and (c) a photograph of an iris (Source: C't magazine).

sition (e.g., lifting residual fingerprint impressions covertly from the sensor or any surface touched by the authorized user, recording the user's voice, or capturing a photograph of the user's face), (c) estimating a close approximation of the user's biometric template through brute-force or hill-climbing attacks, and (d) stealing the biometric template from a database and reverse engineering the template.

While traditional password-based authentication systems work under the assumption of secrecy (i.e., only the legitimate user knows his password), such an assumption is generally not required for a biometric system to work. In contrast, the strength of biometric authentication is derived from the fact that the biometric characteristic is linked to the user physically. Though an attacker may get hold of a legitimate user's fingerprint pattern, it would not be of much use to the attacker if the sensor can ensure that the scanned fingerprint comes directly from the finger of a live user. Therefore, the solution to counter spoof attacks is to incorporate liveness detection capability in the biometric sensor.

7.3.4 Countermeasure: spoof detection

Spoof detection can be broadly defined as differentiating a real biometric trait presented by a live person from a biometric trait presented through any other source. Spoof detection typically involves checking for signs of human vitality or liveness (e.g., blood pulse), a process known as liveness detection. Despite this subtle difference between spoof detection and liveness detection, the two terms are generally used interchangeably in the biometrics literature, which is also the case in this book. Spoof detection can either be decoupled from or integrated into the biometric recognition process. In a decoupled system, no biometric data is acquired until the spoof detection system is convinced that the biometric trait is presented by a live human user. On the other hand, an integrated system detects the spoof while processing the acquired biometric information (either prior to or during feature extraction).

The susceptibility of a biometric system to a spoof attack depends both on the biometric modality and the specific sensor used to capture the biometric trait. For example, a two-dimensional photograph of a human face may be sufficient to fool a camera used in a face recognition system. However, it is usually very difficult to circumvent an optical or capacitive fingerprint sensor by using a 2-D reproduction of a fingerprint because such sensors inherently depend on capturing the 3-D variations in the ridge-valley structures.

While spoof detection is extremely important to ensure the integrity of a biometric system, it also brings in a few disadvantages. Firstly, almost all spoof detection solutions increase the cost of the biometric system. This is because of the need to have additional hardware to capture new information (e.g., spectral or thermal properties) or a software module to process the biometric data already collected and distinguish between a spoof and a live trait. This additional processing also increases the biometric acquisition time, thereby reducing the throughput of the biometric system. Finally, just like biometric systems that are seldom perfect, spoof detection systems are also prone to errors. While a spoof detection system may identify and thwart most of the spoofing attempts, it may also incorrectly classify a few real biometric traits as spoofs, leading to an increase in the failure to capture rate.

Though there are a number of biometric spoof detection algorithms, they can be classified into three main groups based on the mechanism employed for thwarting a spoof attempt. The first approach involves measuring the physiological properties of a live person, which includes blood pulse/pressure, perspiration, spectral/optical properties of the human skin/tissues, electrical/thermal characteristics, and deformation of the muscles/skin. The second approach is based on identifying voluntary or involuntary human behavioral actions like fluctuations in pupil size, blinking, and pupil/eye/head/body movements. The third category is known as the challenge-response mechanism, where the system presents a challenge to the user and measures whether the user responds to the challenge correctly. Examples of challenges include prompting a user to recite a randomly generated phrase/text, asking the user to change his or her facial expression (e.g., smile or frown), and requesting the user to present multiple biometric traits in a randomly generated sequence. Since the last two approaches are fairly straightforward to envision and implement, only the first approach will be discussed in detail.

7.3.4.1 Spoof detection based on physiological properties

While biometric systems are based on physiological characteristics that are unique to each individual (e.g., fingerprint, iris, face), spoof detection algorithms tend to use characteristics that can easily distinguish a human body from innate materials (e.g., silicone gel for fingerprints) used for spoofing. Some of the physiological properties that have been used for spoof detection are discussed below.

- **Pulse rate/ Blood pressure**: This property is generally applicable to biometric traits such as fingerprint and palmprint that require the user to be in physical contact with the sensor. While the pulse rate is a good vitality sign, special hardware may be needed to record this trait. Moreover, the pulse rate and blood pressure vary significantly from one person to another and also within the same person depending on his physical activity and emotional state at the time of acquisition. Furthermore, a single pulse measurement may take up to five seconds. Finally, if a wafer-thin silicone rubber is glued to a real finger, the heartbeat of the underlying finger will result in the detection of a pulse.

- **Perspiration**: Perspiration refers to the sweating process of a live finger. Live fingers exhibit sweating over a period of time whereas fake fingers will not exhibit the sweating process. The perspiration phenomenon starts at the sweat pores on a fingerprint and spreads along the ridge lines, while the valleys do not change. Due to the sweating process in live fingers, the regions around sweat pores can be seen to enlarge over time in a sequence of fingerprint images (see Figure 7.7). One limitation of this procedure to detect a spoof finger is that to observe the sweating process, the finger needs to stay on the fingerprint scanner for a

Live:

Spoof:

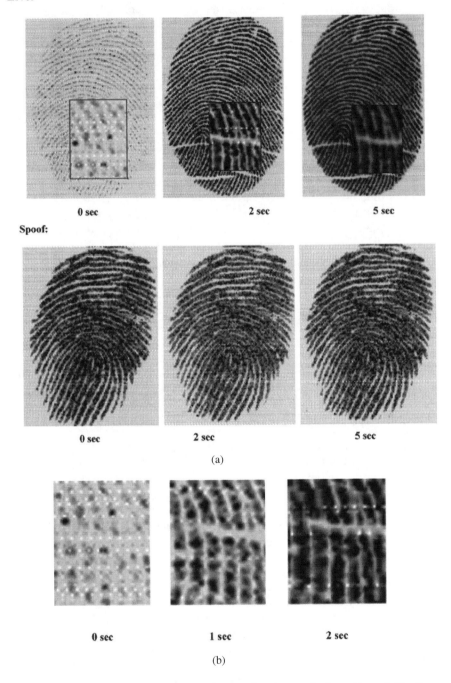

Fig. 7.7 An example of fingerprint spoof detection based on the perspiration pattern of a live finger (adapted from [35]). (a) Example fingerprint images obtained from a live finger (top row) and a fake finger (bottom row) acquired at 0, 2, and 5 seconds after the finger is placed on the sensor, (b) enlarged fingerprint image sequence that demonstrates progression of a perspiration pattern over time in a live finger. ©IEEE

few seconds. The perspiration-based methods are also expected to have some difficulty in dealing with varying amounts of moisture content occurring in live human fingers.

- **Spectral/optical properties of the human skin:** This is one of the most common characteristics that has been successfully used for spoof detection in many biometric systems, including fingerprint, palmprint, face, and iris. The optical properties that may be measured include the absorption, reflection, scattering, and refraction properties under different illumination conditions (such as wavelength, polarization, coherence). In the case of fingerprints, multi-spectral analysis may be used to measure the surface properties as well as sub-surface properties of a finger since components of blood (oxygenated and deoxygenated hemoglobin) absorb different wavelengths of light. Similarly, the tissue, blood, fat, and melanin pigments in the eyes absorb different wavelengths of light. These properties can be leveraged for liveness detection in fingerprint (see Figure 7.8) and iris recognition systems.

  Eyes have a few additional optical properties that can also be used to detect fake irides. For instance, photographs of an iris can be differentiated from a live iris by detecting phenomena like Purkinje reflections and red eye effect. While Purkinje images are reflections of outside objects against the cornea of the eye, the red eye effect is due to retinal reflection. Moreover, analysis of the two-dimensional Fourier spectrum can also be used to identify contact lenses with a fake iris printed on them (see Figure 7.9).

- **Electrical characteristics**: The electrical conductivity of human tissue differs from conductivity of many other synthetic materials such as silicone rubber and gelatin. The conductivity of the material presented to the fingerprint sensor can be measured to differentiate a live finger from a fake finger. However, the conductivity of live fingers varies a lot depending on environmental conditions such as humidity and temperature. If water or saliva is added to a fake finger, its conductivity may be indistinguishable from that of a live finger.

- **Skin deformation**: The deformation pattern of the human skin can be used for differentiating live fingers from fake fingers. Skin is more flexible than most other materials and the ridges and valleys in a fake finger do not deform like a live fingertip. Real live skin deforms only in a certain way because the skin is anchored to the underlying derma and the deformation is influenced by the position and shape of the finger bone. But measuring these deformation patterns is not easy because it requires capturing a video of the fingerprint at a high frame rate as the finger moves on the sensor surface. This is problematic because most fingerprint sensors are designed for single-touch fingerprint acquisition and the users are trained not to move the finger during capture; excessive deformation will affect the matching accuracy of the system.

One of the common criticisms of the liveness detection algorithms employed in commercial biometric systems is that they are based solely on the principle of *se-*

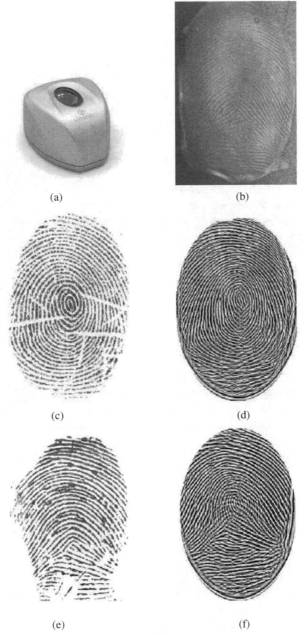

(a)   (b)

(c)   (d)

(e)   (f)

Fig. 7.8 An example of fingerprint spoof detection using the spectral properties of the human tissue. (a) a multi-spectral fingerprint sensor from Lumidigm, Inc. that is capable of capturing the sub-surface properties of a finger, (b) a spoof fingerprint made from glue, (c) an impression of the real finger acquired using a traditional optical fingerprint sensor (based on total internal reflection (TIR) principle), (d) an impression of the real finger acquired using the multi-spectral fingerprint sensor, (e) an impression of the spoof finger (glue spoof overlaid on the real finger) acquired using the optical fingerprint sensor, and (f) an impression of the spoof finger acquired using the multi-spectral fingerprint sensor. It can be observed that the multi-spectral sensor is able to see through the spoof and capture the ridge pattern of the underlying real finger. (Source: Lumidigm, Inc.)

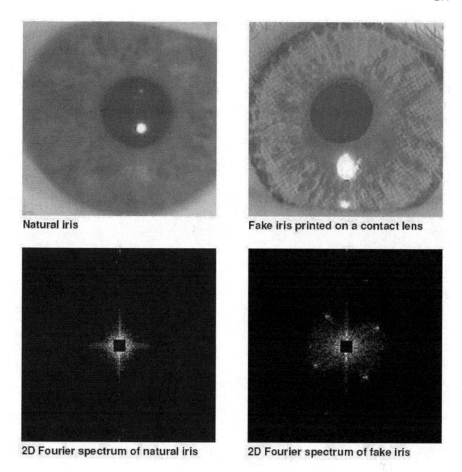

Natural iris

Fake iris printed on a contact lens

2D Fourier spectrum of natural iris

2D Fourier spectrum of fake iris

Fig. 7.9 An example of iris spoof detection (adapted from [13]). A printed iris typically exhibits some artifacts that can be detected by analyzing the 2-dimensional Fourier spectrum of the iris image.

curity through obscurity. In other words, biometric vendors do not generally reveal the algorithm or implementation details about their liveness detection methodology because if the specifics of the spoof detection techniques are revealed, the system can be circumvented easily. Experience in cryptographic systems has shown that this approach does not provide satisfactory results over a period of time. Once an attacker identifies a possible vulnerability and successfully carries out a spoof attack, the complete system falls apart. Therefore, one should assume that the attacker has knowledge about the physiological properties used by the system for detecting spoofs. Consequently, it may be possible for the attacker to create a fake finger with the same properties that are verified by the spoof detector. Of course, the addition of more and more physiological characteristics in the spoof detection process will make it progressively more difficult (though not impossible) for the attacker to fool the system. While biometric sensors should be equipped with as much liveness detection capability as possible, the use of multiple biometric traits (multimodal biometric systems are discussed in Chapter 6) combined with intelligent challenge-response mechanisms may be required to raise the bar to a level that is difficult for an attacker to surmount.

7.4 Attacks on Biometric Processing

The signal processing and pattern matching algorithms that form the crux of automated biometric recognition are implemented in the sensor, feature extractor, matcher, and decision modules. Thus, an attacker can subvert the biometric processing either by directly undermining the core functional modules of the biometric system or by manipulating the communication between these modules. Though the template database is also one of the modules in the biometric system, the motivation and consequences of an attack on the template database are different compared to the other modules. Therefore, the attacks on the template database will be considered separately.

7.4.1 Attacks on the system modules

Attacks on the core functional modules can be mounted either through unauthorized modification or by exploiting the faults in their implementation. The motivation of these attacks could be to cause denial-of-service to legitimate users or facilitate intrusion.

7.4.1.1 Unauthorized modification

The hardware and software components of a biometric system can be modified by attackers. A classic example is the modification of an executable program in a module through a Trojan horse attack. A Trojan horse is malicious software that appears to perform a desirable function for the user, but instead performs some other function that usually facilitates intrusion by unauthorized users. The Trojan horse can disguise itself as one of the modules, bypass that module, and output the values desired by the adversary as input to the subsequent modules. For instance, a Trojan horse program can bypass the feature extractor and send the false features determined by the attacker to the matching module (see Figure 7.10). Similar attacks can also be carried out at the sensing, quality estimation, matching, template database, and decision modules.

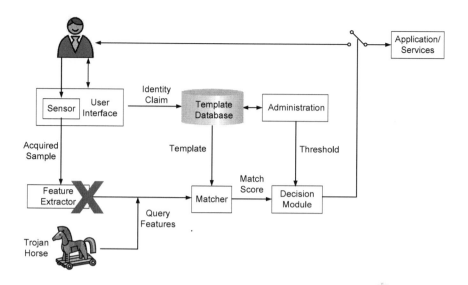

Fig. 7.10 A Trojan Horse attack against the feature extraction module is shown. A Trojan horse is a malicious software that appears to perform a desirable function for the authorized user, but instead performs some other function that usually facilitates intrusion by unauthorized users. In this example, the Trojan horse replaces the feature extractor and outputs the features decided by the attacker instead of the features extracted from the input biometric trait. If the sensor and the matcher modules are unaware of the fact that they are communicating with a Trojan horse, and not with the real feature extractor, it will lead to either denial-of-service to genuine users or intrusion by attackers.

One method to overcome this attack is to employ a trusted biometric system. A trusted biometric system is one in which the different modules are bound together physically and/or logically using mutual authentication between the modules. Mutual authentication implies that the trust is established both ways between two communicating parties. This is usually achieved through public key cryptographic protocols and digital signatures. In addition to mutual authentication, secure code execution practices or specialized tamper-resistant hardware that can enforce secure execution of software can be used to avoid modification of the module functionalities.

7.4.1.2 Exploitation of faults

The attacker may identify and exploit the loopholes in the implementation of the biometric algorithms or insecure configuration to circumvent the biometric system. As an example, consider a matching module in which a specific input value, say $\mathbf{b}_0$, is not handled appropriately, and whenever $\mathbf{b}_0$ is input to the matcher, it always outputs a "match" decision. This vulnerability might not affect the normal functioning of the system because, in practice, the probability of $\mathbf{b}_0$ being generated from a real biometric data may be negligible. However, an adversary can exploit this loophole to easily breach the security without being detected.

Note that the attacker may need to bypass one or more modules in the biometric system to exploit such implementation faults. This attack is also closely linked to the obfuscation attack, because knowledge of the faults in the biometric implementation will allow the attacker to circumvent the system through appropriate alterations of his/her biometric trait. This attack can be prevented by using well-tested biometric algorithms.

7.4.2 Attacks at the interconnections

The following three attacks are possible when an adversary gains control of the communication interfaces between different modules of the biometric system. While the man-in-the-middle and replay attacks are common to the communication channel between any two modules in a biometric system, the hill-climbing attack is specific to the link between the sensor and feature extractor or the link between the feature extractor and matcher.

7.4.2.1 Man-in-the-middle attack

In cryptography, a man-in-the-middle attack is a form of active eavesdropping, where the attacker establishes independent connections between two entities already in communication and relays messages between them. The victims are led to believe that they are directly communicating with each other, when in fact the entire conversation is controlled by the attacker. In biometric systems, a man-in-the-middle attack can be carried out against any two biometric modules and its effect is the same as a Trojan horse attack on a system module, i.e., it allows the attacker to inject false values into the biometric system. Mutual authentication between biometric modules is required to counter this attack.

7.4.2.2 Replay attack

If the channels between the biometric modules are not secured physically or cryptographically, an adversary may intercept the data being transferred and replay it at a later time. The raw biometric data or extracted features can be intercepted and replayed. Replay attacks are possible even if the data is encrypted. A countermeasure against this attack is to use time-stamps or a challenge/response mechanism. Mutual authentication between the modules and use of one-time session keys during every transaction could also mitigate replay attacks.

7.4.2.3 Hill-climbing attack

Hill-climbing attacks are possible when (a) the adversary has the ability to inject raw biometric sample data or features directly through a Trojan-horse attack or a man-in-the-middle attack, and (b) the attacker can obtain the match score output by the matcher (see Figure 7.11). Here, the goal of the attacker is to determine a biometric sample or feature set that matches with that of a targeted identity for the specified biometric algorithm. Clearly, if one can inject arbitrary biometric samples or feature vectors and obtain a match score from the biometric system, one could mount a *brute-force attack*. In this case, the attacker can try different samples from a large biometric database and he is likely to succeed in finding a close match in about (1/FMR) attempts, where FMR is the false match rate of the biometric system. Such a brute-force attack in a biometric system is equivalent to a *dictionary attack* in a password-based authentication system.

It may be possible to improve the efficiency of the brute force attack if the match score information is available. This leads to the hill-climbing attack, where an artificially generated biometric sample or feature set is first introduced into the system and the response (match score) is noted. The adversary then perturbs the initial sample or feature set, submits it to the system, and records the new match score. If the match score in the second iteration is higher than the first one, the changes are retained; else, they are discarded. The above process is iterated several times until the match score exceeds the threshold set by the system administrator. In each iteration where the match score is higher than before, the artificially generated sample or feature set becomes more similar to the template that is being targeted.

One can easily see that a hill-climbing attack is more difficult to implement than a Trojan horse or a man-in-the-middle attack. The reason for this difficulty is that not only access to match scores is needed, the attacker also needs to have some knowledge of the feature/sample distribution to synthetically generate features/samples in such a way that higher match scores can be obtained in the successive iterations. However, the payoff to the attacker resulting from a hill-climbing attack is significantly higher than that of a Trojan horse attack. If a good estimate of the original biometric sample of the target identity can be obtained, it can possibly be used to create a spoof or to identify the same user across different applications that employ the same trait. Thus, a hill-climbing attack not only compromises the integrity of the given biometric system, but it may also compromise other biometric systems using the same trait. Restricting the number of failure attempts allowed within a time-frame, increasing the granularity of the match score, and the use of trusted biometric systems are some of the techniques that can counter the threat of a hill-climbing attack.

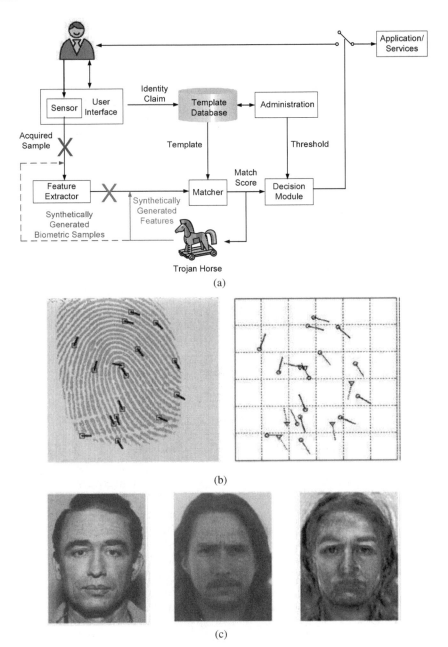

Fig. 7.11 (a) A hill climbing attack can be carried out both in the biometric sample space or in the feature space. Here, the goal of the attacker is to determine a biometric sample or feature set that matches with that of a target identity. Suppose that a Trojan horse replaces the feature extractor and injects synthetically generated features. The feedback obtained through the match score can be used to iteratively modify the synthetic features until a match is found. (b) Regenerated fingerprint minutiae (adapted from [47]). The target fingerprint with labeled minutiae is shown on the left and the minutiae positions learned using hill-climbing attack is shown on the right (solid lines with circle (-o) indicate the original minutiae, dotted lines with triangles (–∇) indicate the synthetic minutiae.). (c) Regenerated face images (adapted from [1]). From left to right: the target face image, the initial selected image for hill-climbing, and the regenerated face image.

7.5 Attacks on the Template Database

Two kinds of attacks are possible on the biometric template database. First, the template database could be hacked or modified by an adversary to gain unauthorized access or to deny access to legitimate users. This unauthorized template modification can be carried out irrespective of the storage location, be it a central server, a remote client (e.g., personal computer, mobile phone, etc.), or a smart-card. A similar attack is also possible in password-based authentication systems. The common technique used to mitigate such a threat is to have strict control on database access. Second, the stored biometric template information may become available to an adversary. Such an attack is referred to as leakage. Leakage is not a serious issue in password-based authentication, because only a cryptographic hash of the password is typically stored in the database, and the adversary gains no useful information from learning this hashed password. However, leakage is a serious problem in biometric systems.

Biometric traits are not always secrets, and the strength of biometric authentication lies in the strong and irrevocable physical link between a live user and his/her biometric trait rather than in the secrecy of biometric data. Therefore, it is natural to wonder why the leakage of a biometric template from the database is a serious security issue. The answer to this question lies in the following observations.

- There are four ways in which the biometric information of a user can be gleaned, namely, (a) collusion or coercion, (b) covert acquisition, (c) brute-force or hillclimbing attacks, and (d) template leakage. Among these four possibilities, the first two require the attacker to be in close physical proximity to the user or get the user's cooperation. The third method requires the attacker to breach the security of the biometric system and mount a successful intrusion attack. Furthermore, the attacker needs to expend significant effort in the first three methods to acquire knowledge about a single user. In contrast, if an attacker can hack into a large biometric database, a task that can be done from a remote location while remaining anonymous, he can easily obtain the biometric information about a large number of users along with their biographic information (such as name, address, etc.).
- The fact that biometric recognition does not rely on the secrecy of biometric data is valid only when the system can reliably distinguish between the presentation of a live user and a spoofed presentation. Another assumption is that the biometric infrastructure is not compromised. If these assumptions are not satisfied, the leaked biometric information will lead to intrusion because the attacker can either reverse engineer the template to create a physical spoof or replay the stolen template to gain unauthorized access.
- Finally, leakage of biometric templates violates the data confidentiality requirement of a biometric system. Furthermore, unlike passwords and tokens, it is not possible to replace compromised biometric traits. Once the biometric information falls into the hands of an adversary, it is lost forever and cannot be reissued, updated, or destroyed. Thus, the irrevocable nature of biometric traits, which is one

of the strengths of biometric recognition, can also be considered a weakness. To further compound this problem, leaked biometric templates can be used for secondary purposes like cross-matching across different databases to covertly track a person without his/her consent, thereby resulting in a function creep. Thus, leakage attack is not only a serious security threat, but also undermines the user's privacy.

Due to these reasons, biometric template protection is a very important issue to be addressed, especially in applications that require storage of biometric data in central servers.

7.5.1 Countermeasure: biometric template security

Since the problem of biometric template security is quite similar to the problem of storing passwords securely, it is natural and intuitive to consider reusing the same techniques developed for password security in order to protect biometric templates. A brief review of the methodologies used in password security is presented (see Figure 7.12) before discussing the biometric template protection algorithms.

7.5.1.1 Techniques for securing passwords

One possible approach for securing passwords is to encrypt them using well-known cryptographic techniques (e.g., Advanced Encryption Standard (AES), Rivest-Shamir-Adleman (RSA) algorithm, etc.) and store only the encrypted password. During authentication, the same encryption algorithm can be applied to the input password and directly matched to the stored encrypted password. Since an encrypted password can be decrypted if the decryption key is known, the security of encryption depends on the secrecy of the decryption key. It is well-known that key management (secure generation, distribution, and storage of cryptographic keys) is probably the most challenging issue in the practical implementation of cryptosystems. Even if the decryption key is held securely, an attacker can choose some arbitrary passwords and obtain the corresponding encrypted passwords. This may allow the attacker to recover the secret key through what is known as a chosen plaintext attack[1]. Due to these limitations, simple encryption of passwords is not sufficient for securing the passwords.

The second alternative is referred to as password-based key generation (see Figure 7.12(b)). In this case, the password is never stored anywhere in the system.

---

[1] A chosen-plaintext attack is one of the attack models used in cryptanalysis. Here, the attacker is assumed to have the capability to choose arbitrary plaintexts (say different passwords) and obtain the corresponding ciphertexts (encrypted passwords). Using these plaintext-ciphertext pairs, the attacker tries to gain some information (e.g., the secret key) that reduces the security of the encryption scheme.

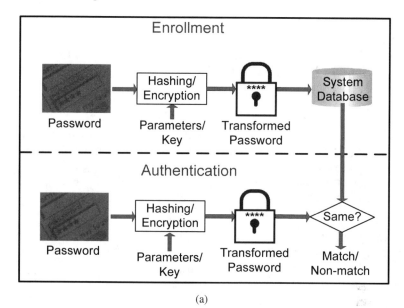

(a)

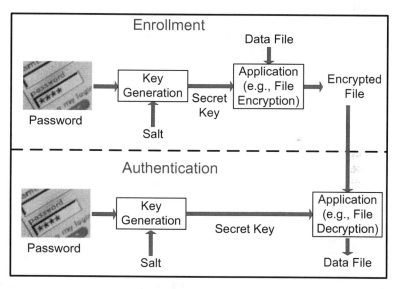

(b)

Fig. 7.12 Approaches used for securing passwords. (a) In password encryption or hashing, only the encrypted password or a cryptographic hash of the password is stored in the database. While the encryption approach requires the decryption key to be held securely, the non-invertibility property of the cryptographic hash function protects the password even if the hash function and its parameters are available to the attacker. Hence, hashing is generally preferred to encryption in the context of password security. (b) In password-based key generation, the password is never stored anywhere in the system. Instead, the password is used to derive a cryptographic key usually in combination with additional random information known as a *salt*. This key generated from the password can be directly used in another application such as a file encryption system.

Instead, the password is directly used to derive a cryptographic key usually in combination with additional random information known as a *salt*. Another application
such as a file encryption system can directly use the key derived from the password for symmetric key cryptography. While this approach is beneficial in the sense
that the password need not be stored anywhere, it can be used only in applications
where the authentication is implicit. For instance, one can decrypt an encrypted file
and read its contents only if the right password is presented.

The third approach used in most modern password-based authentication systems
is to apply a cryptographic hash function to the plaintext password and store only
the hashed password. When the user enters the password during authentication, the
same hash function is applied to the input password and the resulting hash value
is directly matched with the stored hash value (see Figure 7.12(a)). A good cryptographic hash function $\mathbf{h}(.)$ must at least satisfy the following three properties.

1. *Pre-image resistance*: Given a cryptographically hashed password, say $\mathbf{h}(\mathbf{x})$, it
   must be computationally hard to find a password $\mathbf{y}$ such that $\mathbf{h}(\mathbf{y}) = \mathbf{h}(\mathbf{x})$.
2. *Weak collision resistance*: Given $\mathbf{x}$ and $\mathbf{h}(\mathbf{x})$, it must be computationally hard to
   find $\mathbf{y}$, where $\mathbf{y} \neq \mathbf{x}$, such that $\mathbf{h}(\mathbf{y}) = \mathbf{h}(\mathbf{x})$, and
3. *Collision resistance*: It must be computationally difficult to find some arbitrary $\mathbf{x}$
   and $\mathbf{y}$, such that $\mathbf{x} \neq \mathbf{y}$, but $\mathbf{h}(\mathbf{x}) = \mathbf{h}(\mathbf{y})$. In other words, it is difficult to find two
   different passwords that result in the same cryptographic hash. Note that weak
   collision resistance does not imply collision resistance.

Due to the above properties of the hash function, even if the stored (hashed) password becomes available to an adversary, it does not result in a serious security threat.

7.5.1.2 Challenges and requirements in biometric template security

Is it possible to directly apply any of the above three password security approaches
to generate "secure" biometric templates? Unfortunately, the answer to the above
question is negative and the reason lies in the fundamental difference between
password-based and biometric authentication systems highlighted in Chapter 1.
While password-based authentication relies on an exact match between the passwords entered during enrollment and authentication, biometric recognition is based
on inexact match between the enrollment and authentication samples. In fact, as
shown earlier, there can be large intra-user variability in multiple acquisitions of
the same biometric trait and handling these intra-user variations is the most important challenge in designing a biometric template protection scheme. Henceforth, the
term "protected" or "secure" template will be used to refer to those templates that
are obtained after the application of a biometric template security algorithm to the
"unprotected" or "original" template.

A biometric template protection scheme should have the following three properties.

1. **Cryptographic security**: Cryptographic security refers to the pre-image resistance property that is typically satisfied by cryptographic hash functions. Given

a secure template, it must be computationally difficult to find a biometric feature set (commonly known as a *pre-image*) that will match with the secure template. This property defends against the possibility of an attacker intruding into the biometric system under consideration by replaying the pre-image.

The concept of pre-image resistance is also related to *one-way* or *non-invertible* mathematical functions. A function **f** is referred to as a one-way function if it is "easy to compute" (in polynomial time) but "hard to invert" (given **f(x)**, the probability of finding **x** in polynomial-time is small). A non-invertible template protection scheme implies that it will be computationally hard to obtain the original biometric features from the secure template. This prevents an adversary from creating a physical spoof of the biometric trait and intruding another biometric system that makes use of the same biometric trait. Thus, a secure template must be pre-image resistant and non-invertible.

2. **Performance**: The biometric template protection scheme should not degrade the recognition performance (FMR and FNMR) of the biometric system.

3. **Revocability**: It is desirable to have a template protection scheme that can generate multiple secure templates from the same biometric data. These multiple secure templates must be such that even if an adversary obtains two or more of them, it must be computationally hard to (a) identify that they are derived from the same biometric data and (b) obtain the original biometric features of the user. This revocability or cancelability property ensures that cross-matching across biometric databases is not possible, thereby preserving the user's privacy. Revocability also makes it straightforward to discard a compromised template and reissue a new one based on the same biometric data.

Ideally, the template protection scheme should satisfy all the three requirements at the same time. However, it is quite a challenge to design such a technique. The following sections consider different ways of securing biometric templates and analyze how these schemes compare against each other based on the above three requirements. Figure 7.13 presents a broad categorization of the biometric template protection algorithms and Figure 7.14 shows an illustration of major template protection approaches when applied to a fingerprint minutiae template.

7.5.1.3 Standard encryption approach

The simplest way to secure biometric templates is to encrypt them using standard cryptographic techniques like RSA and AES. This is the methodology deployed in most of the existing commercial biometric systems. However, as shown in Figure 7.15, the encryption solution in the case of biometric templates is not equivalent to the password encryption scenario due to the following reason. Recall that multiple acquisitions of the same biometric trait do not result in the same feature set. Typically, standard encryption functions are not smooth functions and a small difference in the values of the feature sets extracted from the raw biometric data would lead to very large difference in the resulting encrypted features (see Figure 7.16). Consequently, unlike password encryption, one cannot perform matching directly in the

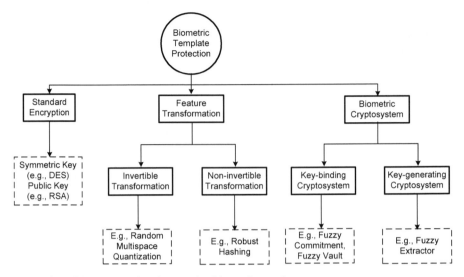

Fig. 7.13 Different approaches for securing biometric templates.

encrypted domain. Rather, the template must be decrypted in order to be matched with the query features. As a result, the original biometric features are exposed during every authentication attempt, irrespective of whether the authentication is eventually successful.

The main advantage of the standard encryption approach is that the recognition performance of the biometric system is not affected at all. Since the matching actually takes place in the decrypted domain, there is no need to re-design or modify the available matching algorithms. This is the reason for the popularity of this approach. However, it must be emphasized the encryption solution is secure and revocable only under ideal conditions (key is kept secret and matching is done at a trusted location). If practical issues such as key management or susceptibility to template theft during a matching attempt are taken into account, the standard encryption technique is not good enough for securing biometric templates.

To overcome this problem, a number of techniques have been proposed, which are specifically designed for biometric template security, keeping in mind the unique characteristics of this domain such as intra-user variations. These techniques can be roughly classified as *feature transformation* approach and *biometric cryptosystem*. But, these two approaches are not mutually exclusive and many of the template protection algorithms proposed in the literature draw upon ideas from both these methodologies. When a template security scheme clearly involves elements from both the basic approaches, it is referred to as a *hybrid biometric cryptosystem*.

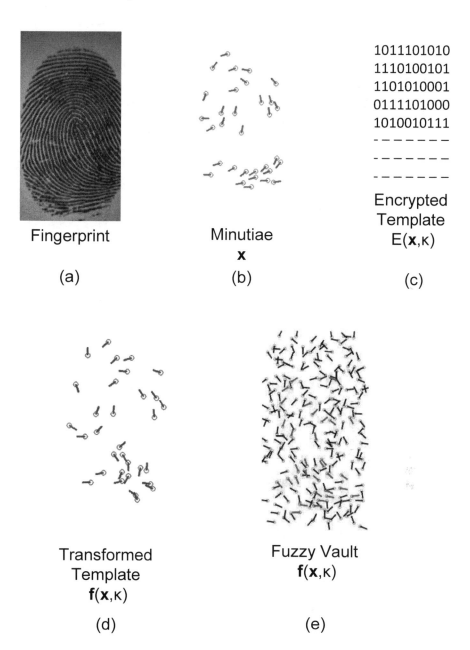

Fig. 7.14 An illustration of different template protection approaches when applied to a finger-print minutiae template. (a) Fingerprint sample acquired during enrollment, (b) minutiae template extracted from the enrollment sample, (c) a fingerprint template encrypted using a standard encryption algorithm such as AES, (d) a transformed minutiae template obtained using a non-invertible transformation scheme, and (e) a fuzzy vault (biometric cryptosystem) that hides the minutiae template among a large set of random chaff points.

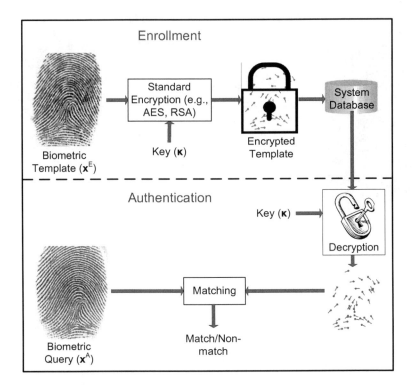

Fig. 7.15 Securing biometric templates through standard encryption techniques. Unlike password encryption, biometric matching cannot be performed in the encrypted domain because of intra-user variations in the biometric data. Since encryption is simple and does not affect the recognition performance, it is widely used in many existing biometric systems. However, the template is secure only if the cryptographic key (κ) is maintained a secret and matching takes place in a trusted environment.

7.5.1.4 Feature transformation approach

In the feature transform approach, a transformation function $\mathbf{f}(.)$ is applied to the biometric template $\mathbf{x}^E$ and only the transformed template $\mathbf{f}(\mathbf{x}^E, \kappa)$ is stored in the database. The parameters of the transformation function are typically derived from a random key, κ, or password. The same transformation function is applied to query features, $\mathbf{x}^A$, and the transformed query, $\mathbf{f}(\mathbf{x}^A, \kappa)$, is directly matched against the transformed template, $\mathbf{f}(\mathbf{x}^E, \kappa)$. From Figure 7.17, one can clearly see that the feature transformation approach is analogous to password encryption or hashing.

Depending on the characteristics of the transformation function $\mathbf{f}$, the feature transform schemes can be further categorized as *invertible* and *non-invertible* transforms.

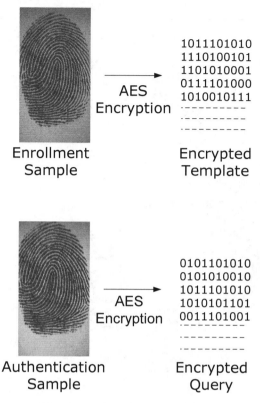

Fig. 7.16 Illustration of the large difference in the encrypted template and encrypted query when features extracted from multiple impressions of the same fingerprint are encrypted using standard encryption techniques (e.g., AES, RSA).

Invertible transformation:

When the transformation function, $\mathbf{f}(.)$, is invertible[2], the security of the transformed template is based on the secrecy of the key κ. In other words, if an adversary gains access to the key and the transformed template, he can recover the original biometric template (or a close approximation of it). Thus, a template protected using the invertible feature transformation approach is similar to an encrypted password. As in the case of password encryption, the practical difficulties in key management limit the security of the invertible transformation approach. Moreover, the matching algorithms need to be re-designed to allow matching in the transformed domain.

However, if the keys are made user-specific and if these user-specific keys are assumed to be secrets known only to the legitimate users, there are two potential advantages. Firstly, the use of additional random information in the form of a user-

---

[2] A transformation function $\mathbf{f}(.)$ is said to be invertible if, given any $\mathbf{f}(\mathbf{x}, \kappa)$ and the corresponding key κ, one can find $\mathbf{x}$ in polynomial time.

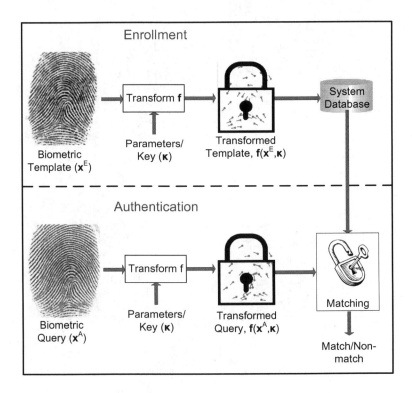

Fig. 7.17 Securing biometric templates using the feature transformation approach. The cryptographic security of the template depends on the characteristics of the transformation function, $\mathbf{f}(.)$. If the transform is invertible, the template is secure only if the key κ is maintained secretly. On the other hand, a template obtained through non-invertible transformation is usually secure, even if the parameters of the transformation are known.

specific key typically increases the separability between the users in the feature space. As a result, the discrimination capability in the transformed domain is higher than in the original feature domain, leading to a lower false match rate. Secondly, user-specific keys facilitate revocability of the transformed templates.

A well-known example of invertible feature transformation approach is the random multi-space quantization technique (see Figure 7.18). This scheme can be used to transform a fixed-length (and typically real-valued) biometric feature vector. Consider a feature vector $\mathbf{x} \in \mathbb{R}^d$. The secret key κ is used as the seed to randomly generate a $m \times d$ orthogonal projection matrix $\mathbf{A}_\kappa$, whose rank is usually less than d. The feature vector $\mathbf{x}$ is projected onto the random orthogonal subspaces ($\mathbf{A}_\kappa \mathbf{x}$) and the individual maps are quantized (usually into a binary value) to compensate for intra-user variations. The threshold for binarization is selected based on the criteria that the expected number of zeros in the template is equal to the expected number of ones so as to maximize the entropy of the template.

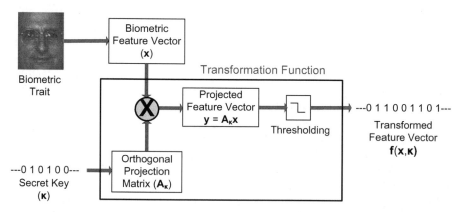

Fig. 7.18 Securing biometric templates using the random multispace quantization technique.

The security in this scheme is provided by the user-specific random projection matrix $\mathbf{A}_K$. If an adversary gains access to this matrix, then the scheme is neither pre-image resistant nor non-invertible. Even though the matrix $\mathbf{A}_K$ does not have an exact inverse because its rank is less than d, one can easily obtain a pre-image by computing the pseudo-inverse of $\mathbf{A}_K$. Further, it may also be possible to recover a close approximation of the original biometric features (some information is lost due to binarization) through a hill-climbing attack. Finally, an attack similar to the chosen plaintext attack may be used to recover the random projection matrix directly.

Another potential technique that can be used as an invertible feature transform is homomorphic encryption. Homomorphic cryptosystems are those where a specific algebraic operation can be performed on the plaintext by performing a (possibly different) mathematical operation on the ciphertext and decrypting the value obtained. For example, the RSA algorithm is homomorphic to multiplication, i.e., if the product of two ciphertexts generated using the same key is decrypted, the result is the same as the product of the corresponding plaintexts. The homomorphic property of the encryption scheme can be exploited to directly perform biometric matching in the encrypted domain, as in the case of password encryption.

Non-invertible transformation:

Non-invertible transformation schemes typically apply a one-way function on the template, and it is computationally hard to invert a transformed template even if the key is known. Ideally, one should employ a transformation function that is both pre-image resistant and non-invertible. If such a transform can be applied, then non-invertible transformation is equivalent to a password hashing scheme. Since it is hard to recover the original biometric template even when the parameters of the transformation are compromised, this scheme provides better security than the invertible transformation approach. By selecting user-specific transform parameters, this approach can also allow revocability.

The main drawback of this approach is the trade-off between discriminability (recognition performance) and non-invertibility (security) of the transformation function. The transformation function should preserve the discriminability (similarity structure) of the feature set, i.e., just like in the original feature space, features from the same user should have high similarity in the transformed space and features from different users should be quite dissimilar after transformation. On the other hand, the transformation should also be non-invertible, i.e., given a transformed feature set, it should be hard for an adversary to obtain the original feature set (or a close approximation of it). It is difficult to design transformation functions that satisfy both the discriminability and non-invertibility conditions simultaneously. Also, one needs to choose an appropriate transformation function based on the characteristics of the biometric features employed in a specific application.

Intra-user variations are usually handled by using transformation functions that are tolerant to input variations. An alternative is to use non-invertible transformation functions that leave the biometric template in the original (feature) space even after the transformation (e.g., fingerprint minutiae can be transformed into another set of minutiae in a non-invertible manner). In this latter scenario, intra-user variations can be handled by applying the same biometric matcher on the transformed features as on the original feature set. Templates that lie in the same space after the application of a non-invertible transform have been referred to as *cancelable templates*.

Examples of non-invertible functions that have been proposed for the purpose of transforming fingerprint minutiae include cartesian, polar, and functional transformations. In cartesian transformation, the minutiae space (fingerprint image) is tessellated into a rectangular grid and each cell (possibly containing some minutiae) is shifted to a new position in the grid corresponding to the translations set by the key κ. The polar transformation is similar to cartesian transformation with the difference that the image is now tessellated into a number of concentric shells and each shell is divided into sectors. Since the size of sectors can be different (sectors near the center are smaller than the ones far from the center), restrictions are usually placed on the translation vector generated from the key so that the radial distance of the transformed sector is not very different than the radial distance of the original position. An illustration of minutiae prior to and after polar and cartesian transformations is shown in Figure 7.19.

For the functional transformation, a mixture of 2D Gaussians or electric potential field in a 2D random charge distribution can be used to determine the translation of the minutiae points. The magnitude of these functions at the point corresponding to a minutia can be used as a measure of the magnitude of the translation and the gradient of a function can be used to estimate the direction of translation of the minutiae. In all the three transforms, two or more minutiae can possibly map to the same point in the transformed domain. For example, in the cartesian transformation, two or more cells can be mapped onto a single cell so that even if an adversary knows the key and hence, the transformation between cells, he cannot determine the original cell to

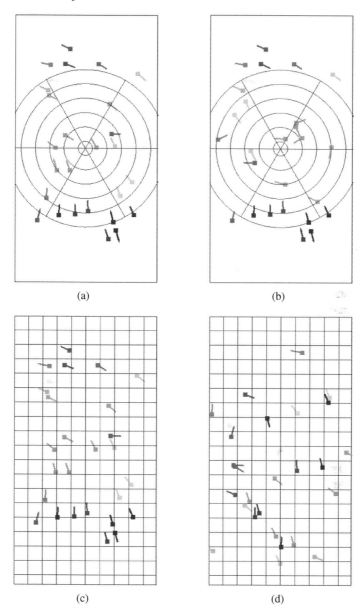

Fig. 7.19 Illustration of cartesian and polar transformation functions for generating cancelable fingerprint templates (adapted from [22]). (a) Original minutiae on radial grid, (b) transformed minutiae after polar transformation, (c) original minutiae on rectangular grid, and (d) transformed minutiae after cartesian transformation. Note that the minutiae are shaded differently to track them after transformation.

which a minutia belongs because each of the minutiae can independently belong to one of the possible cells. This provides a limited amount of non-invertibility to the transform. Also, since the transformations used are locally smooth, the error rates are not affected significantly and the discriminability of minutiae is preserved to a large extent. In the case of fingerprint minutiae transformation, the key to achieving good recognition performance is the availability of an alignment algorithm that can accurately pre-align (register) the fingerprint images or minutiae features prior to the transformation (e.g., based on core and delta in the fingerprints).

7.5.1.5 Biometric cryptosystems

Biometric cryptosystems are somewhat similar to password-based key generation systems because they were originally developed for the purpose of either securing a cryptographic key using biometric features or directly generating a cryptographic key from biometric features. Since the biometric features available during enrollment and authentication are different, these features cannot be directly used for generation of cryptographic keys. In order to facilitate key generation, some public information about the biometric features is stored in the database during enrollment. This public information is usually referred to as *helper data* or *secure sketch* and hence, biometric cryptosystems are also known as helper-data-based methods. The secure sketch is used during authentication to extract a cryptographic key from the query biometric features through a process known as the recovery mechanism. Matching is performed indirectly by verifying the validity of the extracted key or by directly using the key in another application.

Biometric cryptosystems can be further classified as *key binding* and *key generation* systems depending on how the secure sketch is obtained. When the secure sketch is obtained by binding a cryptographic key (that is independent of the biometric features) with the biometric template, it is referred to as a *key binding biometric cryptosystem*. If the helper data is derived only from the biometric template and the cryptographic key is directly generated from the helper data and the query biometric features, it leads to a *key generation biometric cryptosystem*.

It is important to emphasize that the secure sketch is not required to be a secret. Therefore, it must not reveal any significant information about the original biometric template (hence the template is secure) or the cryptographic key (hence the key is secure). Thus, biometric cryptosystems solve the challenging problems of cryptographic key management and biometric template protection simultaneously. Due to this reason, this topic is under active research in both the biometric and cryptographic communities.

The recovery mechanism in a biometric cryptosystem is capable of compensating for intra-user variations in the biometric data, typically through the use of error correction coding techniques. Error correction coding is commonly used in telecommunication systems to enable reliable delivery of digital data over unreliable communication channels. These schemes achieve tolerance against errors by appending additional (redundant) information to the message prior to transmission. In the context of biometric cryptosystems, the biometric features available during enrollment is analogous to the transmitted message in a telecommunication system. The helper data or secure sketch is roughly equivalent to the redundant information that is added to the message. The query biometric features together with the secure sketch constitute the received message. Provided that the query is sufficiently "close" to the enrolled biometric template, the original biometric template can be recovered after error correction.

Naturally, the ability of a biometric cryptosystem to handle intra-user variations directly depends on the amount of redundant information (helper data) used for error correction. Higher redundancy generally leads to higher error tolerance and consequently, greater key stability. Here, key stability refers to the probability of recovering the correct secret key or generating the same cryptographic key during every authentication attempt. This is equivalent to the false non-match rate of a biometric system. On the other hand, storing more redundant information in the form of helper data introduces two major problems. Firstly, a larger error tolerance will typically result in a higher false match rate. Secondly, a larger secure sketch is bound to reveal more information about the biometric features and the cryptographic key. Hence, both the security of the biometric template and the entropy of the generated cryptographic key decrease. Similar to the case of non-invertible feature transform, there is a tradeoff between the security of the biometric template and the recognition performance in a biometric cryptosystem.

Key binding biometric cryptosystem:

In a key binding cryptosystem, the biometric template is secured by monolithically binding it with a secret key within a cryptographic framework. As shown in Figure 7.20, a single entity that embeds both the key and the template is stored in the database as the secure sketch. This secure sketch does not reveal much information about the key or the biometric template, i.e., it is computationally hard to decode the key or the template without any knowledge of the user's biometric data. Matching in a key binding system involves recovery of the key from the helper data using the query biometric features and verifying the validity of the key.

Usually, the helper data is an association of an error correcting code (that is indexed by the secret key) and the biometric template. When a biometric query differs from the template within certain error tolerance, the associated codeword with a similar amount of error can be recovered. This codeword with errors can be decoded to obtain the exact codeword and hence, recover the embedded key. Recovery of the correct key implies a successful match. The tolerance to intra-user variations in the biometric data is determined by the error correcting capability of the associated codeword. Moreover, indirect matching based on the error correction scheme precludes the use of sophisticated matchers developed specifically for matching the original biometric template. This can possibly lead to a reduction in the matching accuracy.

One of the earliest and most well-known key binding biometric cryptosystems is the fuzzy commitment scheme. This scheme can be applied to biometric systems

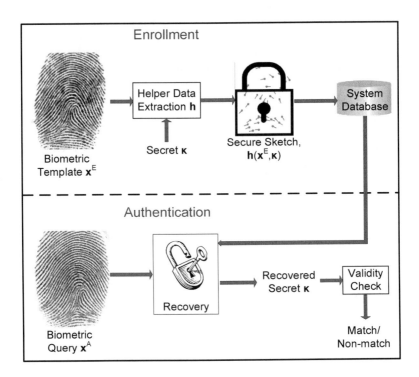

Fig. 7.20 Authentication mechanism when the biometric template is secured using a key binding biometric cryptosystem.

where the feature vector is a fixed-length binary string. Suppose that the enrollment template $\mathbf{x}^E$ is a binary string of length d bits. During enrollment, an error correcting codeword $\mathbf{c}$ of the same length (d bits) is selected. This codeword is uniquely indexed by a secret key κ of length m bits (there is a one-to-one correspondence between $\mathbf{c}$ and κ). Here, m is less than d and the parameter $(d-m)$ is a measure of the redundancy in the error-correction code. The codeword $\mathbf{c}$ is then committed (bound) to the biometric feature vector $\mathbf{x}^E$ to generate the secure sketch. The secure sketch or helper data consists of the fuzzy commitment $(\mathbf{x}^E \oplus \mathbf{c})$ and $\mathbf{g}(\kappa)$, where $\mathbf{g}(.)$ is a cryptographic hash function and $\oplus$ represents exclusive-or (XOR) operation (modulo-2 addition).

During authentication, the user presents a biometric vector $\mathbf{x}^A$. Now one can compute the codeword with errors, $\mathbf{c}'$, as $\mathbf{c}' = \mathbf{x}^A \oplus (\mathbf{x}^E \oplus \mathbf{c})$. If $\mathbf{x}^A$ is close to $\mathbf{x}^E$, $\mathbf{c}'$ is close to $\mathbf{c}$ since $\mathbf{x}^A \oplus \mathbf{x}^E = \mathbf{c}' \oplus \mathbf{c}$. Therefore, $\mathbf{c}'$ can now be decoded to obtain the nearest codeword $\mathbf{c}^*$, which would be equal to $\mathbf{c}$ provided that the distance between $\mathbf{c}$ and $\mathbf{c}'$ is less than the error correcting capacity of the code. From $\mathbf{c}^*$, one can compute κ^*. The matching is successful if $\mathbf{g}(\kappa^*) = \mathbf{g}(\kappa)$.

Key generating biometric cryptosystem:

Direct cryptographic key generation from biometrics is an attractive proposition, but it is a difficult problem because of two reasons: (a) the intra-user variability of the biometric features, and (b) the non-uniform nature of the probability distribution of biometric features. The concept of secure sketch or helper data can be used to solve the first issue. In this scenario, the secure sketch is derived using only the biometric template and the recovery mechanism facilitates exact reconstruction of the template when presented with a query that is close to the template as illustrated in Figure 7.21. Early biometric key generation schemes employed user-specific quantization schemes. Information on quantization boundaries is stored as helper data, which is used during authentication to account for intra-user variations. It is also possible to make use of error correction coding schemes to generate the secure sketch from the biometric features.

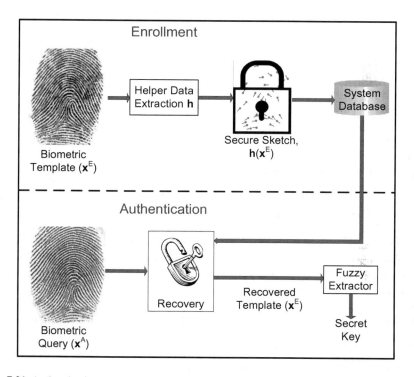

Fig. 7.21 Authentication mechanism when the biometric template is secured using a key generating biometric cryptosystem.

Traditional cryptography also requires the cryptographic keys to have a uniform random distribution. However, it is well-known that biometric features are not uniformly distributed. The fuzzy extractor was proposed as a cryptographic primitive that generates a uniformly random cryptographic key from the biometric features. The secure sketch is an integral component of a fuzzy extractor, which addresses the problem of key stability. The non-uniformity issue can be handled by applying cryptographic hash functions to the biometric template. Recall that a cryptographic hash function has desirable properties such as pre-image resistance and collision resistance. These properties facilitate the extraction of uniformly random binary strings from the biometric features.

7.5.1.6 Discussion on template security schemes

A brief summary of the various biometric template protection approaches is presented in Table 7.1. Apart from the standard encryption and invertible feature transformation schemes, none of the other template protection schemes require any secret information (such as a key) that must be securely stored or presented during matching. Moreover, many template protection techniques proposed in the literature make use of more than one basic approach (e.g., invertible transformation, followed by key-binding). Such hybrid. schemes have not been discussed in detail here.

Table 7.1 Summary of different template protection schemes. Here, $\mathbf{x}^E$ represents the biometric template, $\mathbf{x}^A$ represents the query presented during authentication, and κ is the key (or parameters) used to protect the template or is generated from the template. In feature transformation approach, $\mathbf{f}$ represents the transformation function and m_t represents the matcher that operates in the transformed domain. In biometric cryptosystems, $\mathbf{h}$ is the helper data extraction scheme and $\mathbf{m}$ is the error correction recovery mechanism that allows reconstruction of the key κ.

Approach	Security Feature	Entities Stored	Mechanism to handle Intra-user variations
Invertible transform	Secrecy of key κ	Public domain: Transformed template $\mathbf{f}(\mathbf{x}^E, \kappa)$ Secret: Key κ	Quantization and matching in transformed domain $m_t(\mathbf{f}(\mathbf{x}^E, \kappa), \mathbf{f}(\mathbf{x}^A, \kappa))$
Non-invertible transform	Non-invertibility of the transformation function $\mathbf{f}$	Public domain: Transformed template $\mathbf{f}(\mathbf{x}^E; K)$, key κ	Matching in transformed domain $m_t(\mathbf{f}(\mathbf{x}^E; K), \mathbf{f}(\mathbf{x}^A, \kappa))$
Key-binding biometric cryptosystem	Level of security depends on the amount of information revealed by the helper data H	Public domain: Helper Data $H = \mathbf{h}(\mathbf{x}^E, \kappa)$	Error correction and user specific quantization $\kappa = \mathbf{m}(\mathbf{f}(\mathbf{x}^E, \kappa), \mathbf{x}^A)$
Key-generating biometric cryptosystem	Level of security depends on the amount of information revealed by the helper data H	Public domain: Helper Data $H = \mathbf{h}(\mathbf{x}^E)$	Error correction and user specific quantization $\kappa = \mathbf{m}(\mathbf{h}(\mathbf{x}^E), \mathbf{x}^A)$

As yet, there is no "best" approach for template protection that completely satisfies all the requirements mentioned in Section 7.5.1.2. The application scenario and requirements plays a major role in the selection of a template protection scheme. For instance, in a biometric verification application such as a bank ATM, a simple invertible feature transformation scheme based on the user's PIN may be sufficient to secure the biometric template if it is assumed that both the transformed template and the user's PIN will not be compromised simultaneously. On the other hand, in an airport watch list application, non-invertible transform is a more suitable approach because it provides both template security and revocability without relying on any other input from the user. Biometric cryptosystems are more appropriate in match-on-card applications because such systems typically release a key to the associated application in order to indicate a successful match.

The other major factors that influence the choice of a template protection scheme are the specific biometric trait to be used, its feature representation, and the extent of intra-user variation. In general, more than one template protection scheme may be admissible and the choice of the suitable approach may be based on a number of factors such as recognition performance, computational complexity, memory requirements, and user acceptance and co-operation. Further research in the area of biometric template security is expected to progress along the following three main directions.

1. What is the "optimal" feature transformation function or secure sketch generation technique for a specific type of biometric features and matching function? Optimality generally refers to the best tradeoff between security and recognition performance. Some of the main feature representations include fixed-length binary string (e.g., IrisCode), unordered sets (e.g., fingerprint minutiae), and fixed-length real valued vectors (e.g., LDA features derived from face images). These feature representations may also require different matching functions like Hamming distance, set difference metric, edit distance, etc. Depending on the feature type and matching function, the appropriate template security approach may vary.

2. Suppose that there is a good template protection algorithm for a specific feature type and matching function; what is the best way to embed other types of features in the desired feature domain? For example, most of the error correction schemes can be readily applied for secure sketch generation from binary strings. Therefore, it would beneficial to convert other feature types, say fingerprint minutiae sets, into a binary string so that existing secure sketch algorithms can be used. This question is also relevant in case there is a need to secure templates from multiple biometric traits as a single entity.

3. Finally, one of the important but difficult tasks in the design of a template protection algorithm is: how does the system designer quantify the security provided by the algorithm? Most of the existing methodologies for security analysis are based on unrealistic assumptions (e.g., uniform distribution of biometric features). A related issue is the need to quantify the inherent entropy in (or the individuality of) a biometric trait or the features extracted from it.

7.6 Summary

With large-scale deployments of biometric systems in various commercial and government applications, security issues related to the biometric system itself are becoming ever more important. A biometric system is vulnerable to a number of security threats such as intrusion, denial-of-service, repudiation, and function creep. A systematic analysis of these threats is essential when designing a biometric system. This chapter presented a high-level categorization of the various vulnerabilities of a biometric system and discussed countermeasures that have been proposed to address these threats.

Bibliographical and Historical Remarks

Due to the rapid growth in sensing and computing technologies, biometric systems have become an integral part of modern identity management and information technology (IT) security systems. Naturally, identification of potential vulnerabilities in a biometric system has received increased attention from the biometrics research community. A number of studies have analyzed potential security breaches in a biometric system and proposed methods to counter those breaches [39, 30, 8]. Formal methods of vulnerability analysis such as attack trees [12] have also been used to study how biometric system security can be compromised.

The points of attack in a biometric system were identified in [38]. Attacks at user interface due to the presentation of a spoof biometric trait were studied in [31, 20, 16]. A number of efforts have been made in developing hardware as well as software solutions that are capable of performing liveness detection [35, 3, 41, 34, 29, 28]. Juels et al. [23] outlined the security and privacy issues introduced by insecure communication channels in an e-passport application that uses biometric authentication. Insecure communication channels also allow an adversary to launch replay or hill-climbing attacks [2]. Countermeasures to replay and hill-climbing attacks include time-stamps and challenge/response mechanisms.

Biometric cryptosystems [11] were originally developed for the purpose of either securing a cryptographic key using biometric features or directly generating a cryptographic key from biometric features. One of the earliest references to biometric cryptosystems is a patent issued to Albert Bodo in 1994 that explained a technique to use the biometric template as a cryptographic key [4]. Beginning in 1998, practical template protection schemes started appearing in the literature. Soutar et al. [42] designed a technique that associated an external key with the biometric data. The system effectively ensured recovery of the associated key when a matching biometric image is presented during authentication even in presence of intra-class variations. Davida et al. [14] designed a technique using error correcting codes to secure the biometric templates stored in a smart card in an off-line authentication system.

Fuzzy commitment [25] and fuzzy vault [24] are the two most popular techniques used for constructing biometric cryptosystems. Practical implementation of these two schemes have been proposed for common biometric traits such as fingerprint [33] and iris [19]. Template protection schemes proposed in [5] are examples of hybrid biometric cryptosystems.

Direct cryptographic key generation from biometrics is an attractive proposition but it is a difficult problem because of the intra-user variability. Dodis et al. [15] introduced the concepts of *secure sketch* and *fuzzy extractor* in the context of key generation from biometrics. Sutcu et al. [44] discussed the practical issues in secure sketch construction and proposed a secure sketch based on quantization for the face biometric. The problem of generating fuzzy extractors from continuous distributions was addressed by Buhan et al. [9]. Protocols for secure authentication in remote applications [6] have also been proposed based on the fuzzy extractor scheme.

Biometric cryptosystems offer protection against the recovery of the original biometric template in case an adversary gains access to the system database. However, this approach gives very limited protection against cross-matching of biometric templates across different databases. To address this issue, template transformation techniques were designed. These techniques permanently distort the biometric data using some user specific data while retaining or even enhancing the recognition capacity of the biometric system. Ratha et al. [36] proposed the first such technique to distort a face or a fingerprint images using a user-specific key. A few years later, a number of other techniques were proposed for different biometric modalities such as fingerprint [37], face [17, 46], and iris [49].

As matching performance is one of the main requirements of a biometric recognition system, it is desirable to achieve good performance even when a biometric template protection technique is applied. Techniques were thus designed that incorporated additional features from the same biometric trait [32] in the cryptosystem or combined multiple biometric traits in the same template [26, 18].

There is a natural interest among researchers to estimate the severity of threat to biometric templates and the effectiveness of the proposed techniques in mitigating such risks. A number of techniques have been developed to show that fingerprints could be reconstructed using the stored templates [40, 10]. Other techniques were proposed to explicitly estimate information content (or variability across population) in the biometric features [45]. Techniques were also proposed to evaluate the security capabilities provided by the different techniques [21, 27, 15].

Both biometric cryptosystems and template transformation techniques are not double-blind, i.e., the biometric system is typically aware of which user is being authenticated in a particular transaction, while the user does not know whether he is interacting with the legitimate biometric system. To overcome this limitation, novel authentication techniques and protocols based on homomorphic encryption have been proposed recently [48, 7, 43]. Despite significant research, further improvement to template protection techniques are needed both in terms of both matching performance and security before they can be used in practical biometric systems.

References

1. A. Adler. Sample Images Can Be Independently Restored from Face Recognition Templates. In *Proceedings of Canadian Conference on Electrical and Computer Engineering*, volume 2, pages 1163–1166, Montreal, Canada, May 2003.
2. A. Adler. Vulnerabilities in Biometric Encryption Systems. In *Proceedings of Fifth International Conference on Audio- and Video-Based Biometric Person Authentication (AVBPA)*, volume 3546, pages 1100–1109, Rye Brook, USA, 2005.
3. A. Antonelli, R. Cappelli, D. Maio, and D. Maltoni. Fake Finger Detection by Skin Distortion Analysis. *IEEE Transactions on Information Forensics and Security*, 1(3):360–373, September 2006.
4. A. Bodo. Method for Producing a Digital Signature with aid of a Biometric Feature. German patent DE 42 43 908 A1, 1994.
5. T. E. Boult, W. J. Scheirer, and R. Woodworth. Fingerprint Revocable Biotokens: Accuracy and Security Analysis. In *Proceedings of IEEE Computer Society Conference on Computer Vision and Pattern Recognition*, pages 1–8, Minneapolis, USA, June 2007.
6. X. Boyen, Y. Dodis, J. Katz, R. Ostrovsky, and A. Smith. Secure Remote Authentication Using Biometric Data. In *Advances in Cryptology–EUROCRYPT 2005*, pages 147–163, Aarhus, Denmark, May 2005.
7. J. Bringer and H. Chabanne. An authentication protocol with encrypted biometric data. In *Proceedings of the Progress in Cryptology, AFRICACRYPT*, pages 109–124, 2008.
8. I. Buhan and P. Hartel. The State of the Art in Abuse of Biometrics. Technical Report TR-CTIT-05-41, Centre for Telematics and Information Technology, University of Twente, December 2005.
9. I. R. Buhan, J. M. Doumen, P. H. Hartel, and R. N. J. Veldhuis. Fuzzy Extractors for Continuous Distributions. In *Proceedings of ACM Symposium on Information, Computer and Communications Security*, pages 353–355, Singapore, March 2007.
10. R. Cappelli, A. Lumini, D. Maio, and D. Maltoni. Fingerprint Image Reconstruction From Standard Templates. *IEEE Transactions on Pattern Analysis and Machine Intelligence*, 29(9):1489–1503, 2007.
11. A. Cavoukian and A. Stoianov. Biometric Encryption: A Positive-Sum Technology that Achieves Strong Authentication, Security and Privacy. Technical report, Office of the Information and Privacy Commissioner of Ontario, March 2007.
12. B. Cukic and N. Bartlow. Biometric System Threats and Countermeasures: A Risk Based Approach. In *Proceedings of Biometric Consortium Conference (BCC)*, Crystal City, USA, September 2005.
13. J. Daugman. Recognizing Persons by their Iris Patterns. In A. K. Jain, R. Bolle, and S. Pankanti, editors, *Biometrics: Personal Identification in Networked Society*, pages 103–122. Kluwer Academic Publishers, London, UK, 1999.
14. G. I. Davida, Y. Frankel, and B. J. Matt. On Enabling Secure Applications Through Off-Line Biometric Identification. In *Proceedings of IEEE Symposium on Security and Privacy*, pages 148–157, Oakland, USA, May 1998.
15. Y. Dodis, R. Ostrovsky, L. Reyzin, and A. Smith. Fuzzy Extractors: How to Generate Strong Keys from Biometrics and Other Noisy Data. Technical Report 235, Cryptology ePrint Archive, February 2006. A preliminary version of this work appeared in EUROCRYPT 2004.
16. A. Eriksson and P. Wretling. How Flexible is the Human Voice? A Case Study of Mimicry. In *Proceedings of the European Conference on Speech Technology*, pages 1043–1046, Rhodes, Greece, September 1997.
17. Y. C. Feng, P.C. Yuen, and A.K. Jain. A hybrid approach for face template protection. In *Proceedings of SPIE Conference of Biometric Technology for Human Identification*, volume 6944, Orlando, FL, USA, 2008.
18. B. Fu, S. X. Yang, J. Li, and D. Hu. Multibiometric cryptosystem: Model structure and performance analysis. *IEEE Transactions on Information Forensics and Security*, 4(4):867–882, December 2009.

19. F. Hao, R. Anderson, and J. Daugman. Combining Crypto with Biometrics Effectively. *IEEE Transactions on Computers*, 55(9):1081–1088, September 2006.

20. W. R. Harrison. *Suspect Documents, their Scientific Examination*. Nelson-Hall Publishers, 1981.

21. T. Ignatenko and F. M. J. Willems. Biometric systems: Privacy and secrecy aspects. *IEEE Transactions on Information Forensics and Security*, 4(4):956–973, 2009.

22. A. K. Jain, K. Nandakumar, and A. Nagar. Biometric template security. *EURASIP Journal on Advances in Signal Processing, Special Issue on Advanced Signal Processing and Pattern Recognition Methods for Biometrics*, January 2008.

23. A. Juels, D. Molnar, and D. Wagner. Security and Privacy Issues in E-passports. In *Proceedings of First International Conference on Security and Privacy for Emerging Areas in Communications Networks*, pages 74–88, Athens, Greece, September 2005.

24. A. Juels and M. Sudan. A Fuzzy Vault Scheme. In *Proceedings of IEEE International Symposium on Information Theory*, page 408, Lausanne, Switzerland, 2002.

25. A. Juels and M. Wattenberg. A Fuzzy Commitment Scheme. In *Proceedings of Sixth ACM Conference on Computer and Communications Security*, pages 28–36, Singapore, November 1999.

26. E.J.C. Kelkboom, X. Zhou, J. Breebaart, R.N.J. Veldhuis, and C. Busch. Multi-algorithm fusion with template protection. In *Proc. IEEE 3rd International Conference on Biometrics: Theory, Applications, and Systems, 2009. BTAS '09.*, Washington, DC, September 2009.

27. L. Lai, S. W. Ho, and H. V. Poor. Privacy-security tradeoffs in biometric security systems. In *Annual Allerton Conference on Communication, Control, and Computing (Allerton)*, Monticello, IL, September 2008.

28. E. C. Lee, K. R. Park, and J. Kim. Fake Iris Detection by Using Purkinje Image. In *Proceedings of International Conference on Biometrics*, volume LNCS 3832, pages 397–403, Hong Kong, China, 2006.

29. J. Li, Y. Wang, T. Tan, and A.K. Jain. Live Face Detection Based on the Analysis of Fourier Spectra. In *Proceedings of SPIE Conference on Biometric Technology for Human Identification*, volume 5404, pages 296–303, Orlando, USA, March 2004.

30. M1.4 Ad Hoc Group on Biometric in E-Authentication. Study Report on Biometrics in E-Authentication. Technical Report INCITS M1/07-0185rev, International Committee for Information Technology Standards (INCITS), March 2007.

31. T. Matsumoto, H. Matsumoto, K. Yamada, and S. Hoshino. Impact of Artificial Gummy Fingers on Fingerprint Systems. In *Proceedings of SPIE Conference on Optical Security and Counterfeit Deterrence Techniques*, volume 4677, pages 275–289, February 2002.

32. A. Nagar, K. Nandakumar, and A. K. Jain. Securing Fingerprint Template: Fuzzy Vault with Minutiae Descriptors. In *Proceedings of IEEE International Conference on Pattern Recognition*, Tampa, FL, December 2008.

33. K. Nandakumar, A. K. Jain, and S. Pankanti. Fingerprint-based Fuzzy Vault: Implementation and Performance. *IEEE Transactions on Information Forensics and Security*, 2(4):744–757, December 2007.

34. K. A. Nixon and R. K. Rowe. Multispectral Fingerprint Imaging for Spoof Detection. In *Proceedings of SPIE Conference on Biometric Technology for Human Identification*, volume 5779, pages 214–225, Orlando, USA, March 2005.

35. S. Parthasaradhi, R. Derakhshani, L. A. Hornak, and S. A. C. Schuckers. Time-Series Detection of Perspiration as a Liveness Test in Fingerprint Devices. *IEEE Transactions on Systems, Man, and Cybernetics, Part C: Applications and Reviews*, 35(3):335–343, 2005.

36. N. Ratha, J. Connell, and R. Bolle. Enhancing security and privacy in biometrics-based authentication systems. *IBM Systems Journal*, 40(3):614–634, 2001.

37. N. K. Ratha, S. Chikkerur, J. H. Connell, and R. M. Bolle. Generating Cancelable Fingerprint Templates. *IEEE Transactions on Pattern Analysis and Machine Intelligence*, 29(4):561–572, April 2007.

38. N. K. Ratha, J. H. Connell, and R. M. Bolle. An Analysis of Minutiae Matching Strength. In *Proceedings of Third International Conference on Audio- and Video-Based Biometric Person Authentication (AVBPA)*, pages 223–228, Halmstad, Sweden, June 2001.

39. C. Roberts. Biometric Attack Vectors and Defences. *Computers and Security*, 26(1):14–25, February 2007.

40. A. K. Ross, J. Shah, and A. K. Jain. From Templates to Images: Reconstructing Fingerprints From Minutiae Points. *IEEE Transactions on Pattern Analysis and Machine Intelligence*, 29(4):544–560, 2007.

41. D. R. Setlak. Fingerprint Sensor Having Spoof Reduction Features and Related Methods. United States patent number US 5953441, 1999.

42. C. Soutar, D. Roberge, A. Stoianov, R. Gilroy, and B. V. K. V. Kumar. Biometric encryption using image processing. In *Proc. of SPIE*, volume 3314, pages 178–188, 1998.

43. A. Stoianov. Cryptographically secure biometrics. *Proceedings of SPIE*, 7667(1):76670C, 2010.

44. Y. Sutcu, Q. Li, and N. Memon. Protecting Biometric Templates with Sketch: Theory and Practice. *IEEE Transactions on Information Forensics and Security*, 2(3):503–512, September 2007.

45. Y. Sutcu, H. T. Sencar, and N Memon. How to measure biometric information? In *IEEE International conference on Pattern Recognition*, Istanbul, Turkey, 2010.

46. A. B. J. Teoh, A. Goh, and D. C. L. Ngo. Random Multispace Quantization as an Analytic Mechanism for BioHashing of Biometric and Random Identity Inputs. *IEEE Transactions on Pattern Analysis and Machine Intelligence*, 28(12):1892–1901, December 2006.

47. U. Uludag and A.K. Jain. Attacks on Biometric Systems: A Case Study in Fingerprints. In *Proceedings of SPIE Conference on Security, Seganography and Watermarking of Multimedia Contents VI*, pages 622–633, San Jose, USA, January 2004.

48. M. Upmanyu, A. M. Namboodiri, K. Srinathan, and C. V. Jawahar. Blind authentication: a secure crypto-biometric verification protocol. *IEEE Transactions on Information Forensics and Security*, 5(2):255–268, 2010.

49. J. Zuo, N. K Ratha, and J. H Connell. Cancelable iris biometric. In *Proceedings of the 19th International IAPR Conference on Pattern Recognition (ICPR 2008)*, pages 1–4, 2008.

Index